Drugs and Behavior

Drugs and Behavior
A Sourcebook for the Helping Professions

Rebecca Schilit
Edith S. Lisansky Gomberg

SAGE PUBLICATIONS
The International Professional Publishers
Newbury Park   London   New Delhi

For information address:

SAGE Publications, Inc.
2455 Teller Road
Newbury Park, California 91320

SAGE Publications Ltd.
6 Bonhill Street
London EC2A 4PU
United Kingdom

SAGE Publications India Pvt. Ltd.
M-32 Market
Greater Kailash I
New Delhi 110 048 India

Library of Congress Cataloging-in-Publication Data

Schilit, Rebecca.
    Drugs and behavior : a sourcebook for the helping professions / Rebecca Schilit, Edith S. Lisansky Gomberg.
        p.   cm.
    Includes bibliographical references.
    ISBN 0-8039-3461-0 (cl). — ISBN 0-8039-3462-9 (pb)
    1. Drug abuse—United States.   2. Drug abuse—Treatment—United States.   I. Gomberg, Edith Lisansky 1920–   II. Title.
    [DNLM: 1. Psychotropic Drugs.   2. Substance Abuse.   3. Substance Abuse—therapy.   WM 270 S329d]
HV5825.S36   1991
362.29é18é0973—dc20
DNLM/DLC   91-17558
                                                                                CIP

FIRST PRINTING, 1991

Sage Production Editor: Diane S. Foster

CONTENTS

PREFACE

There is no evidence that the problem of substance abuse is diminishing in American society. Virtually all human service professionals will have to deal with the problem, one way or another—in treatment, in industry, in hospitals, in law enforcement, or in policy. Yet the majority of us know very little about these substances. Perhaps this is because those who are not trained in medical or biological science have neither sought nor received information about drugs that is scientifically correct yet comprehensible and relevant to their lives. Many books have been written about drugs, but how have these been written and for what audience are they intended? There are the standard textbooks of pharmacology, which are intended for students of medicine, pharmacy, dentistry, and other professional and paramedical fields. These books are written with the assumption that the reader has an understanding of anatomy, physiology, biochemistry, and organic chemistry, for much of the material they contain would otherwise be incomprehensible. Textbooks written for undergraduate students have generally approached the topic from a human biology perspective with heavy emphasis on psychobiology and neurology. Although the language in these books might be more accessible, the content falls short of the knowledge base critical to a human service professional.

The present text takes a comprehensive approach to substance abuse education for human service professionals. Relevant psychobiology, psychopharmacology, and central nervous system data will be included, but condensed and in language that is intelligible to readers who may lack scientific background in medical physiology, anatomy, biochemistry, and related subjects. The unique aspect of this text, however, is that it will include topics that have traditionally been excluded from drug texts, namely a range of etiological and explanatory theories, the assumptions involved in different treatment modalities, and alcohol and drug use patterns among special populations.

Organization of the Text

The content of our book will be presented in parts. Part I follows the format of the traditional, higher-level psychopharmacology text. The opening chapters explain the principles of drug action and build a working terminology. Chapter 1 looks at the classification of drugs, trends in drug use, and principles of human behavior as they relate to drug use and abuse. Chapter 2 deals with the slightly more technical aspects of the workings of neurons and the anatomy and physiology of the nervous system. The later chapters of this part make up a pharmacopoeia of psychoactive drugs. Each drug group is examined in terms of its patterns of use and abuse, basic pharmacology and mechanisms of action, therapeutic use, dependence liability, and toxicity.

The etiology of substance abuse is unknown, and research efforts have failed to show a definite, single cause of the disease. It is probable, in fact, that there is no single cause and that various factors interact to produce the disorder. The major theories of etiology can be categorized as physiological (biological/genetic), psychological/psychosocial, and sociological. Part II presents these theories and examines the data presented to support them.

Part III introduces the reader to the most widely used modalities of treatment for substance abuse: individual, family, group, self-help, and medical. The basic assumptions underlying each modality are presented, followed by an evaluation of the modalities based on the available empirical literature.

Part IV examines substance abuse problems and treatment issues among some special populations. The prevalence of drug abuse, the potential for adverse consequences, and the likelihood of receiving effective treatment vary by virtue of gender, race, age, sexual preference, and socioeconomic status. Although less is known about drug use in populations other than those consisting of White middle-class males, it is generally assumed that racism, ageism, sexism, and homophobia contribute to both the unique causes of drug abuse and to the barriers to treatment for special populations. Part V looks at some current issues in the field as they relate to treatment, policy, and prevention.

PART I

Drugs and Their Use

1

OVERVIEW: DRUG USE AND ABUSE

One of the early indicators that a social problem has come of age is the quantity and quality of the research on it. Over the last decade interest in research on the problems of drug abuse has grown dramatically. What is particularly striking is the wide array of scientific disciplines that have explored the problem. Drug abuse is a complex contemporary social problem. Its complexity derives in part from the impact it has on the individual user psychologically, socially, and biologically, and in part from its effects on society, law, economics, and politics. As researchers explore the issue of drug abuse, they must first define the problem within the framework of their discipline.

Drug abuse is not only a term that has been used many different ways in many different contexts but proposed definitions seem immediately to reflect the values of the definer. Some would consider any use of an illegal drug to be abuse; other definitions of abuse rely on the notion of actual or potential harm. Unfortunately, the use of almost any drug, even under the orders of a physician, has at least some potential for harm.

Obtaining clear definitions of some terms pertaining to drug use can be a confusing task. The definition of the term "drug" is a product of social custom and law, both of which change over time (Smith, 1970). Societies throughout the world differ considerably with respect to the rules they follow to classify specific substances, such as drugs, poisons, foods, beverages, medicines, and herbs. The pharmacologist might define a drug as any substance, other than food, whose chemical or physical nature alters structure or function in the living organism (Ray, 1987). This might include such substances as aspirin, tobacco, antacids, or alcohol. Those concerned with the social problem of "drug abuse," however, are likely to seek a narrower definition of the term "drug." Such a

3

definition would highlight the psychoactive properties of certain drugs and the motivation of the user to attain a "high" that characterizes drug-taking behavior in nonmedical contexts.

There are some substances—such as the analgesic Dilaudid—that appear to qualify as a "drug" when used illegally for the purpose of getting high and as a "medicine" when prescribed by a doctor for the treatment of pain. THC (tetrahydrocannabinol), the principal mood-altering chemical in marijuana, is illegal when smoked in marijuana joints to control nausea, but it is legal when prescribed in capsule form by a medical doctor for the same purpose. Should alcohol, which can be used to get high in nonmedical contexts, be considered a drug? Can caffeine and nicotine, which are both mood-altering substances, also be classified as drugs (Roffman, 1987)?

The terms *drug use, drug misuse,* and *drug abuse* are also difficult to define, although we would all probably agree to the distinction between these terms. Drug use will be defined here as the intake of a chemical substance, whether or not the substance is used therapeutically, legally, or as prescribed by a physician. Almost everyone uses a psychoactive substance occasionally, even if it is a socially accepted substance such as coffee, but not everyone misuses or abuses drugs. Misusing a drug indicates that it is being used in a way that can have detrimental effects. There are many definitions of drug abuse. In its most general sense, drug abuse is the continued use of a psychoactive drug despite the occurrence of major problems associated with its use, for example, health, vocational, scholastic, legal, social, or economic difficulties (Resnick, 1979). However, there are many who would argue that any use of illegal drugs constitutes abuse, regardless of the presence or absence of adverse effects. We will define *drug abuse* as the intake of a chemical substance under circumstances or at dosage levels that significantly increase the hazard potential, whether or not the substance is used therapeutically, legally, or as prescribed by a physician.

Drug abuse is often associated with addiction or *dependence,* which the World Health Organization (WHO) defined in 1974 as

> a state, psychic and sometimes also physical, resulting from the interaction between a living organism and a drug, characterized by behavioral and other responses that always include a compulsion to take the drug on a continuous or periodic basis in order to experience its psychic effects, and sometimes to avoid the discomfort of its absence. Tolerance may or may not be present. A person may be dependent on more than one drug. (p. 14)

Discussions of addiction usually include some mention of three important concepts: tolerance, physical dependence, and psychological dependence. *Tolerance* refers to the development of body tissue resistance to the effects of a chemical agent so that larger doses are required to reproduce the original effect. When tolerance develops rapidly (as with LSD), the user is forced to discontinue use until tissues regain their responsiveness to the chemical. When tolerance develops slowly and the chemical also produces physical dependence (e.g., heroin, alcohol), the increased dose requirements speed up and intensify the development of physical dependence. *Physical dependence* is the habituation of body tissues to the continued presence of a chemical agent, revealed in the form of serious, even life-threatening, withdrawal symptoms following cessation of use. The extent of physical dependence and the severity of withdrawal vary according to amount, frequency, and duration of use. *Psychological dependence* can be described as a tendency or craving for repeated or compulsive use of an agent because its effects are deemed pleasurable or satisfying, or because it reduces undesirable feelings, such as anxiety, insomnia, or depression. A person may thus be psychologically dependent on drugs, food, television, sex, relationships, or recreational activities.

Drug Classification

Drugs have been categorized according to a variety of considerations. However, there appears to be little general agreement on the optimal scheme for ordering the universe of biologically active substances. For example, drugs might be organized according to chemical structure, clinical therapeutic use, potential health hazards, liability to nonmedical use (abuse), effects on specific neural or other physiological systems, or influence on certain psychological and behavioral processes. When drugs are categorized on the basis of their tendency to cause similar behavioral outcomes, the following classifications are commonly used: (a) narcotic analgesics, (b) central nervous system depressants, (c) central nervous system stimulants, (d) cannabis, and (e) hallucinogens.

Narcotic Analgesics. These include those drugs that are derivatives of, or are pharmacologically related to products from the opium poppy. The best-known examples are heroin, morphine, and codeine. There are also many synthetic opiates, such as methadone and propoxyphene (Darvon). Narcotics are essential in the practice of medicine: They are the most effective agents known for the relief of intense pain. They are also used as cough suppressants and to stop diarrhea. Most narcotics can be strongly addictive.

It is estimated that 500,000 Americans are dependent on heroin. Approximately 1,000 individuals die each year in the United States as a result of heroin overdose. In 1984, the price tag for heroin sales in the United States was estimated at $4 billion (U.S. Department of State, 1985).

Central Nervous System (CNS) depressants. This group of drugs comprising sedatives and hypnotics generally decreases central nervous system (CNS) arousal, although there may be psychological stimulation at low doses. Most of the drugs in this category are used medically in the induction of anesthesia, in the treatment of epilepsy, in the reduction of excitability and anxiety (sedation), and to induce sleep (hypnosis). The difference between a sedative and a hypnotic often lies in the size of the dose and the route of administration, the hypnotic being a larger dose. When used nonmedically in excessive amounts, the CNS depressants produce an alcohol-like state of intoxication. The barbiturates, of which more than 2,500 formulations have been produced, follow alcohol as the second most commonly used drug in this category.

Central Nervous System Stimulants. These can be divided into three broad groups: the xanithines (among which caffeine is the most common); cocaine; and a third cluster, of which the amphetamines are the prototype. All of these substances have the capacity to increase alertness and wakefulness, to bolster strength and endurance, to decrease appetite, and to enhance one's sense of well-being. It is estimated that 6 million Americans use prescription stimulants and depressants illicitly (Roffman, 1987).

In 1984, approximately 20 million Americans spent an estimated $18 billion on cocaine. "Crack," a highly potent, yet relatively inexpensive form of cocaine that is smoked, began to appear in the United States in 1985 and spread rapidly. Despite efforts by the United States to reduce the worldwide supply of illicit drugs, the State Department reports that the production of coca increased by one third from 1983 to 1984 (U.S. House, 1985).

Cannabis. Marijuana and hashish are products of the cannabis plant. THC, the principal psychoactive component of cannabis, was approved as a prescription medicine in 1985 by the FDA for the control of nausea and vomiting in cancer chemotherapy patients. Other potential but unapproved medical uses are in the treatment of glaucoma, muscle spasm associated with multiple sclerosis, and asthma (Roffman, 1987).

THC is a difficult compound to classify. At low-to-moderate doses, it is a mild sedative-hypnotic agent resembling alcohol and the antianxiety agents in its pharmacological effects. Unlike the sedative-hypnotics, however, higher doses of THC may (in addition to sedation) produce euphoria, hallucinations, and heightened sensation, effects similar to a mild LSD experience. Also unlike the sedatives, high doses of THC do not produce anesthesia, coma, or death.

Americans spent an estimated $44 billion for marijuana in 1984. As many as 25 million Americans may be regular users, with another 40 million using the drug occasionally (Roffman, 1987).

Hallucinogens. Hallucinogens, or psychedelic drugs, are a group of hetero-geneous compounds, all with the ability to induce visual, auditory, or other types of hallucinations and to separate the individual from reality. These agents may induce disturbances in cognition and perception and, in some instances, may produce behavioral patterns that are similar to components found in psychotic behavior. Among the most widely use hallucinogens are (a) LSD, a semisynthetic compound derived from the alkaloid lysergic acid that is found in ergot; (b) mescaline, the principal alkaloid in the peyote cactus; (c) DOM, a synthetic compound with actions of both a hallucinogenic and stimulant nature; and (d) psilocybin, the psychoactive ingredient in the psilocybin mushroom. It is estimated that approximately 1 million Americans are regular users of hallucinogens (Roffman, 1987).

Trends in Drug Use

Although drug use and abuse is not a new phenomenon, today there is more information than ever available concerning patterns of and trends in illicit drug use. Studies from the Social Research Group of George Washington University, the Institute for Research in Social Behavior in Berkeley, California, and others have given us detailed, extensive data showing that drug use is universal. A major purpose of these investigators was to determine the level of psychoactive drug use in the population, excluding those persons hospitalized or in the armed forces. Tables 1.1 and 1.2 are based on data for the specific categories of drugs used.

Over 80% of respondents in the previously mentioned studies reported that they drank coffee, and over 50% said they drank tea during the previous year. Nearly one third of the population was drinking more than five cups of a beverage containing caffeine each day.

The number of cigarettes smoked in the United States in 1979 was about 600 billion. Almost 22 gallons of beer were consumed for each man, woman, and child, as were more than 2 gallons of wine and more than 2.8 gallons of distilled spirits. Studies indicate that large numbers of persons have tried or routinely use marijuana: 51% were between 16 and 17 years of age, and 68% were in the 22- to 25-year range (Petersen, 1980). It is estimated that as many as 40 million or more people have tried marijuana or use it regularly.

Of the many prescriptions written by physicians, approximately one fourth are for drugs that in one way or another modify mood or behavior. Gallup polls show that over half of all adults in the United States report that at some time in their lives they have taken a psychoactive drug (one that affects mood and/or consciousness). Over one third of all adults have used or are using tranquilizers.

TABLE 1.1 Use of Coffee and Sleeping Pills

Item	Coffee			Sleeping Pills	
	Male	Female		Male	Female
Total persons (millions)	64.6	72.9		64.6	72.9
Nonusers (millions)	10.6	14.9		51.8	60.2
Users (millions)	46.1	54.9		4.5	9.4
Percent of total (users)	71.4	75.3		7.0	12.9
1 cup or less daily	18.2	21.8	less than		
2-5 cups daily	40.5	42.9	once/week	3.3	6.2
6 cups or more once/week daily	12.7	10.6	or more	3.7	6.7

Source: U.S. Bureau of the Census (1980).

TABLE 1.2 Drug Use by Type of Drug and by Age Group

Type of Drug	% of Youths (12–17 yr)		% of Youths (18–25 yr)		% of Adults (26 yr and more)	
	Ever used	Current user	Ever used	Current user	Ever used	Current user
Alcohol	70.3	37.2	95.3	75.9	91.5	61.3
Cigarettes	54.1	12.1	82.8	42.6	83.0	36.9
Marijuana	30.9	16.7	68.2	35.4	19.6	6.0
Inhalants	9.8	2.0	16.5	1.2	3.9	0.5

In recent years, the focus of greatest concern among drug experts has been cocaine, for while the use of other drugs was dropping or remained stable, cocaine grew widely in popularity throughout the nation in the late 1970s and early 1980s.

Findings from two major federal studies on drug use in America show that in the last few years, better-educated young people have been reducing their use of cocaine and other drugs. Meanwhile, the least educated have increasingly used cocaine.

Experts caution that their conclusions are tentative and that the rise of a new drug or the appearance of other unpredictable factors could easily upset current trends. And, whatever the trends, drug use is so widespread that it will remain a problem in all sectors of society for years.

However, studies point to a newly emerging picture of drug use in America that carries a mixed message of hope for the well-off and despair for the poor. Among the major conclusions are as follows.

1. With the exception of heroin and crack among the poor, the use of illegal drugs in the nation appears to have peaked, including snorting powdered cocaine.
2. Federally financed studies show that the people turning away from drugs are the most educated and affluent. The poorest and least educated have continued or have increased their drug use.
3. Crack, a smokable form of cocaine, has largely remained a poor person's drug. Its rise in the past 2 years has had devastating effects on poor neighborhoods, but it has failed to make the same inroads into the middle class.
4. The most deadly impact of illegal drug use is probably yet to come, as tens of thousands of intravenous drug users, their sexual partners, and their children contract Acquired Immune Deficiency Syndrome (AIDS). Most of those people will be poor.

Statistics indicate that outside of the poorest neighborhoods, the nation's 20-year affair with illegal drugs is on the decline.

According to the National Institute on Drug Abuse, marijuana use peaked in 1978, and by 1985, 7 out of 10 high school seniors believed marijuana use to be harmful. Young people's use of hallucinogens like LSD and PCP, or "angel dust," has fallen since 1979 as well.

In 1985, a national household survey conducted by the University of Kentucky for the National Institute on Drug Abuse asked 18- to 25-year-olds if they had smoked marijuana in the last month. It found that people who never graduated from high school were most likely to be using the drug. The better educated the young people were, the less likely they were to use marijuana, the survey found.

Among an earlier generation of smokers—people over 35 who probably developed their attitudes toward marijuana in the late 1960s and early 1970s— the findings were just the reverse. It was the college educated who were most likely to be smoking marijuana.

Another study found similar results. The survey, conducted for the National Institute on Drug Abuse by the University of Michigan Institute for Social Research, asked high school seniors what drugs other than marijuana they had used in the previous month.

The survey found that in 1986, seniors of all economic backgrounds were using drugs less than seniors were in 1981. But the greatest change took place among students whose parents had some graduate education: a drop of 13%, from 36.7% to 23.7%. The least change took place among students whose parents had never been to high school: a drop of 2.7%, from 25.4% to 22.7%.

According to the household survey of 18- to 25-year-olds, the people most likely to have used cocaine in the previous month in 1982 were those who graduated from college. Those least likely to have used cocaine were people who never finished high school. Among college graduates, 11% said they had used cocaine in the past month; among those without high school diplomas, only 4% had used cocaine.

But by 1985, the situation was just the opposite. Only 3% of college graduates said they had used cocaine in the last month. But 10% of those who never finished high school said they had used the drug. Because the survey did not include people without homes, it may have understated drug use among the poorest and least educated.

Perhaps the most dire vision of the future concerns the intravenous users of heroin, a drug that has remained predominantly the preserve of the inner-city poor. Although the number of addicts around the nation has remained relatively stable, there has been an alarming rise in the proportion of addicts exposed to the AIDS virus from the sharing of needles. Although only a comparatively small fraction of heroin addicts die from overdoses each year, between 20% and 100% of those exposed to AIDS are expected to die from the disease.

Drug Use and Human Behavior

People turn to drugs in the hope of finding oblivion, peace, expanded consciousness, or euphoria. The fact that few drugs actually produce the effects for which they are taken—or if they do, they do so for only a brief time—seems not to discourage many. People continue to take drugs for many reasons:

1. They are searching for pleasure.
2. Drugs may relieve stress or tension or provide a temporary escape.
3. Peer pressure is strong, especially for young people.
4. The media play a large role in teaching us we can and should avoid pain and maximize pleasure. One national commission studying the drug-abuse problem estimated that by the age of 18 the average American has seen 180,000 television commercials, many of which give the impression that pleasure and relief are to be found in sources outside oneself (Resnik, 1979).

Drug use is a part of human behavior, and as such it follows the same rules and principles as any other behavioral pattern. One basic behavioral principle is that behavior persists when it either increases the individual's pleasure or reduces his or her discomfort (psychic or physical). People do not take just any drug—they take those that affect them pleasurably or that make a situation less intolerable. Further, of those drugs that do increase pleasure or decrease discomfort, the ones chosen must be acceptable within the user's cultural setting.

Behavior, including drug use, is nurtured in several ways. Thus there is no single cause of drug abuse. Studies with animals show that susceptibility to narcotics addiction is partially genetically determined. Strains of laboratory animals have been bred that are either susceptible or resistant to induced addiction. Similarly, strains of laboratory animals have been developed that prefer alcohol solutions over water for drinking, whereas most animals will select tap water if given the choice. This suggests that alcoholism in humans may be partly based on hereditary predisposition (Goodwin, 1979).

Drug use, whether influenced by genetic factors or not, is the result of a complex interaction of past experiences and present environment. This is true of any behavior. It is possible to group some persons together because of a common history and environment and to predict whether or not they will probably use drugs, as well as the class of drug they will most likely use. This does not mean that potential users can be readily identified; rather it means that some groups of individuals can be identified according to the probability of their becoming drug users.

Seevers (1968) believed that the only means by which drug dependence could be eliminated in human society was for people never to come in contact with particular drugs, because, having once experienced certain drug effects, a majority of the world population would inevitably become drug dependent. Many drugs are such powerful, immediate reinforcers that, if all the population were allowed to try every major psychoactive drug and then were permitted free access to the drug of their choice, the effect on society would be disastrous. Part of Seevers's basis for this statement is animal research. If a monkey or rat is allowed to self-administer a drug such as cocaine, it will do so until it dies.

A diagram of how drug dependence is thought to develop is shown in Figure 1.1. If the first drug trial is a rewarding experience, a few more rewarding trials follow until drug use becomes a conditioned pattern of behavior. Continued positive reinforcement with the drug, in the psychological sense, leads in time to primary psychological dependence. Primary psychological dependence is all that is needed to lead to uncontrollable compulsive abuse of any psychoactive drug in certain persons. The effect of drug dependence on the particular person is related to the nature of the psychoactive substance, the quantity used, and the characteristics of the person and of his or her environment. It is often not possible to draw a sharp line between use and abuse.

Possibly 70% of the adult population in the United States is able to use alcohol—a potent psychoactive agent—in moderation, even to the point of strong psychological dependence, with minimal personal injury and social consequences. Many persons use other powerful psychoactive drugs under the

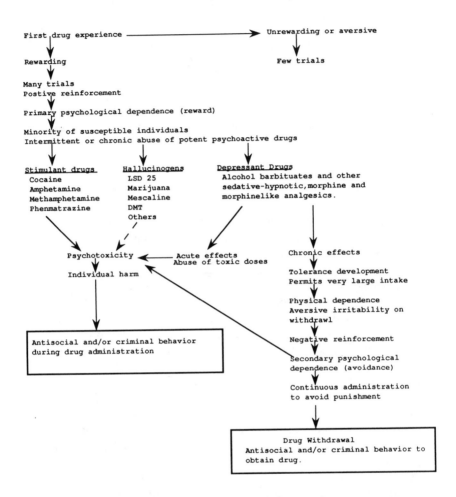

Figure 1.1. Steps in the Process of Drug Abuse or Drug Rejection
Source: Seevers, 1968.

supervision of a physician without becoming drug dependent. The study of the use of these powerful psychoactive drugs is fascinating and surprising. Morphine, for example, produces no significant pain relief for as many as 25% of persons given it; in fact, it may produce unfavorable reactions. Some people can take small amounts of heroin for years without becoming dependent on it, whereas a few become physically addicted after one intravenous dose. Perhaps 5% to 10% of the population would be or could be classified as susceptible to these powerful psychoactive agents; drugs dominate these people's lives.

The user of depressants may develop secondary psychological dependence (see Figure 1.1). This dependence is related to the fact that depressants cause two separate phenomena: *tolerance* and *physical dependence*. Tolerance develops as the drug's action on the vital organs most typically affected, such as the nervous system, the cardiovascular system, and the respiratory system, is lessened. In other words, the same dose has less effect, so the dose must be increased. Not all parts of the body become tolerant at the same rate, and the brain is exposed to larger and larger drug concentrations as tolerance develops in various bodily systems. Not enough is known about brain changes under these conditions.

Continuous exposure of the nervous system to large concentrations of depressant drugs induces physical dependence (see Figure 1.1). This condition is characterized by increased nervous activity but that is evidenced only when the drug is discontinued. The complex of symptoms following cessation of drugs is often referred to as *withdrawal*, or the *abstinence syndrome*.

There are two types of withdrawal syndrome: the morphine type and the alcohol-barbiturate type. The morphinelike drugs may be used interchangeably to give the same effects and to block withdrawal symptoms. The dosage of morphine and morphinelike drugs must be increased as tolerance builds and physical dependence develops. Finally a dose is reached above which further increases will not have any effects on drug dependence. Morphine withdrawal is not life threatening and can usually be accomplished without much difficulty. Alcohol-barbiturate dependence and the subsequent withdrawal syndrome is different from the morphine type in that it usually takes prolonged and continuous administration of large doses over a period of time to develop dependence when the drug is taken orally. However, intravenous administration is different—this way a drug user can become dependent in a few weeks. The alcohol-barbiturate type of withdrawal syndrome is intense, and the severe convulsions associated with it can kill. Withdrawal from alcohol, the barbiturates, and the minor tranquilizers (Valium, Librium)—but not the major tranquilizers (Thorazine, Stelazine, and so on)—cause this condition, and tranquilizers may be given interchangeably to suppress withdrawal symptoms.

The interchangeability of alcohol, barbiturates, and the minor tranquilizers suggests that these drugs work by a common mechanism, but the mechanism is not understood. When a person who is physically dependent on a depressant drug stops taking the drug, symptoms occur that are very similar to those induced by a stimulant. The resulting state of agitation, or hyperexcitability, is apparently due to some action of the central nervous system and is often called the *rebound effect*, or the *paradoxical effect*.

Let us sum up the facts about drug dependence. All drug dependence has as a basis psychological conditioning to the effects of the various drugs. The first characteristic that encourages drug taking is primarily psychological dependence resulting from the positive reinforcement of the reward. In other words, the experience is good, or pleasurable, or it temporarily covers some painful feelings. Each time the person takes the drug in question, the experience is rewarding, and the behavior is positively reinforced. In the case of depressants that may cause physical dependence following repeated use, a second type of behavior, secondary psychological dependence, results. Secondary psychological dependence is a negative experience, sometimes called avoidance or aversive reinforcement because the feelings of withdrawal from the depressant are very unpleasant, and the particular depressant drug is taken to prevent the occurrence of withdrawal symptoms. For example, once a alcoholic starts to experience the symptoms of withdrawal, he or she is motivated to drink to avert the symptoms. The use of depressants is especially difficult to stop because of the buildup of tolerance to the dose taken. As tolerance builds, the dosage needed must be increased, and the reward of taking the drug becomes less important. Then the need to prevent the occurrence of withdrawal becomes the most important factor that will encourage continued use of the drug.

Drugs have multiple effects that vary with the amount of the drug used and the personality of the user, as well as the user's expectations of the drug's effects. Whether or not a person decides to use drugs to solve problems, to obtain a pleasurable experience, or to reduce unhappiness depends on his or her background, present environment, and the availability of drugs.

Special Populations at Risk

Certain groups vulnerable to overinvolvement with drugs have been identified. The ratio of female to male drug abusers is rising, particularly with regard to alcohol, sedatives, tranquilizers, and certain other psychochemicals. Youths have shown dramatic increases in the abuse of all drugs during the past decade. In recent years the increase continues for cocaine, marijuana, and phencyclidine (PCP). The elderly are a group at risk in the misuse of sedative prescription drugs singly and in combination.

Ethnic minorities are usually overrepresented in drug abuse survey data, and special prevention and treatment issues must be devised to deal with this serious issue. All of these populations at risk require careful, thoughtful planning to reduce the prevalence of their dysfunctional drug use.

References

Goodwin, D. W. (1979). Alcoholism and heredity: A review and hypothesis. *Archives of General Psychiatry, 36,* 57-61.

Petersen, R. C. (1980). Marijuana and health. In R. C. Petersen, (Ed.), *Marijuana research findings: 1980* (NIDA Research Monograph No. 31, pp. 1-53). Washington, DC: National Institute on Drug Abuse.

Ray, O. (1987). *Drugs, society, and human behavior.* St. Louis: C. V. Mosby.

Resnick, H. S. (1979). *It starts with people: Experiences in drug abuse prevention* (NIDA Publication No. ADM 79-590). Rockville, MD: National Institute on Drug Abuse.

Roffman, R. (1987). *Marijuana as medicine.* Seattle, WA: Madrona.

Seevers, M. H. (1968). Psychopharmacological elements of drug dependence. *Journal of the American Medical Association, 206,* 1263-1266.

Smith, J. P. (1970). Society and drugs: A short sketch. In P. H. Blachly (Ed.), *Drug abuse data and debate* (pp. 169-175). Springfield, IL: Charles C Thomas.

U.S. Bureau of the Census. (1980). *Statistical abstracts of the United States* (101st ed., p. 130). Washington, DC: Government Printing Office.

U.S. Department of State, Bureau of International Narcotics Matters. (1985, February 14). *The international narcotics control strategy report.* Washington, DC: Government Printing Offfice.

U.S. House Select Committee on Narcotics Abuse and Control. (1985). *Annual report for the year 1984.* Washington, DC: Government Printing Office.

World Health Organization Expert Committee on Drug Dependence. (1974). *Twentieth report* (Tech. Rep. Series No. 551). Geneva, Switzerland: Author.

2

DRUGS AND THE BODY

All psychoactive drugs that are abused produce some alteration in the chemical message sent from one neuron to the next within the synapses of the central nervous system (CNS). As we will see, this alteration in synaptic neurotransmission occurs because each psychoactive drug has a unique chemical structure that causes it to attach to different portions of a neuron or to enzymes located outside the neuron. Once those attachment sites or receptors are occupied by the drug molecules, the normal chemical message between two neurons becomes either inhibited or enhanced. The alteration in chemical neurotransmission produces a concomitant alteration in electrical neurotransmission within the CNS and this may be expressed ultimately as an alteration in mood or behavior.

Before altering chemical neurotransmission within the CNS, however, a psychoactive drug must enter the bloodstream and cross into the brain from capillaries that offer a structural resistance known as the *blood-brain barrier*. Once absorbed into the brain, a drug will continue to produce its psychoactive effect until it diffuses back into the bloodstream, where it can be carried to the liver and be metabolized to an inactive compound that is excreted readily. The following sections outline briefly these basic pharmacological principles.

Routes of Drug Administration

Drugs of abuse are typically self-administered either orally, by injection, or by inhalation. The oral route is the most commonly used method of drug self-administration among the general population. Unlike the injection and inhalation routes, there is little social stigma associated with taking drugs orally,

16

either in pills containing prescription and nonprescription remedies or in the form of beverages containing alcohol or caffeine. The primary advantage of the oral route is that the drug effect is prolonged because the cells lining the gastrointestinal tract provide a structural barrier that slows absorption of the drug into the bloodstream. However, some drugs are deactivated by acids or enzymes within the gastrointestinal tract and thus produce a weak effect by the oral route. In addition, drugs administered orally must first pass through the liver, where they may be metabolized to inactive compounds before reaching the brain. Surprisingly, the problems of oral absorption are not obviated completely by "snorting" drugs like cocaine through the nose, as cocaine administered intranasally is partially passed through the nasopharynx and swallowed into the gastrointestinal tract before it is absorbed (Van Dyke, Jatlow, Ungerer, Barash, & Byck, 1978).

The injection route involves administering a soluble drug either intravenously (IV), intramuscularly (IM), or subcutaneously (SC). In medical practice, the injection route offers several advantages over the oral route. First, the concentration of the drug within the bloodstream is easier to control because individual differences in the rate of absorption are minimized. Second, the injection route can be used when the patient is unconscious. Third, the onset of the drug effect is rapid, especially when administered intravenously. The rapid onset of the drug effect is a major reason why drugs of abuse are often self-administered by injection. In addition, some drugs of abuse, such as heroin, may be injected because they are poorly absorbed via the oral route. A major problem with injecting drugs of abuse involves the use of nonsterile syringes that may transmit various infectious diseases, including hepatitis and Acquired Immune Deficiency Syndrome (AIDS).

The inhalation route is also used to self-administer a variety of drugs of abuse, including anesthetic gases such as nitrous oxide, volatile hydrocarbons such as those found in some glues, and small particles such as nicotine and THC that are found in cigarette and marijuana smoke, respectively. These drugs cross the cells that line the lungs and rapidly enter the bloodstream to penetrate the brain. Unfortunately, the inhalation of drugs may irritate the lung tissue, and chronic use may produce permanent tissue damage. Moreover, anesthetic gases may induce oxygen deprivation or hypoxia, and prolonged use of volatile hydrocarbons has been linked to irreversible brain damage.

Blood-Brain Barrier

Once absorbed into the blood, most drugs diffuse readily into various body tissues and internal organs. However, not all drugs will penetrate the brain, as the blood capillaries within the brain provide a protective barrier that is not found in peripheral circulation. In peripheral capillaries, the endothelial cells that make up the capillary wall are separated by pores that allow most drugs to pass readily between cells. In contrast, the endothelial cells of capillaries within the brain are packed closely, leaving tight junctions that allow only small drug molecules but not plasma proteins to pass between cells. This so-called blood-brain barrier may be reinforced further by the end-foot processes of the nonneural astrocytes that surround the brain capillaries. Another distinction between capillaries in the periphery and the brain is that the endothelial cells of brain capillaries have many more mitochondria, the intracellular organelles that convert glucose and oxygen into energy utilized by the cell. The large number of mitochondria present in the brain capillaries provide the energy required to remove various molecules from the brain via active transport systems.

Although the tight junctions of the blood-brain barrier inhibit the passage of many drugs, most psychoactive drugs penetrate the brain readily by passing directly across the membrane surface of the capillary endothelial cell. The outer membrane of the endothelial cell as well as most other cells throughout the body consist of a bilayer of fat that has many proteins embedded within its surface. This membrane has a fluidlike quality that makes it permeable to drugs that are soluble in fat and relatively impermeable to drugs that are soluble in water. In addition, drugs that are not bound to plasma proteins and that have a neutral ionic charge rather than an ionized charge are most likely to cross the membrane of the endothelial cell. In general, drugs of abuse tend to be lipid (fat) soluble, nonionized small molecules that penetrate the brain by passing directly across the endothelial cells of the capillaries.

Metabolism and Excretion of Drugs

The major organ responsible for deactivating psychoactive drugs circulating within the blood is the liver. Cells within the liver contain numerous microsomes, which are intracellular organelles specialized in synthesizing the enzymes that can metabolize psychoactive drugs. Drugs can be metabolized by either microsomal or nonmicrosomal liver enzymes by the process of either oxidation, reduction, hydrolysis, or conduction (see Mayer, Melmon, & Gilman, 1980). In general, these four different metabolic reactions convert the drug to a watersoluable product that is readily excreted from the body. However, in some cases, a drug is excreted in an unchanged form. The kidneys are the major organ responsible for excreting drug metabolites from the body.

Neurotransmitters

The CNS of mammals contains many different chemical messengers or neurotransmitters. Each individual neuron usually has the capacity to synthesize and release only one particular neurotransmitter, although recent evidence indicates that two or more different neurotransmitters may coexist within the same neuron (Hokfelt, Johansson, Ljungdahl, Lundberg, & Schultzberg, 1980). The synthesis of a neurotransmitter occurs in the cell body of a neuron, where the nucleus containing the genetic program required to construct neurotransmitter molecules is located. Neurotransmitter molecules are packaged into small spherical storage compartments called vesicles.

Although a neurotransmitter substance is synthesized and packaged into vesicles within the neuronal cell body, it is not used as a chemical messenger until it is transported to a portion of the neuron known as the presynaptic terminal. The presynaptic terminal is an enlarged knob, found at the end of each axon that is specialized for releasing the neurotransmitter into the synapse. Neurons that have branching axonal projections that contact many other neurons have a multitude of presynaptic terminals.

Once deposited into the presynaptic terminal, the vesicle awaits its turn to release its neurotransmitter content into the synapse by a process called exocytosis. Exocytosis involves the rupturing of a vesicle such that its content is released into the synapse. The process of exocytosis is not a random occurrence but instead is directly linked to the arrival of an electrical signal or action potential at the presynaptic terminal. The exact mechanism involved in the conversion of an electrical signal into a chemical release is not known at present. However, the process of exocytosis remains hypothetical as there is some evidence to suggest that neurotransmitters may be leaked slowly from vesicles rather than discharged rapidly in quanta as expected from exocytosis (Tauc, 1982).

Nonetheless, once a neurotransmitter is released into the synapse, it is subject to one of three different fates. First, the neurotransmitter may attach itself to a receptor located on the membrane surface of the next neuron, postsynaptic neuron. As will be discussed in the next section, this receptor occupation by the neurotransmitter can produce a functional alteration in the firing rate of the postsynaptic neuron. Second, the neurotransmitter may be deactivated by local enzymes present in the extracellular fluid. These metabolic enzymes are relatively specific for which neurotransmitters they will deactivate. Once deactivated, some extracellular metabolites, or by-products, are transported into the blood and excreted through the kidneys. Finally, if a neurotransmitter is not deactivated, it may be taken into a vesicle and used again in exocytosis. This reuptake mechanism is evident with many, but not all, neurotransmitter systems.

The mechanism of the neurotransmitter function that has been described thus far may be altered by a variety of psychoactive drugs. Some drugs block the biosynthesis of neurotransmitters within the neuronal cell body, whereas others block the transport of the neurotransmitter from the cell body to the presynaptic terminal. By blocking either the normal synthetic or transport processes, the stores of neurotransmitters become depleted, as the reuptake process does not recover all of the neurotransmitter within the synapse. In addition, some psychoactive drugs alter normal neurotransmitter function by disrupting the storage, release, or reuptake processes at the presynaptic terminal. Amphetamines, for example, stimulate the release of the neurotransmitter dopamine, whereas cocaine blocks the reuptake of dopamine into the presynaptic terminal. Thus, both amphetamine and cocaine increase the availability of dopamine within the synapse, albeit by different mechanisms of actions. An increase in dopamine within the synapse is also obtained following the administration of a drug that inhibits the degradative enzyme, monoamine oxidase (MAO), which normally inactivates dopamine within the synapse. Finally, many psychoactive drugs of abuse alter the normal function of neurotransmitters located on the postsynaptic neuron.

In order to understand the biochemical substrates of drug abuse, a few of the specific neurotransmitters that have been identified within the brain are discussed here. In particular, various drugs of abuse involve the neurotransmitters dopamine, norepinephrine, serotonin, and gamma-aminobutyric acid (GABA). The biosynthetic pathways for each of these different neurotransmitters share several common features. First, each of these neurotransmitters is synthesized from an amino acid precursor (tyrosine, tryptophan, or glutamate) that is either found in our diet or that is synthesized readily from an essential amino acid found in our diet. Second, the synthesis and metabolism of each neurotransmitter is controlled by the availability of different endogenous enzymes that are required to perform the different biochemical reactions. The enzymes involved in synthesizing the neurotransmitter are found generally within the neuron, whereas enzymes involved in metabolizing the neurotransmitter after it is released from the presynaptic terminal are found generally outside the neuron, within the synapse. The names of these enzymes usually have suffixes ending in -ase, which means to decompose chemically. Finally, the decomposition or metabolism of each of these neurotransmitters ends in a product that can be removed from the brain and excreted.

Recent evidence indicates that peptides, which are chains of amino acids, may also function as neurotransmitters in the brain (Guillemin, 1978; Snyder, 1980). In particular, the endorphin and enkephalin opioid peptides may be involved in the action of drugs of abuse. Both the endorphins and enkephalins can produce a number of behavioral effects that are similar to those produced by morphine. (Recent reviews of the psychopharmacological aspects of opioid peptides can be found in Frederickson & Geary [1982] and Olson, Olson, Kastin, & Coy [1984].)

Acetylcholine

Acetylcholine was first identified as a transmitter chemical in the peripheral nervous system. It is now known also to be present in large amounts in brain tissue. Following synthesis, acetylcholine is thought to be stored inside the nerve terminal within synaptic vesicles until it is released into the synapse upon arrival of an action potential from the axon. The acetylcholine then diffuses across the synaptic gap and attaches itself to receptors on the dendrite of the next neuron, which results in the transmission of information between the two neurons. This attachment is important because some psychoactive drugs may either mimic the action of acetylcholine at the dendrite receptor or else block access of the transmitter to the receptor. Drugs that mimic the action of acetylcoholine at the receptor include compounds such as nicotine, which may alter behavior. Agents thought to block access to acetylcholine to the receptors include atropine and scopolamine. Once acetylcholine has exerted its effect on the postsynaptic dendrite, its action is terminated by an enzyme. Drugs which inhibit the destructive enzyme induce nightmares, confusion, hallucinations, feelings of agitation, confusion, and a slowing of intellectual and motor functions.

Norepinephrine and Dopamine

The term *catecholamine* refers to a group of chemically related compounds, the most important of which are epinephrine, norepinephrine, and dopamine. In the peripheral nervous system, epinephrine is a neurotransmitter important in the maintenance of such major body functions as blood pressure and heart rate. Epinephrine is not commonly found in the brain. Norepinephrine and dopamine appear to be the catecholamine neurotransmitters in the brain. Many drugs that profoundly affect brain function and behavior exert their effects by altering the synaptic action of norepinephrine and dopamine in the brain.

In recent years, much has been learned about the precise localization of dopamine and norepinephrine neurons and synapses within the brain. The cell bodies and dendrites are situated in one area of the brain, and the axons travel to other sites in the brain, where they synapse with the dendrites of other cells. It appears that most norepinephrine cell bodies are situated in the brainstem and that these cell bodies send axons to certain brain structures. Other cell bodies send axons from the brainstem down to the spinal cord. Because the lower brain and the brainstem appear to be essential to the display of basic instinctual behavior in hunger, thirst, emotion, and sex, norepinephrine may be a neurotransmitter important in the regulation of these functions.

Dopamine cell bodies are primarily situated in the *substantia nigra*. These cells send axons to a group of structures called the *basal ganglia*. The dopamine neurons play an important role in movement, and loss of dopamine is associated with the disorder called Parkinson's disease. Some drugs are capable of blocking the reuptake of norepinephrine from the synapse back into the nerve terminal, thus increasing the action of norepinephrine at the synapse. Such compounds include cocaine and a series of drugs that elevate mood and reverse depression (the tricyclic antidepressants). Some drugs are capable of blocking the movement of norepinephrine from the presynaptic nerve terminal into the synaptic vesicle where the transmitter is stored and protected from the enzyme MAO. An example of such a drug is reserpine. As a result of this blockage, norepinephrine may be metabolized by MAO and the nervous system depleted of the transmitter, resulting in sedation and emotional depression. Some drugs, such as amphetamine, are capable of inducing the release of norepinephrine from the nerve terminal.

Serotonin

Serotonin, like acetylcholine, norepinephrine, and dopamine, is believed to be a neurotransmitter in the brain. Several hallucinogenic compounds (LSD, for example) have been found to resemble serotonin structurally, and the hypothesis has been suggested that at least some drug-induced hallucinations are due to alterations in the functioning of the serotonin neurons. In the brain, significant amounts of serotonin are found in the upper brainstem. Serotonin appears to be involved in the regulation of body temperature, sensory perception, and sleep. Its other functions are less clear. Like norepinephrine and dopamine, serotonin is destroyed by the enzyme MAO.

GABA

GABA (gamma-aminobutyric acid) is the major inhibitor of neurotransmission in the brain. In drug studies, it has been shown that the antianxiety effects of benzodiazepine tranquilizers occur when the synaptic actions of GABA are facilitated. These studies initiated a search for a "natural Valium," which would correspond to the discovery of enkephalins, which we call "natural opiates." Although no endogenous antianxiety compounds have been identified yet, it is generally agreed that the benzodiazepines potentiate the actions of GABA within the brain.

Receptors

Embedded within the outer membrane surface of each neuron are numerous receptors, which are protein structures specialized in recognizing specific neurotransmitter substances at the synapse. Although each neuron typically synthesizes and releases only one neurotransmitter, there may be a variety of different receptor types on the surface of a single neuron, depending upon how many different neurons synapse upon it. In general, each receptor is capable of recognizing only one particular type of neurotransmitter, thus preventing "cross-talk" between two synapses that reside close together but utilize different neurotransmitters. To date, receptors have been isolated for each one of the neurotransmitters found within the brain.

When a receptor is occupied by a neurotransmitter that alters neurotransmission, the receptor is said to be activated. Receptor activation involves some change within the postsynaptic neuron that leads ultimately to an increase or decrease in the permeability of the postsynaptic membrane to ions involved in electrical transmission. Excitatory neurotransmitters are those that increase the firing rate of postsynaptic neurons by increasing membrane permeability to ions, whereas inhibitory neurotransmitters decrease the firing rate of postsynaptic neurons by decreasing membrane permeability to ions. The exact nature of the intraneural events responsible for transforming a chemical message at the receptor into an electrical message at the postsynaptic membrane is not known at present.

Many drugs of abuse produce their effect on the brain by occupying receptors normally utilized by neurotransmitters or by altering the second messenger system. In general, for a drug to occupy a receptor site, it must have a strong chemical attraction or affinity for the receptor, such that it can displace the natural neurotransmitter from its own receptor. Many drugs found in plant extracts or synthesized in the laboratory have greater affinity for the receptor than the endogenous neurotransmitter. Perhaps it seems surprising that the endogenous neurotransmitter may not have maximal affinity for its own receptor site. However, it should be realized that an essential property of neurotransmitter-receptor interactions is that they are reversible (Burt, 1985). The most efficient chemical message sent across the synapse is by a neurotransmitter that attaches to and detaches from the receptor optimally. This contrasts with a number of psychoactive drugs that attach readily to the receptor but do not detach readily. In some cases, drugs may even attach or bind to receptors irreversibly.

When a drug attaches to postsynaptic receptors to alter synaptic neurotransmission, then the drug is said to have a *direct action*. This contrasts with the *indirect action* of some drugs, in which an alteration in synaptic neurotransmission is obtained even though the drug does not attach to postsynaptic receptors. Drugs that have a direct action on receptors are classified as either *agonists* or *antagonists,* and they often have chemical structures similar to that of the natural neurotransmitter. Agonist drugs activate the receptors in a manner that mimics the action of the natural neurotransmitter. In contrast, antagonist drugs occupy the receptors but do not activate them, thus producing a functional blockade of the postsynaptic neuron. One cannot determine a priori whether an agonist or antagonist drug will increase or decrease the firing rate of the postsynaptic neuron. If the natural neurotransmitter is excitatory on the firing rate of a postsynaptic neuron, then an agonist drug will increase the firing rate, and an antagonist will decrease it. However, if the neurotransmitter is inhibitory, then an agonist drug will decrease the firing rate, and an antagonist will increase it. Both agonist and antagonist drugs are used extensively by psychopharmacologists to investigate the neurochemical processes that mediate various behaviors. In addition, antagonist drugs offer a potentially useful pharmacologic tool to treat some cases of drug abuse.

Brain Mechanisms of Drug Reinforcement

Perhaps the most important psychopharmacologic factor involved in the self-administration of drugs of abuse involves a drug's capacity to produce a positive affective state, or reinforcement. Until recently, very little was known about the brain mechanisms involved in drug reinforcement. However, the demonstration that laboratory animals will self-administer a variety of drugs of abuse has provided an important model by which the brain mechanisms of drug reinforcement have been investigated.

Strong evidence now indicates that the *mesolimbic system* of the brain is involved in drug reinforcement. The mesolimbic system consists of dopamine-containing neurons that have their cell bodies in the mid-brain area. These cell bodies project long axons forward via the medial forebrain bundle to innervate the *nucleus accumbens* and other diffuse structures of the limbic system, including the septum, amygdala, and olfactory tubercle (Issacson, 1974). Electrical stimulation of the mesolimbic pathway along the medial forebrain bundle is reinforcing, and this reinforcing effect is thought to be produced by the release of dopamine from the presynaptic terminals that innervate the target limbic structures.

The dopamine mesolimbic system appears to play an essential role in mediating the reinforcing effect of stimulant drugs such as amphetamine and cocaine. As mentioned previously, both amphetamine and cocaine activate dopamine systems by increasing the availability of dopamine within the synapse. Dopamine antagonists such as pimozide, which are effective in blocking the reinforcing effect of electrical stimulation of the medial forebrain bundle (Wauquier & Niemegeers, 1972), are also effective in reducing the reinforcing effect of stimulant drugs (Risner & Jones, 1976; Yokel & Wise, 1976). It is not clear at present, however, whether other dopamine systems (such as the nigrostriatal and tuberohypophyseal systems) are also involved in the maintenance of self-administration of stimulant drugs.

In addition to mediating the reinforcing effect of stimulant drugs, recent evidence indicates that the dopamine mesolimbic system may mediate, at least in part, the reinforcing effect of opiate drugs such as heroin and morphine (Bozarth, 1983). Opiate receptors have been localized on dopamine-containing neurons in the mesolimbic system (Pollard, Lelorens, Bonnet, Costentin, & Schwartz, 1977). In general, the administration of morphine produces an excitatory effect on the firing rate of neurons within the major dopaminergic pathways to the brain, and this excitatory effect is accompanied by an increase in the synthesis and release of dopamine (Iwamoto & Way, 1979). Most important, however, morphine is reinforcing when injected directly into the ventral tegmental areas of the mesolimbic system but not when injected into a brain region just outside the ventral tegmental area (Phillips & LePiane, 1980). Also, the reinforcing effect of morphine in the ventral tegmental area is blocked by the administration of the opiate antagonist naloxone, suggesting that opiate receptors in this brain region are involved in drug reinforcement.

In contrast to stimulant and opiate drugs, the brain mechanisms involved in the reinforcing effects of other drugs of abuse are less well understood. The most widely abused class of drugs today is the sedative hypnotics, which include alcohol, methaqualone (Quaalude), the barbiturates (e.g., Seconal, Nembutal, and Amytal), and the benzodiazepines (e.g., Librium, Valium, and Dalmane). Despite their wide abuse, little is known about the neuroanatomical pathways involved in the action of sedative hypnotics. However, it is thought that alcohol and barbiturates have a general, depressant action on neuronal membranes, whereas the benzodiazepines have a more selective action at inhibitory GABA synapses (Harvey, 1980).

Finally, the brain mechanisms involved in the reinforcing effects of the hallucinogens and THC are poorly understood, in large part because laboratory animals will not readily self-administer these drugs. However, it is known that the lysergic acid diethylamide (LSD) is an agonist drug at serotonin receptors located on cell bodies of serotonin-containing neurons in the raphe nucleus (Cooper, Bloom, & Roth, 1982). In addition, recent evidence indicates that acetylcholine pathways within the limbic system mediate, at least in part, some of the behavioral effects of THC (Miller & Branconnier, 1983). It remains to be determined whether hallucinogenic drugs influence the mesolimbic system or some other reward system within the brain.

References

Bozarth, M. A. (1983). Opiate reward mechanisms mapped by intracranial self-administration. In J. E. Smith & J. D. Lane (Eds.), *The neurobiology of opiate reward processes* (pp. 331-359). Amsterdam: Elsevier.

Burt, D. R. (1985). Criteria for receptor identification. In H. I. Yamamura, S. J. Enna, & M. J. Kuhar (Eds.), *Neurotransmitter receptor binding*. New York: Raven.

Cooper, J. R., Bloom, F. E., & Roth, R. H. (1982). *The biochemical basis of neuropharmacology*. New York: Oxford University Press.

Frederickson, R. C. A., & Geary, L. E. (1982). Endogenous opioid peptides: Review of physiological, pharmacological, and clinical aspects. *Progress in Neurobiology, 19*, 19-69.

Guillemin, R. (1978). Peptides in the brain: The new endocrinology of the neuron. *Science, 202,* 390-402.

Harvey, S. C. (1980). Hypnotics and sedatives. In A. G. Gilman, L. S. Goodman, & A. Gilman (Eds.), *The pharmacological basis of therapeutics* (5th ed., pp. 102-136). New York: Macmillan.

Hokfelt, T., Johansson, O., Ljungdahl, A., Lundberg, J. M., & Schultzberg, M. (1980). Peptidergic neurones. *Nature, 284,* 515-521.

Issacson, R. L. (1974). *The limbic system.* New York: Plenum.

Iwamoto, E. T., & Way, E. L. (1979). Opiate actions and catecholamines. In H. H. Loh & D. H. Ross (Eds.), *Advances in biochemical psychopharmacology: Vol. 1. Neurochemical mechanisms of opiates and endorphins* (pp. 357-407). New York: Raven.

Mayer, S. E., Melmon, K. L., Gilman, A. G. (1980). The dynamics of drug absorption, distribution, and elimination. In A. G. Gilman, L. S. Goodman, & A. Gilman (Eds.), *The pharmacological basis of therapeutics* (5th ed.) New York: Macmillan.

Miller, L. L., & Branconnier, R. J. (1983). Cannabis: Effects on memory and the cholinergic limbic system. *Psychological Bulletin, 93,* 441-456.

Olson, G. A., Olson, R. D., Kastin, A. J., & Coy, D. H. (1984). Endogenous opiates: 1983. *Peptides, 5,* 975-992.

Phillips, A. G., & LePiane, F. G. (1980). Reinforcing effects of morphine microinjection into the ventral tegmental area. *Pharmacology, Biochemistry, & Behavior, 12,* 965-968.

Pollard, H., Llorens, D., Bonnet, J. J., Costentin, J., & Schwartz, J. C. (1977). Opiate receptors on mesolimbic dopaminergic neurons. *Neuroscience Letters, 7,* 295-299.

Risner, M. E., & Jones, B. E. (1976). Role of noradrenergic and dopaminergic processes in amphetamine self-administration. *Pharmacology, Biochemistry, & Behavior, 5,* 447-482.

Snyder, S. H. (1980). Brain peptides as neurotransmitters. *Science, 209,* 976-983.

Tauc, L. (1982). Nonvesicular release of neurotransmitter. *Physiological Reviews, 62,* 857-893.

Van Dyke, C., Jatlow, P., Ungerer, J., Barash, P. G., & Byck, R. (1978). Oral cocaine: Plasma concentrations and central effects. *Science, 200,* 201-213.

Wauquier, A., & Niemegeers, C. J. E. (1972). Intracranial self-stimulation in rats as a function of various stimulus parameters: II. Influence of haloperidol, pimozide and pipamperone on medial forebrain bundle stimulation with monopolar electrodes. *Psychopharmacologia, 27,* 191-202.

Yokel, R. A., & Wise, R. A. (1976). Attenuation of intravenous amphetamine reinforcement by central dopamine blockade in rats. *Psychopharmacology, 48,* 311-318.

3

NARCOTICS

Definition of Narcotic

The narcotic drugs include some of our most valuable medicines, as well as some of the most abused. The term *narcotic* originally referred to opium and the drugs made from opium, such as heroin, codeine, and morphine. Opium is obtained from the opium poppy; morphine and codeine are extracted from opium, and heroin is made chemically from morphine. Medical science subsequently synthesized drugs that have properties similar to heroin, codeine, or morphine. These drugs are also classified as narcotic drugs. To clarify terminology further, "opiate" refers to any substance of natural or synthetic origin that has morphinelike effects. (Federal law classifies the coca leaf and a chemical derived from it, cocaine, as narcotics, but these drugs are stimulants and medical science does not consider them narcotics. Cocaine is treated in Chapter 6.)

Extent of Use

Since the late 1960s several sophisticated statistical techniques have been brought to bear to estimate the number of heroin users in the United States. Different groups of researchers have estimated the number of heroin addicts from 1970 to the mid-1980s, and the estimates mostly range between 400,000 and 500,000 (Brodsky, 1985).

Indicators of heroin use changed during the 1970s. When those admitted for treatment were asked in what year they began heroin use, relative "peaks" were seen in the periods 1968-1972 and 1974-1976. Although few people report heroin use in household surveys or in the national survey of high school seniors, those figures indicated peaks during the same time periods (Crider, 1985). The Drug Abuse Warning Network (DAWN) reports also indicated higher levels of heroin-related medical emergencies and deaths at those times. Those two periods of somewhat higher heroin use, perhaps among those experimenting with heroin or using it for the first time, have been referred to as "epidemics." They seem to correspond with times at which heroin prices were relatively low and purity relatively high, both indicating a greater supply.

In 1970 public and federal concern began to focus on the problem of heroin addiction among service personnel stationed in Southeast Asia (U.S. House of Representatives Committee on Armed Services, 1971). Heroin was about 95% pure and almost openly sold in South Vietnam. Not only was the Southeast Asia heroin undiluted, it was inexpensive. The high purity of the heroin make it possible to obtain psychological effect by smoking or sniffing the drug. This fact, coupled with the misconception that addiction occurs only when the drug is used intravenously, resulted in about 40% of the users sniffing, about 50% smoking, and only 10% mainlining their heroin (U.S. House of Representatives Committee on Foreign Affairs, 1971).

Some early 1971 reports estimated that 10% to 15% of the American troops in Vietnam were addicted to heroin. However, an excellent follow-up study of veterans who returned from Vietnam in September 1971 showed that most of the Vietnam heroin users did not continue heroin use in this country. Only 1% to 2% were using narcotics 8 to 12 months after returning from Vietnam and being released from the service, approximately the same percentage of individuals found to be using narcotics when examined for induction into the service (Robins, 1974).

Substances of Abuse

Heroin. Heroin is a white or brown powder. It produces an intense euphoria, making it the most popularly abused narcotic. Similar to all narcotic drugs, a tolerance develops rapidly and the abuser must ingest increasingly larger quantities to get "high."

Heroin is administered in a variety of ways, including sniffing ("snorting"), smoking, and injection under the skin ("popping") or into a vein ("mainlining"). For the latter two methods, the powder is liquified before it is administered. The first emotional reaction is an easing of fears and relief from worry. This is often followed by a state of inactivity bordering on stupor.

Heroin is synthesized from morphine and, weight for weight, is up to 10 times more potent in its pharmacologic effects. Pure heroin is "cut" or diluted by the trafficker with such substances as milk sugar or quinine, or both. The drug sold to the addict as heroin usually contains one part heroin and nine or more parts other substances.

Morphine. For many years, morphine was the drug of choice for the relief of pain. It is often used by street drug users when heroin is difficult to obtain. Euphoria can be produced with small doses. Tolerance and physical dependence build up rapidly.

Codeine. Most commonly abused in the form of cough preparations, codeine is less addictive than morphine or heroin and less potent, in terms of producing euphoria. When withdrawal symptoms occur, they are less severe than with the more potent drugs.

Hydromorphone (Dihydromorphinone). This drug is made from morphine. Although it is almost as potent as heroin, its use does not seem to produce the same thrill as mainlining heroin does.

Oxycodone (Dihydrohydroxycodeinone). This drug is made from codeine. It is classified as a drug with high addiction potential. Although effective orally, most users dissolve tablets in water, filter out the insoluble binders, and mainline the active drug.

Meperidine. A product of chemical laboratories rather than poppy fields, this drug was claimed to be without addicting potential when first produced. Experience, however, has proved otherwise. Dependence on this drug is slower to develop and less intense than with morphine.

Methadone. Methadone was invented by German chemists in 1941, when the supply of morphine to Germany ran low. It has many properties similar to those of morphine, among which is the ability to relieve pain and to produce physical and psychologic dependence. A major difference between methadone and morphine and heroin is that when it is taken orally, under medical supervision, it prevents withdrawal symptoms for approximately 24 hours, but it is quite addictive when taken by itself over years.

Pharmacology
Chemistry

Raw opium contains about 10% by weight of morphine and a smaller amount of codeine. The addition of two acetyl groups to the morphine molecule results in diacetylmorphine, otherwise known as heroin. The acetyl groups allow heroin to penetrate the blood-brain barrier more readily, and heroin is therefore two to three times more potent than morphine. Other natural opiate derivatives are obtained by modification of the two hydroxyl groups.

Medicinal chemists have worked hard over the decades to produce compounds that would be effective pain relievers, trying without success to separate the analgesic effect of the narcotics from their dependence-producing effects. As a result there are several synthetic narcotics sold as prescription pain relievers.

In addition to the narcotic analgesics, this search for new compounds led to the discovery of *narcotic antagonists,* drugs that block the action of morphine, heroin, or other narcotics. The administration of a drug such as naloxone or naltrexone can reverse the depressed respiration resulting from a narcotic overdose. If given to an individual who has been taking narcotics and has become physically dependent, these antagonists can precipitate an immediate withdrawal syndrome, as though the previously taken narcotic had been removed from the body.

Mechanism of Action

The pharmacologic actions of morphine and related opiates are extremely complex. Although great advances have been made, the exact mechanism by which opioids exert their effects remains uncertain. The definitive research showing that all vertebrates have built-in antipain compounds in the CNS is one of the most exciting discoveries in the field of drug abuse. Furthermore, these compounds act on specific receptor sites at nerve cell synapses, the same binding sites occupied by the drugs we call narcotics.

These receptors would be fashioned like locks, to accept only key-shaped internal or injected compounds with pain-relieving or euphoriant effects, such as opiatelike molecules. Slight modification of the structure of opiates, or of their electric charges, will not permit a "fit" with the receptor molecule, and all narcotic activity will be lost.

The distribution of these receptors in the nervous system does not correlate precisely with the distribution of any one neurotransmitter or any recognized neural system, although the limbic system and periaqueductal gray matter, areas that may play a role in opioid analgesia, are particularly enriched.

In a general way, the distribution of opiate receptors in the brain resembles the distribution of a neurotransmitter. For example, dopamine is packaged in granules of certain nerve endings; its overall distribution in the brain is patchy, with small regions of high concentrations and other areas with no detectable amounts at all. Dopamine receptors are distributed to correspond with the dopamine in nerve endings, as a neurotransmitter, and when it is released, it has to combine with a specific receptor in order to cause its typical biologic effect; for the endogenous opioid, it might be euphoria or relief of pain.

It is known that minor manipulations of the spatial configuration of a narcotic can change it from a strong narcotic agonist to a narcotic antagonist that will prevent any narcotic from producing its effects. This occurs because a narcotic antagonist such as naltrexone can displace or prevent an agonist such as morphine from occupying the available narcotic receptor sites.

The unusually high structural specificity of the opiates and of the opiate receptors, as well as the actual presence of the receptors and their distribution, which suggested they might be neurotransmitter receptors, raised the question as to why they should exist. Other neurotransmitter receptors are activated by endogenous neurotransmitters, and so logically it would seem that there are natural opioid substances that activate the opiate receptors. Thus the search for an "endogenous ligand" of the opiate receptor began (*ligand* means a molecule that binds to a receptor).

In 1975, a pair of molecules, leu-enkephalin and met-enkephalin, were isolated from animal brain extracts. These *enkephalins* acted like morphine but were many times more potent. It was interesting that these enkephalin molecules were from a chemical class known as *peptides,* sequences of amino acids linked together, and it was soon recognized that the same sequence of amino acids occurred in a larger molecule that had been isolated from the pituitary gland. This led to the discovery of a group of *endorphins* (endogenous morphinelike substances) that are also found in brain tissue and that also have potent opiate effects.

Since this discovery, endorphin-containing neurons and opiate receptors have been located in the pain pathways in the brain and spinal cord and in the nerves supplying the intestines. The endorphins are in the nerve terminals, like neurotransmitters. This means they can be released by nerve activity to act on the opiate receptors of adjacent neurons. Thus release of endorphin in the spinal cord can shut down pain messages and prevent their ascent to the brain by inhibiting other neurons. Suppose a nerve cell uses acetylcholine or dopamine as its neurotransmitter. If this acetylcholine- or dopamine-containing nerve cell has opiate receptors, and if endorphin is released nearby, the release of acetylcholine or dopamine will be decreased. Thus the function of the nerve cell on which the acetylcholine or dopamine would have acted will be depressed. However, we still know very little about what kinds of circumstances turn the release of endorphins on or off, and where this occurs in the brain or spinal cord (Goldstein, 1979).

Effects

Morphine and the morphinelike analgesic agents produce major effects on the CNS and the gastrointestinal system. The outstanding effect of morphine on humans is the relief of pain. This action is very selective; other senses are altered very little or not at all. Although morphine is effective for all types of pain, it is more so against continuous dull pain than against sharp intermittent pain. In the study of analgesic action in humans, pain is separated into two components: (1) as a specific sensation, which you feel; and (2) as suffering, or how you react to the specific sensation. Morphine and morphinelike compounds decrease the perception of pain, and also alter the individual's reaction to it.

The latter effect is undoubtably part of the euphoria. The individual is aware of the pain but is not bothered by it. The administration of morphine to certain individuals, particularly to those not experiencing pain, may result in an unpleasant experience consisting of mild anxiety, or even fear, and frequently nausea, sometimes with vomiting. This state is called dysphoria. Sleep is produced with larger doses of morphine, but the central depressant actions of morphine do not decrease anticonvulsant activity or cause slurred speech or significant motor incoordination, as do barbiturates. A person's respiratory center is quite sensitive to the actions of morphine, and death from morphine overdose is attributable to respiratory failure. Morphine can contract bronchial smooth muscle, thereby decreasing the individual's ability to obtain oxygen. It will also constrict the pupil of the human eye, and pinpoint pupils are of diagnostic value. In opiate dependence, tolerance to this effect of morphine does not develop. Morphine can cause excitation in some individuals.

Therapeutic Uses

Natural and synthetic morphinelike drugs are effective pain relievers. They are among the most valuable drugs available to physicians and are widely used for short-term acute pain resulting from surgery, fractures, burns, and the like, as well as to reduce suffering in the later stages of terminal illnesses, such as cancer.

Analgesia. The major therapeutic indication of morphine and the other narcotics is the reduction of pain. The effects of narcotics are relatively specific to pain. Fewer effects on mental and motor ability accompany analgesic doses of these agents than with equipotent doses of other analgesic and depressant drugs.

Antitussive actions. The narcotics also have the effect of decreasing coughing. Codeine has been widely used for its antitussive properties and is still available in some prescription cough remedies. Nonprescription cough remedies contain dextromethorphan, a narcotic analogue that is more selective in its antitussive effects.

Gastrointestinal. Regarding diarrheal disorders, synthetic opioids are proving effective agents for decrease of bowel motility. The opiates remain at the forefront of treatment for these disorders.

Causes for Concern

Acute toxicity. In acute morphine poisoning, the individual is comatose and cyanotic, with slow respiration and pinpoint-size pupils. The major development in the treatment of acute morphine poisoning has been the discovery of the antidotal action of nalorphine or naltrexone.

Most opiate-dependent individuals take heroin. However, heroin, by the time it reaches the user, is grossly contaminated with such things as starch, quinine, baking soda, and mannitol. Its strength is seldom known, and thus it is not surprising that heroin overdose accounts for about 1% of the deaths of heroin users. Nonsterile drugs and equipment, and faulty techniques, cause much damage. The practice of sharing the same needle to inject drugs into the veins can result in the spread of such blood-borne diseases as serum hepatitis and AIDS. Hepatitis was the most frequent complication observed by Louria, Hensle, and Rose (1967) and was seen in 42 of the 100 cases of complications of heroin dependence studied by this group. Bacterial infection of the heart occurs quite often, and is fatal more often than hepatitis. Acute pulmonary congestion and edema are also frequent findings.

Chronic toxicity. Prolonged misuse of opiates usually results in physical dependence, withdrawal, and tolerance to the actions of the narcotic being abused.

Physical Dependence

Morphine produces a strong physical dependence. The withdrawal symptoms appear a few hours after the last dose and reach peak intensity in 36 to 72 hours. The time of onset, peak intensity, and duration of the withdrawal phenomenon vary with the degree of dependence, the characteristics of the drug, and the individual using it. Methadone has effects that last much longer than those of morphine, and has a much slower and less traumatic withdrawal syndrome. Administration of a specific antagonist, such as nalorphine, promptly precipitates a rapid and intense withdrawal syndrome.

The classic 1950s stereotype of "cold turkey" withdrawal is not indicative of the contemporary heroin experience. Today's chronic heroin user develops only a mild degree of physical dependence on heroin, reflecting the common practice of extreme dilution so evident on the streets. The addict admitted to a medical ward for withdrawal or medical complication can usually be treated with mild sedation without resorting to substitute narcotics such as methadone.

Cross-addiction is a common phenomenon with today's heroin user, whether "speedballing" with an intravenous combination of heroin and cocaine, or indulging simultaneously with barbiturates and alcohol.

Abstinence Syndrome

There is considerable information available concerning the characteristics of withdrawal to narcotics. The person dependent on these drugs seeks them for their euphorogenic effects as well as to ward off the unpleasant withdrawal syndrome that occurs about 4 to 8 hours after the last dose, and which reaches a peak in 36 to 72 hours. Depending on the severity of the withdrawal syndrome, disturbances will subside in 5 to 10 days.

At first, the seeking of euphorogenic effects is the reason for repeated use of the drug. Warding off withdrawal does not come into play until the individual has received a number of doses of the narcotic. Once the dependence is established, the fear of withdrawal becomes a predominant reason for the continued use. In many instances, the opiate-dependent individual will maintain the "addiction" to avoid withdrawal.

The opiate withdrawal is characterized by abdominal pain, irritability, cold sweats, yawning, gooseflesh, diarrhea, nausea, perspiration, and vomiting. These effects will be noticed within the first 24 hours of abstinence. They are uncomfortable but not life threatening in healthy individuals. The user may also fall asleep for several hours. "Rebound" excitability of the CNS, manifested by pupillary dilation, increases in heart rate, a rise in blood pressure, involuntary twitching and kicking, and spontaneous sexual orgasms, may occur. Tremors and pain in the back and extremities are common complaints. A user can lose 10 pounds in 24 hours and also suffer from disturbances in acid-base balance and dehydration.

A number of medical disorders can complicate matters and increase the severity of withdrawal. These disorders include arthritis, damage to the liver, peptic ulcer, ulcerative colitis, epilepsy, and diabetes. A number of cardiovascular diseases such as congestive heart failure, severe hypertension, and anginal syndrome, as well as respiratory disease or asthma and pneumonia, also can potentiate the danger of withdrawal.

Tolerance

With the morphine-type analgesics, tolerance evolves primarily to the respiratory depressant, analgesic, sedative, and euphorogenic effects. The rate of tolerance development depends on the pattern of use. Intermittent use lessens the possibility of development of tolerance while continuous use increases it. However, the dose is still limited, and even in the tolerant opiate-dependent individual, death from an overdose will result from respiratory depression. Significant tolerance does not develop to the constipating effect of the bowels. Individuals who are tolerant to one of the opiate analgesics will be tolerant to the others; this is called *cross-tolerance,* as previously defined. Tolerance is rapidly lost upon withdrawal of the opiates, so that reinstitution of the drug at the prewithdrawal dose may result in overdose. In this regard, chronic users have been known to take as much as 4 grams of a drug in 24 hours—far greater than the lethal dose for a nontolerant person. The duration of tolerance is 1 to 2 weeks, and following this period of abstinence, the individual again responds to a small dose of the drug.

References

Brodsky, M. D. (1985). History of heroin prevalence estimation techniques. In National Institute on Drug Abuse, *Self-report methods of estimating drug use* (Research Monograph No. 57). Washington, DC: Government Printing Office.

Crider, R. A. (1985). Heroin incidence: A trend comparison between national household survey data and indicator data. In National Institute on Drug Abuse, *Self-report methods of estimating drug use* (Research Monograph No. 57). Washington, DC: Government Printing Office.

Goldstein, A. (1979). Recent advances in basic research relevant to drug abuse. In R. L. Dupont, A. Goldstein, & J. O'Donnell (Eds.), *Handbook on drug abuse* (pp. 439-446). Washington, DC: National Institute on Drug Abuse.

Louria, D. B., Hensle, T., & Rose, T. (1967). The major medical complications of heroin addiction. *Annals of Internal Medicine, 67,* 1.

Robins, L. N. (1974). *The Vietnam user returns* (Monograph Series A, No. 2, Contract No. HSM-42-72-75). Washington, DC: Special Action Office for Drug Abuse Prevention.

U.S. House of Representatives Committee on Armed Services. (1971). *Inquiry into alleged drug abuse in the armed services* (Report of special subcommittee). Washington, DC: Government Printing Office.

U.S. House of Representatives Committee on Foreign Affairs. (1971). *The world heroin problem* (Committee print). Washington, DC: Government Printing Office.

4

CENTRAL NERVOUS SYSTEM DEPRESSANTS:

Sedative-Hypnotics

The purpose of this chapter is to review available information on central nervous system (CNS) depressants, including pharmacology, prevalence, and abuse potential.

This discussion is limited to the barbiturates, the nonbarbiturate sedative-hypnotics, the benzodiazepines, and inhalents. Alcohol, one of the most widely used CNS depressants, presents a problem of such magnitude and is so unique in nature that it requires independent attention.

Drugs that induce a ready sleep are hypnotic. For centuries, the only such drugs known were alcohol, opium, and belladonna. The hypnotic-type drugs are general CNS depressants, depressing both the CNS and a wide range of cellular functions in many vital organ systems. In small doses, hypnotics have a sedative effect with a tendency to produce drowsiness or apathy; with an overdose, they are anesthetic, and ultimately fatal. In prescribed dosage, they usually induce sleep. These drugs do not relieve pain, as do morphine or aspirin. The hypnotic drugs are primarily abused by the adult community. Many people who have lost the habit of sleep without the assistance of drugs become very dependent on them.

Barbiturates

The barbiturates refer to any of the derivatives of barbituric acid. More than 2,500 barbiturates have been synthesized but, although approximately 50 of these have been approved for clinical use, only about a doxen are widely used. These drugs, however, are the most common, and perhaps the most valuable, CNS depressants utilized in medicine today.

The traditional method of classifying the barbiturates is based upon their relative duration of action. The ultrashort-acting barbiturates, sodium methoxital (Brevital), sodium thiamylal (Surital), and sodium thiopental (Pentothal), are employed primarily as intravenous anesthetics, often in conjunction with nitrous oxide or other inhalational agents. The short- to intermediate-acting barbiturates are used primarily as sedative-hypnotic agents; they include amobarbital (Amytal), sodium butabarbital (Butisol), sodium pentobarbital (Nembutal), secobarbital (Seconal), and vinbarbital (Delvinal). Phenobarbital (Luminal), mephobarbital (Mebaral), and metharbital (Gemonil) are long-acting barbiturates and are used as sedative-hypnotics and as agents in the emergency room treatment of convulsions.

Although it must be kept in mind that the action of these drugs upon the CNS depends on the particular barbiturate, the dosage, the route of administration, the state of the CNS at the time of administration, and the degree of tolerance that may exist, it is possible to present some general information about the pharmacology and effects of the barbiturates.

Pharmacology

Although barbituates may be injected, oral administration is the safest and most common method of introducing them into the body. These drugs are absorbed rapidly from the stomach and, because there is no impenetrable barrier to their diffusion, they enter the bloodstream and tend to be distributed uniformly throughout the body. The further distribution and concentration of the barbiturates in various tissues and organs are largely dependent upon lipid solubility and protein bonding. Thus fat depots and protein-rich organ tissues accumulate the highest concentrations of the barbiturates. Great variations exist among the different barbiturate compounds. The highly lipid-soluble and protein-bound drugs, such as thiopental, are absorbed more rapidly by the brain and other organs, and thus are of quicker onset and shorter duration of action.

Mechanisms of Action

Barbiturates depress the reticular activating system (RAS) by interfering with oxygen consumption and energy-producing mechanisms in the neurons. Like other cells, neurons take up oxygen and glucose from the blood and convert the glucose into a usable form of energy, the ATP molecule. Barbiturates inhibit the breakdown and the formation of ATP. Thus the neurons are deprived of their usable form of energy and become inactive. The depression of the RAS greatly reduces the number of impulses reaching the cerebral cortex, thus promoting calmness, drowsiness, and sleep, depending on the dosage.

Effects

Whereas peripheral structures will not be directly affected until significantly higher dose levels are attained, the CNS is extremely sensitive to the depressant effects of the barbiturates and will exibit physiologic responses to sedative-hypnotic doses. The barbiturates produce a general reduction in CNS activity at sedative doses, leading to drowsiness and muscular uncoordination. In some instances, however, certain individuals have experienced anxiety and excitement rather than sedation following the administration of low doses of barbiturates. In hyperkinetic children, for example, both barbiturates and amphetamines produce effects opposite to those found in the normal population. Thus, whereas barbiturates produce excitability in these children, amphetamines are used to calm the hyperactive child. The aftereffects of barbiturate-induced sleep may include drowsiness, hangover, headache, overt excitement, and decrements in motor performance, which might last for several hours.

Although the ultrashort-acting barbiturates are administered intravenously to induce anesthesia for surgery, they do not (nor do other barbiturates) relieve pain. In fact, in the presence of severe pain, the barbiturates are often incapable of producing sedation or sleep. In small doses, they may cause hyperalgesia, an increase in the reaction to painful stimuli.

Barbiturates can exert a depressant effect on the respiratory, renal, hepatic, cardiovascular, and other biologic systems, but these effects are not significant until doses well above therapeutic levels are reached. The toxic state produced by these drugs is discussed later.

The psychologic effects observed following the ingestion of the barbiturates are remarkably similar to those produced by alcohol. As with all psychoactive drugs, the set (the personality and emotional state of the user) and the setting (the environment in which the drug is taken) greatly affect the outcome of the drug experience. Thus one individual may find a pleasant, serene, and relaxed enjoyment, whereas another may feel hostile and aggressive. While low doses produce variable effects, moderate doses commonly reduce reaction time, impair mental functioning and memory, and result in slurred speech, a loss of inhibitions, a reduction in emotional control, and other effects resembling alcohol intoxication.

Continued excessive doses of barbiturates result in slurring of speech, staggering, loss of balance and falling, faulty judgment, quick temper, and a quarrelsome disposition. Overdoses, particularly when taken in conjunction with alcohol, result in unconsciousness and death unless the user receives proper medical treatment.

The appearance of drunkenness without an alcoholic breath may indicate excessive use of depressant drugs. However, an unsteady gait and speech problems may also be signs of neurologic disorders.

CNS Depressants Other than Barbiturates

Nonbarbiturate drugs are classified as sedative-hypnotic drugs. They are used therapeutically to induce sleep. Although there are a variety of chemical structures and pharmacologic properties that are exclusive to these drugs, they are in some ways similar to barbiturates in their activity. Therefore what is known about the barbiturates is also representative of the hypnotics. Drugs included in the nonbarbiturate sedative-hypnotic group are chloral hydrate (Noctec, Somnos); bromide (Bromo-Seltzer, Nervine, Sleep-Eze, Sominex); ethchlorvynol (Placidyl); paraldehyde (Cylic ether); glutethimide (Doriden) and methyprylon (Noludar); methaqualone (Quaalude, Sopor); fluthenazine (Prolixin); and carbamates (urethan and related drugs, including alcohol).

Chloral hydrate is the oldest of the nonbarbiturates. It is advantageous because it suppresses the rapid-eye-movement (REM) phase during sleep. However, its popularity has decreased with the introduction of the barbiturates. It takes about 30 minutes for chloral hydrate to take effect. Chloral hydrate is rapidly metabolized to trichloroethanol, which is the active hypnotic agent. Alcohol accelerates the rate of conversion and potentiates the CNS depressant effect. Chloral hydrate does not depress the CNS as much as a comparable dose of barbiturates. It is an excellent hypnotic, but it has a narrow margin of safety. Chloral hydrate is a stomach irritant, especially if given repeatedly and in large doses. Chloral addicts may take enormous doses of the drug; they develop tolerance and physical dependence (Harvey, 1980).

The bromides are used very little now because of their slow onset of action and their toxicity. Bromides are still available in a few over-the-counter preparations (Bromo-Seltzer, Nervine, Sleep-Eze, and Sominex). It has a half-life of 12 days and is therefore excreted slowly from the kidneys.

Paraldehyde is effective as a CNS depressant with little respiratory depression and a large safety margin. However it has a bad taste and a strong odor that saturates the breath. It is irritating to the throat and stomach. Currently paraldehyde is mainly used in institutions, most often in treatment of delirium tremens in alcoholics. The paraldehyde addict usually gets started on the drug during treatment for alcoholism and comes to prefer it to alcohol. It causes tolerance and dependence (Harvey, 1980).

Glutethimide and methyprylon are similar to secobarbital in their actions. However, glutethimide is useful in motion sickness and exhibits anticholinergic actions.

Methaqualone includes Quaaludes, which are among the most popular of the illicit drugs in the United States. It has a rapid absorption rate in the gastrointestinal tract, and its duration of action is longer than chloral hydrate. Unlike other drugs of its kind, it acts centrally on the brain and does not depress the brain reticular system or medulla.

Some of the risks of using hynotics other than for therapeutic purposes are quite apparent. Chloral hydrate may produce unconsciousness if taken in combination with alcohol. Bromides may accumulate in the body if taken daily for a period of weeks. Chronic bromide intoxication includes impaired memory, drowsiness, dizziness, irritability, skin rash, and gastrointestinal distress. Delirium, hallucinations, mania, or coma may occur in severe cases. Paraldehyde has significant effects upon the respiratory and cardiovascular systems after therapeutic doses are surpassed. At high concentrations, it inhibits the release of acetylcholine from the nerve endings and may lead to muscle weakness and fatigue. Doriden, Quaalude, and Prolixin accumulate in the body fat and thus are harder to expel from the system. The stored compound further complicates toxicity. Doriden is highly toxic. The only nonbarbiturates that rarely have any side effects include the piperidine derivatives, glutethimide and methyprylon. The nonbarbiturates are useful in producing sleep; however, precautionary measures must be taken when surpassing therapeutic levels.

Tolerance to Barbiturates and Other CNS Depressants

The CNS depressants have all been shown to be capable of producing both tolerance and, if used chronically, physical dependence. Several mechanisms are involved in the development of tolerance to these agents. The barbiturates—chloral hydrate, glutethimide, methyprylon, and meprobamate—stimulate the production of metabolic enzymes in the liver, which inactivate these drugs. Adaptation of nervous tissue to the presence of the CNS depressants also occurs. As the individual becomes experienced as to the effects produced by these drugs, a certain amount of psychologic control can be exerted. Acquired tolerance disappears almost completely after 1 or 2 weeks of abstinence. Unlike tolerance to opiates, barbiturate tolerance does not significantly increase the lethal dose. Therefore, as the individual increases the doses to maintain the same level of intoxication, the margin between the intoxicating dose and the fatal dose becomes smaller.

Because of the similarity in action of these substances, one CNS depressant is often substituted for another. Thus, for example, if one develops a dependence on one CNS depressant, the physical or psychological demands associated with the dependence may be met by using another depressant drug; that is, a cross-dependence develops. In a similar manner, if tolerance has developed to the use of a barbiturate, resistance to the effects of other CNS depressants (including alcohol) will be observed (cross-tolerance). Because of this cross-tolerance, withdrawal symptoms from dependence upon one CNS depressant may be prevented or diminished by administration of another.

Abstinence. Compared to opiate-induced withdrawal symptoms, the abstinence syndrome that develops following abrupt withdrawal of the barbiturates in a chronic user is much more dangerous. Effects observed during the barbiturate abstinence syndrome include (a) insomnia, (b) tremulousness, (c) weakness, (d) cramps, (e) vomiting, (f) hyperthermia, (g) confusion, (h) chronic blink reflex, and (i) low blood pressure. In some cases delayed convulsions and death have occurred. Alcohol is similar to the barbiturates, particularly with regard to resultant delirium tremens. Short-acting barbiturates, when abused, could lead to convulsions after the second and third day of abstinence, whereas the long-acting barbiturates might induce convulsions between the third and eighth day of abstinence (Goth, 1974).

Barbiturate Poisoning and Toxicity

Acute use of barbiturates may induce violent behavior, and overdosage will cause death due to respiratory failure. The barbiturates are the most frequent chemical agents used to commit suicide. Medical examiners are well acquainted with accidental deaths due to sublethal combinations of barbiturates and alcohol.

Unlike other addicting drugs, there is no pure antagonist to barbiturate poisoning. Even if overdosage does not result in death, other serious complications must be monitored such as cyanosis of skin, slowed respiration, hypothermia, reduced reflexes, coma, circulatory impairment, and hyperstatic pneumonia.

Benzodiazepines

The benzodiazepine family of depressants relieve anxiety, tension, and muscle spasms; produce sedation; and prevent convulsions. These substances are marketed a anxiolytics (mild or minor tranquilizers), sedatives, hypnotics or anticonvulsants based to some extent on differences in their duration of action. The first benzodiazepine, chlordiazepoxide (Librium), was introduced in 1960. Twelve members of this group currently are marketed in the United States. They are alprazolam (Xanax), chlordiazepoxide (Librium), clonazepam (Clonopin), clorazepate (Tranxene), diazepam (Valium), flurazepam (Dalmane), halazepam (Paxipam), lorazepam (Ativan), midazolam (Versed), oxazepam (Serax), prazepam (Restoril), and triazolam (Halcion).

During the first 20 years of their availability, benzodiazepines were thought to resemble closely the barbiturates in their pharmacological action. However, these drugs facilitate GABA neurotransmission. Thus they are considered to be superior to the barbiturates for most uses for which they are prescribed. They are effective and safe and overdosage is less lethal than that of other sedatives. There are two warnings, however: (a) the additive effects of benzodiazepines and alcohol can lead to serious depression of respiration and reduced visual-motor and driving skills, and (b) benzodiazepines should not be used during pregnancy.

The popularity of these compounds is indicated by the fact that diazepam and chlordiazepoxide are currently two of the most widely prescribed drugs in the United States. More than 45 million prescriptions for diazepam (Valium) are filled each year. Such use also leads to extensive misuse. Diazepam is one of the primary drug-related reasons for visits to hospital emergency rooms across the nation. It is the first or second most abused drug in many cities, and it is mentioned in more than 54,000 episodes of drug abuse. Seventy percent of these episodes involved women, and suicide attempts were involved in 51% of all incidents (Julien, 1988).

Mechanisms of Action

The benzodiazepines seem to have their primary action on the limbic system. The limbic system is considered to be the intermediary between the hypothalamus and the cerebral cortex, and it appears to control emotion. The antianxiety drugs may depress information transfer between these regions of the brain and blunt emotion. Like barbiturates (but to a lesser extent), they decrease both the spontaneous activity of the reticular activating system and its response to incoming sensory input.

The exact mechanism by which these drugs work is not known. Diazepam (Valium) and other benzodiazepines potentiate the effects of the neurotransmitter GABA. This transmitter is believed to act as an inhibitor for certain parts of the brain. An increase in GABA may lower the amount of norepinephrine and serotonin in the brain. These latter two neurotransmitters are believed to be responsible to some of the symptoms of anxiety. If they are reduced it could possibly explain the reduction of anxiety effected by the benzodiazepines. Interestingly, the brain has specific receptor sites for diazepam, chlordizepoxide, and the other benzodiazepines, even though no similar chemicals have been discovered to be produced by the body. None of the known neurotransmitters combines with these receptors (Tallman, Paul, Skolnick, & Gallagher, 1980).

Effects

Although they produce sedation, sleep, and stupor, benzodiazepines differ from the barbiturates in that they are not general neuronal depressants. That is, they act selectively at specific synapses in certain locations rather than depress every CNS neuron. Also, unlike the barbiturates, the benzodiazepines do not produce true general anesthesia at high does. However, at low to moderate doses, they all have sedative-hypnotic properties to some extent.

The benzodiazepines show only two significant peripheral effects: dilation of the blood vessels of the heart with intravenous use and, at very high doses, blockage of the nerves to the muscles.

Not all the benzodiazepines have muscle-relaxing properties, but it is a powerful and selective effect in those that do. The muscle relaxation is not peripheral but centrally mediated, although the exact sites of action are unknown. Humans develop tolerance to this effect.

Some benzodiazepines affect the reticular formation at moderate dosages, blocking arousal and causing sleep. For this reason, they are among the most commonly prescribed sleeping pills. The drowsiness they produce, however, diminishes over the course of a few days as tolerance develops. This is ultimately an advantage, since it means that benzodiazepines can soon calm a person without sedation, and therefore they are more selective than the barbiturates. Tolerance for the anxiety relieving effects have not been shown.

The behavioral effects of the benzodiazepines run the same gamut as those of the barbiturates. Sensitivity to these drugs increases with age and in the presence of liver disease, and it decreases with alcohol use, cross-tolerant drugs, or recent use of other benzodiazepines.

Side Effects

Daytime sedation and drug hangover are the most common side effects of the benzodiazepines, but their incidence is somewhat lower than that seen with the barbiturates. Other side effects include dizziness, fatigue, prolonged physical and psychomotor reaction times, incoordination, staggering, interruption of thought and psychomotor function, confusion, and amnesia. Judgment and motor performance are significantly impaired because a drug-induced "brain syndrome" occurs in a manner similar to that seen in individuals taking barbiturates. Cumulative interaction with alcohol is of special significance and especially serious. In the elderly, the drug action is prolonged and the magnitude of the "brain syndrome" is intensified.

Sleep patterns are disrupted; REM sleep is depressed; and REM rebound occurs upon drug discontinuation. It is usually less severe than that seen following cessation of barbiturate therapy, however, because the duration of action of most benzodiazepines is quite prolonged.

Despite these side effects, the benzodiazepines are remarkably safe compounds. Even when taken in huge amounts (as in suicide attempts), benzodiazepines are rarely fatal unless they are combined with other sedative drugs, such as alcohol. Cardiovascular and respiratory depression rarely occur.

Tolerance and Dependence

Their pharmacological similarity to the barbiturates and the other sedative-hypnotic compounds makes it seem likely that the benzodiazepines would induce tolerance and dependence. Indeed, after repeated use, tolerance usually develops to most of the effects of the minor tranquilizers, and the dose must be increased to obtain the desired results. Both psychological and physiological dependence on these drugs resemble dependence on alcohol and the barbiturates. The benzodiazepines used for anxiety (like Librium and Valium) and converted to active metabolites. This conversion markedly extends the effective biological half-life. High doses must be given for long periods of time and then abruptly withdrawn before marked withdrawal symptoms appear. Because of the formation of active metabolites. Withdrawal symptoms may not appear for up to a week. Withdrawal symptoms are nearly identical to those of barbiturate addition.

Cross-tolerance and cross-dependence exist among the benzodiazepines and other sedative drugs. Cross-tolerance does not appear to affect the lethal dose. Because these compounds are sedative agents, their effects are additive with those of other sedative-hypnotic compounds.

Inhalants

In 1773 nitrous oxide, or "laughing gas," was introduced. In the eighteenth and nineteenth centuries, "ether frolics" and laughing gas demonstrations were popular parlor games among the elite. Later, as medical professionals observed the participants "feeling no pain," nitrous oxide became a legitimate tool of medicine.

Although nitrous oxide was one of the first volatile substances to be abused, inhaling certain substances to get high has been a dangerous pasttime since ancient days. And it is even more risky today.

In 1978, more than 150 Americans died after sniffing fumes from volatile substances such as gasoline, spray paint, thinner, or transmission fluid. About 1,800 people needed emergency room treatment. These casualties did not happen through accidental exposure on the job. These people deliberately inhaled fumes for the intoxicating effect.

Inhalant use by high school seniors has increased steadily at a time that most other drug use has declined. Annual inhalant use, for example, increased from 4.3% in 1983 to 6.9% in 1987 (Johnson, O'Malley, & Bachman, 1987). Annual use among youth in the National Household Survey of Drug Abuse also increased from 2.9% in 1972 to 4.6% in 1979 and 5.0% in 1985 (NIDA, 1988). Yet, perhaps because inhalant abuse is often thought to be confined to special populations, or because the prevalence is low compared to abuse of other drugs, this increase has gone practically unnoticed.

Initial use of inhalants starts very young, sometimes preceding the initial use of alcohol or tobacco. Beauvais and Oetting (1988) report lifetime prevalences of inhalant use ranging from 5% to 15% among young children. Approximately half of those who try inhalants show signs of continuing use. Their results suggest there may be significant inhalant experimentation by children under the age of 12.

Research suggests that youths who begin with inhalants are more likely to continue to serious levels of drug involvement than those whose first drug is marijuana. From a geographic perspective, the highest prevalence is found in relatively isolated communities such as Indian reservations or small Hispanic communities.

Although data from the various surveys show that the typical abuser is a young teenager, inhalant-abusing emergency room patients are concentrated among 20- to 29-year-olds (DAWN, 1986). Inhalant abusers seen in emergency rooms are predominantly adult males. A substantial portion of these adults also use other drugs (NIDA, 1988). Thus the dominance of the emergency room data by adult males may reflect years of exposure or the adverse effect of combinations of drugs rather than the size of the adult population in the prevalence pool.

Like most other CNS depressants, inhalants develop a tolerance, impair judgment, distort reality perceptions, and in high concentration produce anesthesia and subsequent death. No physical dependence has been reported. Symptoms include exhilaration, lightheadedness, and hallucinations.

There are an estimated 23 chemicals involved in inhalation or "sniffing" abuse. It is nearly impossible to arrive at an accurate number because every year thousands of new products appear on the shelves of stores that sell groceries, hardware, painting, office supplies, auto parts, and nonprescription drugs. Most of the compounds fall into one of eight categories: alcohols, esters, ketones, aromatic hydrocarbons, aliphatic hydrocarbons, anesthetics, freons (fluorocarbons), and aliphatic nitrites.

Prospects for inhalation abuse include cleaning fluids, lighter fluids, spray paints, paint thinners, shoe polish, nail polish, spot removers, solvents, nonstick frying pan sprays, aerosol sprays of all kinds, typewriter correction fluid, glues, gasoline, deodorants, kerosene, and hundreds of other products. Inhalant abuse can be found at home, school, work, or just about any place.

One of the preferred chemicals is toluene, widely used in various products. In the 1970s, nitrous oxide was rediscovered as an inhalant mostly by health professionals and college students. Use of butyl nitrite fumes, sometimes found in room deodorizers, was also evident.

Butyl nitrite is closely related to amyl nitrite, a prescription drug used since 1867 to treat heart pains. When amyl nitrite became an over-the-counter drug in 1960, it was immediately popular for abusive use. Glass vials of amyl nitrite make a distinctive noise when crushed, which accounts for their nickname, "poppers." When popped and inhaled, amyl nitrite fumes give the sniffer a quick high. The Food and Drug Administration (FDA) then reclassified amyl nitrite as a prescription drug in 1969. Because butyl nitrite was readily available, it became the new favorite. Butyl nitrite is sold in capsule form or in aerosol cans in novelty stores, drug paraphernalia shops, and some record stores. Butyl nitite is favored as a sexual stimulant and euphoriant.

Methods of Use

Sticking a substance in your nose appears to be a simple operation, yet the methods of administering inhalants vary.

Hydrocarbon sniffers prefer the "bagging" technique. The user puts the inhalant into a plastic bag, places the bag tightly over the nose and mouth, and breaths deeply. This method differs from sniffing soaked rags, cotton, tissues, or sniffing from a cup or glass filled with the substance. Some people will put the substance in an empty soft drink can so they appear to be sipping a beverage. A danger in the bagging method is inhaling carbon dioxide fumes along with the hydrocarbon gases. There have been cases of suffocation when the user passed out after putting the bag over his or her head.

"Huffing," or inhaling through the mouth, is another way to absorb the inhalant when the user is concerned about irritating nasal membranes. Some people use a "flute," which is a rolled paper designed to enclose the substance at one end and direct the fumes into the mouth or nose.

How much does it take to get high from inhalants? Usually, a third of a tube of glue or adhesive is squeezed into the bag. Or, an ounce of liquid solvent will thoroughly soak a rag or handkerchief. Some people like to heat the liquids to raise the vapor output.

For aerosols, the gases have to be separated from the particulate matter in order to inhale them. The aerosol container can be turned upside down to release the gas from an upside-down position. Or, a cloth can be put over the mouth and nose to act as a filter. The more avid hydrocarbon users sniff directly from the container, or put the inhalant in a soft drink container. The less cautious aerosol sniffers bypass filtering.

Effects

Because no legal or medical requirements dictate how pure the ingredients of these store-bought products should be, potential toxicity is difficult to determine. Furthermore, there is no control of impurities. The retention, metabolism, and excretion of different substances and combinations remain unestablished.

Usually, the body absorbs substances through the stomach and intestines. This allows the digestive system to break down and direct substances to the liver, where poisons are removed. This process takes time. But when the substances are inhaled, they enter the body through the lungs and respiratory system, where materials are absorbed rapidly, sending chemicals to the brain. This method bypasses the usual, safer way of putting substances into the system. The effects, good and bad, are immediate.

Inhalants are depressants, which slow the brain and the nervous system. Like alcohol, inhalants produce giddiness or euphoria, reduce inhibitions, and induce delusions of well-being and grandeur. When used frequently or in volume, inhalants numb senses, cause hallucinations, or result in unconsciousness.

The commonly abused volatiles do not cause significant tolerance or physical dependence but can cause a wide variety of adverse effects and physical abnormalities. These include changes and damage to the kidney, liver, bone marrow, and brain. Gastroenteritis, hepatitis, jaundice, and blood abnormalities are among the complications that occur following use of these substances. Alteration of consciousness and cardiac arrhythmias are immediate whereas persistent organic brain syndrome, peripheral nerve injury, reduction in blood cell formation, and liver and kidney damage are delayed. Long-term effects may not appear for 10 to 30 years and consist primarily of an increased risk of cancer.

Chronic exposure to benzene can cause leukemia and severe anemia. Glue and contact cement contain hexane, which can damage the nervous system and cause numbness, loss of touch sensation in the feet, and limb weakness. Ketones in rubber cements, printing ink, and paint can cause similar nerve damage. Methylene chloride, used as a solvent in spray paints and thinners, is converted to carbon monoxide in the body. Freon aerosol propellants in such products as frying pan spray *(PAM)* have caused sudden death by cardiac arrhythemias when sniffing was followed by vigorous exercise. Freon has been removed from most consumer aerosol products. Gasoline additives such as TCP cause degeneration of motor nerves, and the lead additives cause lead poisoning (Comstock & Comstock, 1977). Heavy users of volatile substances commonly have slow-healing ulcers around the mouth and nose. Loss of appetite and poor eating habits may cause nutritional deficiencies as they do in the chronic alcoholic.

A study by the Addiction Research Foundation (ARF) in Canada links long-term toluene use to short-term memory loss and motor skills impairment. Brain scans have shown the cerebellum being "eaten away." Because abusers are usually young and the neurological damage is irreversible, the possible long-term effects are frightening. Another complication, "metabolic acidosis," reduces the body's potassium level to a point of total weakness.

Nitrous oxide seems to be the least toxic of the abused volatile substances. Repeated exposure for 24 hours or more may depress the bone marrow and cause death from impaired ability to form blood cells. Anesthesiologists and surgical personnel exposed to anesthetics over long periods of time have an increased risk of miscarriage, birth defects, and kidney and liver disease.

No one is certain of the safety or hazard of nitrites, the so-called recreation drugs. The immediate side effects of nitrites are well-known and not too serious. They are headaches, dizziness, nausea, and fainting. However, no data exist on long-term, continuous use, and experts caution against combining nitrites with other substances. Other experts warn against possible harm to the cardiovascular system, especially among those with potential heart disease problems.

Overdose treatment, if the abuser survives long enough to be taken to the hospital, consists of using supportive measures until he or she excretes the toxic substance. The person taken to the emergency room may have acute organic brain syndrome entailing a loss of muscular coordination, lethargy, irritability, confusion, and possible disorientation and impaired short-term memory. This condition clears up gradually as the lipid-soluble inhalant comes out of fat stores and is excreted. Most of the volatile hydrocarbons (toluene, hexane, and so on) and nitrous oxide are eliminated unchanged through the lungs.

A number of deaths have been attributed to volatile-solvent abuse. The fatalities have usually occurred when the user was alone. Death may be caused by respiratory failure or suffocation from the plastic bag used to contain the inhalant. Some types of aerosol propellant may cause cardiac arrest and kill the user that way. Other inhalants, such as hairspray, kill by coating the lungs and preventing the exchange of oxygen and carbon dioxide. An estimated 700 people died in the 1970s from inhaling all types of aerosols.

References

Beauvais, F., & Oetting, E. R. (1988). Inhalant abuse by young children. In R. A. Crider & B. A. Rouse (Eds.), *Epidemiology of inhalant abuse: An update* (DHHS Publication No. ADM 88-1577). Rockville, MD: National Institute on Drug Abuse.

Comstock, E. G., & Comstock, B. S. (1977). Medical evaluation of inhalant abuser. In C. W. Sharp & M. L. Brehm, (Eds.), *Review of inhalants: Euphoria to dysfunction* (NIDA Research Monograph No. 15). Washington, DC: U.S. Government Printing Office.

Drug Abuse Warning Network. (1984). *Quarterly report* (DHHS Series G, No. 12). Washington, DC: Government Printing Office.

Goth, A. (1974). *Medical pharmacology* (7th ed.). St Louis: C. V. Mosby.

Harvey, C. S. (1980). Hypnotics and sedatives. In A. G. Gilman, L. S. Goodman, & A. Gilman (Eds.), *The phenomenological basis of therapeutics* (6th ed.). New York: Macmillan.

Johnson, L. D., O'Malley, P. M., & Bachman, J. G. (1987). *National trends in drug use and related factors among American high school students and young adults, 1975-1986* (DHHS Publication No. ADM86-1535). Washington, DC: Government Printing Office.

Julien, R. M. (1988). *A primer of drug action* (5th ed.). New York: W. H. Freeman.

National Institute on Drug Abuse. (1988). *1985 National household survey on drug abuse*. Rockville, MD: Author.

Tallman, J. F., Paul, S. M., Skolnick, P., & Gallagher, D. W. (1980). Receptors for the age of anxiety: Pharmacology of the benzodiazepines. *Science, 207*, 274-281.

5

ALCOHOL

The use, misuse, and abuse of alcohol is one of the major health problems in the United States. Alcoholism ranks as the third most prevalent public health problem in this society. But the problems associated with alcohol are not limited to the health problems of alcoholic persons, for their alcoholic behavior leads to familial, social, vocational, and legal problems. Thus alcoholism contaminates many persons associated with the target alcoholic.

Next one must consider the fact that people use, misuse, and abuse alcohol, yet may never become alcohol dependent nor defined as alcoholic. Still these patterns of alcohol utilization contribute to health impairment, vehicular and pedestrian accidents, criminal behavior, destructive social behavior, and other adverse community consequences. Alcohol problems are therefore not limited to just alcoholics.

Alcohol is part of this overmedicated society, in which the use of psychoactive substances of many kinds is viewed as personally desirable and socially acceptable. The current widespread use of alcohol is supported by legal, personal, professional, social, and cultural sanctions—or perhaps more accurately the lack of either positive or negative sanctions. There are few social rules or guidelines about the safe and proper use of alcohol, or the avoidance and deterrence of adverse consequences of use. Thus the problems of alcohol use do not respect age, sex, ethnicity, geography, or legality. Everyone encounters the use, misuse, and abuse of alcohol in daily life.

Patterns of Use

A national survey of alcohol consumption conducted in 1982 consisted of personal interviews with over 5,000 randomly selected respondents from the household population of the contiguous United States (Miller & Cisin, 1983). This survey found that for all age groups, the use of alcohol was significantly less prevalent than it had been in 1979. Past-month use of alcohol was reported by 27% of youths aged 12 to 17 years, 68% of young adults aged 18 to 25 years, and 57% of adults over age 25. Current daily alcohol use was reported by 11% of the older adults and 7% of the younger adults.

The data on the correlates of heavy drinking provided by the 1979 national survey of alcohol consumption (National Institute on Alcohol Abuse and Alcoholism [NIAAA], 1981) indicated that drinking patterns differed by sex, religious affiliation, education, and income. Twenty percent of male drinkers and 10% of female drinkers reported experiencing some symptoms of alcohol dependence in the year prior to the survey. Jews evidenced low-to-moderate rates of alcohol dependence or addiction, whereas Roman Catholics, Protestants, and those with no religious affiliation indicated relatively high proportions of heavy drinkers (defined in the 1979 survey as those who sometimes drink five or more drinks per occasion and who drink on at least 10 occasions per month). The proportion of abstainers was high among the fundamentalist Protestant groups, but among those in this category who did drink, the rate of alcohol dependence was quite high. The proportion of heavy drinkers increased with education among men, but there was no difference for either sex in alcohol dependence between the lower and higher educational categories. Higher income was related to the amount of drinking only with regard to the number of abstainers, which decreased with income; the survey showed no relationship between heavy drinking and income for either sex.

Alcohol

Ethyl alcohol (ethanol) occurs naturally as a decomposition product of plant carbohydrates; the breakdown to alcohol is facilitated by the presence of the yeast fungi, which are added by nature, or deliberately by man. The intoxicating effects of alcohol have been known since ancient times; there are few cultures that have not consumed alcoholic beverages to induce states of altered consciousness. Fermentation with the catalytic aid of yeast permits a maximum alcohol concentration of about 10% by volume; higher concentrations are not possible from fermentation because the alcohol would kill off the yeast. More concentrated preparations, for industrial use or for drinking, are produced by using alcohol obtained from distillation.

The properties of alcoholic beverages are modified by congeners. These are substances other than ethyl alcohol; chemically many are higher alcohols. Congeners affect the aroma and taste of alcoholic drinks; they are thought to increase the intoxicating results and hangovers, but they are present in such small amounts relative to ethyl alcohol that their contribution to the abuse and dependence potential of alcoholic beverages is minimal.

Effects of Alcohol

The consumption of alcohol results in a wide variety of biochemical changes in the body. Although the principal target organs of alcohol in the body are the cerebral and the hepatic tissue, other organs are also affected to some extent. Pharmacologically, alcohol is a central nervous system (CNS) depressant and produces effects similar to the general anesthetics, which have dissimilar structures. What gives ethyl alcohol (ethanol) this potency is its lipid solubility and extremely rapid penetration of the blood-brain barrier.

When alcoholic beverages are drunk, their aroma and the alcohol itself stimulate the salivary and gastric secretions through excitation of nerve endings in oronasal and gastric mucosa; in addition, the psychological aspects attached to alcoholic drinks can psychically increase the same secretions. Moderate amounts of alcohol in the stomach directly induce gastric secretion through release of gastrin or histamine. Strong alcoholic beverages inhibit gastric secretions except for mucus, and produce the inflammatory changes of gastritis. This in part accounts for the experience of nausea and upset stomach.

Absorption of alcohol rapidly takes place through the mucosa of the gastro-intestinal tract and lungs. Inhalation of alcoholic fluids that have been vaporized by being poured onto a hot surface is a rapid means of intoxication. The effects of drinking alcohol are pronounced within half an hour. The cutaneous vessels become dilated and perspiration is increased; heat loss through the skin is therefore augmented but makes the drinker feel warm. The heat loss and cooling of the interior of the body are great enough to cause a slowdown in some biochemical processes.

Initially, there may be quickening of respiration; heart rate and blood pressure also increase, partly because of a rise in circulating noradrenaline (norepinephrine). Depression of the vital centers in the nervous system by large quantities of alcohol produce slow breathing and a drop in blood pressure. Alcohol inhibits the release from the posterior pituitary of antidiuretic hormone (ADH) and oxytocin; suppression of ADH release contributes to the diuresis that results from drinking alcoholic beverages. This action probably means that the body excretes more fluid than is taken in with the alcoholic beverages. However, this does not seem to be the only basis for the thirst experienced the next day. Another cause may be that alcohol causes fluid inside the cells to move outside the cells. This cellular dehydration, without decrease in total body fluid, is known to be related to, and perhaps to be the basis of, an increase in thirst.

The depressant actions of alcohol on the central nervous system affect first the higher cerebral functions responsible for concern about personal behavior and for self-restraint. The resultant freedom from anxiety and inhibition produces euphoria and apparent stimulation, with vivacity of speech and action. As drinking progresses, responses to stimuli are slowed and muscle control is impaired; clumsiness, ataxia, and nystagmus develop. Decrements of motor function are detectable at a blood-alcohol concentration (BAC) of 50 mg/dl; they are more severe at greater concentrations and arise from impairment of many structures, including the cerebellum and cerebellar tracts. Alcohol adversely affects information processing powers, such as the abilities to solve problems or to memorize, and reduces performance in complex reactions like those needed for driving. The oculomotor nuclei are impaired, so that squint and double vision develop. Very large amounts of alcohol, producing a BAC over 400 mg/dl, sedate to the extent of coma; fatalities occur from rapid excess ingestion of alcoholic beverages.

Alcohol releases the sexual drive from restraint of the cerebral cortex but inhibits conduction along the neuronal pathways responsible for sexual function. The result has been described succinctly by Shakespeare in *Macbeth*: "It provokes the desire, but it takes away the performance."

Although alcohol diffuses throughout the brain, several regions of the organ are especially susceptible to the substance. They are the cerebral cortex, reticular formation, and hippocampus. But a major research difficulty in the elucidation of the differential effects of alcohol on localities within the brain is that changes monitored in one area may reflect alterations produced elsewhere in the nervous system by alcohol. In particular there are considerable gaps in knowledge of the effects of alcohol on the cerebellum and its connecting tracts.

Research on the results of alcohol on brain cells has concentrated on neurons. Alcohol does not directly influence energy processes within neurons to an extent that inhibits nerve activity; in common with other sedatives its significant actions are considered to take place largely in the nerve cell membrane and at the synaptic junction between cells. Alcohol acts against the initiation and conduction of nerve impulses through a depressant effect on the rate of rise and the amplitude of the action potential; this effect is probably related to alcohol-induced decrease of sodium conductance across the nerve membranes.

Another possibility relevant to synaptic activity is that alcohol may bind calcium to the terminal vesicles of axons, which could in turn induce the release of neurotransmitter at the synapses. It has also been suggested that alcohol can promote attachment of released neurotransmitter to the postsynaptic receptor sites, with excitation at low alcohol concentrations giving way to depression at high levels of alcohol (Ehrenpreis & Teller, 1972).

Distribution, Excretion, and Metabolism

Alcohol is 30 times more soluble in water than in fat; after absorption it is quickly distributed in water throughout the body. Although small amounts of absorbed alcohol are excreted unchanged in the breath, perspiration, and urine, most of the alcohol that enters the bloodstream is metabolized. The rate of elimination of alcohol from the blood varies between and within individuals. The average rate of fall of blood alcohol concentration is about 0.23 to 0.3 ounces per hour. Many factors, such as body weight, the presence of food in the stomach, speed and duration of drinking, and the proportion of alcohol in drinks, affect the blood-alcohol concentration.

The major pathway in the body for the initial biotransformation of alcohol involves the enzyme alcohol dehydrogenase. The enzyme is concentrated in the liver, where over 80% of absorbed alcohol is metabolized. Alcohol dehydrogenase converts alcohol to acetaldehyde and hydrogen ions. Acetaldehyde is further metabolized to acetate, which then enters the energy-producing pathways and ultimately is excreted as carbon dioxide and water. Between 90% and 98% of the alcohol is completely oxidized, unlike many other drugs that may be excreted unchanged in the urine. About 2% to 5% may be removed by exhalation and excretion in the urine, tears, or sweat, but the rest must be oxidized. The metabolism rate of alcohol differs from that of most other substances in that the rate of oxidation is nearly constant with time.

Alcohol can also be metabolized to a small extent by the microsomal mixed-function oxidase enzymes in the liver. The liver responds to chronic intake of alcohol by increasing production of a certain type of membrane: endoplasmic reticulum. This increase in endoplasmic reticulum is associated with increased levels of the microsomal drug metabolizing enzymes. This explains the known interaction between alcohol and the many other drugs oxidized by this enzyme system, such as the barbiturates (Ritchie, 1980). As long as there is alcohol in the system, alcohol gets preferential treatment, and the metabolism of other drugs is slower than normal (Hoyumpa et al., 1981). When heavy alcohol use stops and the alcohol has disappeared from the body, the high activity of the enzymes continues for 4 to 8 weeks. During this time drugs are metabolized more rapidly (Iber, 1977).

One of the enzymes that increases is the microsomal ethanol oxidizing system (MEOS). Thus alcohol increases the activity of one of the two enzyme systems responsible for its own oxidation. The increased activity of this MEOS pathway may be a partial basis for the tolerance to alcohol that is shown by heavy users of alcohol.

Another reason why it is important to know about the MEOS is that it is part of the indirect cause of the fatty liver that develops in alcohol users. Fatty acids are the usual fuel for the liver. When alcohol is present, it has higher priority and is used as fuel. As a result, fatty acids (lipids) accumulate in the liver and are stored as small droplets in liver cells. Sometimes the droplets increase in size to the point where they rupture the cell membrane (and pour lipids into the bloodstream, which may have serious effects on the cardiovascular system), causing death of the liver cells.

The metabolism of alcohol also curtails the conversion of glycogen to glucose. Hypoglycemia can therefore follow the excess consumption of alcohol, especially in children and poorly nourished individuals. Paradoxically, alcohol is also able to produce the opposite condition of glucose intolerance or hyperglycemia (Dornhurst & Ouyang, 1971). The effect does not depend on the caloric value of alcohol or on impaired secretion of insulin. One possible factor is that acetate, which is released from the liver as a breakdown product of alcohol, competes with glucose, particularly in the muscles; the peripheral utilization of glucose and its uptake from the blood are thereby prevented. Another factor may result from the effect of alcohol in promoting the release of catecholamines from the adrenal medulla; the increase of circulating adrenaline (epinephrine) induces glycogenolysis and might thereby favor a rise of blood sugar.

Tolerance

Alcohol tolerance develops in a way comparable to tolerance to the barbiturates. Drug-disposition tolerance results from enzyme induction in the liver, which causes more rapid metabolism of alcohol. Pharmacodynamic tolerance causes the nervous system to adapt to the continual presence of alcohol (thus more and more of the drug is needed to produce the same effects). In the advanced stages of dependence on alcohol, tolerance can drop. Like enhancement in tolerance, erosion of tolerance is presumably due for the most part to changes in the target sites within the nervous system at which alcohol acts. Behavioral tolerance allows the person to adjust to the effects of alcohol on speech, vision, and motor control (Jaffe, 1980). Some persons can learn to cover up the typical signs of intoxication. Alcoholics also display cross-tolerance to other CNS depressant drugs, but the mechanism responsible for this is not understood.

Physical Dependence and Alcohol Withdrawal

Dependence on alcohol has psychological and physical aspects. Physical dependence on alcohol is not always easy to distinguish in practice from psychic dependence, nor is it necessarily the most important of the two, but it will be described here, so that later it may be fitted into the general picture of the alcohol dependence syndrome. The presence of physical dependence is shown and recognized by the abstinence effect that develops when the concentration of alcohol in the body drops below the level necessary to ward off withdrawal features. The desire to suppress abstinence symptoms contributes to ongoing alcohol ingestion by alcoholics.

Tremor is an early feature that commonly develops within a few hours of the last drink. At first it is only present in the fingers and hands, though it may be accompanied by a feeling of internal muscular quivering. A fine tremor can be apparent to the individual on performing a delicate motor task such as carrying a cup and saucer. A more marked tremor interferes with shaving and dressing. Gross tremor involves other regions than the hands; at first the tongue and finally the whole of the limbs and trunk are involved in shaking.

Sweating is an acute result of alcohol intake, but it is also a withdrawal feature. Alcoholics may notice that their night clothes and bed sheets are soaked in perspiration. Anxiety, depression, irritability, and restlessness may develop. A sensation as if the stomach were shaking, anorexia, nausea, and vomiting are other features of the alcohol abstinence syndrome. Blood pressure and pulse rate are increased while taking alcohol; their elevation continues after cessation of drinking as a sign of the withdrawal phase.

Insomnia is common. When sleep occurs, it is accompanied by frequent vivid dreams. During the periods of falling asleep and waking, visual and auditory hallucinations are often present. The sleep phenomena are associated with a decrease of the interval between the onset of sleep and the commencement of REM sleep, and with an increase in the quantity of REM sleep and dreams (Greenberg & Pearlman, 1967). The dreams and hallucinations experienced while going to sleep or waking are heralds of the severe form of the alcohol abstinence syndrome—delirium tremens (DT).

In most cases the features of alcohol withdrawal do not progress to delirium tremens but run a benign course. The symptoms and signs are pronounced by the second day, reach a peak on the third day, and then subside, so that by the end of the first week only minor alterations remain. The majority of individuals do not develop delirium or withdrawal convulsions.

Delirium Tremens

Like many descriptive titles for diseases and syndromes, the term "delirium tremens" is evocative and informative. The tremor is generalized and communicated to adjacent structures, so that when the individual is lying down even the bed can shake. Consciousness is clouded; there is disorientation about time and place; attention span is shortened, so that the individual is distracted by external and internal (psychic) events and is unable to concentrate for long on one topic.

Illusions may be present. The illusional misinterpretations of perceived stimuli are frequently of a kind that reassure the individual that familiar surroundings and people are present, so that the nurse can be mistaken for a relative, the doctor mistaken for a friend.

Visual hallucinations are common. The images are occasionally of large objects; the alcoholic may be terrified, for example, because a life-size elephant is visualized in the hallway. More usually the visual hallucinations involve small images; sometimes they are also rapidly moving and interpreted by the alcoholic as perceptions of small animals or birds. Hallucinations of an auditory nature are also frequent in delirium tremens. On occasion, the coarse sounds that are sometimes heard in DT (cracking, banging, whistling, roaring) might be produced by contractions of the middle ear muscles, *tensor tympani* and *stapedius*. But complex sounds, in the form of voices or often of music, occur in DT; they arise from hallucinatory disturbances of perceptual functions within the brain. If the hallucinated sounds accompany visual images, then the two kinds of hallucinations are commonly synchronized.

Delusions, when they are present, are paranoid in type; in part they can be understood as attempts by the alcoholic to account for the delirious phenomena, in part they arise within a mood setting of fear, and they aggravate the individual's terror.

The predominant affect is anxiety, progressing to fear. Suspicion and anger are often present. Interspersed with these unpleasant moods are periods of alcoholic euphoria. Marked restlessness may develop.

The second stage of alcohol withdrawal syndrome is seen infrequently and only in a small number of individuals. These symptoms include convulsive seizures. Convulsive seizures may be fatal if they reach the epileptic stage where there is one seizure following another. Seizures are usually of the grand mal type and may begin as early as 12 hours after abstinence, but more often they appear during the second or third day.

The abstinence syndrome from alcohol deprivation is similar to that arising from withdrawal of the other CNS depressants that are not morphinelike in their actions. Cross-dependence occurs between individual members, including alcohol, of the nonopioid or general class sedatives; that is, the administration of suitable quantities of one substance in this category suppresses the features consequent on stopping the prolonged excessive consumption of another substance in the group. Cross-dependence permits the treatment of alcohol withdrawal by another sedative, which is then gradually withdrawn.

The Alcohol Dependence Syndrome (Alcoholism)

The diagnosis of alcoholism is problematic because there are many different conditions that can be diagnosed as alcoholism. The attempt to reach agreement on a core definition of alcoholism continues to be difficult and confusing. This is aptly reflected in the report of a special committee of the Royal College of Psychiatrists (1979):

> The word "alcoholism" is in common use, but at the same time there is general uncertainty about its meaning. Where is the dividing line between heavy drinking and this "illness"? Is it a matter of quantity drunk or damage sustained, or of what else besides? This confusion is not limited to the layman, for final clarification has eluded the many experts and expert committees that have grappled with the terms to be used about drinking problems. (p.1004)

The underlying problems center upon a delineation of the critical elements to be included in a definition of alcoholism. As Mendelson and Mello (1979) observe, "Criteria for the diagnosis of alcohol abuse are imprecise and ambiguous."

The attempt to define critical elements has a long and checkered history among various official bodies; this history is briefly reviewed below.

The Jellinek Classification

Jellinek (1952) attempted to provide a set of provisional diagnostic categories of alcoholism, which he labeled alpha, beta, gamma, delta, and epsilon. These are descriptive patterns of drinking. Jellinek did not consider all these five types forms of alcoholism, but five types of alcohol use and abuse. Subsequent research has demonstrated that the five types are not useful for prescription of treatment or prediction of prognosis, for they are too vague and generalized.

Jellinek himself was well aware of the limitations of his descriptive approach to diagnosis and even expressed dire concerns over the simplistic application of his typologies.

The lay public uses the term "alcoholism" as designation for any form of excessive drinking, instead of as a label for a limited and well-defined area of excessive drinking behavior. Automatically, the disease conception of alcoholism becomes extended to all excessive drinking, irrespective of whether or not there is any physical or psychological pathology involved in the drinking behavior. Such an unwarranted extension of the disease conception can only be harmful, for, sooner or later, the misapplication will reflect on the legitimate use, too, and, more important, will tend to weaken the ethical basis of social sanctions against drunkenness (Jellinek, 1952).

In a very real sense, Jellinek anticipated the diagnostic work of the next 20 years with his emphasis on differentiation between different patterns of alcohol abuse, the difference between dependence on alcohol and the consequences of alcohol use, and the importance of sociocultural variations in patterns of alcohol use, misuse, and abuse.

The World Health Organization Definition

Through the work of a series of expert committees, the World Health Organization (WHO) has grappled with producing a universally and cross-culturally valid definition of alcoholism, for which diagnostic criteria could be developed. The first salient report (WHO, 1952), focused on the quality of psychic dependence, with secondary physical dependence, as the critical elements of alcoholism.

But what constituted dependence? In another WHO report (WHO, 1964) the term "dependence" was defined as

A state, psychic, and sometimes also physical, resulting from the interaction between a living organism and a drug, characterized by behavioral and other responses that always include a compulsion to take a drug on a continuous or periodic basis in order to experience its psychic effects, and sometimes to avoid the discomfort of its absence. Tolerance may or may not be present.

These reports gave rise to the ensuing formulation of alcoholism as a syndrome, termed the "alcohol dependence syndrome," with the following cardinal elements (Edwards & Gross, 1976; Edwards, Gross, Keller, & Moser, 1976):

1. Narrowing of drinking repertoire
2. Salience of drink-seeking behavior
3. Increased tolerance to alcohol
4. Repeated withdrawal symptoms
5. Relief-avoidance of withdrawal
6. Subjective awareness of compulsion to drink
7. Reinstatement of syndrome after abstinence

However, the definition of the syndrome did not resolve matters. Further research revealed that many persons with some degree of alcohol dependence syndrome were quite socially functional, while other persons, with little if any evidence of the syndrome, engaged in severe abuse of alcohol in terms of disordered behavior and adverse consequences of drinking. To address this situation the 1976 WHO report (Edwards, Gross, Keller, Moser, & Room, 1976) and the Royal College of Psychiatrists' report (1979) recommended that two basic classifications be employed: (a) the alcohol dependence syndrome, and (b) the alcohol-related disabilities. Both reports suggest an overlap between the two sets, yet they define two distinct types of alcohol problems.

In brief, the WHO reports present a substantial attempt to clarify the definition or definitions of alcoholism. Yet the current flux reflects the unresolved conceptual issues of definition (Davies, 1979).

The Diagnostic and Statistical Manual
of the American Psychiatric Association Definition

The 1980 diagnostic criteria of American psychiatry (APA, 1980) are explicitly atheoretical in that they do not attempt to infer how a disorder develops. Rather, diagnosis is based on the description of clinical features. In this sense, the third edition of the *Diagnostic and Statistical Manual of Mental Disorders* (DSM-III) approaches the definition of alcoholism in terms of observed typologies like Jellinek's. The WHO definitions are built upon etiologic assumptions.

DSM-III classifies alcohol intoxication, alcohol withdrawal, and alcohol organic mental disorders, as well as alcohol abuse and alcohol dependence. Alcohol abuse is defined as pathological use for at least 1 month that causes impairment in social or occupational functioning; alcohol dependence in addition includes either tolerance or withdrawal.

As with the other definitions, the DSM-III categories are too general and imprecise for the purposes of treatment prescription or prognosis.

In retrospect one can observe that there are multiple definitions of alcoholism. This is not necessarily undesirable, as long as one specifies the context, goals, and purposes for which a specific definition of alcoholism is employed.

Physical and Psychosocial Consequences of Alcohol Use and Abuse

Approximately 10% of adult drinkers will develop alcoholism at some point in their lives, with profound health and psychosocial consequences. The NIAAA survey (1981) reported that mortality rates for alcoholics were 2.5 times higher than for the general population, and alcoholism ranked behind only heart disease as a leading cause of death. Long-term use of substantial amounts of alcohol can result in heart muscle disease (Ritchie, 1980) and high blood pressure.

Liver damage commonly results from heavy drinking. Liver disease occurs because metabolizing alcohol has priority over the liver's normal functions. Its final stage, cirrhosis (scarring) of the liver, occurs about six times more frequently in alcoholics than in nondrinkers. Cirrhosis is the general name for many types of liver damage that are similar in appearance. The heavy drinker first develops a fatty liver, which is reversible if he stops drinking. When alcohol is present, the liver uses it, and the liver's regular fuel (fatty acids), as well as proteins, accumulate. The engorged liver cells die, triggering the next stage, an inflammatory process called *alcoholic hepatitis*. Cellular death and inflammation cause the last stage: cirrhosis.

Alcoholism results in the loss of brain cells, and studies report brain atrophy in anywhere from 50% to 100% of alcoholics. Korsakoff's syndrome is a characteristic psychotic condition caused by the associated nutritional and vitamin deficiencies. Polyneuritis—an inflammation of the nerves that causes burning and prickly sensations in the hands and feet—has the same origin (Seixas, 1980).

Heavy drinkers have lowered resistance to pneumonia and other infectious diseases. Malnutrition is a factor, but lowered resistance may also occur in well-nourished drinkers. Heavy drinking appears directly to interfere with the bone marrow, where various blood cells are formed. The suppression of the bone marrow contributes to alcoholic anemia in which red blood cell production cannot keep pace with the need. Heavy drinkers are also more likely to develop alcoholic bleeding disorders because they have too few platelets to form clots (Seixas, 1980). Heavy drinking is furthermore related to increased risk of cancer of the mouth, pharynx, larynx, and esophagus.

Heavy drinking during pregnancy can result in harm to the fetus ranging from mild physical and behavioral deficits to fetal alcohol syndrome (FAS). Alcohol is involved in the majority of fatal traffic accidents and in deaths from falling, fires, and drowning. The risk of suicide among alcoholics is 30 times greater than in the general population; accidental lethal overdoses frequently occur when alcohol is combined with other drugs.

It is estimated that 25% of all families in the United States will be affected by alcoholism at some time. Alcoholism increases the likelihood of family violence, incest, and divorce. More than 12 million children live in alcoholic families, and they are at greatly increased risk of developing alcoholism themselves, as well as eating disorders, learning disabilities, and delinquent behavior.

References

American Psychiatric Association. (1980). *Diagnostic and statistical manual of mental disorders* (3rd ed.). Washington, DC: Author.

Davies, D. L. (1979). Defining alcoholism. In M. Grant & P. Gwinner (Eds.), *Alcoholism in perspective*. Baltimore, MD: University Park Press.

Dornhurst, A., & Ouyang, A. (1971). Effect of alcohol on glucose tolerance. *Lancet, 2,* 957-959.

Edwards, G., & Gross, M. M. (1976). Alcohol dependence: Provisional description of a clinical syndrome. *British Medical Journal, 1*(6017), 1058-1066.

Edwards, G., Gross, M. M., Keller, M., & Moser, J. (1976). Alcohol-related problems in the diability perspective: A summary of consequences of the WHO group of investigators on criteria for identifying and classifying disabilities related to alcohol consumption. *Journal of Studies on Alcohol, 37*(9), 1360-1382.

Edwards, G., Gross, M. M., Keller, M., Moser, J., & Room, R. (1976). *Alcohol-related disabilities* (Offset Publication No. 32). Geneva, Switzerland: World Health Organization.

Ehrenpreis, S., & Teller, D. N. (1972). Interaction of drugs of dependence with receptors. In S. J. Mule & H. Brill (Eds.), *Chemical and biological aspects of drug dependence* (pp. 177-207). New York: Raven Press.

Greenberg, R., & Pearlman, C. (1967). Delirium tremens and dreaming. *American Journal of Psychiatry, 124,* 133-142.

Hoyumpa, A., et al. (1981). Effect of short term ethanol administration on lorazepam clearance. *Hepatology, 1,* 47-53.

Iber, F. L. (1977). Drug metabolism in heavy consumers of ethyl alcohol. *Clinical Pharmacology and Therapeutics, 22*(5), 735-742.

Jaffe, J. H. (1980). Drug addiction and drug abuse. In A. G. Gilman, L. S. Goodman, & A. Gilman (Eds.), *The pharmacological basis of therapeutics* (6th ed., pp. 535-584). New York: Macmillan.

Jellinek, E. M. (1952). Phases of alcohol addiction. *Quarterly Journal of Studies on Alcohol, 13,* 673-684.

Mendelson, J. H., & Mello, N. K. (Eds.). (1979). *The diagnosis and treatment of alcoholism.* New York: McGraw-Hill.

Miller, J. D., & Cisin, I. H. (1983). *Highlights from the National Survey on Drug Abuse: 1982.* Rockville, MD: National Institute on Drug Abuse.

National Institute on Alcohol Abuse and Alcoholism. (1981). *Alcohol and health: Fourth special report to the Congress.* Washington, DC: Government Printing Office.

Ritchie, J. M. (1980). The aliphatic alcohols. In A. G. Gilman, L. S. Goodman, & A. Gilman (Eds.), *The pharmacological basis of therapeutics* (6th ed., pp. 376-390). New York: Macmillan.

Royal College of Psychiatrists. (1979). Alcohol and alcoholism. *American Journal of Psychiatry, 137,* 1004.

Seixas, F. A. (1980). The medical complications of alcohol. In S. E. Gitlow & H. S. Peyser (Eds.), *Alcoholism: A practical treatment guide* (pp. 165-180). New York: Grune & Stratton.

World Health Organization. (1952). *Expert Committee Report No. 48.* Geneva, Switzerland: Author.

World Health Organization. (1964). *Expert Committee Report on Mental Health* (Tech. Rep. No. 273). Geneva, Switzerland: Author.

6

CENTRAL NERVOUS SYSTEM STIMULANTS

Stimulants are substances that act on the central nervous system (CNS), causing the person who takes the drug to feel both physically and mentally more lively. Other than coffee and nicotine, the most widely used stimulants in the United States are amphetamine and cocaine.

Amphetamines

Amphetamines are synthetic amines that are similar to the body's own neurotransmitter, norepinephrine, and the hormone for emergencies, epinephrine (adrenalin). The amphetamines generally cause an arousal or activating response not unlike one's normal reaction to emergency situations or to stress. The CNS-stimulating properties of amphetamines were discovered in 1927, and these drugs were used medically in the 1930s. Although a variety of related drugs and mixtures currently exist, the most common amphetamine substances are amphetamine (Benzedrine by trade name), dextroamphetamine (Dexedrine), and methamphetamine (Methadrine or Desoxyn). Generally, if doses are adjusted, the psychological effects of these various drugs are similar, so they will be discussed as a group. Other drugs with similar pharmacological properties are phenmetrazine (Preludin), and methylphenidate (Ritalin). Common slang terms for amphetamines include speed, crystal, meth, and uppers.

Mechanism of Action

Amphetamines stimulate the reticular activating system. The activation is transmitted to all parts of the brain, and the individual becomes aroused, alert, and hypersensitive to stimuli. This activation may be a very pleasant experience in itself, but a continual high level of activation may produce anxiety.

Amphetamines have potent effects on the reward (pleasure) center in the medial forebrain bundle. Increases in this system are experienced as pleasurable; thus the user is encouraged to continue the experience. The "flash" or sudden feeling of intense pleasure that is experienced when amphetamine is taken intravenously probably results from the delivery of a high dose of the drug to the reward center.

Amphetamine has three actions on neurotransmission. First, it causes the neurotransmitter norepinephrine to leak spontaneously from the presynaptic sites. This leakage causes stimulation of the next neuron across the synapse, as if a normal impulse were being transmitted. Second, the electrical impulses occur in the presynaptic fiber, and the presence of amphetamine increases the amount of neurotransmitter released with each impulse. Third, amphetamine enhances its own effects as well as those resulting from electrical stimulation by blocking the reuptake of dopamine and norepinephrine, so that the stimulus is continuous across the synapse to the next neuron.

A curious condition that has been reported many times in heavy amphetamine users is behavioral stereotypy. This means that a simple activity is repeated over and over again. An individual will get caught up in a repetitious thought or act for hours. This phenomenon seems to be peculiar to the amphetamines, although it may occur to a lesser extent in the course of a psychedelic trip.

Behavioral stereotypy may occur because amphetamines inhibit the uptake of dopamine in the brain. Dopamine is the neurotransmitter associated with the complex controls for some of the motor functions of the body. When the reuptake of dopamine or norepinephrine is blocked, the neurons become more sensitized (Sulser & Sanders-Bush, 1971). This change is not rapidly reversed. Chronic use of high doses of amphetamines causes dramatic decreases in the neurotransmitter dopamine that persist months after the drug is stopped (Jaffe, 1980). The accumulation of dopamine might also explain the hallucinogenic effects of large doses of amphetamines.

Absorption and Elimination

Amphetamines may be taken by a variety of different routes. When taken orally the peak effects are found 2 to 3 hours after ingestion. The half-life is 10 to 12 hours, so that a fairly stable blood level can be achieved with oral administration at 4 to 6 hour intervals, and virtually complete elimination of the drug would occur within 2 days after the last dose. With intravenous injection, peak effects are much more rapid. With higher doses a tachyphylaxis (rapid tolerance) may be seen. Because amphetamine produces its effects largely by displacing the catecholamine transmitters from their storage sites, with large doses the catecholamines may be sufficiently depleted so that another dose within a few hours may not be able to displace as much catecholamine, and reduced effect is obtained.

Medical Uses of Amphetamines

Until 1970 amphetamines had been prescribed for a large number of conditions, including depression, fatigue, and long-term weight reduction. In 1970 the Food and Drug Administration (FDA), acting on the recommendation of the National Academy of Sciences, restricted the legal use of amphetamines to three types of condition: narcolepsy, hyperkinetic behavior, and short-term weight reduction programs.

Narcolepsy or sleep epilepsy. The use of amphetamine for the treatment of narcolepsy is of minor importance because it is not a widespread ailment. A person who has narcolepsy goes to sleep as frequently as 50 times a day if he or she stays in one position very long. Taking amphetamine will keep this person alert to normal daily existence. The usual dose of dextroamphetamine is 30 to 50 mg per day, in divided doses.

Hyperkinesis. This common behavioral problem in children and adolescents involves an abnormally high level of physical activity. About 4 out of every 100 grade school children and 40% of school children referred to mental health clinics because of behavioral disturbances are hyperactive. Boys are much more likely to be diagnosed as hyperactive than girls. Such children have short attention and concentration spans. Their behavior is aggressive, irrelevant, without clear direction, and hard to predict. Their aggressiveness, talkativeness, and restless, impulsive behavior disrupt the classroom and often their home life as well.

The drug commonly used to treat the hyperkinetic child is methylphenidate (Ritalin). Ritalin is a mild stimulant of the CNS that counteracts physical and mental fatigue while having only slight effects on blood pressure and respiration. Its potency is intermediate between that of amphetamine and caffeine. Methylphenidate and amphetamine are about equally effective in treating hyperkinesis, but methylphenidate is thought to stunt growth less than amphetamine (Weiner, 1980). Stimulants are believed to work on hyperactive children by stimulating inhibitory areas of the brain, thus facilitating better control of motor activity and concentration.

Weight reduction. One of the legal uses of amphetamines is for the treatment of obesity. According to accepted medical and health standards, over 35% of Americans are overweight. This is a major health problem, for statistics show that being overweight is an important factor in heart disease, coronary artery disease, and cerebrovascular disease.

Amphetamine and chemically similar compounds are used for appetite control because they decrease hunger. A drug that suppresses appetite is called an anorectic drug, or an anorexiant. Amphetamines are thought to act by affecting the appetite center in the hypothalamus. They do not affect blood-sugar levels, but they do decrease food intake. This is the reason why the FDA approved short-term use of amphetamines for weight-loss programs. Unless the dose is continuously increased, the appetite-suppressing action of this drug, together with the pleasant stimulating effects, usually wears off after about 2 weeks. At high doses the anorectic effect returns, but an even higher tolerance will then develop. Because of this buildup of tolerance, the FDA issued a warning about the danger of long-term use of amphetamines.

Amphetamine Misuse and Abuse

At the 1970 hearing on amphetamines before the Select Committee on Crime, it was estimated that over 5 billion amphetamine doses had been manufactured legally the year before. The Department of Justice reported in 1970 that it was unable to account for 38% of the total amount of amphetamines manufactured in the United States—nearly 2 billion doses. About 8% of all prescriptions in the United States were for amphetamines. The amounts manufactured far exceeded the needs for medical purposes. Nearly 99% of amphetamines sold were for weight control. In 1972 a new law took effect setting a quota for amphetamine production: 235 million units—a sizeable drop in volume. Accurate figures on the amount of illegal amphetamine manufactured and sold were not available, but estimates run from 10% to 25% of the amount on the legal market.

Today there are many fewer people using prescription amphetamines, but there is still a fair-sized market in oral doses of illicitly made speed. Although many purchasers may have in mind an occasional small dose to help them stay awake to study or drive, it is probably the case that most oral users are out to get high. This is more dangerous, for to get an obvious effect in a hurry, there is a tendency to start with higher doses. A dose of 10 mg to 30 mg of Dexedrine will make a person feel quite good—alert, talkative, and "high." Unfortunately this dosage is likely to cause hyperactive and nervous or jittery feelings that can encourage the use of another drug, such as methaqualone (sopors) or a barbiturate to relieve the discomfort of those feelings.

There are still some people using amphetamines intravenously. Intravenous amphetamine use may begin with only 30 mg. In a binge of using speed (methamphetamine in liquid form) every 2 or 3 hours for 3 or 4 days, tolerance develops rapidly, and 500 mg to 1000 mg may be injected at one time. Initially the user may feel energetic, talkative, enthusiastic, happy, confident, and powerful, and may initiate and complete highly ambitious tasks. He or she does not sleep and usually eats very little. The pupils of the eyes are dilated, the mouth is dry, and the body temperature is elevated (hyperpyrexia).

After the first day or so, toxic, unpleasant symptoms become prominent as the dosage is increased. The toxic effects are similar to those found in people who use lower doses less frequently, but they are intensified. Symptoms commonly reported at this stage are teeth-grinding, confused and disorganized patterns of thought and behavior, compulsive repetition of meaningless acts, irritability, self-consciousness, suspiciousness, and fear. Hallucinations and delusions similar to a paranoid psychosis occur. The person is likely to show aggressive and antisocial behavior for no apparent reason. Severe chest pains, abdominal pain that mimics appendicitis, and fainting from overdosage are sometimes reported.

"Cocaine bugs" are one bizarre effect of high doses of amphetamines: The individual feels something, like insects, crawling under his or her skin. Amphetamine and cocaine probably stimulate nerve endings in the skin, thus causing this sensation. Toward the end of the "run," which usually lasts less than a week, the toxic symptoms dominate.

After a few days of high doses, it appears that new catecholamines cannot be synthesized fast enough. Because the amphetamine effect depends of the availability of dopamine and norepinephrine, the drug will eventually lose its effect. When the drug is discontinued, prolonged sleep follows, sometimes lasting several days. On awakening, the person is lethargic, quite hungry, and often severely mentally depressed. He or she may overcome these effects with another injection, initiating a new cycle. Barbiturates, tranquilizers, or opiate narcotics are sometimes used to ease the "crash" or to terminate an unpleasant run.

Continued use of massive doses of amphetamines often leads to considerable weight loss, sores and nonhealing ulcers, liver disease, hypertensive disorders, cerebral hemorrhage (stroke), and kidney damage. It is often impossible to tell whether these effects are a result of the drug, poor eating habits, or other factors associated with the life-style of people who inject methamphetamine. Experiments in which rhesus monkeys were injected intravenously with methamphetamine every other day for 1 week, or twice a week for a month, or twice a week for a year, have shown that methamphetamine is capable of producing direct injury to arteries and veins, which causes severe brain damage. Oral methamphetamine given to monkeys and rats results in cerebral vascular changes and kidney damage as serious as that caused by intravenous methamphetamine (Rumbaugh, 1977).

Heavy use of amphetamines or cocaine may induce a psychosis that is indistinguishable from paranoid schizophrenia. In addition, several investigators contend that schizophrenics and others with borderline psychotic conditions are more likely to use the drug intravenously than are other individuals. In one study, 41% of those requiring hospital treatment for amphetamine use were thought to have been schizophrenic before taking the drug (Hekimian & Gershon, 1968).

Cocaine

Cocaine is currently the major stimulant of abuse in the United States, with epidemic levels of addiction becoming evident. Similarly, the abuse of amphetamines exists on a worldwide basis and threatens to resurface in the United States if or when cocaine use wanes. Indeed, there is a substantial demand for CNS stimulants that undoubtedly stems from their euphorogenic property. The natural history of stimulant abuse includes intoxication and withdrawal states, progressive repercussions of addiction, and psychological features of chronic use. Pharmacological actions of CNS stimulants on endogenous reward centers produce acute intoxication effects, while protracted neurochemical disruptions in the brain appear to be associated with withdrawal and craving states. Compelling evidence now exists that cocaine is physically addictive based on measurable neurochemical alterations and clinical observations.

According to 800-COCAINE surveys (Washton & Gold, 1987), point prevalence and lifetime prevalence were relatively stable from 1985 to 1987. However, cocaine use by adolescents is on the rise, as evidenced by a 6% frequency of cocaine use by high school seniors in a 1984 survey. There now appears to be a core group of 4 to 5 million regular cocaine users. Because cocaine often progresses to severe and entrenched addiction, a stable and younger group of users would be expected to yield increasing numbers of seriously addicted users over time. Consistent with this notion is the finding by the Drug Abuse Warning Network (DAWN) that cocaine emergency room visits are increasing at an alarming rate (from 10 per 100,000 visits in 1983 to 75 per 100,000 in 1986). Similarly, there has been a tremendous increase in hospitalizations and outpatient treatments for cocaine abuse. These epidemiological data support the concept of "progression," or the automatic worsening of addiction over time, that is well appreciated in alcoholism and opiate dependence. However, with cocaine abuse, a much shorter time appears sufficient for the development of entrenchment patterns of addiction and lack of control over drug use.

Currently 5,000 adults in the United States daily try cocaine for the first time, according to the Minnesota Institute for Public Health and Prevention Resource Center (1985). "Today, it is estimated that 22 to 25 million people have tried cocaine at least once . . . Conservative estimates indicate that there are over two million cocaine addicts in the United States today" (p. 2).

In order to evaluate present trends in cocaine abuse two surveys were conducted in the New York area. The first was done in May 1983 and the second in May 1984. The more recent survey shows an increase in the number of female users and a shift toward younger age groups. A higher percentage of lower-income users was also evident. Less than 50% are now earning over $25,000 per year, with more students, blue-collar, and clerical workers.

Looking at survey respondents who had used the drugs for periods ranging from several months to 15 years, the frequency of use and route of administration were examined. Most were intranasal users, although nearly all intravenous and freebase users began as intranasal users. In the year between surveys, the freebase route of administration had increased, and the intravenous method had decreased. The incidence of intranasal use had remained virtually unchanged. Because freebase and intravenous routes are essentially interchangeable with regard to brain cocaine delivery, a shift from intravenous use does not represent a decrease in addiction severity. The weekly amount of cocaine used by callers had increased, as had concomitant abuses of other drugs and alcohol. This represents a progression of polysubstance abuse, or "chemical dependency," in these individuals. Other drugs were often used to counter adverse effects of cocaine, such as restlessness, irritability, depression, paranoia, and overstimulation. It should be noted that the combined use of cocaine and other drugs or alcohol can be extremely dangerous. One example of this is seen in users who become rapidly stuporous from previously ingested depressants when the acute effects of cocaine wear off. This situation can occur when users are driving, or engaged in other critical activities.

Pharmacology

There are two distinct pharmacological actions of cocaine: first, it acts as a powerful CNS stimulant, and second, it is a highly effective anesthetic.

Cocaine's popularity as an illicit recreational drug is due to its first pharmacological action, that of inducing euphoria as a stimulant. Initial stimulation begins in the cortical cells of the brain, resulting in feelings of euphoria and excitation. When the dose is increased, lower brain center cells are stimulated, sometimes resulting in convulsions and tremors. The effects on the brain cells are of short duration and are followed by a period of depression, despondency, and confusion. (Some of the "addictive" properties of cocaine may be explained by the fact that users clamor for repeated doses in order to avoid the depression that comes with abstinence; Eiswirth, Smith, & Wesson, 1980.)

The pharmacologic action of blocking the generation and transmission of nerve impulses has made cocaine valuable throughout history as a local anesthetic. The duration of the local blocking action is only from 20 to 40 minutes. Once the drug is absorbed into the bloodstream and circulated throughout the body, the blocking action is reversed, and the neurons return almost immediately to normal functioning. Anesthesia of mucous membranes can be achieved with small doses, but larger doses are needed to anesthetize larger areas of mucous membranes or nerve trunks (Eiswirth et al., 1980).

Some of the pharmacologic effects of cocaine make its use riskier than other illicit drugs. Unlike other local anesthetics, cocaine constricts blood vessels, causing a rise in blood pressure and a depression of the heart rate. An overdose can result in sudden cardiac arrest because of the drug's toxic effect on the heart muscle.

Absorption and Elimination

Because it constricts the blood vessels, the liver detoxifies cocaine at a much slower rate than other local anesthetics—about 30 mg to 40 mg an hour. Some of the drug is even excreted unchanged in the urine (Eiswirth et al., 1980).

The cocaine molecules are metabolized by enzymes found in the blood and the liver, and the activity of these enzymes is highly variable from one person to another. Because of this variability, estimates of the half life of cocaine in humans vary from about 20 minutes to over 2 hours (Jones, 1984).

Cocaine can be absorbed by any body tissue—including mucous membranes—and the rate of absorption varies, making cocaine a dangerously unpredictable drug. For example, it would take 1,200 mg of cocaine to cause death if it is taken orally—the acids and enzymes in the stomach destroy most of the cocaine before it can be absorbed into the body. But it would take only 30 mg to cause death if the cocaine was "snorted"—inhaled into the nose. As tolerance builds and the doses are increased, the user plays a risky game: The margin is narrow between euphoria and death (Eiswirth et al., 1980).

Methods of Use

Four main methods of use are employed by cocaine users.

Injection. The drug is injected under the skin, into muscle tissue, or directly into the veins. The effects of the cocaine are felt most rapidly from injection, especially injection into the veins; the user can tolerate a slightly higher dose of cocaine through injection than through all other methods except oral ingestion.

Inhalation. Called "snorting," this method is accomplished by inhaling a small amount of cocaine powder into one nostril while pinching the other nostril shut. Snorting allows for the smallest dose—absorption through the mucous membranes is rapid, and generally very complete. A user can tolerate 40 times the dose if he swallows it, and more than 20 times the dose if he injects it, compared to snorting.

Ingestion. Because the enzymes in the stomach rapidly destroy cocaine, oral ingestion allows for the greatest dose with the least effect. Oral ingestion is the least popular method of cocaine use, probably because the effects are only obtained with large doses.

Smoking. Users who want to smoke cocaine convert it into freebase by extracting it into a volatile organic solvent, such as ether. Although the greatest "high" is achieved by smoking cocaine, it packs intense health hazards, and accidental overdosing is common. Because of the procedure used in manufacturing freebase, it is extremely difficult to control dosages. Smoking also brings with it greater dependency on cocaine and more intense psychological effects; paranoid psychosis is most frequently seen in freebase smokers but is relatively rare among cocaine users who inject, swallow, or snort the drug.

The popularity of this form of freebasing began to decline with the discovery that cocaine freebase could be made by mixing cocaine with baking soda and water. When a piece of this cocaine "crack" or "rock" is heated, cocaine vapors are produced and may be inhaled.

Effects

Physiological effects. Cocaine is used illicitly mainly for the psychological and behavioral effects it produces, because they, as a whole, are perceived as being pleasant. Most of the physiological effects of cocaine use, on the other hand, are detrimental to health; in improper doses or incorrect administration, in fact, cocaine can cause death.

One of the most important effects of cocaine is on the circulatory system. Cocaine is a vasoconstrictor—it causes a constriction of the blood vessels. When used intranasally over a period of time, this constriction effect can cause death of the cells of the mucous membrane lining the nose, resulting in ulceration of the tissue. In mild cases, the user experiences a stuffy or runny nose; in more severe cases, it is difficult or impossible to breathe through the nose. Heavy cocaine use can cause perforation of the septum, the wall dividing the two halves of the nose; in extreme cases, the septum may collapse completely.

As a result of the drug's vasoconstrictive action, blood pressure rises within a few minutes of the cocaine's infiltration of the bloodstream. The increase in blood pressure depends on the method of administration: Smoking the drug can within a few minutes produce what it would take an hour of snorting to produce. As the effects of the cocaine wear off, the blood pressure drops to below-normal levels; if the dosage was high enough, the resulting drop in blood pressure could cause death.

Because of the drug's stimulant effect on brain cells, cocaine causes variations in breathing rate. With an increased dose, breathing becomes rapid and shallow; if the dose is high enough, complete respiratory failure occurs as the drug's effects wear off and the body systems become depressed.

Additional common physiological effects of cocaine use include vomiting (in increased doses, the drug stimulates the brain's vomit reflex), insensitivity to temperature, change in body temperature, hyperactivity, tremors, convulsions, severe weight loss, insomnia, dryness of the mouth and throat, and dizziness.

When cocaine is used as a base and smoked, it causes minor lung irritation, swollen glands in the floor of the mouth, and soreness in the chest, neck, and cheeks. Long-term use can cause deterioration of the lung tissue.

Psychological effects. It is cocaine's psychological effects that have elevated it to such popularity: It causes exhilaration, euphoria, a burst of energy, increased mental capabilities, increased sociability, sexual stimulation, and excitation.

But that is only half the story: Unfortunately, the adverse psychological effects have received much less publicity and are, in many cases, much more powerful than the favorable effects.

One of the most common adverse psychological effects of cocaine use is the depressive state that follows the initial euphoria. It also causes confusion, despondency, anxiety, lethargy, and irritability. Behavioral changes occur at much lower doses than do physiological changes, and users often crave repeated doses in an effort to avoid the depression that follows the elation. Some establish a frenzied cycle, repeating injections as often as every 10 minutes to escape the depression.

Use of cocaine on a chronic or daily basis often results in perceptual disturbances, including hallucinations and delusions. The hallucinations suffered by a heavy cocaine user resemble those of an alcoholic in delirium tremens; with prolonged use, the user experiences extreme paranoia. Suffering these adverse psychological effects, many users become alarmed at the sensation of the cocaine injected under the skin; fully convinced that there are insects, snakes, or other animals burrowing under their skin, they tear frantically at their skin in an attempt to "dig out the cocaine bugs."

Unfortunately, psychotic behavior can result from relatively low doses of cocaine; even minute doses that are snorted or smoked can result in hallucination and severe psychosis.

Addiction and Dependence

A great deal of controversy still surrounds the issue of cocaine addiction: Do users develop a dependence or an addiction to cocaine, or is this a product of hysteria?

There is no literal physical addiction to cocaine—in other words, a user who is deprived of cocaine will not suffer physical withdrawal symptoms like those generally suffered by heroin users.

There is, however, a great deal of evidence indicating psychological dependence on cocaine. Users tend to develop a craving for the drug—a tendency that can be explained by the cycle of the drug's effects on the body and the mind. Following the initial euphoria and burst of energy created by cocaine, the user falls into a depressive state characterized by despondency, anxiety, depression, and dizziness. The higher the dose, the worse the depression that follows. Many chronic users develop a strong psychological addiction to cocaine, probably out of an attempt to avoid the depressive state that occurs when cocaine's effects vanish (Eiswirth et al., 1980).

Regardless of the source, the extreme psychological craving develops among chronic users—and the more frequently cocaine is used, the more intense the craving becomes, particularly among those who inject the drug intravenously. Animal experiments indicate that cocaine is one of the most powerful, possibly *the* most powerful, of drug reinforcers.

One recent experiment is particularly illuminating. A group of monkeys were allowed unrestrained access to intravenous injections of cocaine 23 hours a day; the monkeys were able to give themselves injections of 0.2 mg per kg of weight per injection during the testing periods. As the monkeys continued to inject the drug, they developed severe weight loss, hyperactivity, hallucinations, tremors, and convulsions. Food and water became unimportant, and they stopped eating, drinking, and sleeping in their frenzy to continue giving themselves injections. Within 5 days, all were dead.

Cocaine users do develop a tolerance to the drug, but it is unlike the tolerance developed in response to almost all other drugs. With chronic use, no tolerance develops toward the euphoric properties of the drug, but users do develop a tolerance for the drug's ability to ease anxiety and alleviate stress. In addition, cocaine bears a reverse tolerance effect: Occasional users find themselves becoming less tolerant, not more tolerant, of the drug's effects. An occasional user who continues to use the same dose of cocaine increases his chances of accidental overdose, acute cocaine poisoning, and possible death (Dupont, Goldstein, & O'Donnell, 1978).

Medical Uses

Cocaine's properties as a local anesthetic and as a vasoconstrictor have rendered it valuable in several different medical applications. Its use today is limited to anesthetic and pain-killing applications.

The only recognized and legal medical use for cocaine in the United States today is as a local anesthetic in surgery involving the eye, ear, nose, throat, and upper respiratory passages (Dupont et al., 1978). In addition to its ability to anesthetize the mucous membranes involved in such surgery, cocaine provides other benefits. Because it acts to constrict the blood vessels, it prevents massive blood loss during surgery that would otherwise occur in membranes richly supplied with blood vessels; in addition to minimizing blood loss, it allows for more accurate surgery by keeping the area free of vision-obstructing blood and the surgical field clear (Petersen, 1979).

When used under controlled medical conditions, cocaine has an excellent record for safety. A recent report of its use in approximately 93,000 operations revealed severe reactions to the cocaine in only 14 of the patients; none of them died (Petersen, 1979).

Cocaine has been used on an experimental basis in the treatment of depression and other mental or psychotic disorders. The use of cocaine in the treatment of depression has been generally disappointing and, although it may help some patients, its use for depression is not recommended (Wesson & Smith, 1977).

Minor Stimulants

Xanthines are the oldest stimulants known to man. The three xanthines of primary importance are caffeine, theophylline, and theobromine. Caffeine is found in coffee, tea, and cocoa. It is added to many carbonated soft drinks and over-the-counter medications as well. Theophylline is found in tea, and theobromine is found in chocolate.

The cured coffee bean contains about 1% caffeine. Dried tea leaves have about 5% caffeine plus theophylline. Cocoa has little caffeine, but about 2% theobromine.

These minor stimulants, especially caffeine and theophylline, have proven medicinal value. They stimulate the CNS, act on the kidneys as a diuretic, stimulate cardiac muscle, and relax smooth muscle. Persons who have bronchial spasms or asthma probably have noticed that they can breathe a bit easier after drinking a cup of tea.

The three chemicals are methylated xanthines and are closely related alkaloids. Most alkaloids are insoluble in water, but these are unique, because they are slightly water soluble.

These xanthines have similar effects on the body, with caffeine having the greatest and theobromine almost no stimulant effect on the CNS and the skeletal muscles. Theophylline is the most potent and caffeine the least potent agent on the cardiovascular system. Caffeine has been the most extensively studied and, unless otherwise indicated, is the drug under discussion here.

Caffeine

Absorption, Metabolism, and Excretion

Caffeine is readily absorbed from the gut, distributed throughout the body, and rapidly taken up by the brain. It is metabolized by the liver, and is excreted both free and as a metabolite by the kidneys. The primary use of caffeine in the United States is as a CNS stimulant to increase alertness and to reduce fatigue. There is a potential tolerance that leads to an increasing dosage and a moderate psychologic dependency. Although no specific physical dependency appears to arise, many people experiencing withdrawal complain of increased insomnia, irritability, cardiac palpitation, tremor, flushing, anorexia, dehydration, diuresis, fever, albuminuria, and abdominal discomfort (Reimann, 1967).

Pharmacology

Some 150 mg to 250 mg of caffeine, or about two cups of coffee, is sufficient to activate the CNS. The observation that the cortical neurons are stimulated is shown by the cortex activation and EEG arousal pattern. In the absence of tolerance, there is an increase in the wakeful state, mood elevation, and the length of time it takes to fall asleep. At higher doses, about 500 mg, caffeine stimulates the autonomic centers of the brain, heart rate, and respiration. The cardiovascular system works in opposition to the effect of caffeine upon the autonomic centers. Hypertensive headaches may be reduced by caffeine. This may be due to the effects of vascular muscular dilation and blood vessel constriction caused by the autonomic centers. Although peripheral dilation usually occurs, blood vessel constriction takes place in the brain. Caffeine users have a lower heart rate, higher blood pressure, and a slightly higher basal metabolic rate than nonusers. Nonusers of caffeine experience a significantly reduced heart rate at about 150 mg to 250 mg of caffeine. A higher blood level of lipids and glucose develops in heavy coffee users, and this may cause a higher incidence of angina and myocardial infarction than in moderate coffee users or abstainers.

Even higher doses, about eight cups of coffee, cause an increase in synthesis of microsomal enzymes in the liver that metabolize the drug. Caffeine is not very toxic, but high doses (from 1 g to 10 g) can cause convulsions and respiratory failure. Six deaths in humans have been reported in the literature, one following an intravenous injection of 3.2 g (the oral dose that would generally be fatal has been estimated at over 10 g; Syed, 1976). Toxic effects of caffeine can result from taking 1 g in a single dose (Stillner et al., 1978). The central stimulation and toxic effects can be blocked by CNS depressants (Peters, 1967).

Behavioral Actions

Stating precisely how caffeine affects behavioral performance is difficult because individuals are affected in various ways. One report shows contrasting effects between users and nonusers. Heavy coffee drinkers experienced irritability and sleepiness when given a placebo, but were alert and content with caffeine (Goldstein, Kaiser, & Warren, 1965a, 1965b). Nonusers given 150 mg to 300 mg of caffeine had upset stomachs and were jittery and nervous. Caffeine works much like amphetamines, increasing the individual's level of physical performance, mitigating boredom, and increasing attention. There is cortical stimulation, reduced drowsiness, and greater alertness and reactivity, but there may be irritability and excitability, which can disrupt behavior.

Generally 200 mg to 300 mg of caffeine, or about two cups of coffee, is a sufficient therapeutic dose to offset fatigue and improve performance of motor tasks. This may be partly due to caffeine's action on the agent muscle.

Tolerance and Dependency on Caffeine

A strong tolerance does not develop from caffeine. There is usually less tolerance to the CNS stimulation effect of caffeine than to most of its other effects. The tolerance that develops to caffeine can be eliminated either by increasing the dose or by completely abstaining. Increasing the dose two or four times also eliminates tolerance buildup. Caffeine's effect on the kidneys shows an increase in urine output and in the salivary flow; there is no tolerance development.

Dependence on caffeine is real, and one withdrawal symptom that has been well substantiated is headache, which generally develops in habitual users (five cups or more of coffee per day) after about 18 hours of abstinence. Some reports suggest that nausea and lethargy may precede the actual headache, but the only clear symptom is the headache. It has been produced experimentally by giving caffeine chronically to noncaffeine users and then substituting a placebo, as well as by withholding coffee from habitual users (Goldstein, 1964; Goldstein & Kaiser, 1969).

Adverse Reactions

Caffeinism. In 1974 the world was introduced to a new term: Caffeinism (Greden, 1974):

> High intake of caffeine ("caffeinism") can produce symptoms that are indistinguishable from those of anxiety neurosis, such as nervousness, irritability, tremulousness, occasional muscle twitchings, insomnia, sensory disturbances, tachypnea, palpitations, flushing, arrhythmias, diuresis, and gastrointestinal disturbances. The caffeine withdrawal syndrome and the headache associated with it may also mimic anxiety. (Elkins et al., 1981)

Many studies show that individuals with psychiatric or emotional problems have those problems intensified by high caffeine intake. Similarly, some of the problems may be the result of high caffeine intake (Bezchlibnyk et al., 1981).

Physiological toxicity. Caffeine has been shown to be mutagenic and teratogenic in experimental animals (Goyan, 1980), but only at concentrations much in excess of those used therapeutically or those resulting from drinking coffee or tea. It is not considered a significant toxic hazard in humans.

Nevertheless, pregnant women should be cautious about consumption of large amounts of caffeine, such as those in over-the-counter stimulant preparations and carbonated beverages. Coffee consumption has also been tentatively linked with cancer of the pancreas (MacMahon et al., 1981). However, in 1984 the American Cancer Society's nutritional guidelines indicated there was no reason to consider caffeine a risk factor in human cancer.

References

Bezchlibnyk, K. S., et al. (1981). Should psychiatric patients drink coffee? *Canadian Medical Association Journal, 124,* 357.

Dupont, R. I., Goldstein, A., & O'Donnell, J. (1978). *Handbook on drug abuse* (pp. 241-244). Rockville, MD: National Institute on Drug Abuse.

Eiswirth, N., Smith, D., & Wesson, D. (1980). Current perspectives on cocaine use in America. *Grassroots, 2*(80), 1.

Elkins, R. N., et al. (1981). Acute effects of caffeine in normal prepubertal boys. *American Journal of Psychiatry, 138*(2), 178-183.

Goldstein, A. (1964). Wakefulness caused by caffeine. Nauncyn- Cchiedebergs Arch. fur *Exper. Pathol. Pharmakol.* 248-269.

Goldstein, A., & Kaiser, S. (1969). Psychotropic effects of caffeine in man: III. A questionnaire survey of coffee drinking and its effects in a group of housewives. *Clinical Pharmacology and Therapeutics, 10*(4), 477.

Goldstein, A., Kaiser, S., & Warren, R. (1965a). Psychotropic effects of caffeine in man: I. Individual differences in sensitivity to caffeine-induced wakefulness. *Journal of Pharmacological and Experiental Therapy, 149*(1), 156.

Goldstein, A., Kaiser, S., & Warren, R. (1965b). Psychotropic effects of caffeine in man: II. Alertness, psychomotor coordination, and mood. *Journal of Pharmacological and Experiental Therapy, 150*(1), 146.

Goyan, J. E. (1980, September 5). Statement FDA release.

Greden, J. F. (1974). Anxiety of caffeinism: A diagnostic dilemma. *American Journal of Psychiatry, 131,* 1089-1092.

Hekimian, L. J., & Gershon, S. (1968). Characteristics of drug abusers admitted to a psychiatric hospital. *Journal of the American Medical Association, 205,* 125-130.

Jaffe, J. H. (1980). Drug addiction and drug abuse. In A. G. Gilman, L. S. Goodman, & A. Gilman (Eds.), *The pharmacological basis of therapeutics* (6th ed., pp. 535-584). New York: Macmillan.

Jones, R. T. (1984). The pharmacology of cocaine. In J. Grabowski (Ed.), *Cocaine: Pharmacology, effects, and treatment of abuse* (NIDA Research Monograph No. 50). Washington, DC: Government Printing Office.

MacMahon, B., et al. (1981). Coffee and cancer of the pancreas. *New England Medical Journal, 304*(11), 630-633.

Minnesota Institute for Public Health and Prevention Resource Center. (1985). *Cocaine.* Anoka, MN: Author.

Peters, J. M. (1967). Factors affecting caffeine toxicity. *Journal of Clinical Pharmacology, 7,* 131-141.

Petersen, R. C. (1979, July 24). *Cocaine* (pp. 2-3; statement before the U.S. House of Representatives Select Committee on Narcotics Abuse and Control). Washington, DC: Government Printing Office.

Reimann, H. A. (1967). Caffeinism, a cause of long-continued low-grade fever. *Journal of the American Medical Association, 202,* 131.

Rumbaugh, C. L. (1977). Small vessel cerebral vascular changes following chronic amphetamine intoxication. In H. E. Ellinwood, Jr., & M. M. Kilbey (Eds.), *Cocaine & other stimulants* (pp. 241-251). New York: Plenum.

Stillner, V., et al. (1978). Caffeine-induced delirium during prolonged competitive stress. *American Journal of Psychiatry, 135*(7), 855-856.

Sulser, F., & Sanders-Bush, E. (1971). Effects of drugs on amines in the CNS. *Annual Reviews of Pharmacology, 11,* 209-230.

Syed, I. B. (1976). The effects of caffeine. *Journal of the American Pharmaceutical Association, N.S. 16,* 568-572.

Washton, A. M., & Gold, M. S. (1987). Recent trends in cocaine abuse: A view from the national hotline, "800-COCAINE." *American Journal of Drug and Alcohol Abuse, 6*(2), 31-47.

Weiner, N. (1980). Norepinephrine, epinephrine, and the sympathetic amines. In A. G. Gillman, L. S. Goodman, & A. Gilman (Eds.), *The pharmacological basis of therapeutics* (6th ed., pp. 138-175). New York: Macmillan.

Wesson, D. R., & Smith, D. E. (1977). Cocaine: Its use for central nervous system stimulation including recreational and medical uses. In *Cocaine* (Research Monograph No. 13, pp. 137-152). Rockville, MD: National Institute on Drug Abuse.

7

MARIJUANA AND HASHISH

An official government report released in 1977 disclosed that 11% of the nearly four million high school seniors in the United States were smoking marijuana every day (Rogers, 1978). A report issued in 1978 by the National Institute on Drug Abuse (NIDA) reported that marijuana use in the United States had increased 25% in just 1 year.

The sharpest rise in users was among the 12 to 17 age group; the second sharpest rise was among those ages 18 to 25. More than one in four of the latter group uses marijuana regularly. The use of marijuana continues to be strongly related to age: Only 7% of those aged 34 have ever even tried marijuana (Petersen, 1980).

Statistics released by the Department of Health, Education, and Welfare in 1975 demonstrate that the use of cannabis (marijuana and hashish) among Americans is increasing sharply. A majority (53%) of those between the ages of 18 and 25 have tried marijuana; almost one in four under the age of 18 has experimented with the drug. Of those under 18, 12% regularly used the drug in 1975.

Marijuana usage is not as prominent among Americans over the age of 25. Although over half of those younger have tried cannabis, only a third of the older population has experimented with marijuana. The older the age group, the less common the marijuana usage: Of those over the age of 35, less than one in a hundred used the drug regularly. This trend may not continue, however, because over half of America's college students use marijuana regularly, and over a third of those who do use it plan to continue using it (NIDA, 1975).

Marijuana has lost some of its nontraditional and nonconservative stigma, with the result that its users come from all classes, socioeconomic groups, and ages. Current government estimates for 1979 conclude that 43 million Americans have smoked marijuana at least once, and the number of current users exceeds 16 million ("Facts," 1979).

A 1975 report by the Secretary of Health, Education, and Welfare asserted that "marijuana users as compared to nonusers are more likely to use or have used other, both licit and illicit, psychoactive drugs. The more heavily a user smokes marijuana, the greater the probability he has used or will use other drugs."

A survey taken in 1976 disclosed that 85% of marijuana users also use hashish; none of the nonusers used hashish. Although none of the nonusers used amphetamines, LSD, cocaine, opiates, barbiturates, or tranquilizers, of those who used marijuana three times a week, 52% used amphetamines, 51% used LSD, 44% used cocaine, 24% used opiates, 20% used barbiturates, and 28% used tranquilizers (included in the last two categories were prescription medicines; Jones & Jones, 1977). A study of 367 heroin addicts in the United States revealed that all but 4 had used marijuana before they had used heroin.

Cannabis

Marijuana and hashish are preparations of materials from the Cannabis plant. The primary psychoactive agent, THC, is concentrated in the resin of the plant, with most of the resin in the flowering tops, less in the leaves, and little in the fibrous stalks. The psychoactive potency of a Cannabis preparation depends on the amount of resin present and therefore varies depending on the part of the plant used. Americans are most familiar with marijuana, dried plant material that varies considerably in its makeup. Some samples are made from the entire plant, including stems, whereas higher samples contain mostly materials from the tops of plants with flowers. Hashish is widely known around the world, and in its purest form is pure resin. It may be less pure, depending on how carefully the resin has been removed from the plant material.

Pharmacology

The most common method of using marijuana is by smoking dried plant parts. A less common, but still prevalent method of drug use involves eating the plant parts (usually mixed in cakes, brownies, or other food). Eating provides a slower effect, but temperatures required for baking alter the chemistry of the Cannabis, resulting in stronger, more potent drug actions.

The chemical components of the Cannabis plant include a specific and unique group of chemicals called the cannabinoids. As far as potency is concerned, the five most important cannabinoids are delta-9-THC (delta-9-trantetrahydrocannabinol), delta-8-THC, THCacid (delta-9-transtetrahydro-cannobinolic acid), CBN (cannabinol), and CBD (cannabidiol).

The primary ingredient—and the one that causes the major psychoactive reaction—in Cannabis is delta-9-THC; the other four ingredients listed above (and still other negligible ingredients) have little biologic effect.

Absorption and Elimination

Smoking the dried and chopped stems, leaves, and flowers of the Cannabis plant, as mentioned earlier, provides the most effective administration; the amount of delta-9-THC absorbed into the bloodstream from the lungs varies considerably among smokers, but major psychoactive and physiologic effects usually appear within 2 to 3 minutes (and sometimes less). The peak effect occurs within 10 to 20 minutes, and the psychoactive and physiologic effects last from 1-1/2 to 2 hours. Approximately 5 mg of delta-9-THC is contained in one marijuana cigarette.

Onset of effects is slower when the plant parts are eaten (either alone or as part of a confectionery). Onset begins 30 to 60 minutes after consumption; the peak is reached 2 to 3 hours after eating, and the effects last 3 to 5 hours. When administration is oral—that is, when the plant parts are eaten in some form—three times as much marijuana is required to produce the effects derived from smoking.

Almost all of the delta-9-THC is metabolized by the body: Less than 1% is found unchanged in the urine or feces of the marijuana user, regardless of whether the Cannabis is smoked, ingested, or drunk. Once in the bloodstream, delta-9-THC is rapidly changed in the liver to a compound called 11-hydroxy-THC (11-OH-THC), which is also psychoactive. The 11-OH-THC is then transformed rapidly into the inactive 8, 11-dihydroxy-THC. THC leaves the blood rapidly through metabolism and through rapid uptake into the tissues. There is a tendency for THC and its metabolites to bind to proteins and to remain stored for long periods of time in body fat. As the two chemicals disappear from the bloodstream, they are distributed to the various body organs, where they accumulate: delta-9-THC to the lungs, salivary glands, jejunum, kidneys, adrenal glands, muscles, liver, and testes (in decreasing order of concentration levels), with high concentrations found in the brain for the first 7 days following inhalation or ingestion; 11-OH-THC remains bound to the albumin.

After the initial distribution to various body organs, relatively high concentrations of radioactivity are found in the liver, the bile, the gastrointestinal tract, the kidneys, and the bladder. The delta-9-THC can cross the placenta in pregnant women, resulting in sizable concentrations of delta-9-THC in the fetus.

Although 99% of the delta-9-THC is metabolized by the body, the 1% that is not metabolized—the metabolic waste—is excreted through the urine and feces, with radioactive traces visible in the urine and feces for days after the administration of a single large dose (making it possible for forensic teams to detect the presence of marijuana with much greater accuracy than the presence of alcohol).

Five days after a single injection of THC, 20% remains stored, whereas 20% of its metabolites remain in the blood. Complete elimination of a single dose can take up to 30 days. Measurable levels of THC in blood from chronic users can be detected for up to 6 days after their last marijuana cigarette. The biological half-life (the time it takes for the body to eliminate half of the drug) of THC was reported to be 56 hours in subjects who had never before had cannabis, and 28 hours in those who had used it repeatedly (Lemberger, Tamarkin, Axelrod, & Kopin, 1971). In recent work with more sensitive measurement methods, the biological half-life for THC in chronic users was found to be 19 hours, whereas metabolite half-life was 50 hours (Jones, 1980).

The presence of delta-9-THC in the body affects the heart rate, the intraocular pressure, and the color of the conjunctiva; it has no evident effect on the body temperature, respiratory rate, or deep tendon reflexes. It has no evident effect on blood sugar or plasma levels and has a minute effect on pupillary size.

Mechanism of Action

THC has effects on the electrical properties of nerve membranes, alters turnover rates of serotonin and dopamine (Hamon, 1984), and has effects on prostaglandin synthesis ("Prostaglandins," 1985), to note a few of its effects. Whether any of these is the basic effect or whether all are secondary to some other direct action is not known.

Effects

Any form of drug abuse will have more devastating effects on individuals who are especially vulnerable—and children and adolescents are among the group deemed inherently more vulnerable. Children and adolescents, who are still in various stages of physical and psychological development, suffer more pronounced and chronic effects from Cannabis use than do adults, but the following effects are common to all age groups. Their severity and intensity will probably vary according to the age, health, and general vulnerability of the user. A person who is already ill or who is suffering from a chronic disease will always suffer more intense effects from Cannabis use.

Physical Effects

Effects on the brain. Because of the metabolization of delta-9-THC and its tendency to accumulate in the fatty tissues, marijuana accumulates in concentrated amounts in the brain tissue; significant amounts can be found in the brain up to 8 days after ingestion. Findings on the effect of marijuana on the brain are not clear cut and are subject to some controversy, but the results of some experiments conducted in the United States and in England indicate that marijuana leads to significant atrophy of brain tissue. During intoxication, significant changes in the normal EEG pattern of brain activity occur, but the long-range implications of such brain-activity pattern change is not known. Currently, X-ray techniques have not conclusively shown permanent damage to brain tissue.

Some effects of intoxication are also being suggested as possible permanent effects—including loss of memory, slowdown of the learning process, and inability to control motor and involuntary motor processes. Marijuana use also leads to a dulling of time perception, depth perception, distance perception, and speed perception.

Other long-term effects on the brain function include upset in motor coordination, causing a change in gait, uncontrolled laughter, a lag between thought and facial expressions, and unsteady hands. Once thought to be only temporary effects of intoxication, research has shown that these effects may in many cases be long-term and may increase as frequency of marijuana use increases.

Marijuana use also affects the deep control centers located in the brain. Users find that marijuana causes the white of the eyes to turn red, facial skin to turn red, pupils to dilate (making the eyes extremely sensitive to light), appetite to increase or decrease markedly, mouth and throat to get extremely dry, extremities to grow cold, and symptoms of nausea, vomiting, and diarrhea to develop.

Marijuana residue tends to accumulate in greater concentration in the brain's gray matter than in the white matter, with resulting impairment in abstract thinking. Subjects who have used marijuana heavily over an extended period of time are unable to distinguish between abstract and concrete thinking.

Accumulation of delta-9-THC in the fatty tissues of the brain may cause actual destruction of brain cells and actual dissolution of the thin membranes essential in preserving brain structure. Damaged cells cannot be replaced; in some cases, alternate pathways around destroyed cells can be formed through the brain. In many cases, users make adjustments for chemical disturbances and brain cell destruction.

Studies involving a number of healthy young male subjects who had smoked marijuana heavily over a long period of time showed brain atrophy comparable to that normally found in 90-year-old men. The brain damage is progressive—cannabinoids accumulated in the brain take so long to be eliminated that atrophy continues long after marijuana use is discontinued. This progressive atrophy is responsible for the psychic changes that accompany marijuana use (Campbell, Thomson, Evans, & Williams, 1972).

Still other studies involving healthy young male long-term users indicated that brain atrophy results in literal shrinkage of the cerebral structures; study subjects had lost the fluid in the inner cavity of the brain, and that fluid had been replaced with air.

Brain damage has also been exhibited in moderate users of marijuana. Those who smoked two marijuana cigarettes a day for a period of 2 years suffered major disturbances in brain wave activity; those disturbances (measured by EEG) corresponded to behavioral changes. Even among moderate users—those who had used marijuana for up to 2 years—the effects were observed up to 2 years after discontinued use.

Marijuana also disturbs blood flow in the brain. Cerebral blood flow is not uniform—the two parts of the brain that receive (and require) the greatest blood flow are the cerebral cortex and the deep brain area, which require up to four times the amount of blood required by other sections of the brain. Those two areas are also those areas most affected by marijuana, and accumulation of delta-9-THC in those areas causes tissue starvation due to inadequate blood flow. If continued over a period of time, such tissue starvation leads to cell destruction and brain atrophy.

Because the brain controls all body systems, the effect of marijuana on the brain also affects all other body systems—some generally, and some more specifically.

Effects on cells. Moderate use of marijuana—smoking as few as three cigarettes a week—may seriously interfere with the body's production of RNA and DNA in the cells. Reduction of RNA and DNA synthesis sharply reduces the mitotic index, or the rate at which cells generate new cells. Even as little as three cigarettes a week can result in a 41% reduction of new cell production.

Slowing down the body's vital DNA production may lead to two conditions: chromosome breakage and breakdown of the body's immune response system.

Studies at the University of Utah Medical Center revealed that more than 60% of those who used marijuana moderately suffered a significant number of chromosome breaks—up to three times as many as nonusers. Unfortunately, because marijuana use has been widespread for only 2 decades, and because the heaviest use has been among adolescents, the incidence of possible birth defects has yet to be witnessed. Result of studies leads to the conclusion that such birth defects may become evident.

Marijuana's interference with the body's production of DNA also lowers resistance to disease, disrupting the body's immune response system. Immune-globulin G, a chemical vital to immunity, has been found to be reduced among moderate marijuana users. T-lymphocytes, also critical to immunity, are destroyed by marijuana and can be destroyed in those who smoke one to three cigarettes a week for a period of at least 1 year. Moderate marijuana users are more likely to be affected by disease and are less likely to be able to fight off disease than are nonusers. Among those who use marijuana heavily, the tendency to develop disease can be 68% higher.

Implications of DNA and RNA destruction run deeper than just possible chromosome damage to offspring and increased susceptibility to disease. The chromosomes carry the genetic information for each cell, and that genetic information is passed not only to offspring but to each new cell that is formed within the body. Each new cell (with rare exceptions) is identical to the cell from which it was derived. Marijuana use (as little as twice a week) can lead to chromosome breakage that affects the cells manufactured in the body, leading to mutations, tumors, virus disease, anemia, and early aging. Normally, chromosomes break at a very low rate; this rate is accelerated sharply by exposure to radiation, certain viruses, and toxic chemicals (including delta-9-THC).

Studies have recently indicated that marijuana use causes the chromosome breakage that occurs normally as a part of the aging process. Moderate use of marijuana can cause as much chromosome breakage in 2 years as would normally occur in 50 years.

Marijuana's effects on production of RNA and DNA is apparently a result of the drug's deterioration of the cell's outer membranes.

Effects on the reproductive system. Marijuana use has been shown to affect both male and female reproductive systems and to have serious implications for the health of the fetus during pregnancy.

Smoking two marijuana cigarettes a day can disturb the level of ovarian hormones and can interfere with the ovarian cycle in as few as 12 days of use. Marijuana use can also lead to early menopause, triggering hormone levels that cause menopause onset to be six times as high as in nonusers.

Marijuana also has deleterious effects on levels and production of testosterone—the hormone that causes development of facial hair, development of muscle tissue, and the development of the reproductive system in the male. Researchers are unsure about the permanency of this effect, and some studies indicate that testosterone levels return to normal slowly after discontinuance of the drug (Harclerode, 1980).

Evidence also suggests that long-term marijuana use may lead to a decrease in the tissue mass of the testes, resulting in interference with testosterone production as well as sperm production. Sperm count is lower among users of marijuana than among nonusers; in 35% of the users the sperm count was low enough to render the users sterile. Marijuana users in general had a 44% lower testosterone level than did nonusers.

Sperm may also be destroyed or altered by marijuana. Studies of marijuana users reveal that delta-9-THC may cause degeneration of sperm, fragmentation of sperm, and improper sperm formation due to impairment of protein synthesis critical to the formation of the head of the sperm.

Delta-9-THC and other chemicals (most of them toxic) found in marijuana accumulate in high concentrations in the placenta and embryonic tissue, causing a reduction in birth weight and a sharp increase in the incidence of stillbirths. Fetal death and fetal abnormality have been shown to be directly related to marijuana use, and the severity of fetal abnormality (and incidence of fetal death) is directly related to the doses and frequency of marijuana used by the mother.

Nursing babies of mothers who use marijuana are also subject to all of the toxic effects of marijuana. Such babies suffer from physical damage as well as marked decline in mental vigor. Marijuana can be detected in nursing infants as soon as 4 hours after the mother inhaled or ingested Cannabis.

Effects on the respiratory system. Because marijuana must be inhaled deeply and held longer in the lungs than tobacco smoke, the lungs of marijuana users are more blackened than the lungs of tobacco smokers. The concentration of delta-9-THC is greater in the lungs than in any other body tissue, and examination reveals serious breakdown in lung tissue among marijuana users.

In normal, quiet breathing, air is not drawn into the small air sacs, but is drawn instead only into the smaller airway tubes (bronchioles) that ventilate the air sacs. The modules of oxygen and carbon dioxide rapidly diffuse between the air sacs and the air tubes during normal breathing; nicotine, which enters the lungs on particles of tobacco cigarette smoke, dissociates readily with the oxygen and enters the bloodstream without needing to be drawn into the air sacs. But THC is tightly bound to the surface of the carbon particles; those carbon particles must be deeply inhaled into the lungs, where they are drawn into the air sacs and held until they adhere to the walls of the air sacs next to microscopic capillaries that feed the air sacs. Over a period of several minutes the THC molecules are absorbed from the carbon particles directly into the bloodstream.

Almost half of those who smoke marijuana suffer from chronic sore throat, laryngitis, and pharyngitis. The same proportion suffer from respiratory disease; a few less have chronic bronchitis and emphysema. Some suffer from restrictive lung disease (such as interstitial fibrosis), and all suffer some impairment of lung function (Jones, 1980).

Over the long term, marijuana use leads to degeneration of the cell nuclei in the lungs and can result in a condition leading to lung cancer. Long-term use also results in tissue destruction (necrosis) and in destruction of the membranous linings of the lungs (Jones, 1980; Turner, 1980).

Effect on liver. Because many marijuana users also drink alcohol, it is difficult to determine how much liver damage is caused by marijuana and how much is caused by alcohol. In one study of marijuana users who did not use alcohol or who used alcohol in only moderate and infrequent doses, definite liver damage was indicated by biopsy in those who had smoked marijuana for

2 to 6 years. A study of those who had smoked marijuana for 6 months to 2 years showed little damage to the liver and little (if any) impairment of liver function, leading to the conclusion that liver damage results only after years (instead of months) of marijuana use.

Effect on the immune system. In animal experiments it is possible to show that THC, Cannabis extracts, and marijuana smoke in doses comparable to typical use by humans suppress the immune system reactions. In humans, some studies, but not all, indicate that heavy use of marijuana may interfere with the T-lymphocyte part of the immune system. This component is known to play a role in resistance to viral infection and to cancer.

Effects on the heart. Although marijuana does not lead to the development of heart disease in normal, healthy young adults, it can lead to the onset of critical heart problems in those who had a tendency for heart disease or in those whose hearts were less than healthy. Particularly serious is the effect of lowering the exercise tolerance in those who have anginal syndrome.

When administered in high doses, marijuana can cause a lowering of blood pressure. High doses of marijuana can also cause racing of the heart (sharply increased heart rate), but the heart beat generally returns to normal after discontinuance of use. In most cases, cardiac output is decreased during use.

Other physical effects. Moderate marijuana use also causes an inability of the blood to be properly oxygenated, abnormal dilation or constriction of the pupils, decrease of intraocular pressure, decrease in body temperature, increase of REM sleep, and reduction of sympathetic nerve activity.

Psychological Effects

Although marijuana's physical effects have not been widely acknowledged among users, its psychological effects are acknowledged and hailed—and in many cases are the reason for the use.

Marijuana users report vivid changes in sensation, including ability to see patterns, forms, figures, or meaningful designs in visual material that normally has no particular form; ability to visualize objects more sharply; ability to see things in three-dimensional depth; visualization of new colors or shades of color; acquisition of a sensual quality to vision that makes it seem as though the user can "touch" an object he is looking at; the ability to hear more subtle changes in sounds; the ability to understand song lyrics that are usually unclear; ability to hear greater spatial separation between musical instruments; vivid auditory images; variance in the sound quality of the user's voice; more exciting, sensual sense of touch; increase in the heaviness of objects; increase in taste sensations; increased enjoyment of eating; craving of sweets; increase in sense of smell; and increase in the distance between the user and other objects or people.

Marijuana users claim a different feeling toward their own body, describing a "pleasant warmth" inside the body; awareness of the beating of the heart; feeling of lightness, as if the user were floating in midair; a feeling of flowing energy in the body; awareness of air filling the lungs; ability to tolerate pain easily; and a tingling or vibration in the body. Users also describe an effect on physical movement, saying that their emotions seem exceptionally well coordinated with their physical movement.

In connection with interpersonal relations, users say that they experience deep insight into other people, difficulty playing ordinary social games, tremendous empathy, feelings of isolation, and desires to interact more with people.

Much less acclaimed by users are the less pleasant psychological effects of marijuana: antisocial behavior, reduction of attention span, propensity toward mental illness, schizophrenia, mania, personality deterioration, loss of motivation, inability to form normal thought processes, inability to concentrate, loss of affection for loved ones, loss of inhibition, loss of willpower, paranoia, and loss of learning ability.

Study of the psychological effects of marijuana use have led researchers to identify the "Cannabis syndrome," a behavior disorder characterized by "diminished drive, lessened ambition, decreased motivation, and apathy." Mental tasks requiring concentration and attention—specifically the ability to read—are greatly impaired among those who use marijuana.

Heavy usage over long periods of time, or usage by an individual who is psychologically unstable prior to usage, can result in hallucinations, delusions, and auditory misperceptions (Petersen, 1980). Other psychological effects, evident as both long-range effects and as effects during intoxication, include confusion, restlessness, excitement, delirium, disorientation, and clouding of consciousness.

Therapeutic Uses

Marijuana's potential therapeutic uses have been indicated as possibly beneficial in treatment of the following diseases and disorders:

Glaucoma. Intraocular pressure, which permanently damages the retina and the optic nerve, has been isolated as the cause of glaucoma, a disease of the eye that accounts for 14% of all new reported cases of blindness in the United States each year.

Marijuana acts to reduce intraocular pressure in a number of ways:

1. It causes vasoconstriction of the small arteries supplying the ciliary body of the eye, thereby reducing both the capillary pressure and the rate of aqueous fluid secretion.
2. It increases the eye's ability to drain aqueous fluid.
3. It slightly alters ocular tissues to decrease the rate of aqueous fluid production further and to increase aqueous fluid drainage further.
4. It inhibits prostaglandin synthesis (which is not directly related to treatment of primary glaucoma, but which is important in the treatment of secondary glaucoma).
5. It causes a change in the patient's psychophysiologic state, allowing relaxation and euphoria, both demonstrated as significant to treatment (Goldberg, Kass, & Becker, 1978-1979).

Studies indicate that reduction in intraocular pressure is significant; 30 minutes after smoking marijuana, pressure in experimental subjects was reduced from 29% to 34%. Studies in Europe indicate that the effect of a single marijuana cigarette on reduction of intraocular pressure is effective for up to 1 month (depending on dose-tolerance levels) (Goldberg et al., 1978-1979).

Asthma. In normal subjects, marijuana has the tendency to dilate the bronchioles, which during asthma attacks become constricted and make intake of sufficient air difficult or impossible. Although several other drugs are effective in bringing about dilation of the bronchioles, THC—the active ingredient in marijuana—lasts longer and tends to require less frequent administration.

Unfortunately, THC is only completely effective when administered in cigarette form—and the smoking of cigarettes is seriously contraindicated for asthma due to the irritating effect on the lungs, throat, and bronchial airways. Furthermore, intake of marijuana smoke into the lungs decreases the natural bacterial activity of the lungs, making them susceptible to bacterial infection (including pneumonia). Asthma, emphysema, and lung cancer have been confirmed as frequent side effects of smoking marijuana.

Cancer. Marijuana has several applications for treatment of cancer victims. Initial experimental studies have shown that Cannabis retards the growth of certain strains of tumors, but THC is generally less effective than other chemotherapeutic agents already on the market for the reduction of tumor growth. Of significant value to cancer victims is marijuana's therapeutic action to control nausea, vomiting, and loss of appetite that normally accompanies conventional chemotherapy (Petersen, 1980). Standard antiemetics used to treat nausea and vomiting have been ineffective against the nausea and vomiting that follow chemotherapy, while initial treatments with marijuana have proven effective in providing complete relief. Also helpful with cancer victims is the tranquilizing, mood-elevating property of marijuana.

Muscle spasticity. Marijuana has been shown to be effective in controlling the spasticity of muscles common in cerebral palsy, multiple sclerosis, and certain kinds of stroke. The ability of THC to reduce and control muscle spasticity is related to its inhibitory effect on the nerve reflexes.

Epilepsy. Several of the chemical constituents of marijuana have effectiveness as anticonvulsives; cannabidiol seems to be more effective and to have fewer hazardous side effects in seizure-prone individuals than does THC.

Use of marijuana in controlling seizures resulting from epilepsy needs to be critically monitored by the prescribing physician, for large doses of THC in a seizure-prone individual can cause the onset of seizures (Cohen, 1980).

Transplanting/skin grafts. Administration of marijuana has proven effective in lessening the body's tendency to reject organ transplants and skin grafts, making it a potentially useful and important drug in treatment of plastic surgery patients.

Marijuana's beneficial therapeutic actions—reduction of pain, reduction of inflammation, control of convulsions, deadening of nerve impulses, control of nausea and vomiting, and dilation of bronchioles—make it a possible drug-of-importance in the treatment of certain diseases and disorders. However, its undesirable side effects—including transient anxiety, altered perception, interference with normal thought processes, visual and auditory hallucinations, tachycardia, hypotension, hypothermia, hyperglycemia, frequency of urination, diarrhea, and significant reductions in heart and liver weight over a long period of use—call for careful monitoring and close examination of cases in which marijuana is used. In some cases, the undesirable side effects may contraindicate the use of marijuana.

Still another serious consideration in the use of marijuana as a therapeutic agent is the development of tolerance to the drug; patients who initially require only a small dose that carries with it few side effects may quickly require larger doses, increasing the occurrence of undesirable side effects.

Currently, those who desire to do research on marijuana's therapeutic effects must receive clearance from the Food and Drug Administration and from the Drug Enforcement Administration.

Dependence

It has not been conclusively demonstrated that dependence occurs as a result of marijuana usage. Physical dependence has been demonstrated in laboratory experiments with humans given large doses of THC every 4 hours for 10 to 20 days. Beginning several hours after the last oral dose, subjects showed irritability, restlessness, nausea, and vomiting. These symptoms peaked at 8 hours, and declined over the next 3 days. Sleep disturbances and loss of appetite were also reported (Jones & Benowitz, 1976). Such withdrawal symptoms are virtually never reported outside the research laboratory. It is much easier to show psychological dependence in heavy users of marijuana (Jones, 1980).

Tolerance

For years there was debate over whether tolerance developed to the effects of THC and/or marijuana. Whereas animal studies repeatedly demonstrated tolerance to the behavioral disruption produced by large doses of marijuana, the experiences of human marijuana smokers seemed to indicate that experienced users could get high more readily than inexperienced users, possibly implying reverse tolerance. The reverse tolerance syndrome, however, only applies to initial use of the drug and is experienced only with the first few doses. We know that learning plays an important role in the psychological reaction, particularly to low doses of marijuana. That, combined with the fact that THC may build up in the tissues of chronic users, might account for any increased reaction.

With continued use of the drug, tolerance develops at a fairly rapid pace. Findings of the Report of the Indian Hemp Drugs Commission revealed that heavy users of marijuana required four times the amount of the drug to obtain the same effect as moderate users of the drug. In one experimental study, subjects were given marijuana several times daily for a month in dosages of their own choosing; the subjects increased the dosages steadily (although slowly) over the period of the experiment. Although the number of cigarettes smoked daily over the month increased, the pulse rate and other symptoms of euphoria actually decreased, even though the users were slowly increasing the dosage.

Experiments on animals revealed that once tolerance had developed, increasing the drug by one hundred times had little physical effect on the animals that had developed tolerance.

Tolerance to one chemical ingredient of marijuana generally indicates tolerance to its other chemical ingredients—for instance, tolerance to delta-9-THC also signifies tolerance to delta-8-THC, even when the chemicals are administered separately instead of as parts of the drug—but tolerance to marijuana does not in most cases cross over to tolerance to other drugs. In some cases, a person may develop tolerance to some effects of delta-9-THC, but not to other effects of the same chemical.

References

Campbell, A. M. G., Thomson J. L. G., Evans, M., & Williams, M. J. (1972). Cerebral atrophy in young cannabis smokers. *Lancet, 1,* 202-203.

Cohen, S. (1980). Therapeutic aspects. In R. C. Peterson (Ed.), *Marijuana research findings: 1980* (NIDA Research Monograph No. 31, pp. 199-221). Rockville, MD: National Institute on Drug Abuse.

Facts about a weed called pot. (1979, March). *Changing Times,* p. 21.

Goldberg, I., Kass, M. A., & Becker, B. (1978-1979, winter). Marijuana as a treatment for glaucoma. *The Sightsaving Review,* 147-154.

Hamon, M. (1984). Common neurochemical correlates to the action of hallucinogens. In B. L. Jacobs (Ed.), *Hallucinogens: Neurochemical, behavioral, and clinical perspectives.* New York: Raven Press.

Harclerode, J. (1980). The effect of marijuana on reproduction and development. In R. C. Petersen (Ed.), *Marijuana research findings: 1980* (NIDA Research Monograph No. 31, pp. 137-166). Rockville, MD: National Institute on Drug Abuse.

Jones, R. T. (1980). Human effects: An overview. In R. C. Petersen (Ed.), *Marijuana research findings: 1980* (NIDA Research Monograph No. 31, pp. 54-88). Rockville, MD: National Institute on Drug Abuse.

Jones, R. T., & Benowitz, N. (1976). The 30-day trip—Clinical studies of cannabis tolerance and dependence. In M. C. Graude & S. Szara (Eds.), *Pharmacology of marijuana.* New York: Raven Press.

Jones, H., & Jones, H. (1977). *Sensual drugs* (pp. 215-249). London: Cambridge University Press.

Lemberger, L., Tamarkin, N. R., Axelrod, J., & Kopin, I. J. (1971). Delta-9-tetrahydrocannabinol: Metabolism and disposition in long-term marijuana smokers. *Science, 173,* pp. 72-74.

National Institute on Drug Abuse. (1975). *Marijuana and health: Fifth annual report to the United States Congress from the Secretary of Health, Education, and Welfare* (pp. 2-3). Rockville, MD: Author.

Petersen, R. C. (1980). Marijuana and health. In R. C. Petersen (Ed.), *Marijuana research findings: 1980* (NIDA Research Monograph No. 31. pp. 1-17). Rockville, MD: National Institute on Drug Abuse.

Prostaglandins and cannabis, XIV. Tolerance to the stimulatory actions of cannabinoids on arachidonate metabolism. (1985). *Journal of Pharmacology and Experimental Therapeutics, 235,* 87.

Rogers, R. (1978, December 10). *Reading, writing and reefer* [Transcript of an NBC news report, p. 11]. The National Broadcasting Company, Inc.

Turner, C. E. (1980). Chemistry and metabolism. In R. C. Petersen (Ed.), *Marijuana research findings: 1980* (NIDA Research Monograph No. 31, pp. 81-97). Rockville, MD: National Institute on Drug Abuse.

8

HALLUCINOGENS

A hallucinogenic or psychotomimetic drug may be defined as one that will consistently produce changes in thought, perception, and mood, alone or in concert, without causing major disturbances of the autonomic nervous system or other serious disability.

It is important to realize that psychotomimetics, as the word implies, are substances that in an animal's body cause symptoms similar to those of schizophrenia. They are not necessarily similar and do not even act in a similar manner to those substances that may be responsible for causing mental disorders.

Additionally the hallucinogens (the term primarily used here except for an occasional reference to "psychedelics" [mind-manifesting]) cause visual, auditory, tactile, gustatory, and olfactory hallucinations and produce ecstatic states in some individuals. A variety of agents currently available (including LSD, mescaline, and psilocybin), which have been known in natural forms, such as certain mushrooms, cactus buttons, and seeds, have the property of permitting experiences of expanding consciousness.

Although research in the past has focused on legitimate medicinal uses of hallucinogens, to date there is no evidence that drugs such as LSD can be employed safely in humans in a beneficial way. And it is very unlikely that an understanding of the mechanisms of action of hallucinogenic drugs will be of much value in the study of the biochemical basis of mental function.

Extent of Use

LSD (d-lysergic acid diethylamide) ushered in the current wave of non-medical drug excesses almost three decades ago. Since the 1960s, its use has waxed and waned. Recent reports indicate a resurgence of LSD use may be under way.

The psychedelic "revolution" began 25 years ago. Within 7 years it had reached its peak and began to decline. The use of typical hallucinogens has declined, but a certain amount of consumption remains (Johnson, Bachman, & O'Malley, 1982; Miller, Cisin, Gardner-Keaton, et al., 1983). During the 1970s, phencyclidine (PCP) usage rose and the number of adverse reactions were impressive in those West Coast cities that experienced large-scale utilization. PCP is now on the decline although it, too, retains some adherents.

The latest psychedelic drug to hit the streets is the "designer drug" MDMA. In 1985, *Newsweek* ("Getting High," 1985), *Life* ("Trouble," 1985), *Time* ("Crackdown," 1985), and numerous other popular magazines printed major stories on the subject, often sensationalizing the reputed euphoric and therapeutic qualities of MDMA. With the rise in popularity has come an increased street demand. In testimony submitted for the federal administrative hearings to determine final scheduling, psychopharmacologist Ronald Siegel (1985) stated that street use "escalated from an estimated 10,000 doses distributed in all of 1976 to 30,000 doses distributed per month in 1985" (p. 2).

Types of Hallucinogenic Drugs

There are three major chemical classes of hallucinogens, organized according to the neurotransmitter they are thought to affect most: norepinephrine, acetylcholine, or serotonin. Some of the psychoactive agents probably influence more than one neurotransmitter, but this method of organization can help keep in mind the more important mechanisms through which they work. The first category of hallucinogen has psychoactive chemicals that are similar in structure to norepinephrine; mescaline and the synthetic compound dimethoxymethylamphetamine (DOM, or STP) are examples. The second type of drug is structurally similar to acetylcholine and may influence acetylcholine neurotransmission. This group of drugs includes such hallucinogens as henbane, nightshade, Datura, and a few others. These drugs are sometimes called anticholinergics because neurons that release acetylcholine are called cholinergic neurons. The third category of hallucinogenic drugs may structurally mimic serotonin's indole structure and cause the body to react as if more, or in some cases less, serotonin were released from its neurons.

Indole Type Hallucinogens

The basic structure of the neurotransmitter serotonin is referred to an as indole nucleus. The hallucinogens LSD and psilocybin also contain this structure. For that reason and because some other chemicals with this structure have similar hallucinogenic effects, this group is referred to as the indole hallucinogens.

d-Lysergic Acid Diethylamide (LSD). The mental results of LSD are a paradigm for the effects on the mind of the other hallucinogens. LSD is a product of research into the ergot alkaloids. Ergot is the resting stage of the fungus *Claviceps purpurea*. From medieval times there are recorded outbreaks of ergotism caused by eating rye bread contaminated with the fungus. The manifestations usually take the form of painful gangrene of the fingers, toes, and ears due to peripheral vasoconstriction, but psychotic features have also occurred. Although the nature of the natural hallucinogen is undetermined, lysergic acid is the basic structure in several of the alkaloids found in ergot; lysergic acid diethylamide (LSD-25, LSD) is its derivative. The psychoactive properties of LSD were discovered by Dr. Albert Hofmann, who in 1943 during the course of investigations consumed some of the drug and then cycled home under its influence.

LSD is taken orally. Its effects on mental processes develop gradually, reach their height in 2 to 4 hours, and begin to subside after about 12 hours. Perception is influenced in many ways. Illusions develop: Objects may appear larger or smaller than normal, walls or ceilings recede or grow near, colors and outlines become more vivid and impressive. On closing the eyes, afterimages are prolonged, or brightly colored and realistic images may be seen.

Hallucinations are frequent; they are predominantly visual. With open eyes realistic or fantastic images are perceived, to which strong effects of pleasure or fear are attached. Synaesthesia occur, that is, sensations evoked by one sensory modality are transformed into perceptions from another modality. Thus noises may evoke colored patterns, or colors are experienced as sounds. Appreciation of the body image is distorted; the body as a whole, or a portion, such as a limb, appears to enlarge or to shrink.

Affective disturbance is extensive and varied. Elation, depression, mild euphoria, or anxiety may be elicited; an evoked mood can rapidly increase in intensity or be transformed into a dissimilar affect. Injuries have occurred to elated persons who overestimated their physical powers; self-harm has been inflicted by subjects suicidally depressed from LSD; users attempting to escape from the psychomimetic effects of the drug have accidently injured themselves. Through these several routes fatalities have ensued from LSD.

The passage of time is subjectively slowed by the drug. Ideas that stimulate profound religious insight occur; the user may consider that under LSD he gains insight into the fundamental concepts of life. Objects seen or heard in the environment can seem to acquire a significant or mystical meaning and importance.

The somatic effects of LSD are mainly sympathomimetic. They include tachycardia (rapid heart beat), hypertension, increased body temperature, pupil dilatation, and tremor. Muscle weakness, nausea, and dizziness can also develop.

LSD resembles other psychoactive drugs with respect to the concordance of its mental effects and the drug experience and expectations of the user, with the subject's current mood, and with the social setting in which the drug is taken.

The LSD experience is always interesting to the user, and often enjoyable, but in a sizable proportion of instances it is unpleasant. A distressful experience under LSD represents the most common hazard of the drug; it is unpredictable and a "bad trip" can ensue after a series of "good trips." The subject of an adverse reaction should be reassured and verbally calmed; a benzodiazepine or phenothiazine drug is helpful.

The results of LSD develop in a person who has not recently taken the drug after a dose on the order of 50 mg. Tolerance supervenes quickly and markedly. After half a dozen administrations spaced over a few weeks doses up to 800 mg or slightly higher may be needed to produce a full reaction.

The mechanism of action of LSD is unclear. The structure of the drug resembles the neurotransmitter serotonin. Conceivably LSD could exert psychotomimetic effects through one of two contrasting processes. The drug may activate the serotoninergic receptors in the brain; alternatively, LSD could inertly occupy serotonin receptors and thereby inhibit activity normally induced by the neurotransmitter. Although animal experiments support either view, the concept that the effects of LSD develop through stimulation of serotoninergic synapses is in conformity with the antipsychotic effect of some major tranquilizers that block serotonin receptors.

LSD may affect the normal balance of norepinephrine, dopamine, and serotonin in the reticular activating system of the brainstem. In addition to its effects on serotonin, LSD may also mimic the action of dopamine. DOM has similar effects on serotonin and dopamine. Thus the most potent hallucinogens may be those that both inactivate brain serotonin and mimic brain dopamine (Jacobs & Trulson, 1979).

Experiments with radioactive LSD show that about half of it is cleared from the body within 3 hours, and more than 90% is excreted within 24 hours. Tolerance develops rapidly to repeated doses, probably because of a change in sensitivity of the target cells in the brain rather than a change in liver enzymes. Tolerance wears off within a few days after the drug has been discontinued. Because there are no withdrawal symptoms, a person does not become physically dependent but can become psychologically dependent on LSD.

Repeated use of LSD can lead to a prolonged psychosis that resembles schizophrenia (Bowers, 1972; Hatrick, 1970). The condition requires admission to a psychiatric unit and therapy with a major tranquilizer. The psychosis is often at first indistinguishable from schizophrenia, but it usually clears completely and permanently within weeks or months.

The acute effects of LSD on mental processes can recur suddenly and briefly at intervals of days, weeks, or months after taking the drug. Physical or psychological stresses and certain drugs such as marijuana and antihistamines may also trigger flashbacks. Treatment consists of reassurance that the condition will go away and use of a minor tranquilizer if necessary to control the anxiety (Cohen, 1978). Frequent use of LSD has also been claimed to produce defects in the capacity for abstract thought (McGlothlin, Arnold, & Freedman, 1969).

The attribution, on doubtful evidence, of a toxic effect of LSD to human chromosomes illustrates a tendency to exaggerate some of the hazards of unconventional drugs. Chromosomal impairment from any cause can have serious results; the subject is more likely to develop leukemia, and if the germ cells are affected, then progeny subsequently conceived are prone to developmental defects. Around 1970 statements were issued that authoritatively described chromosomal damage from LSD.

Chromosome harm from LSD is, however, unsubstantiated. It is not established that persons who have taken the drug exhibit a higher proportion of chromosomal irregularities than controls. LSD damages the fetus in more than one species of experimental animals, but it has not been confirmed that children born to LSD users possess an increased incidence of congenital defects (Dishotsky, Loughman, Mogar, & Lipscomb, 1971).

There are several hallucinogens that, like LSD, bear a structural similarity to serotonin. Psilocybin and psilocin are the active alkaloids of the Mexican mushroom *Psilocybe mexicana,* which is noted for psychotoxic effects when ingested. Dimethyltryptamine, or DMT, is not active by mouth and is taken either as snuff, by smoking, or by injection.

Adrenergic Type Hallucinogens

Mescaline (Peyote). Peyote is a small, spineless, carrot-shaped cactus, which grows wild in the Rio Grande valley and southward. It is mostly subterranean, and only the grayish-green pincushion-like top appears above ground. Only the part of the cactus that is above ground is easily edible, but the entire plant is psychoactive. This upper portion, or crown, is sliced into disks that are dried and are known as "mescal buttons." Over 30 psychoactive alkaloids have been identified in peyote, but mescaline is the most active, and is the one that induces intensified perception of colors and euphoria in the user.

The average dose of mescaline that will cause hallucinations and other physiological effects is from 300 mg to 600 mg (an aspirin is about 325 mg). It may take up to 20 peyote buttons to get 600 mg of mescaline. Effects include dilation of the pupils, increase in body temperature, anxiety, hallucinations, and alteration of body image. Mescaline induces vomiting in many people, and some muscular relaxation. Apparently there are no aftereffects or drug hangover at low doses.

High doses induce cardiac depression, headaches, slowing of respiratory rhythm, contraction of the intestines and the uterus, difficulty in coordination, dry skin with itching, and hypertension. It is estimated from animal studies that from 10 to 30 times the lowest dose that will cause behavioral effects in humans may be lethal. Death in animals results from convulsions and respiratory arrest. Mescaline is perhaps 1000 to 3000 times less potent than LSD, and 30 times less potent than psilocybin.

Mescaline is readily absorbed if taken orally but passes the blood-brain barrier only very poorly (which explains the high dose required). Within 30 minutes to 2 hours after ingestion mescaline reaches a maximum concentration in the brain, and the drug may remain in the brain up to 9 or 10 hours. The effects obtained with low doses, about 3 mg/kg, are primarily euphoric, while doses in the range of 5 mg/kg give rise to a full set of hallucinations. Hallucinations may last up to two hours and are dependent to some extent on the dose level. About half the dose is excreted unchanged in the urine in about 6 hours. A slow tolerance builds up after repeated use, and there is cross-tolerance to LSD. As with LSD, mescaline intoxication can be alleviated or stopped by a dose of chlorpromazine (Thorazine, a major tranquilizer) and to a lesser extent with diazepam (Valium, a minor tranquilizer).

Mescaline acts at least partly by decreasing brain levels of norepinephrine, although its effects are not as strong or consistent in this regard as those of LSD. In addition, mescaline alters the turnover rate of serotonin, thus increasing the amount in brain tissue. LSD also increases serotonin, probably by depressing the release of the neurotransmitter. Mescaline does not appear to affect all the tryptaminergic neurons, unlike LSD and DMT (Bridger, Barr, Gibbons, & Gorelick, 1978). Serotonin, believed to function as a neurotransmitter, is found almost exclusively within neurons of the raphe nuclei. These nuclei are clusters of neurons on the midline of the brainstem that send some of their axons to portions of the visual cortex and to portions of the limbic system. The visual and the limbic systems are known to be important in emotional experience and expression. Thus, altering the activity of these neurons is thought to be the basis for the effects of hallucinogens like mescaline and LSD.

MDA (3,4-methylenedioxy-amphetamine). MDA was first synthesized in 1910 and is structurally related to both mescaline and amphetamine. The drug is usually classified as a hallucinogen, but it also has some stimulatory characteristics. In early research it was found that MDA is an anorexiant (causing loss of appetite) and is a mood elevator in some persons.

MDA first appeared on the streets in 1967 and became known as a drug that produced a sensual, easily managed psychedelic high (Meyers, Rose, & Smith, 1967-1968). People who take this drug usually report experiencing a sense of well-being and heightened tactile sensations and thus increased pleasure through sex and expression of affection. The MDA experience is usually devoid of the visual and auditory distortions that mark the LSD experience. Those under the influence of MDA often focus on interpersonal relationships and demonstrate an overwhelming desire or need to be with or to talk to people. The unpleasant side effects most often noted are nausea, periodic tensing of muscles in the neck, tightening of the jaw and grinding of the teeth, and dilation of the pupils. After MDA was placed in Schedule I of the Controlled Substances Act in 1970, its use seemed to level off and gradually decline.

Research shows that the mode of action of MDA is similar to that of amphetamine in some respects. It may cause extra release of norepinephrine and block its reabsorption for a period of time. It also depletes dopamine. Just how the drug modifies brain activity is not known.

MDMA. MDMA, along with other amphetamine and methamphetamine analogues, is often regarded as a "designer drug." However, MDMA was first synthesized and patented in 1914. It became more popular than its cousin, MDA, primarily because its effects were much more desirable. MDMA, also known as "Adam," "Ecstasy," or "XTC," seems to possess a multiple personality. Many physicians and therapists view the drug as a valuable therapeutic aid, see minimal harm associated with carefully monitored use, and claim successful results in most cases (Greer, 1985; Grinspoon, 1985; Lynch, 1985; Wolfson, 1985). Drug enforcement officials, on the other hand, see a dangerous substance with potentially harmful adverse effects, accompanied by increasing abuse outside the therapeutic community (Drug Enforcement Administration, 1985; Sapienza, 1985).

The uniqueness of this substance can also be seen in the controversy generated over the proper terminology for MDMA (Beck, 1986; Seymour, 1986). As an analogue of MDA, it is related to both mescaline and the amphetamines. Although MDMA most commonly has been labeled a psychedelic drug, it possesses stimulant properties as well. Moreover, although the drug has been used for "mind altering" experiences, it is not hallucinogenic (except at very high doses) and thus rarely produces delusions or the mental confusion common to other psychedelics.

In terms of popular use, MDMA is essentially the successor to MDA. Although MDMA first appeared on the street in the early 1970s, use remained very limited until the end of the decade. Of those who had experienced both drugs, the majority preferred MDMA. Beck (1986) gives three major reasons for this: First, the stimulant side effects of MDA are more troublesome; second, MDMA has a greater perceived euphoric and therapeutic effect; and finally, the illegality of MDA undoubtedly drew some users toward MDMA, which was a legal substance until July 1985.

The oral route is by far the most common method of ingestion, although some individuals occasionally inhale the drug. Intravenous use seems to be rare; users describe its effects as less satisfying than that provided by methamphetamine injection (Seymour, 1986). The oral method is generally preferred because it produces the longest, smoothest high with the least amount of stimulant side effects. At times a small quantity of MDMA will be swallowed or inhaled as a "booster" after the initial oral dose begins to wear off. A continuous use of boosters, however, generally leads to great fatigue the next day.

The MDMA dosage range between effectiveness and toxicity is fairly narrow. The effectiveness threshold is around 50 mg, and toxic effects begin to increase sharply over the 200-mg-dose level. The usual dose ranges from 100 mg to 150 mg, with 125 mg about average. Effects generally appear within 20 to 60 minutes, when the user experiences a "rush" usually described as mild but euphoric. The "rush" may last from a few minutes to half an hour or not occur at all, depending on the user's mental set and the environment, the dose ingested, and the MDMA's quality. After the rush, the high levels off to a plateau usually lasting from 2 to 3 hours and followed by a gradual "coming down" sensation, ending with a feeling of fatigue. Insomnia, however, may persist long after the fatigue stage, depending on the dosage and the user.

MDMA, although milder and shorter-lasting than MDA, still exerts strong amphetamine-like effects on the body, including dilated pupils, dry mouth and throat, tension in the lower jaw, grinding of the teeth, and overall stimulation. The side effects are less troublesome when a small or moderate dose is taken by a healthy individual. Moreover, MDMA usually exerts a strong paradoxical effect of relaxation, bringing less attention to the side effects (Beck, 1986).

Other psychological side effects are also noted. Users cite a dramatic drop in defense mechanisms and increased empathy for others. Combined with the stimulant effect, this generally produces an increase in intimate communication. Although both MDA and MDMA have been labeled "aphrodisiacs," users most often report a more sensual experience. Researchers, too, have noted that both compounds enhance the pleasure of touching but interfere with erection in men and inhibit orgasm in both men and women (Beck, 1986; Klein, 1985; Seymour, 1986; Weil, 1976).

Several potentially serious psychological problems have also been associated with the use of MDMA. Rare episodes of hyperventilation have been noted (Beck, 1986; Seymour, 1986; Siegel, 1985). These almost always occur during the onset of the experience as part of a generalized panic reaction.

Although little is known about the potential toxicity for humans of MDA, MDMA, or any of the other amphetamine psychedelics, some research has assessed toxic and legal doses in animals (Davis & Borne, 1984; Hardman, Haavik, & Seevers, 1973). Assuming the results of the data on animals can be generalized to humans, indications are that a lethal IV dose for 50% of 150-pound individuals would be about 1100 to 1780 mg. Thus a lethal dose for injected MDMA may be a little over 10 times the usual 100 mg to 150 mg dose. A recent study, however, suggested a much lower toxicity level when MDMA is ingested orally, approximately corresponding to 150 times the human therapeutic level (Goad, 1985).

The potential for dependency and/or abusive use patterns must also be addressed. Although Seymour (1986) states that MDMA does not seem to pack a "euphoric punch" or "rush" comparable to other drugs, Beck (1986) finds just the opposite to be true. Among individuals who have tried both MDMA and cocaine, the majority usually express a strong preference for the longer, smoother euphoria provided by MDMA.

The strong euphoria associated with MDMA points toward a high abuse potential. Recent studies at Johns Hopkins found that primates will self-administer MDMA at regular intervals (although not quite as frequently as cocaine; cited in Beck & Morgan, 1986). In sharp contrast to cocaine, however, there appear to be relatively few cases of what might be considered heavy abuse of MDMA (Greer, 1983; Meyers et al., 1967-1968; Seymour, 1986; Siegel, 1985). In an ongoing study of MDMA users, Siegel (1985) stated that the most common patterns of use are "experimental" (10 times or less in a lifetime) or "social-recreational" (one to four times per month). He also noted that "compulsive patterns marked by escalating dose and frequency of use have not been reported with MDMA users" (pp. 2-3).

DOM or STP (Dimethoxymethylamphetamine). Although the basic structure of DOM is amphetamine, it is discussed here because of its hallucinogenic effects that seem to work through mechanisms similar to those of mescaline and LSD. DOM probably mimics the effect of dopamine and depress the activity of serotonin-containing neurons (Jacobs & Trulson, 1979). Doses of less than 3 mg produce heartbeat increases, pupil dilation, and increased blood pressure and body temperature. It causes a mild euphoria that may last from 8 to 12 hours, with peak reactions after 3 to 5 hours. A dose of 3 mg to 5 mg will cause a 6- to 8-hour hallucinogenic period. Higher doses of around 10 mg will cause "trips" lasting from 16 to 24 hours. These long trips are more likely to cause panic reactions.

DOM produces a higher incidence of acute and chronic reactions than any of the other commonly used hallucinogens, with the possible exception of PCP. The effects of DOM are like a combination of amphetamine and LSD, with the hallucinogenic effects of the drug very often putting the peripheral amphetamine-like physiological effects out of perspective. (Peripheral—outside the nervous system—effects of amphetamine may include headache, sweating, irregular heartbeat, nausea, vomiting, diarrhea, increased breathing rate, and pain and difficulty in urination; Smith & Meyers, 1969.) As with LSD and mescaline, chlorpromazine will ease the experience of the long trip very rapidly, but it can also interfere with breathing. Bourne (1976) recommends using Valium because there are fewer shock reactions than with chlorpromazine.

Phencyclidine (Phenylcyclohexylpiperdine, or PCP). PCP was developed in the late 1950s as an intravenous anesthetic. Although it was found to be an effective anesthetic, it had side effects that led to its being discontinued as a drug for human use. Sometimes persons coming out of the anesthetic had delirium and near manic states of excitation lasting 3 to 18 hours. PCP is now legitimately available only as an animal anesthetic. The street source is mainly synthesized in illicit laboratories from readily available chemical precursors.

Phencyclidine has depressant, stimulant, hallucinogenic, and analgesic properties. The effects of PCP on the central nervous system (CNS) vary greatly. At low doses the most prominent effect is similar to that of alcohol intoxication, with generalized numbness; the person becomes less sensitive to pain. As the dose of PCP is increased, the person becomes even more insensitive and may become fully anesthetized. Large doses can cause coma, convulsions, and death.

The majority of peripheral signs of PCP effects are apparently related to activation of the sympathetic nervous systems. Flushing, excess sweating, and a blank stare are common, although the size of the pupils are unaffected. The cardiovascular system reacts by increasing blood pressure and rapid heart action. Analgesia, side-to-side eye movements, muscular incoordination, double vision, dizziness, nausea, and vomiting occur in many people taking medium to high doses.

The drug has negative effects most of the time it is used. Why, then, do people use PCP repeatedly as their drug of choice, instead of another street drug? The fact that PCP has the ability markedly to alter the person's subjective feelings may be reinforcing, even though that alteration is not always positive. PCP may give the user feelings of strength, power, and invulnerability. Other positive effects include heightened sensitivity to outside stimuli, a sense of stimulation and mood elevation, and dissociation from the surroundings. PCP is a social drug; virtually all users report taking it in groups rather than as a solitary experience (Petersen & Stillman, 1978).

Some users develop a profound psychological dependence on PCP, in spite of its unpredictability and the behavioral impairment it produces. The dependence-producing properties of PCP have also been studied in monkeys, who will learn to produce intravenous injections of the drug (Balster & Chait, 1978). This is in contrast to LSD and other hallucinogens, which will not support animal self-administration and do not produce behavioral dependence in most users.

The mechanism of PCP's action on the brain was a mystery for several years, for PCP does alter many neurotransmitter systems but did not appear to act directly on any of them. In 1979 it was reported that a specific receptor for PCP was present in the brain, and in 1981 the identity between that receptor and another that had previously been considered a subtype of opiate receptor was reported (Quirion, Hammer, Herkenham, & Pert, 1981). The drug cyclazocine, which has some opiate activity and has also been reported to produce halluci-nations, binds well to this PCP receptor, but morphine, naloxone, and other opiates do not. Thus the receptor is probably better characterized as being selective for PCP, ketamine, and other similar drugs rather than as a type of opiate receptor. The presence of such a receptor has led to speculation about a possible endogenous substance that would normally act on the receptor. It is not far from there to the speculation that excessive amounts of this hypothetical substance in some individuals might be responsible for schizophrenia.

Evidence clearly shows that PCP can cause a psychosis in some subjects similar to that seen in schizophrenics. It may last for days or weeks and characteristically becomes more severe during the first few days of its course. During initial clinical trials of PCP as an anesthetic, one sixth of the volunteers became severely psychotic for several hours after they woke up. PCP has no equal in its ability to produce brief psychoses nearly indistinguishable from schizophrenia. The psychoses, induced with moderate doses given to normal, healthy volunteers, lasted about 2 hours and were characterized by changes in body image, thought disorders, estrangement, autism, and occasionally rigid inability to move (catalepsy). Subjects reported feeling numb, had great diffi-culty differentiating themselves from their surroundings, and complained after-ward of feeling extremely isolated and apathetic. They were often violently paranoid during the psychosis.

Anticholinergic Hallucinogens

The nightshade family (Solanaceae), which includes potatoes, contains all the naturally occurring agents included in this category. Four of these plants, *Atropa belladonna, Mandragora officinarum, Hyascyamus,* and *Datura,* are well known throughout history. Each of these plants contains active alkaloids that are responsible for their mind-altering effects. Three in particular are potent central and peripheral cholinergic blocking agents: (a) scopolamine, or hyo-scine; (b) hyoscyamine; and (c) atropine. These drugs occupy the acetylcholine receptor site but do not activate it; thus their effect is primarily to block muscarinic cholinergic neurons, including the parasympathetic system.

Scopolamine may produce excitement, hallucinations, and delirium even in therapeutic doses, whereas with atropine, doses bordering on the toxic are usually required to obtain these effects. The drug atropine is actually a mixture of the two stereochemical forms of hyoscyamine and may not occur naturally in the plant (Schultes & Hoffman, 1973).

These agents have potent peripheral and central effects, and some of the psychological responses to these drugs are probably a reaction to peripheral changes. These alkaloids block the production of mucus in the nose and throat and prevent salivation, so the mouth becomes uncommonly dry, and perspiration stops. Temperature may increase to fever level, and heart rate may show a 50-beat-per-minute increase with atropine. Even at moderate doses these chemicals cause considerable dilation of the pupils of the eyes with an inability to focus on nearby objects. The anticholinergics depress the reticular activating system and slow the brain waves considerably, as shown on an electroencephalogram (EEG). At larger doses, a condition occurs that is similar to a psychosis, in which there is delirium, loss of attention, mental confusion, sleepiness, and loss of memory of recent events. These two characteristics—a clouding of consciousness and no memory of the period of intoxication—plus the absence of vivid sensory effects separate these drugs from the indole and catechol hallucinogens. Hallucinations may also occur at higher doses. At very high doses, paralysis of the respiratory system may cause death.

Synthetic Anticholinergics. Anticholinergic drugs were once used to treat Parkinson's disease (before the introduction of L-dopa) and are still widely used to treat the pseudoparkinsonism produced by antipsychotic drugs. Particularly in older people there is concern about inadvertently producing an "anticholinergic syndrome," characterized by excessive dry mouth, elevated temperature, delusions, and hallucinations. Drugs such as Artane (trihexyphenidyl) and Cogentin (benztropine) have only rarely been abused for their delirium-producing properties.

References

Balster, R. L., & Chait, L. D. (1978). The behavioral effects of phencyclidine in animals. In R. C. Petersen & R. C. Stillman (Eds.), *Phencyclidine (PCP) abuse: An appraisal* (NIDA Research Monograph 21, pp. 53-65). Washington, DC: U.S. Department of Health and Human Services.

Beck, J. (1986). The popularizaton and resultant implications of a recently controlled psychoactaive substance. *Contemporary Drug Problems, 13,* 1.

Beck, J., & Morgan, P. A. (1986). Designer drug confusion: A focus on MDMA. *Journal of Drug Education, 16*(3), 287-302.

Bourne, P. G. (Ed.). (1976). *Acute drug emergencies: A treatment manual.* New York: Academic Press.

Bowers, M. B. (1972). Acute psychosis induced by psychotomimetic drug abuse: I. Clinical findings. II. Neurochemical findings. *Archives of General Psychiatry, 27,* 437-442.

Bridger, W. H., Barr, G. A., Gibbons, J. L, & Gorelick, D. A. (1978). Dual effects of LSD, mescaline, and DMT. In R. C. Stillman & R. E. Willete (Eds.), *The psychopharmacology of hallucinogens* (pp. 150-180). New York: Pergamon.

Cohen, S. (1978). Psychotomimetics (hallucinogens) and cannabis. In W. B. Clark & J. del Giudice (Eds.), *Principles of psychopharmacology* (2nd ed., pp. 357-369). New York: Academic Press.

A crackdown on ecstasy. (1985, June 10). *Time*, p. 64.

Davis, W. M., & Borne, R. F. (1984). Pharmacologic investigation of compounds related to 3, 4 Methylenedioxyamphetamine (MDA). *Substance and Alcohol Actions/Misuse, 5*, 105-110.

Dishotsky, N. I., Loughman, W. D., Mogar, R. E., & Lipscomb, W. R. (1971). LSD and genetic damage. *Science, 172*, 431-440.

Drug Enforcement Administration. (1985). *Fact Sheet*. Washington, DC: Author.

Getting high on "ecstasy." (1985, April 15). *Newsweek*, p. 96.

Goad, P. T. (1985, April). *Preliminary report on the acute and subacute oral toxicity of MDMA in rats* [Written testimony, Docket No. 85-48]. U.S. Department of Justice, Drug Enforcement Administration hearings, Disposition.

Greer, G. (1983). *MDMA: A new psychotropic compound and its effects in humans*. Santa Fe: NM: Author. (333 Rosario Hill, Santa Fe, New Mexico 87501)

Greer, G. (1985, April). [Written testimony, Docket No. 84-48]. U.S. Department of Justice, Drug Enforcement Administration hearings.

Grinspoon, L. (1985, April). [Written testimony, Docket No. 84-48]. U.S. Department of Justice, Drug Enforcement Administration hearings.

Hardman, H., Haavik, C., & Seevers, M. (1973). Relationship of the structure of mescaline and seven analogs to toxicity and behavior in five species of laboratory animals. *Toxicology and Applied Pharmacology, 25*(2), 299-309.

Hatrick, J. K. (1970). Delayed psychosis due to LSD. *Lancet, 2*, 742-744.

Jacobs, B. L., & Trulson, M. E. (1979). Mechanisms of action of LSD. *American Scientist, 67*, 396-404.

Johnson, L. D., Bachman, J. G., & O'Malley, P. M. (1982). *Student drug use, attitudes and beliefs*. Washington, DC: Government Printing Office.

Klein, J. (1985, May). The new drug they call ecstasy. *New York*, pp. 38-43.

Lynch, R. D. (1985, April). [Written testimony, Docket No. 84-48]. U.S. Department of Justice, Drug Enforcement Administration hearings.

McGlothlin, W. H., Arnold, D. O., & Freedman, D. X. (1969). Organicity measures following repeated LSD ingestion. *Archives of General Psychiatry, 21*, 704-709.

Meyers, F. H., Rose, A. J., & Smith, D. E. (1967-1968). Incidents involving the Haight-Asbury population and some uncommonly used drugs. *Journal of Psychedelic Drugs, 1*(1), 140-146.

Miller, J. D., Cisin, I. H., Gardner-Keaton, et al. (1983). *National survey on drug abuse: Main findings, 1982*. Rockville, MD: National Institute on Drug Abuse.

Petersen, R. C., & Stillman, R. C. (1978). Phencyclidine: An overview. In R. C. Petersen & R. C. Stillman (Eds.), *Phencyclidine (PCP) abuse: An appraisal* (Research Monograph No. 21, pp. 1-17). Rockville, MD: National Institute on Drug Abuse.

Quirion, R., Hammer, R. P., Herkenham, M., & Pert, C. B. (1981). Phencyclidine (angel dust)/sigma "opiate" receptor: Visualization by tritium-sensitive film. *Proceedings of the National Academy of Sciences, U.S.A., 78*, 5881-5885.

Sapienza, P. (1985, April). [Written testimony, Docket No. 84-48]. U.S. Department of Justice, Drug Enforcement Administration hearings.

Schultes, R. E., & Hoffman, A. (1973). *The botany and chemistry of hallucinogens*. Springfield, IL.: Charles C Thomas.

Seymour, R. B. (1986). *MDMA*. San Francisco: Haight Ashbury Publications.

Siegel, R. K. (1985, April). [Direct testimony, Docket No. 84-48]. U.S. Department of Justice, Drug Enforcement Administration hearings.

Smith, D., & Meyers, F. (1969). The psychomimetic amphetamine with special reference to STP (DOM) toxicity. In D. Smith (Ed.), *Drug abuse papers,* 1969 (Section 4). Berkeley: University of California Press.

The trouble with ecstasy. (1985, September). *Life,* pp. 88-94.

Weil, A. T. (1976). The love drug. *Journal of Psychedelic Drugs, 8*(4), 33.

Wolfson, P. E. (1985, April). [Written testimony, Docket No. 84-48]. U.S. Department of Justice, Drug Enforcement Administration hearings.

9

NICOTINE

A summary of trends in drug use, comparing the 12 graduating classes of 1975 through 1986, gives us some interesting facts on the prevalence of cigarette smoking among high school students (Johnson, O'Malley, & Bachman, 1987). The peak years of smoking appear to have been 1976 and 1977 in this age group, as measured by lifetime, 30-day, and daily prevalence. Over the four subsequent graduating classes, 30-day prevalence dropped substantially from 38% in the class of 1977 to 29% in the class of 1981. More important, daily cigarette use dropped over that same interval from 29% to 20%, and daily use of half a pack per day or more dropped from 19.4% to 13.5% between 1971 and 1981 (nearly a one-third decrease). In 1981 the decline decelerated; in 1982 and 1983 it halted. There was a brief resumption of the earlier decline in 1984, with daily use falling from 21% to 19%, and daily use of half a pack per day dropping from 13.8% to 12.3%. Since 1984, there has been practically no change in most of these statistics, with the exception that smoking at the level of half pack per day fell by less than 1.0% from 12.3% in 1984 to 11.4% in 1986. What seems most noteworthy is the lack of appreciable decline rates since 1981, despite (a) the general decline that has occurred for most other drugs (including alcohol), (b) some rise in the perceived harmfulness and personal disapproval associated with smoking, and (c) a considerable amount of restrictive legislation that has been debated and enacted at state and local levels in the past several years.

Most of the initial experiences with cigarettes took place before high school. For example, regular cigarette smoking was begun by 11% prior to 10th grade versus 10% in grades 10 through 12.

Cigarette smoking among American college students has declined modestly in the period 1980 to 1985. The 30-day prevalence fell from 25.8% to 21.5% between 1980 and 1984, then rose slightly (to 22.4%) in 1985, where it stayed in 1986. The daily smoking rate fell from 18.3% in 1980 to 14.3% in 1984, though the rate of decline decelerated after 1983. In 1986, this figure declined further to 12.7% (Johnson et al., 1987).

Although the trends in substance use among American college students closely parallel those occurring among their age group as a whole, there are some important differences in absolute levels. By far the greatest difference between college students and others their age occurs in cigarette smoking. For example, the prevalence of daily smoking among college students is only 13%, versus 30% for all high school graduates that age who are not in college. Smoking at the rate of half a pack a day stands at 8.3% versus 24.2% for these two groups, respectively. High school senior data show the college-bound to have much lower smoking rates in high school than the noncollege-bound; thus most or all of the differences observed at college age actually preceded college attendance (Johnson et al., 1987).

Smoking trends for adults have also been well documented (U.S. Bureau of the Census, 1987). In 1970, 36.7% of adults over the age of 25 reported being current smokers. In 1980 this figure had declined to 32.6%, and in 1985 it stood at 29.8%.

Chemical Composition of Tobacco

At the onset, smoking cigarettes may seem fairly innocent. Advertising encourages cigarette smoking as soothing and relaxing, something to be enjoyed. Subsequent serious health complications are well known, however. Lung cancer, a number-one risk in cigarette smoking, is thought to be caused by polonium-210 and nickel present in the smoke of tobacco (Volle & Koelle, 1975).

Interestingly, carbon monoxide (CO) may turn out to be a more toxic component in cigarette smoke than nicotine. It is well known that smoking one pack of cigarettes yields about 260 mg of CO to the user, and this amount can convert 5% to 10% of the normal hemoglobin to carboxyhemoglobin. Nicotine, the main toxic ingredient, comprises from 0.5% to 8.0% of toxic components.

Smoking one cigarette yields at least 6 mg to 8 mg of nicotine (compared with a cigar, which yields from 15 mg to more than 40 mg of nicotine) and about 90% of the nicotine is absorbed when inhaled, whereas only 25% to 50% of nicotine is absorbed when drawn into the mouth and then exhaled.

The amount of nicotine found in tobacco depends upon the brand of tobacco, humidity, the nature of the soil in which the tobacco grew, and the species of tobacco, as well as on the habits of the smoker (Bogen, 1929). Unless the tobacco is chewed or snuffed, it is the amount of nicotine that appears in the smoke that is critical (Bailey, 1928). The least noxious form of tobacco smoking is the pipe, and the most harmful is the cigarette.

Toxicology of Tobacco Components

Carbon monoxide. Carbon monoxide is a colorless, odorless, nonirritant gas. Its toxicity stems from its binding to hemoglobin to form carboxyhemoglobin, which is 2.10 times stronger than the binding of oxygen to hemoglobin to form oxyhemoglobin. Thus, repeated exposure to even small amounts of carbon monoxide can dramatically reduce the amount of hemoglobin available for combination with oxygen and cause anoxemia of all tissues. Certainly the heart and brain, which are heavily dependent on aerobic respiration for function, are the first victims of anoxemia. Goldsmith and Landau (1968) reported that carbon monoxide binds not only to hemoglobin but also to many other iron proteins, including major electron transporters.

Other compounds. The fermentation of the polysaccharide pectin, found in the tobacco plant, yields methyl alcohol. It is estimated that 40 mg of methyl alcohol is absorbed after smoking 20 unfiltered cigarettes and 42 mg is absorbed after smoking 10 cigars.

Other tobacco by-products include ammonia, formaldehyde, phenols, creosote, anthracene, and pyrene and hydrocyanic acids. It is noteworthy that fertilizers and insecticides may add arsenic and lead to the tobacco.

Nicotine. In 1928, nicotine was isolated from tobacco. There is no therapeutic indication for its use. The naturally occurring liquid alkaloids l-methyl-1-(3-pyridyl) pyrrolidine, commonly known as nicotine, is volatile and colorless. An ingredient in tobacco; upon oxidation it turns brown and smells like burning tobacco. Nicotine is very poisonous; in fact, a cigar contains enough nicotine for two lethal doses. However, through smoking, the nicotine is not delivered rapidly enough to prove fatal to an individual. Death due to nicotine poisoning, like cyanide poisoning, is very quick.

Metabolism

Absorption of the nicotine from tobacco seems to take place via most of the membranes of the body (Butler, Goldstein, & Ross, 1972; Konturek et al., 1971). Those of particular interest are in the mouth, nose, and lungs. The absorption of nicotine through the mucosa is very dependent on the form in which the alkaloid is present.

Studies of the frequency of inhalation or puffing by cigarette smokers have indicated that there is a tendency to optimize the amount of nicotine delivered to the smoker. These studies can be extended to the other forms of tobacco use. Although nicotine is less readily absorbed by the oral mucosa, cigar smoke is more alkaline than cigarette smoke, and thus presents more of the nicotine in the freebase form. As such, it is more soluble in the fat-rich mucosal cell walls and accordingly is more readily absorbed. Snuff and chewing tobacco use involve prolonged contact with the mucosa and thus more chance for nicotine absorption.

Smoking one cigarette causes small increases in heart rate and blood pressure. These effects can be credited to the fact that nicotine causes a release of adrenaline from the adrenal gland and other storage sites. One cigarette contains about 25 mg of nicotine, of which some 10% is absorbed by the inhaling smoker. The same effects can be approximated by the intravenous injection of 1 mg of nicotine.

Once nicotine has been absorbed into the bloodstream, it is circulated throughout the systemic blood. It is then available to its various sites of pharmacologic action. At the same time, the drug is passing through the liver, where it is metabolized. Metabolism of a drug results, generally, in its conversion into chemicals that are less toxic and more water soluble than the precursor. The increase in water solubility renders the compound more soluble in urine, and thus it is more readily excreted from the body. Nicotine is converted into a number of such metabolites. Some 10% to 20% of ingested nicotine is excreted unchanged via the urinary tract.

The liver is the major organ that deactivates nicotine. It is well established that approximately 85% of the drug is modified prior to excretion via the kidneys. Because nicotine acts on the hypothalamus to cause a release of the hormone that reduces the loss of body fluids, it tends to slow excretion of itself.

Today the typical filter cigarette still contains between 1 mg and 20 mg of nicotine. The individual who smokes and inhales will absorb 10% of that. In this regard, a 1-mg intravenous injection of nicotine can induce the physiologic effects of smoking. Usually, 90% of inhaled nicotine is absorbed.

A significant fraction of inhaled nicotine is metabolized by the lungs. The major metabolites of nicotine are cotinine and nicotine-1-N-oxide. The half-life of nicotine following inhalation is 30 to 60 minutes. These nicotine metabolites are rapidly eliminated in the kidneys. Nicotine is also excreted in the milk of lactating women who smoke. The milk of heavy smokers may contain up to 0.5 mg of nicotine per liter.

Pharmacology of Nicotine

Nicotine is considered one of the most toxic of all drugs. Generally, the major pharmacologic effects include elevated blood pressure, increased bowel activity, and an antidiuretic action. Nicotine, after prolonged use, produces moderate tolerance and a mild to moderate development of physical dependence.

Nicotine is a curious drug, for it first stimulates and then depresses the nervous system. The stimulatory effect is due to release of norepinephrine and to the fact that nicotine mimics the action of acetylcholine. Nicotine thus stimulates cholinergic nerves first, but is not removed from the receptors very rapidly, so the next effect is depression, caused by blocking nerve activity. Nicotine will actually increase the respiration rate at low dose levels because it stimulates the receptors in the carotid artery that monitor the brain's need for oxygen. At the same time, nicotine stimulates the cardiovascular system by release of epinephrine, causing increases in coronary blood flow, heart rate, and blood pressure. The effect is to increase the oxygen requirements of the heart muscle, but not the oxygen supply. This may trigger heart attacks in susceptible persons.

In animal studies, nicotine has been shown to alter the electrical discharge of the reticular formation. The drug shifts the EEG to an arousal pattern, thereby acting at the level of the cortex to augment the frequency of the electrical activity.

Low doses of nicotine stimulate oxygen receptors in the carotid artery. The signs associated with acute nicotine poisoning include paralysis of respiratory muscle, convulsions, and tremors.

General brain effects. Nicotine has been proposed as the primary incentive in smoking (Jarvic, 1973). It is rapidly extracted by the alveolar capillaries, enters the pulmonary circulation, and is pumped to the aorta, where it stimulates the aortic and carotid chemoreceptors and may produce reflex stimulation of the respiratory and cardiovascular centers in the brain stem. Within one circulation time, one fourth of the nicotine inhaled passes through the brain capillaries and, because the blood-brain barrier is highly permeable to nicotine, the nicotine passes quickly into the brain (Oldendorff, 1977).

Once in the brain, nicotine markedly stimulates nicotinic cholinergic (ACH) synapses and produces tremors, and even convulsions, in both laboratory animals and humans. In terms of mechanism of action, nicotine also releases various biogenic amines, including catecholamines and serotonin. The excitation of respiration is a particularly prominent action of nicotine, although large doses act directly on the *medulla oblongata*. Smaller doses work indirectly via chemoreceptors. Stimulation of the central nervous system (CNS) is followed by depression, and death results from failure of respiration due to both central paralysis and peripheral blockade of muscles of respiration.

Nicotine stimulates the emetic chemoreceptor trigger zone in the medulla, and it causes nausea and vomiting in novices. It exerts an antidiuretic action as the result of stimulation of the hypothalamic system, with the concomitant release of antidiuretic hormone (ADH).

Studies from a number of laboratories indicate that nicotine can have a facilitating effect upon learning and memory in animals, and possibly in humans. Centrally, nicotine may even act as a mild tranquilizer, allowing individuals to make proper choices.

Heart and circulatory actions. Nicotine and other products in smoke, such as carbon monoxide, are picked up by the red blood cells where they bind to the hemoglobin molecules and form carboxyhemoglobin. Up to 10% of all hemoglobin in smokers may be in the carboxyhemoglobin form, which cannot carry oxygen, so up to 10% of smokers' blood is ineffective as far as normal oxygen-carbon dioxide exchange is concerned. This situation could easily cause a smoker to become out of breath from exertion. It is a factor in heart attacks and in the lower birth weight and survival rates of infants born to women who smoke during pregnancy.

Effects on the gastrointestinal tract. In contrast to the cardiovascular effects of nicotine, the actions of the drug on the gastrointestinal tract are largely the result of parasympathetic stimulation. The combined activation of parasympathetic ganglia and cholinergic nerve endings results in increased tone and motor activity of the bowels. Systemic absorption of nicotine may produce nausea, vomiting, and diarrhea. Inhibition of stomach contractions resulting from hunger is another pharmacologic effect of nicotine. This partially explains the increased hunger and weight gain when one ceases cigarette consumption.

One report showed that when smokers of over a pack per day stopped smoking, there was a decrease in the heart rate of three beats per minute and a 10% decrease in oxygen consumption. Slowing of the heart rate decreases, to some extent, the energy needs of the body. It seems more probable that the decrease in oxygen consumption resultes from a general decrease in the rate at which food is utilized for energy, so that with the same food intake, more will be shifted into fat-storage depots (Glauser et al., 1970).

Acute Tobacco and Nicotine Poisoning

The acutely fatal dose of nicotine for an adult is probably about 60 mg of the base. Smoking tobacco usually contains 1% to 2% nicotine. When smoked, cigarettes currently manufactured in the United States usually deliver 0.25 to 2.5 mg of nicotine.

The symptomatology of acute nicotine or tobacco poisoning is quite variable. Generally nicotine-poisoned individuals exhibit nausea, vomiting, dizziness, and general weakness. These conditions, to some extent, are all too familiar to the novice smoker attempting to enjoy that first strong cigar. Severe nicotine poisoning can quickly result in convulsions, unconsciousness, and possibly death. In fact, it appears that in some instances coma and death occur before all the symptoms of nicotine poisoning manifest themselves. This may in some measure account for the observed variety in symptom patterns.

Documentation of the past medical therapeutic usage of tobacco is replete with cases of nicotine overdose. Infusion of a tobacco decoction into the rectum sometimes resulted in fatal nicotine poisoning due to rapid absorption of nicotine by the rectal tissue. Application of hot tobacco leaves to the skin sometimes gave the same result, but often over a longer period of time owing to the slower absorption of nicotine through the skin. Cases of serious nicotine poisoning have been recorded wherein users of nicotine sulfate insecticide spray inadvertently allowed their skin to come into contact with the solution.

Small children who play with old smoking pipes provide sometimes receive fatal dosages of nicotine. The child who uses an old pipe to blow soap bubbles is courting death with an intensity that is not generally appreciated.

Chronic Toxicity of Tobacco and Nicotine

Not only does cigarette smoking cause cancer of the lungs (Public Health Service, 1967), it also causes cancer of the oral cavity, larynx, esophagus, and the mucosal epitheliomas. Heavy cigarette smoking takes its toll, with male smokers versus nonsmokers in America dying from lung cancer at a ratio of 11:1. Women also suffer from cigarette-smoking health complications. Reproductive disorders include preeclampsia, fewer pregnancies, more spontaneous abortions, and a higher incidence of neonatal mortality, as well as low-birth-weight infants (Butler et al., 1972). Many of the health problems associated with cigarette smoking are also found in nonsmokers; however, the risks for the smokers are obviously higher. Smokers, for example, have higher incidences of respiratory, pulmonary, cardiovascular, ulcer, and even vision problems. The respiratory syndrome is characterized by dyspnea, wheezing, pharyngeal constriction, pain in the chest, and frequent upper respiratory infections, often mistaken for asthma, which disappear after smoking is eliminated. It is thought that the respiratory syndrome is caused by a depression of the ciliary defense mechanism of the respiratory tract. Ventilatory efficiency may also by impaired. Chronic obstructive pulmonary disease was observed in smokers, and pulmonary damage occurred in high school students who had smoked for at least 1 to 5 years (Seely, Zuskin, & Bouhuys, 1971).

Another considerable health risk from cigarette smoking involves the cardiovascular system. More and more smokers are dying from coronary disease. Levine (1973) found evidence of increased thrombus formation due to tobacco smoke, which also contributed to coronary heart disease.

Psychologic factors and high levels of gastric acid cause the development of peptic ulcers. Although an increase in gastric acid does not occur from cigarette smoking, there is a decrease in bicarbonate in the small intestine, apparently due to nicotine, and this may contribute to the formation of peptic ulcers as a result of cigarette smoking (Department of Health, Education, and Welfare [DHEW], 1979, Doll, Jones, & Pygott, 1958). A gradual or sudden decrease in visual acuity, mostly in the central field and especially for colored objects, may eventually lead to optic nerve atrophy and permanent injury to vision. Fortunately, this is not a frequent occurrence.

Tolerance development and toxicity of nicotine and other chemicals in tobacco are extremely dangerous effects that cannot be overemphasized. A person's life is shortened by 14 minutes for every cigarette smoked; moreover, in the United States alone, it is estimated that 360,000 persons die each year from tobacco use (Vogt, 1977). The high incidence of a variety of medical problems from tobacco smoking is detailed and described in authoritative reports by the Surgeon General of the U.S. Public Health Service in *Smoking and Health* (DHEW, 1979) and *The Health Consequences of Smoking* (Public Health Service, 1967). Yet a large population still abuses cigarette smoking, which could be the nation's most preventable cause of death (Jaffee, 1974; Ochsner, 1971).

Tolerance and Dependence Liability

Although any substance may, under some conditions, be compulsively used, substances characterized by a certain constellation of features are likely to be compulsively used and abused under a much broader range of conditions, including those that lead to damage. In brief, the compound must be psychoactive, must have euphoriant qualities similar to those of reference drugs (e.g., morphine, amphetamine, ethanol), and must serve as a biologic reinforcer (be voluntarily self-administered). Other qualities such as the ability to produce tolerance and physiologic dependence are interesting and may be of functional significance but are neither necessary nor sufficient determinants of drug dependence.

Two lines of study involving human subjects were undertaken by the Addiction Research Center of the National Institute on Drug Abuse. The first involved pharmacodynamic analyses that assessed the psychoactivity of nicotine and its possible qualities as a euphoriant. A variety of parameters were assessed when nicotine was given in the form of tobacco smoke and intravenous injections. The second line of study assessed the reinforcing properties of intravenous nicotine in cigarette smokers. The intravenous studies were critical in determining whether nicotine, in the absence of the usual confluence of stimuli involving the cigarettes themselves (e.g., social and cultural), was characterized by the constellation of pharmacologic properties typical of those of known drugs of abuse.

Psychoactivity and Euphoriant Properties of Nicotine

The initial study showed that nicotine was psychoactive and produced orderly effects on measures of psychoactivity (Henningfield, Miyasato, & Jasinski, 1983). Following either smoke inhalation or intravenous administration, nicotine was discriminated from placebo, and dose strength estimates were directly related to nicotine dose. These self-reported effects peaked within about 1 minute and dissipated within 3 to 5 minutes. Certain physiologic responses were also dose-related and showed similar temporal patterns of onset and offset: heart rate, pupil diameter, and electroencephalographic response (Lukas & Henningfield, 1983). A subsequent study showed that the ganglionic blocker, mecamylamine, attenuated physiologic and self-reported effects of nicotine (Henningfield et al., 1983). Variability of response on self-report measures was lower when nicotine was given intravenously than when it was given in the form of tobacco smoke, suggesting that the stimuli provided by smoking confound discrimination of the effects of nicotine.

Euphoria is objectively defined by the observation that administration of the drug, under controlled experimental conditions, produces dose-related increases in scores on the Liking scale off the Single-Dose Questionnaire, and scores on the Morphine Benzedrine Group (MBG or Euphoria) scale of the Addiction Research Center Inventory (ARCI) (Jasinski et al., 1984). In this study, nicotine, like drugs known to be abused, produced significant dose-related increases in scores on both the Liking and MBG scales (Jasinski, Johnson, & Henningfield, 1984). Additionally, intravenous injections of nicotine were most commonly identified as a prototypic euphoriant drug (cocaine) by subjects with extensive drug abuse histories.

These studies confirmed that nicotine produced critical functional effects of tobacco smoke and that nicotine is a psychoactive drug with properties of a euphoriant. These findings are consistent with those obtained in animal drug discrimination studies in which it has been shown that nicotine is readily discriminated and that its discriminative properties are more stimulant-like than depressant-like.

Reinforcing Properties of Intravenous Nicotine

The ultimate test of whether nicotine is a dependence-producing drug is, in the abstract, very simple: namely to determine if nicotine injections serve as positive reinforcers and thereby strengthen behavior leading to their administration. The critical finding of this study was that intravenously available nicotine was self-administered by each of the subjects tested (Henningfield et al., 1983). Furthermore, patterns of self-administration were similar to those of humans smoking cigarettes or of animals self-injecting cocaine in analogous experimental preparations (Griffiths, Bigelow, & Henningfield, 1980).

The number of injections gradually increased across sessions; then, when saline was substituted for nicotine, the number of injections rapidly declined across sessions. Subsequent studies showed that nicotine was preferred to saline when both substances were concurrently available (Henningfield & Goldberg, 1983a), and that mecamylamine pretreatment attenuated the nicotine preference (Henningfield, 1983).

The human self-administration study findings are consistent with animal studies in which nicotine has been shown to serve as a positive reinforcer in a variety of species, including primates and nonprimates, and under a variety of experimental conditions (see review by Henningfield & Goldberg, 1983b).

Cigarette Smoking as a Form of Drug Dependence

Russel (1976), in discussing tobacco smoking as a form of drug dependence, suggested that the modern cigarette is a highly efficient device for self-administering the drug nicotine. Unknown to most, by inhaling, the smoker can get nicotine to the brain more rapidly that the heroin-dependent person can get a "buzz" by shooting heroin into a vein. For example, it takes only 7 seconds for nicotine in the lungs to reach the brain compared with the 14 seconds it takes for blood to flow from arm to brain. Additionally the smoker gets a "shot" of nicotine after each inhaled puff. It has been estimated that at 10 puffs per cigarette, the pack-a-day smoker gets more than 70,000 nicotine shots to the brain in a year.

As with other addictive psychoactive substances, such as alcohol and heroin, the notion of "once a smoker, always a smoker" is only a slight exaggeration. Only 25% of smokers succeed in giving up the habit for good before reaching the age of 60. There is only a small minority—2% according to one study—for whom smoking is a take-it-or-leave-it affair, and who limit themselves to intermittent or occasional smoking, once or twice a week or less.

The dependence liability of tobacco smoking clearly is strong, and few other forms of drug taking are as addictive as the puff-by-puff shots of nicotine obtained by smoking cigarettes. Tobacco addiction is so easily acquired relative to alcohol, and possibly even heroin, that cigarette smoking is a drug-addiction problem.

There is a variety of reasons why cigarette smoking is so addictive. These include (a) rapid and numerous pharmacologic reinforcements afforded by the puff-by-puff bolus of intake from inhaled cigarette smoking, (b) rapid clearance and metabolism of nicotine in the brain, (c) the sharp "letdown" from these effects that depend on a direct action, (d) the fact that cigarette smoking not only does not impair performance but actually enhances socialization, and (e) its social acceptability. Although the social climate has changed, cigarette smoking is still, in most social circles, far more acceptable than the use of other drugs, with the exception perhaps of tea and coffee, sleeping pills (taken at night but not by day), and tranquilizers that are medically prescribed. Among other reasons is that, in modern societies, cigarettes are one of the most readily available of all commodities. This availability is linked to low cost. Also, cigarette smoking combines a pharmacologic effect with a sensorimotor ritual that includes the mouth as a locus of pleasurable self-indulgence.

Chronic Effects of Smoking and Disease

Cardiovascular disease. Nicotine has a triple effect on the cardiovascular system. It causes a hemodynamic response of the heart, it leads to increased circulation of free fatty acids, and it causes an increase in platelet stickiness and aggregation (Hatchell & Collins, 1980). Coronary heart disease is the major cause of death among both males and females in the American population. The 1979 surgeon general's report clearly demonstrated the close association of cigarette smoking and increased coronary heart disease among males. Furthermore, a report of the surgeon general in 1980 revealed that coronary heart disease, including acute myocardial infarction and chronic ischemic heart disease, occurs more frequently in women who smoke. In general, smoking increases the risk by a factor of about two; in younger women, cigarette smoking may increase the risk severalfold. The use of oral contraceptives by women who smoke cigarettes increases the risk of a myocardial infarction by a factor of approximately 10.

It is known that increased levels of high-density lipoprotein (HDL) are correlated with a reduced risk of an acute myocardial infarction and that cigarette smokers have decreased levels of HDL.

Smoking cigarettes is a major risk factor for arteriosclerotic disease and for death from arteriosclerotic aneurysm of the aorta (an aneurysm is a weakened area in a blood vessel that forms a blood-filled sac). Smokers have a higher incidence of atherosclerosis of the coronary arteries that supply blood to the heart, which blocks these arteries with fat deposits. Both the carbon monoxide and the nicotine in cigarette smoke can precipitate angina attacks (painful spasms in the chest when the heart muscle does not get the blood supply it needs).

Cigarette smokers experience an increased risk for subarachnoid hemorrhage. In females, the use of both cigarettes and oral contraceptives appears synergistically to increase this risk.

Cigarette smokers may be more likely to develop severe or malignant hypertension than nonsmokers.

Respiratory system. Three types of diseases are classified under the term *chronic obstructive lung disease* (COLD): chronic bronchitis, pulmonary emphysema, and reversible obstructive lung disease, or bronchial asthma.

A majority of patients suffering from COLD are cigarette smokers (Crowdy & Snowden, 1975). Women's total risk of COLD appears to be somewhat lower than men's, which may be the result of differences in prior smoking habits.

Ventilatory functions have been shown to be decreased in smokers as compared with nonsmokers. The prevalence of chronic bronchitis varies directly with cigarette smoking, increasing with the number of cigarettes smoked per day.

Among patients with pulmonary emphysema, 98% are smokers (Anderson, Ferris, & Zickmantel, 1965). The presence of emphysema at autopsy exhibits a dose-response relationship (one pack per day) with cigarette smoking during life (Auerbach et al., 1972).

There is a close relationship between cigarette smoking and chronic cough or chronic sputum production in both males and females, which increases with total pack-years smoked. Current smokers show poorer pulmonary functions than do ex-smokers or nonsmokers, a relationship that is dose related to the number of cigarettes smoked.

Cancer. The use of tobacco in any form may cause cancer of the lip, tongue, tonsils, larynx, lung, stomach, intestine, pancreas, and bladder (Hammond, 1975; Rothman, 1975; Wynder et al., 1975). In almost all countries where the incidence of lung cancer has been studied, the number of cigarettes smoked is seen to have risen with the incidence of the cancer.

Tennant (1980) reported the synergistic effects of smoking tobacco and of smoking hashish on the development of precancerous cells on lung tissue. A similar combined effect of alcohol and smoking has been observed for cancer of the larynx. The risk of developing cancer of the larynx is 10 times greater among tobacco smokers who are also heavy drinkers.

The exact mechanisms by which tobacco or its components cause cancer are unknown. It is believed that chemical carcinogens initiate the alteration of gene expression that is characteristic of cancer by modifying DNA molecules. Some carcinogens enter the cell and bind directly to the DNA, but most substances that act as carcinogens are metabolically converted before binding to DNA. Definite identification of the chemical promoters in cigarette smoke is inconclusive. However, volatile phenols, aldehydes, and acids are likely candidates.

There are alarming statistics concerning the interrelationship between tobacco utilization and cancer. Cigarette smoking accounts for 18% of all cancers newly diagnosed and 25% of all cancer deaths in women. The rise in lung cancer death rates is currently much steeper in women than in men. This probably reflects the fact that women first began to smoke in large numbers 25 to 30 years after the increase in cigarette smoking among men. Women cigarette smokers have been reported to have between 2.5 and 5 times greater likelihood of developing lung cancer than nonsmoking women.

The use of filter cigarettes and cigarettes with low levels of tar and nicotine is correlated with a lower risk of cancer of the lung and larynx as compared with the use of high-tar and -nicotine or unfiltered cigarettes. After cessation of smoking, the risk of developing lung and laryngeal cancer has been shown to drop slowly, equaling that of nonsmokers after 10 to 15 years.

Effects of Smoking on the Fetus

Infants born to women who smoke during pregnancy are from 70g to 250 g lighter than children born to comparable nonsmoking women. Maternal smoking during pregnancy may adversely affect the child's long-term growth, intellectual development, and behavioral characteristics. Furthermore maternal smoking during pregnancy exerts a direct growth-retarding effect on the fetus; this effect does not appear to be mediated by reduced maternal appetite, eating, or weight gain.

The mortality of babies of smokers is significantly higher than for babies of nonsmokers for both stillbirths and neonatal deaths. Up to 14% of all preterm deliveries in the United States may be attributable to maternal smoking.

An infant's risk of developing the "sudden infant death syndrome" is increased by maternal smoking during pregnancy. In addition, studies suggest that cigarette smoking might impair fertility in both women and men.

References

Anderson, D. O., Ferris, B. G., Jr., & Zickmantel, R. (1965). The Chilliwack Respiratory Survey, 1963: IV. The effect of tobacco smoking on the prevalence of respiratory disease. *Canadian Medical Association Journal, 92*, 1066.

Auerbach, O., et al. (1972). Relation of smoking and age to emphysema: Whole-lung section study. *New England Journal of Medicine, 186*(286), 853.

Bailey, E. M. (1928). The thirty-second report on food products and the twentieth report on drug products. *Connecticut State Agricultural Station Bulletin, 295*, 300.

Bogen, E. (1929). Composition of cigarettes and cigarette smoke. *Journal of the American Medical Association, 93*, 1110.

Butler, N. R., Goldstein, H., & Ross, E. M. (1972). Cigarette smoking in pregnancy: Its influence on birth rate and perinatal mortality. *British Medical Journal, 2*, 127.

Crowdy, J. P., & Snowden, R. R. (1975). Cigarette smoking and respiratory ill-health in the British army. *Lancet, 1*, 1232.

Department of Health, Education, and Welfare. (1979). *Smoking and health: A report of the surgeon general* (DHEW Publication No. PHS 79-50066, p. 1251). Washington, DC: Author.

Doll, R., Jones, F. A., & Pygott, F. (1958). Effect of smoking on the production and maintenance of gastric and duodenal ulcers. *Lancet, 1,* 657.

Glauser, S. C., et al. (1970). Metabolic changes associated with the cessation of cigarette smoking. *Archives of Environmental Health, 20,* 377.

Goldsmith, J. R., & Landau, S. A. (1968). Carbon monoxide and human health. *Science, 162,* 1352.

Griffiths, R. R., Bigelow, G. E., & Henningfield, J. E. (1980). Similarities in animal and human drug taking behavior. In N. K. Mello (Ed.), *Advances in substance abuse: Behavioral and biological research* (pp. 1-90). Greenwich, CT: JAI.

Hammond, E. C. (1975). Tobacco. In J. F. Fraumeni, Jr. (Ed.), *Persons at high risk of cancer: An approach to cancer etiology and control.* (p. 131). New York: Academic Press.

Hatchell, P. C., & Collins, A. C. (1980). Influence of genotype and sex on behavioral sensitivity to nicotine in mice. *Psychopharmacology* (Berlin), *71,* 45.

Henningfield, J. E. (1983). Measurement issues in cigarette smoking research: Basic behavioral and physiologic effects and patterns of nicotine self-administration. In J. Grabowski & C. Bell (Eds.), *Measurement in the analysis and treatment of smoking behavior* (NIDA Research Monograph No. 48, pp. 27-38). Washington, DC: Government Printing Office.

Henningfield, J. E., & Goldberg, S. R. (1983a). Control of behavior by intravenous nicotine injections in human subjects. *Pharmacology, Biochemistry, and Behavior, 19,* 989-992.

Henningfield, J. E., & Goldberg, S. R. (1983b). Nicotine as a reinforcer in human subjects and laboratory animals. *Pharmacology, Biochemistry, and Behavior, 19,* 1021-1026.

Henningfield, J. E., Miyasato, K., & Jasinski, D. R. (1983). Cigarette smokers self-administer intravenous nicotine. *Pharmacology, Biochemistry, and Behavior, 19,* 887-890.

Jaffee, E. S. (1974). Nodular lymphonia: Evidence for organ for follicular B lymphocytes. *New England Journal of Medicine, 290*(4), 813-819.

Jarvic, M. E. (1973). Further observations on nicotine as the reinforcing agent in smoking. In W. L. Dunn, Jr. (Ed.), *Smoking behavior: Motives and incentives* (p. 33). Washington, DC: Winston.

Jasinski, D. R., Johnson, R. E., & Henningfield, J. E. (1984). Abuse liability assessment in human subjects. *Trends in Pharmacological Science, 5,* 196-200.

Johnson, L. D., O'Malley, P. M., & Bachman, J. G. (1987). *National trends in drug use and related factors among American high school students and young adults, 1975-1986.* (NIDA Publication No. ADM 87-1535). Washington, DC: Government Printing Office.

Konturek, S. J., et al. (1971). Effects of nicotine on gastrointestinal secretions. *Gastroenterology, 60,* 1098.

Levine, P. H. (1973). An acute effect of cigarette smoking on platelet function. A possible link between smoking and arterial thrombosis. *Circulation, 48,* 619.

Lukas, S., & Henningfield, J. E. (1983). *EEG correlates of physiological and behavioral effects of intravenous nicotine in humans.* Paper presented at the 2nd World Conference on Clinical Pharmacology and Therapeutics, Washington, DC.

Oldendorff, W. H. (1977). Distribution of drugs to the brain. In M. E. Jarvic (Ed.), *Psychopharmacology in the practice of medicine* (p. 167). New York: Appleton-Century-Crofts.

Ochsner, A. (1971). Bionchogenic carcinoma, a largely preventable lesion assuming epidemic proportions. *Chest, 59,* 358-359.

Public Health Service. (1967). *The health consequences of smoking* (Publication No. 1696). Washington, DC: Government Printing Office.

Rothman, K. J. (1975). Alcohol. In J. F. Fraumeni, Jr. (Ed.), *Persons at high risk of cancer. An approach to cancer etiology and control* (p. 139). New York: Academic Press.

Russell, M. A. H. (1976). Tobacco smoking and nicotine dependence. In R. J. Gibbins et al. (Eds.), *Research advances in alcohol and drug problems* (Vol. 3, p. 1). New York: John Wiley.

Seely, J. E., Zuskin, E., & Bouhuys, A. (1971). Cigarette smoking: Objective evidence for lung damage in teen-agers. *Science, 172*, 741.

Tennant, F. S., Jr. (1980). Histopathologic and clinical abnormalities of the respiratory system in chronic hashish smokers. *Substance and Alcohol Action/Misuse, 1*, 93.

U.S. Bureau of the Census. (1987). *Statistical abstract of the United States: 1988* (108th ed.) Washington, DC.

Vogt, T. M. (1977). Smoking behavioral factors as predictors of risk. In M. E. Jarvik, et al. (Eds.), *Research on smoking behavior* (NIDA Research Monograph No. 17, p. 122). Rockville, MD: National Institute on Drug Abuse.

Volle, R. L., & Koelle, G. G. (1975). Ganglionic stimulating and blocking agents. In L. S. Goodman & A. Gilman (Eds.), *The pharmacological basis of therapeutics* (5th ed., p. 565). New York: Macmillan.

Wynder, E. L., et al. (1975). Interdisciplinary and experimental approaches: Metabolic epidemiology. In J. F. Fraumeni, Jr. (Ed.), *Persons at high risk of cancer: An approch to cancer etiology and control* (p. 139). New York: Academic Press.

PART II

Theories of Etiology

10

BIOLOGICAL AND GENETIC
EXPLANATIONS

Most people working on the frontier of alcohol and drug research accept an explanation of alcohol or drug dependency in terms of multiple cause. There are exceptions (Goodwin, 1986), and it is probably true that a widely held popular explanation of alcoholism or drug dependency is that a person is "born that way." But while biological and genetic bases are included in most theories of etiology, the extent to which other explanatory concepts are added to biology/genetics varies widely. This chapter discusses etiology-by-biology.

Jellinek reviewed a number of "physiopathological or physical etiologies" (Jellinek, 1960), summarized under these headings: allergy, biochemistry/physiology, brain pathology, nutrition, and endocrinology. An *allergy* explanation of alcoholism persists to this day and is frequently held by members of Alcoholics Anonymous. One *biochemical* explanation viewed alcoholism as a pathological symptom of mental disorder in which two cholinergic substances played a key role. These substances were termed *tension substance* and *resentment substance,* and consumption of alcohol by alcoholics apparently reduced these substances significantly more than similar consumption by nonalcoholic persons (Fleetwood, 1955; Fleetwood & Diethelm, 1951). *Brain pathology* theories sometimes viewed "a cerebral condition" as predispositional and sometimes perceived brain damage, as a consequence of heavy drinking and nutritional deficiencies, to be linked with "loss of control over drinking." *Nutritional* theories varied, sometimes viewing alcoholism as rooted in thiamine deficiency (Mardones, 1951), sometimes positing alcoholism as based on an inherited pattern of individual metabolic peculiarities leading to increased vitamin requirement (Williams, 1947). *Endocrinological* explanations were usually in terms of endocrinological dysfunction with hypoadrenocorticism frequently mentioned. And the current generation, often holding strong views about sugar, will respond to an early view that emotional tensions produced hypoglycemia and that alcohol acted as sugar substitute for people in whom that occurred (Berman, 1938).

Recent developments in biomedical technology and expanded interest in alcohol have stimulated research in alcohol/endocrine interactions; alcohol and drug effects on the cardiovascular, immune, and central nervous systems; the pathogenesis of alcoholic liver disease; liver transplants; and the application of molecular biology. The major emphasis within the last two decades, however, has been on the role of genetic endowment and the search for a biological marker. It is often repeated in the alcohol literature, for example, that a person with a positive family history of alcoholism has four times greater likelihood of developing alcoholism than a person with a negative family history although this is misleading, based on a misinterpretation of available data. The search for a biological marker has more practical implications than does the work on genetic endowment; if one could identify potential alcoholics with a biochemical marker or markers, the work of primary preventers would be greatly advanced.

Role of Genetic Endowment

The role of genetic endowment has been examined primarily by studies of twins, and more recently by adoption studies. Although there are also many animal studies demonstrating genetic preference and level of alcohol consumption, these have not commanded as much public attention.

Twin Studies

Studies of identical twins reared apart or comparison of identical and fraternal twin pairs for the development of alcoholism have yielded mixed results. Four major studies are usually cited. In the earliest of such studies, Kaij (1960) reported that identical twins were significantly more concordant for alcoholism than fraternal twins, and the more severe the alcoholism, the greater the difference. This study has been criticized and the results questioned (Lester, 1989). A second study has found identical versus fraternal twin differences among the youngest alcoholics studied but no difference in the total sample (Partanen, Brunn, & Markkanen, 1966). A third study reported no identical/ fraternal twin differences (Murray, Clifford, & Gurlin, 1983), and a fourth study supported a genetic factor, that is, identical twins were more often concordant for alcoholism than fraternal twins (Hrubec & Omenn, 1981).

Some questions have been raised about the assumptions that underlie twin studies of the genetics of alcoholism, for instance, the assumption that greater concordance for monozygotic or identical twins over dizygotic or fraternal twins is attributable to heredity. With these and other methodological questions, conclusions about the genetic basis of alcoholism derived from twin studies are limited.

Adoption Studies

During the 1970s, results from three adoption studies, conducted separately and by different investigators in Denmark, Sweden, and the United States, reported findings that provided some support for a genetic predisposition toward severe alcoholism, at least among males. Sons of alcoholics were more likely to be alcoholic than were sons of nonalcoholics, whether raised by their biological parent or by nonalcoholic, adoptive parents. Sons of alcoholics, however, did not as adults manifest more psychiatric symptomatology than sons of nonalcoholics, both samples having been raised by adoptive parents. The results for male adoptees were clear in the Danish research (Goodwin et al., 1974), but the same kind of study, conducted with Danish women adoptees, gave ambiguous results (Goodwin, Schelsinger, Knop, Mednick, & Guze, 1977). The Swedish data showed low rates of alcoholism among adopted daughters of alcoholics as well, but a later analysis of the data showed a correspondence between alcoholism in the biological mothers and alcoholism in the adopted daughters (Bohman, Sigvardsson, & Cloninger, 1981).

Several questions have been raised. Methods in different adoption studies vary; some have utilized face-to-face interviews, and others have relied on records such as hospitalizations and arrests. There are population trends that need to be considered in genetic interpretations: Recent analysis shows that younger age cohorts, compared with older cohorts, show more expected lifetime prevalence of alcoholism and earlier age at onset (Reich, Cloninger, Van Eerdewegh, Rice, & Mullaney, 1988). There are different definitions of "alcoholism" in different studies. There is a problem in interpreting the genetic transmissibility of alcoholism from alcoholic mothers because the mother's drinking may produce fetal alcohol effects that will appear among some of the adoptees being studied.

In dealing with the heterogeneity of history and clinical picture presented by persons diagnosed as alcoholic, Cloninger and his colleagues have developed a typology that they believe includes both genetic and environmental variables (Cloninger, 1983; Gilligan, Reich, & Cloninger, 1987). Type II alcoholism has a relatively early onset, occurs more often in males, and is presumably more strongly related to underlying genetic factors. Type I alcoholism occurs in both men and women, has a later stage of onset, and presumably is more susceptible to environmental factors.

The adoption study that was conducted in the United States reported a higher rate of childhood conduct disorders in the male offspring of alcoholics (Cadoret, Cain, & Grove, 1979). Without speaking to the issue of nature versus nurture in the transmission of alcoholism, similar findings reported a frequent history of hyperactivity or conduct disorder during the childhood of men who later became alcoholic. Similarly for women, a history of emotional and/or behavioral disorder in early life is reported by a sample of alcoholic women in treatment when compared with a sample of matched, nonalcoholic women (Gomberg, 1989). The alcoholic women are significantly more likely to have a positive family history than the nonalcoholic women. Clearly, positive family history and childhood behavioral disorders are linked, whether genetically or environmentally.

Genetic Marker Studies

These studies seek to establish a relationship between a biological trait known to be inherited and alcoholism. A variety of biological traits, including blood groups and serum proteins and color vision defects, has been studied. Results have been ambiguous.

Two recent lines of investigation are reported to be promising. Schuckit (1988) reports investigation of the effects of alcohol on sons of alcoholic fathers and a comparable group of young men: The sons of alcoholics are described as family-history-positive (FHP) and the control group as family-history-negative (FHN). The FHP subjects demonstrate less intense reactions to alcohol, measured by self-report, measures of body sway, changes in several hormones after drinking, and "the intensity of persistence of ethanol-related changes on two electrophysiological measures." Although FHP and FHN groups show no significant difference in the apparent rate of absorption (e.i., the disappearance of alcohol) some small but statistically significant differences between the groups appear in their levels of acetaldehyde, suggesting possible differences in their "mode" of ethanol metabolism (Schuckit, 1984).

A second line of investigation focuses on the event-related potential of the specific electrical response of the brain to external sensory stimuli (Begleiter & Porjesz, 1988). When 25 young sons of alcoholic fathers and 25 boys matched for age, school placement, and socioeconomic status—but no family history of alcoholism—are compared with ERP performance, the sons of alcoholic fathers show a significantly reduced amplitude of "the late positive component . . . of the ERP," a result similar to that obtained among abstinent alcoholics. Both the reaction-to-alcohol studies and the event-related potential studies are seeking the biological marker that would predict who is more vulnerable and who is less vulnerable in the future development of alcoholism.

Other Drugs

It is clear from the theories and investigators cited that most of the theorizing and research has been about the etiology of *alcohol* dependency. Etiological theorizing about dependency on other drugs seems to appear more readily in explanations in psychological or sociological terms. But there has been at least one explanation of narcotics addiction in biological terms: an explanation of narcotics addiction vulnerability by an unspecified metabolic deficiency (Dole & Nyswander, 1967). Although initial experimentation with drugs begins with curiosity about effects, those people who have this unspecified biological susceptibility respond to heroin, for example, with euphoria instead of aversive side effects. Dole and Nyswander (1967) explained their positive findings with methadone maintenance, in part, by the assumption that methadone corrected the metabolic deficiency.

Caveat

It is of interest that biology and genetics researchers caution about a simplistic interpretation of the inheritability of alcoholism. Schuckit (1988) describes alcoholism as "a genetically influenced disorder." Begleiter and Porjesz (1988) spell this out:

It is becoming increasingly obvious that the development of alcoholism is not likely to be the result of a single biological or behavioral factor. Indeed the disease of alcoholism is likely to reflect the complex interactions of biological and behavioral predisposing factors in conjunction with environmental precipitating factors. (p. 492)

These cautions have not been characteristic of media reporting. Thus, a headline of an article by Blakeslee (1984) reads, "Scientists Find Key Biological Causes of Alcoholism," and Kolata (1987) reports, "Alcoholism: Genetic Links Grow Clearer." Heath (1987) has called heredity versus environment, "a false antithesis" and comments:

It is . . . striking to discover that the people who are most intimately and seriously concerned with investigating the significance of genetic factors with respect to alcoholism are not nearly so confident or assertive about causality as are journalists, policy-makers, members of organizations of children-of-alcoholics, and many others.

References

Begleiter, H., & Porjesz, B. (1988). Potential biological markers in individuals at high risk for developing alcoholism. *Alcoholism: Clinical and Experimental Research, 12,* 488-493.

Berman, L. (1938). *New creations for human beings.* New York: Doubleday Doran.

Blakeslee, S. (1984, August 14). Scientists find key biological causes of alcoholism. *New York Times,* pp. 1, 4.

Bohman, M., Sigvardsson, S., & Cloninger, R. (1981). Maternal inheritance of alcohol abuse. Cross-fostering analysis of adopted women. *Archives of General Psychiatry, 38,* 965-969.

Cadoret, R. J., Cain, C. A. & Grove, W. M. (1979). Development of alcoholism in adoptees raised apart from alcoholic biologic relatives. *Archives of General Psychiatry, 37,* 561-562.

Cloninger, C. R. (1983). Genetic and environmental factors in the development of alcoholism. *Journal of Psychiatric Treatment and Evaluation, 5,* 487.

Dole, V. P., & Nyswander, M. E. (1967). Rehabilitation of the street addict. *Archives of Environmental Health, 14,* 477-480.

Fleetwood, M. F., & Diethelm, O. (1951). Emotions and biochemical findings in alcoholism. *American Journal of Psychiatry, 108,* 433.

Gilligan, S. B., Reich, T., & Cloninger, R. (1987). Etiologic heterogeneity in alcoholism. *Genetics Epidemiology, 4,* 395-414.

Gomberg, E. S. L. (1989). Alcoholic women in treatment: Early histories and early problem behaviors. *Advances in Alcohol and Substance Abuse, 8,* 133-147.

Goodwin, D. W. (1986). Speculations on the cause(s) of alcoholism. *Digest of Addiction Theory and Application, 5,* 57-64.

Goodwin, D. W., Schulsinger, F., Knop, J., Mednick, S., & Guze, S. B. (1977). Alcoholism and depression in adopted-out daughters of alcoholics. *Archives of General Psychiatry, 34,* 751-755.

Goodwin, D. W., Schulsinger, F., Moller, N., Hermansen, L., Winokur, G., & Guze, S. B. (1974). Drinking problems in adopted and nonadopted sons of alcoholics. *Archives of General Psychiatry, 31,* 164-169.

Hrubec, Z., & Omenn, G. S. (1981). Evidence of genetic predisposition to alcoholic cirrhosis and psychosis: Twin concordance for alcoholism and its biological end points by zygosity among male veterans. *Alcoholism: Clinical and Experimental Research, 5,* 207-215.

Jellinek, E. M. (1960). *The disease concept of alcoholism.* New Haven, CT: Hillhouse.

Kaij, L. (1960). *Studies on the etiology and sequences of abuse of alcohol.* Lund, Sweden: University of Lund Press.

Kolata, G. (1987, November 10). Alcoholism: Genetic links grow clearer, *New York Times,* pp. 1, 2.

Lester, D. (1989). The heritability of alcoholism. *Drugs and Society, 3,* 29-68.

Mardones, R. (1951). On the relationship between deficiency of B vitamins and alcohol intake in rats. *Quarterly Journal of Studies on Alcohol, 12,* 563-575.

Murray, R. M., Clifford, C., & Gurlin, H. M. (1983). Twin and alcoholism studies. In M. Galanter (Ed.), *Recent developments in alcoholism* (pp. 29-49). New York: Plenum.

Partanen, J., Brunn, K., & Markkanen, T. (1966). *Inheritance of drinking behavior: A study on intelligence, personality and use of alcohol of adult twins.* Helsinki: Finnish Foundation for Alcohol Studies.

Reich, T., Cloninger, C. R., Van Eerdewegh, R., Rice, J. P., & Mullaney, J. (1988). Secular trends in the familial transmission of alcoholism. *Alcoholism: Clinical and Experimental Research, 12,* 458-464.

Schuckit, M. A. (1984). Prospective markers for alcoholism. In D. W. Goodwin, K. T. Van Dusen, & S. A. Mednick (Eds.), *Longitudinal research in alcoholism* (pp. 147-164). Boston: Kluwer-Nijhoff.

Schuckit, M. A. (1988). Reactions to alcohol in sons of alcoholics and controls. *Alcoholism: Clinical and Experimental Research, 12,* 465-470.

Williams, R. J. (1947). The etiology of alcoholism: A working hypothesis involving the interplay of hereditary and environmental factors. *Quarterly Journal of Studies on Alcohol, 7,* 567-587.

11

PSYCHOSOCIAL AND SOCIOCULTURAL EXPLANATIONS

Personality

No matter how many times and in what fashion "the addictive personality" is buried, it seems necessary to state and restate that there is no unique personality that antedates alcoholism or drug abuse. A wide variety of persons becomes involved with alcohol and/or drugs. They vary in gender, age, social class, ethnicity, drugs used, patterns of use, accompanying psychiatric symptomatology, and so on—to say nothing of the wide range of societal and legal attitudes toward different groups of users, different drugs, different patterns of usage (e.g., public versus private). So how can one speak of "the addictive personality"? This could be a case of the expert "doth protest too much," although the argument that "the addictive personality" does *not* exist is not confined to experts.

Separate from the idea of a total, unique addictive personality is the concept of some *predisposing behavior traits*. Such traits may be embedded in a variety of personalities. Behavior traits that have been associated with the development of substance abuse are

Difficulty in impulse control
Difficulty in coping with stress, including problems in frustration tolerance
Passive-dependent patterns of behavior
Egocentricity with manipulative, demanding behaviors
Antisocial behaviors

This is not a complete list, but there are investigators and theorists who would argue in favor of one or another of these behaviors as antecedent. This is really the critical question; without longitudinal, carefully monitored studies, reliance must be placed on the study of individuals *after* they have become drug abusers, and the critical question then becomes one of separating the behaviors and traits that were *antecedent* to the substance abuse and those that are *consequential,* or following from the substance abuse. To find low self-esteem in the detoxifying patient with a long history of alcohol or drug abuse is hardly surprising considering how long social punishment and self-punishment have been in progress. To the practitioner, the question of what preceded and what followed the years of drug abuse may be academic. The practitioner must deal with what he or she assesses as the present situation. The question of antecedent behavior is perhaps most relevant to those who would *prevent* abuse, and this includes practitioners in all branches of health care as well as educators.

Three descriptions of personality-as-explanation are (a) the psychoanalytic perspective, (b) the dependency perspective, and (d) the need-for-power theory.

The *psychoanalytic interpretation* of drug abuse and addiction has been modified by many psychoanalytic theorists, yet the core of the interpretation was well stated by Fenichel (1945) who wrote, "The reasons for reverting to alcohol are either the existence of external frustration . . . or internal inhibitions, that is, states in which one dare not act against the superego without such artificial help." Fenichel and the other psychoanalysts described alcoholism as an *impulse neurosis* that derived from "difficult family constellations [that] created specific oral frustrations in childhood." The person who would become alcoholic or drug addicted was narcisstic and demanding, and Knight (1937) described a cycle of demand-frustration-rage-guilt-demand and pointed out the multiple roles that alcohol played for the alcoholic:

> The use of alcohol as a pacifier for disappointment and rage, as a potent means of carrying out hostile impulses to spite his parents and friends, as a method of securing masochistic debasement, and as a symbolic gratification of the need for affection, is now interweaving itself in the neurotic vicious circle.

A more detailed exposition of the psychoanalytic perspective has been written by Barry (1988).

The *dependency perspective* was articulated early by a research team (McCord & McCord, 1960) who followed a sample of men studied in the Cambridge-Somerville project in Massachusetts. These sociologists argued, and produced data to support the argument, that alcoholism was preceded by dependency conflict early in life. This conflict and confusion about the mother's role produced stress, intense need for affection, and a blurring of self-image, which generated anxiety, the base of developing alcoholism.

To some extent, this view seemed to be substantiated by a cross-cultural study of 110 preliterate societies, which found linkages between child training in different societies and the drinking patterns of those societies (Child, Bacon, & Barry, 1965). Bacon (1974) reanalyzed the cross-cultural data on 53 societies and concluded that the evidence in support of a dependency-conflict hypothesis was sound, that frequency of drunkenness appeared to be related to societal customs that discouraged dependent behavior in childhood and adulthood and emphasized demands for achievement.

The *need-for-power model* was developed from a series of experiments that included observations of fraternity parties, interviews, and projective techniques (McClelland, Davis, Kalin, & Wanner, 1972). In postulating the linkage between drinking and power, the model was relevant only for males and probably only for urbanized, educated males in Western culture. The investigators distinguished between "personalized power" and "social power"; failure to gain "social power" creates a state like anxiety, which produces drinking to gain "a primitive and narcissistically gratifying sense of personal power."

Both dependency perspective and the need-for-power model are described by Heath (1988) in his summary of anthropological theories and models of alcohol use of alcoholism.

Behavioral Theories

Under the heading of behavioral theory, four kinds of models are presented here: (a) the tension reduction hypothesis, (b) expectancy and cognitive models, (c) biobehavioral theories, and (d) conditioning theories.

The *tension-reduction hypothesis* involves concepts of tension (a heightened drive state, an aversive state), anxiety, and reinforcement. The drinking of alcohol becomes the reinforcer because it produces a reduction in tension (Cappell & Greeley, 1987). Although this seems to fit with common sense observation, there are a number of problems. One problem is the assumption that drinking reduces tension; the experimental literature shows results that vary with (a) the kind and duration of the stress that is presumed to be the basis of the tension, (b) the amount of alcohol consumed, and (c) individual differences in vulnerability to stress. In some experiments, if subjects are given alcohol while they *anticipate* a stressful event, the effect of alcohol can be tension inducing as well as tension alleviating (Ager, 1989). There are several experiments that suggest that there are differences between problem drinkers and moderate drinkers in the amount of alcoholic beverage that gives maximal relief from pain (Cutter, Maloof, Kurtz, & Jones, 1976) and differences between high-risk and low-risk (for alcoholism) subjects in sensitivity to alcohol under conditions of stress (Sher & Levenson, 1982).

The tension-reduction hypothesis also assumes that people drink alcohol for its tension-reducing qualities. Research results about this assumption are unclear. If a questionnaire asks a leading question—whether the respondent drinks for relief or in order to feel better—a sizable percentage of both problem drinkers and moderate drinkers tends to answer affirmatively. But recent studies that query adolescent drinkers and college student drinkers about their motivation for drinking suggest that there are more positive reasons for drinking than those posited by the tension-reduction hypothesis. Young people report drinking for celebration, for sociability, for pleasure. Research on age differences, gender differences, and ethnic differences in motivation to drink remains to be done.

Expectancy and cognitive models have, in central place, the major role of cognitive factors. The term *expectancy* usually refers to anticipation of a predictable, regular relationship between event X or object Y and an outcome; outcome expectancies are a person's belief that consuming alcohol or drugs, in this instance, will produce a desired outcome. A commonly held view of alcohol is seeing it as "a magic elixir" (Marlatt, 1987). In American society, alcoholic beverages are expected to reduce tension, enhance pleasure, and increase sexuality, aggressiveness, and social assertiveness.

Expectancy theory seeks to explain the initiation of alcohol use, the maintenance of alcohol use, the increased alcohol intake of some individuals, and the continuing drinking in the face of destructive consequences. Expectancies about alcohol and drugs clearly are learned and developed early in life. Such a concept obviously overlaps with sociocultural factors because expectancies are learned from the family and the groups in which a person participates.

Alcoholics appear to have stronger positive expectations associated with alcohol than do moderate drinkers, and there is evidence that suggests that alcoholics who expect alcohol to provide positive global effects and increase assertiveness were *more* likely to discontinue the course of treatment (Brown, 1985). Apparently, in treating alcoholism, strong expectation of alcohol as a powerful reinforcer predicts early termination of treatment and less successful outcome.

Biobehavioral theories about the etiology of alcoholism anticipate integrative approaches, such theories seek to integrate biological and behavioral science approaches. Straus (1986) has linked this need for integrative, interdisciplinary biobehavioral research to alcohol dependency, the heritability of alcoholism, the life cycle and aging, and gender comparison.

Seeking to explain smoking behavior and the effects of nicotine in a biobehavioral framework, a formulation is described that tries to explain how smoking is established and maintained (Pomerleau & Pomerleau, 1988).

Reinforcement from nicotine, it is suggested, might involve both pleasurable states as well as relief from withdrawal; evidence shows that opiate reinforcement can involve both, and that separate neuronal pathways might be involved (among heroin addicts, the effect of heroin in terminating unpleasant withdrawal symptoms does show tolerance but the effect of heroin in producing euphoria does not). The combination of biological and behavioral variables in explanation provides a useful rationale for combining pharmacological and behavioral techniques.

Neuropsychology, a "hybrid discipline," has evolved from efforts to interrelate brain and behavior processes; neurobehavioral theories of the etiology of alcohol/drug abuse are developed within the framework of neuropsychology (Tarter, Alterman & Edwards, 1988). They hypothesize that certain neurobehavioral disturbances, manifested in childhood and adolescence, are inherited and increase the risk for alcoholism in adulthood. These behavioral deficits are seen as pointing to a dysfunction of specific neural systems (prefrontal-midbrain brain axis). Although the specific brain dysfunction has been noted and seen as a *consequence* of alcoholism, it is the view of Tarter and colleagues (1988) that the brain dysfunction is inherited and precedes alcoholism "in certain vulnerable individuals." Although the neurobehavioral theory draws from data taken from high-risk persons and from alcoholics, the theory awaits further testing.

A variant of biobehavioral theory is Wikler's (1973) conditioning theory of narcotic addiction. There are two central concepts: pharmacological reinforcement and direct reinforcement. Pharmacological reinforcement occurs as the result of interaction between pharmacological drug effects and sources of reinforcement. A distinction is made between *direct* reinforcement, where the source of reinforcement is not drug-produced, and *indirect* reinforcement, that is, the central nervous system changes produced as a consequence of drug dependence. In narcotic addiction, the addiction is seen as a result of conditioning of "central processing events" produced by the action of a narcotic at a neuronal receptor site along the different pathways. Wikler suggested that the treatment of drug addiction be a combination of experimental extinction and the substitution of socially approved reinforcers (Platt, 1986).

Conditioning theories are based on the association between drug effects and the stimulus situation in which the drug is taken. It is argued that classical conditioning, as originally described by the Russian physiologist Pavlov, may serve as the paradigm to explain the acquisition, maintenance, and extinction of drug-taking behaviors. Pavlov's work goes back to the 1920s, but Wikler, whose work is described above, was one of the first to use classical conditioning in explaining the motivation to use drugs (Wikler, 1948). He posited the idea that a drug/unconditioned stimuli "could support both drug isodirectional and drug antagonistic" conditioned responses and also argued that the conditioning of drug antagonistic conditioned responses could explain drug tolerance and drug dependence (Sherman, Jorenby, & Baker, 1988). The latter researchers have examined the relevance of Pavlovian principles in acquired preference and aversion for alcohol-associated stimuli, in alcohol tolerance, and in the development of urges or craving for alcohol, and conclude that Pavlovian principles contribute "significantly" to the understanding of these phenomena. A Pavlovian perspective also suggests that alcohol- or drug-dependent behaviors may be modified by "experimental extinction," particularly if the extinction efforts are directed at conditioned alcohol effects adversely influencing abstinence.

Psychosocial Theories

As psychosocial theories, three models will be described: (a) a social-learning model, (b) a family model: family interaction approach, and (c) a family model: development/systems approach.

The *social-learning model* of alcohol use and alcoholism is an integrative model that draws on the principles of classical and operant conditioning but differs from traditional models in several ways: (a) it emphasizes the importance of symbolic, vicarious, and self-regulatory processes in human behavior; and (b) it emphasizes cognitions that play a central role in this model (Wilson, 1988). Social-learning theory also incorporates aspects of other etiological models, for instance, the tension-reduction hypothesis, the concept of expectancy, and genetics. It is well summarized by Nathan (1983), who has described alcohol use as a socially acquired, learned behavior pattern, maintained by antecedent cues (classical conditioning and expectancies), consequent reinforcements (operant conditioning and tension reduction), cognitive factors, modeling influences, and the interaction of behavioral and genetic mechanisms.

Arguing that earlier applications of learning theory were narrowly based on few learning principles derived from animal conditioning, Bandura (1969) extended learning theory to encompass the treatment of clinical disorders and stimulated researchers and practitioners to move beyond aversive conditioning methods. From these early beginnings, a variety of treatment techniques— including relapse prevention—and some innovative research strategies have developed, for instance, single-case experimental design and multicomponent treatment programs. Reinforcement methods that involve community resources have been developed, and there has been recent emphasis among social-learning-theory-oriented practitioners on the development of social and self-regulatory skills for coping with psychological and social situations associated with problem drinking. It is of interest that this emphasis is beginning to appear among therapists who treat cocaine-dependent people (Kolata, 1989).

Although the social-learning model does *not* necessarily set moderate drinking as a goal in the treatment of alcoholics, it does include controlled drinking as a possible goal in the treatment of some alcoholics. The question then becomes: What characteristics does the latter group of alcoholics display that indicate that they may be candidates for controlled drinking? Miller (1982) summarized the evidence, which suggests that early-stage problem drinkers with fewer signs of alcohol-related problems, fewer signs of "addiction," fewer medical problems, and less family history of alcoholism are the best patients for such a goal, that is, controlled, moderate drinking. This has probably been the most controversial aspect of the social-learning model (Pendery, Maltzman, & West, 1982; Sobell & Sobell, 1984).

The *family model: family interaction approach* tends to emphasize the marital dyad. Like many contemporary approaches, it is really an integrative approach with emphasis on parental behavior in the alcoholic family, behaviorism, classifications of alcoholics in terms of drinking patterns and drinking locations, and communication theory.

Such an approach includes study of parental influences, and reviews of relevant literature suggest that alcoholism is consistently associated with deficits in parenting, such as absence, family tension, rejection, emotional distancing, and parental alienation and unresponsiveness to the child's needs. In a study of children of recovering and active alcoholics, the children of recovering alcoholic parents functioned as well as normal control children, whereas the children in alcoholic families functioned relatively poorly (Moos & Billings, 1982).

There has been a fair amount of study of marital interactions and communications of couples in which one member is alcoholic: Such interactions suggest that such couples are different from "normal" families, although it is unclear how they differ from other kinds of "distressed" couples. Interestingly, there is some evidence that when the alcoholic spouse in a marriage is drinking, the interactions are sometimes more positive than during sober periods when both alcoholic and spouse are more tense. This suggests some support for a view of alcohol as, at times, serving an *adaptive* function in a marriage by facilitation of interaction (Steinglass, Davis, & Berensen, 1977). Jacob and his colleagues (Jacob & Leonard, 1988; Jacob, Ritchey, Cyitkovic, & Blane, 1981) have reported differences in marital interaction based on high consumption/low consumption and on binge versus daily drinking patterns. Generally, where drinking is regular and steady, spouse response is less negative than when the drinking is intermittent.

The most significant etiological factor in this family interaction approach is probably parenting deficits that occur as a product of parental alcoholism. Although the support for this comes largely from clinical samples and studies with methodological weaknesses, the role of negative early family experience as a significant etiological variable cannot be ruled out.

The *family model: developmental systems approach* has developed a series of conceptualizations that are relevant. One conceptualization is of *boundaries,* that is, the family has a boundary that separates inside and outside, such a boundary having varying degrees of permeability in different families. Another concept used is that of *homeostatic regulation*—there is a range of conflict beyond which a family does not go. Perhaps basic to a systems approach is the conceptualization of the family as a *gestalt,* meaning that the whole is more than the sum of its parts. The family cannot be understood by separately examining individual members.

Steinglass, Bennet, Wolin, and Reiss (1987) posit three developmental stages of the family—early, middle, and late—and a primary focus of their research is the extent to which this model fits the alcoholic family. Their work supports the idea of alcoholism as "a family disease" or a family disorder. Alcoholism is associated with far-reaching effects for all family members, although the children raised in such a family are less vulnerable and less likely to become alcoholic themselves when certain conditions prevail, for instance, if family rituals are observed (Wolin, Bennet, Noonan, & Teitelbaum, 1980).

Although "systems theory" and "family treatment" are often used interchangeably (Pearlman, 1988), they are clearly not the same. The former refers to a conceptual framework emphasizing wholeness, the latter describes techniques and interventions. Interventions with marital dyads, entire families, other systems extending beyond the nuclear family are all adaptations of system theory. In systems theory, behavior is determined and maintained by the ongoing demands of the key interpersonal systems in which an individual interacts, not by his/her intrapsychic state. Causality, furthermore, is viewed as circular rather than linear: cause-effect is not "reductionistic" but rather based on complex formulations involving "feedback loops and interaction" (Pearlman, 1988). Etiology, then, is based on behavior observed in family contexts, such behavior resulting from the interactions between relevant family members.

Sociocultural Theories

The sociocultural theories have been a joint contribution of sociologists, such as Bacon (1943), Bales (1946), Gusfield (1963), Pittman and Snyder (1962), Ullman (1958) and others, and the work of anthropologists. The emphasis has been on social and cultural factors; socially shared beliefs and behaviors as they relate to alcoholic beverages are assumed to be vital in the study of alcohol and alcohol-related problems (Bennett, 1988; Heath, 1988). More recently, anthropological and sociological study of alcohol has expanded to include ethnographic studies of family culture (Bennett, 1988).

Bales's (1946) early work identified three sociocultural variables influencing rates of alcoholism and suggested that the rate of such problems in a given society was determined by their interaction: dynamic factors or the degree to which tension is created by a culture; norms about drinking (whether typically abstinent, ritual, convivial, utilitarian, or symbolic); and the degree to which a culture provides alternative ways of dealing with stress. The work of MacAndrew and Edgerton (1969) was another major contribution; they concluded that "drunken comportment is an essentially learned affair. . . . Over the course of socialization, people learn about drunkenness what their society "knows" about drunkenness . . . [and] they become the living confirmation of their society's teachings."

Although early work in anthropology relating to alcohol use was primarily fieldwork and the study of other cultures, more recent work has focused on cross-cultural study *and* alcohol-related issues in mainstream American society and its ethnic and racial subcultures (Bennett & Ames, 1985). One of the contributions, in fact, of people working in the area of subcultural norms about drinking and drug use has been the development of "culturally appropriate" treatment modalities (although this work is in its early stage and such treatments need to be studied and evaluated).

Some sociocultural theorists distinguished between etiological factors, which are called *predisposing* and are usually genetic/biological in nature, and those called precipitating factors, most often environmental and/or cultural.

Heath (1988) has distinguished a number of different sociocultural models: (a) a normative model, (b) the single distribution model, (c) the anxiety model, (d) the social organization model, (e) the conflict-over-dependency model, (f) the power model, (g) the symbolic interactionist model, and (h) the social-learning model.

In the *normative model,* norms, prescriptive and proscriptive, are guidelines for behavior, and different ways of viewing the norms about alcohol may involve social deviance behaviors, the labeling approach, reference groups, anomie, ambivalence, and the "time out" hypothesis. This last norm was derived by MacAndrew and Edgerton (1969), who concluded that drunkenness provides "time out" during which many normative rules are temporarily suspended; this is demonstrated in legal decisions in which a person is held less responsible for acts performed while under the influence.

The *single distribution model* is based on the per capita consumption of alcohol beverages, which has been hypothesized as crucial in the determination of the prevalence of alcoholism.

The *anxiety model* has as central theme the primary function of alcoholic beverages in all societies as the reduction of anxiety. This model emphasizes anxiety, stress, and tension. The extension of this model encompasses sociocultural deprivation and "anomic depression" and has been used in explanations of drinking patterns of Blacks and American Indians.

The *social organization model* is an elaboration of the anxiety model; drinking behavior has been related to elements of social structure and social organization, for instance, village settlement patterns. The work upon which this model is based is cross-cultural comparison.

The *conflict-over-dependency model* is discussed above, under personality explanations.

The *power model* is also discussed above under personality explanations.

The *symbolic interactionist model* is a recent variant on the normative model in which more allowance is made for individual variation, such as innovation and deviance.

The *social-learning model* emphasizes social learning, both content and process. Such a model is discussed above under psychosocial explanations.

Fundamentally, sociocultural explanations emphasize beliefs, values, and attitudes held by a group about alcohol, which play a very significant role in the way members of that group will drink. One of the difficult questions raised by Bennett (1988) concerns the *definition* of alcoholism. As she points out, the same symptoms do not surface for all alcoholics, and the question is how to distinguish between alcoholism, heavy drinking, drunkenness, problem drinking, and alcohol-related problems. Among the anthropologists surveyed by Bennett, most would distinguish between alcoholism on the one hand, and alcohol-related problems or problem drinking on the other. The biomedical model of alcoholism as a disease was seen as "too limiting, especially since behavior is often used to infer a biomedical diagnosis" (Bennett, 1988, p. 117).

References

Ager, R. (1989). *Three models about the etiology and maintenance of alcoholism: Description and analysis.* Unpublished manuscript.

Bacon, M. K. (1974). The dependency-conflict hypothesis and the frequency of drunkenness: Further evidence from a cross-cultural study. *Quarterly Journal of Studies on Alcohol, 35,* 363-376.

Bacon, S. D. (1943). Sociology and the problems of alcohol: Foundations for a sociological study of drinking behavior. *Quarterly Journal of Studies on Alcohol, 4,* 399-445.

Bales, R. F. (1946). Cultural differences in rates of alcoholism. *Quarterly Journal of Studies on Alcohol, 6,* 480-499.

Bandura, A. (1969). *Principles of behavior modification.* New York: Holt, Rinehart & Winston.

Barry, H., III (1988). Psychoanalytic theory of alcoholism. In C. D. Chaudron & D. A. Wilkinson (Eds.), *Theories on alcoholism* (pp. 103-141). Toronto: Addiction Research Foundation.

Bennett, L. A. (1988). Alcohol in context: Anthropological perspectives. *Drugs and Society, 2,* 89-131.

Bennett, L. A., & Ames, G. M. (Eds.). (1985). *The American experience with alcohol.* New York: Plenum.

Brown, S. A. (1985). Reinforcement expectancies and alcohol treatment outcome after one year. *Journal of Studies on Alcohol, 46,* 304-308.

Cappell, H., & Greeley, J. (1987). Alcohol and tension reduction: An update on research and theory. In H. T. Blane & K. E. Leonard (Eds.), *Psychological theories of drinking and alcoholism* (pp. 15-22). New York: Guilford.

Child, I. L., Bacon, M. K., & Barry, H., III (1965). A cross-cultural study of drinking. *Quarterly Journal of Studies on Alcohol,* (Suppl. 3).

Cutter, H. S., Maloof, B., Kurtz, N. R., & Jones, W. C. (1976). "Feeling no pain": Differential response to pain by alcoholics and nonalcoholics, before and after drinking. *Journal of Studies on Alcohol, 37,* 273-277.

Fenichel, O. (1945). *The psychoanalytic theory of neurosis.* New York: Norton.

Gusfield, J. R. (1963). *Symbolic crusade: Status politics and the American temperance movement.* Urbana, IL: University of Illinois Press.

Heath, D. B. (1988). Emerging anthropological theory and models of alcohol use and alcoholism. In C. D. Chaudron & D. A. Wilkinson (Eds.), *Theories on alcoholism* (pp. 353-410). Toronto: Addiction Research Foundation.

Jacob, T., & Leonard, K. E. (1988). Alcohol-spouse interaction as a function of alcoholism subtype and alcohol consumption interaction. *Journal of Abnormal Psychology, 97,* 231-237.

Jacob, T., Ritchey, D., Cvitkovic, J. F., & Blane, H. T. (1981). Communication styles of alcoholic and nonalcoholic families when drinking and not drinking. *Journal of Studies on Alcohol, 42,* 464-482.

Kolata, G. (1989, August 24). Experts finding new hope on treating crack addicts. *New York Times,* pp. 1, 9.

Knight, R. P. (1937). The psychodynamics of chronic alcoholism. *Journal of Nervous and Mental Disease, 86,* 538-548.

MacAndrew, C., & Edgerton, R. B. (1969). *Drunken compartment: A social explanation.* Hawthorne, NY: Aldine.

Marlatt, G. A. (1987). Alcohol, the magic elixir: Stress, expectancy and the transformation of emotional states. In E. Gottheil, A. Druley, S. Pashko, & S. P. Weinstein (Eds.), *Stress and addiction.* New York: Brunner/Mazel.

McCelland, D. C., Davis, W. N., Kalin, R., & Wanner, E. (1972). *The drinking man.* New York: Free Press.

McCord, W., & McCord, J. (1960). *Origins of alcoholism.* Palo Alto, CA: Stanford University Press.

Miller, W. R. (1982). Treating problem drinkers: What works? *Behavior Therapist, 5,* 15-18.

Moos, R. H., & Billings, A. G. (1982). Children of alcoholics during the recovery process: Alcoholic and matched control families. *Addictive Behaviors, 7,* 1551-1563.

Nathan, P. E. (1983). Behavioral theory and behavioral theories of alcoholics. In M. Galanter (Ed.), *Recent developments in alcoholism* (Vol. 1). New York: Plenum.

Pearlman, S. (1988). Systems theory and alcoholism. In C. D. Chaudron & D. A. Wilkinson (Eds.), *Theories on alcoholism* (pp. 289-324). Toronto: Addiction Research Foundation.

Pendery, M., Maltzman, I., & West, L. J. (1982). Controlled drinking by alcoholics? New findings and a re-evaluation of a major affirmative study. *Science, 217,* 169-174.

Pittman, D. J., & Snyder, C. R. (Eds.). (1962). *Society, culture, and drinking patterns.* New York: John Wiley.

Platt, J. J. (1986). *Heroin addiction, theory, research and treatment* (2nd ed.). Malabar, FL: Krieger.

Pomerleau, O. F., & Pomerleau, C. S. (1988). A biobehavioral view of substance abuse and addiction. In S. Peele (Ed.), *Visions of addiction* (pp. 117-139). Lexington, MA: Lexington Books.

Sher, K. J., & Levenson, R. W. (1982). Risk for alcoholism and individual differences in the stress-response-dampening effect of alcohol. *Journal of Abnormal Psychology, 91*, 350-367.

Sherman, J. E., Jorenby, D. E., & Baker, T. B. (1988). Classical conditioning with alcohol: Acquired preferences and aversions, tolerance, and urges/craving. In C. D. Chaudron & D. A. Wilkinson (Eds.), *Theories on alcoholism* (pp. 173-237). Toronto: Addication Research Foundation.

Sobell, M. B., & Sobell, L. C. (1984). The aftermath of heresy: A response to Pendery et al.'s (1982) critique of "Individualized behavior therapy for alcoholics." *Behavior Research & Therapy, 22*, 413-440.

Steinglass, P., Bennet, L. A., Wolin, S. J., & Reiss, D. (1987). *The alcoholic family.* New York: Basic Books.

Steinglass, P., Davis, D. I., & Berensen, D. (1977). Observation of conjointly hospitalized "alcoholic couples" during sobriety and intoxication: Implications for theory and therapy. *Family Process, 16*, 1-16.

Tarter, R. E., Alterman, A. I., & Edwards, K. L. (1988). Neurobehavioral theory of alcoholism etiology. In C. D. Chaudron & D. A. Wilkinson (Eds.), *Theories on alcoholism* (pp. 73-102). Toronto: Addiction Research Foundation.

Ullman, A. D. (1958). Sociocultural backgrounds of alcoholism. *Annals of the American Academy of Political and Social Science, 315*, 48-54.

Wikler, A. (1948). Recent progress in research on the neurophysiological basis of morphine addiction. *American Journal of Psychiatry, 105*, 329-338.

Wikler, A. (1973). Conditioning of successive adaptive responses to the initial effects of drugs. *Conditioned Reflexes, 8*, 193-210.

Wilson, G. T. (1988). Alcohol use and abuse: A social learning analysis. In C. D. Chaudron & D. A. Wilkinson (Eds.), *Theories of alcoholism* (pp. 239-287). Toronto: Addiction Research Foundation.

Wolin, S. J., Bennett, L. A., Noonan, D. L., & Teitelbaum, M. A. (1980). Disrupted family rituals: A factor in the intergenerational transmission of alcoholism. *Journal of Studies on Alcohol, 41*, 199-214.

12

THEORIES OF ETIOLOGY

Thirty years ago, Jellinek (1960) wrote the following:

> The etiquette of the American alcoholism literature demands that the psychiatrist should acknowledge that physiopathological, cultural and social elements have a role in the genesis of alcoholism. On the other hand, the physiopathologist is required to admit the existence of social, cultural, and possibly some individual psychological factors. With few exceptions, however, after having made the prescribed bow, specialists proceed to formulate their etiological theories exclusively in terms of their respective disciplines. Sociologists and anthropologists, too, go their way and give a casual nod to psychology and physiopathology. (p. 13)

Things have not changed very much over 30 years. If we assume that an *integrative* approach to etiology encompasses biochemical, psychological, and sociocultural variables, many of those working in the field of alcohol and drug studies observe the "etiquette" described by Jellinek and formulate theories not in biopsychosocial terms but in terms of their own discipline. Research in etiology has many hazards even when maintained in one discipline; for example, the assumption that because event A precedes event B, it is a *cause* of event B. If one adds to these hazards the complexity of biochemistry + psychology + culture, the challenge seems overwhelming. Perhaps it is best conceived as a kind of predictive equation. Fundamentally, the aim of any etiological theory is to predict with precision who will or will not develop alcohol or drug problems. If the predictive equation is conceived as having three sets of components, each of these components in turn being quite complex and multifactored, some idea of the task can be obtained.

The problem inherent in the etiology of drug abuse could be lessened were all researchers and practitioners to agree on the term *drug abuse*. Are we talking about the *initiation* and early use of a substance? Are we talking about the steps or *phases* as a person goes from exploration to steady use to dependency? Are we talking about the *maintenance* of drug dependency? The motivation as well as the behaviors associated with drug-taking may vary from one stage to the next, and human beings are not easily divided into drug abusers and non-drug abusers. People may, for example, drink heavily and problematically for a period of time and then move out of the population of heavy/problem drinkers. Some people use illegal drugs sporadically, even weekly (heroin "chippers") but do not form what we think of as dependency.

With these caveats, what are the trends toward integrative theories of etiology?

Integrative Theories

Let us assume that we have three major disciplines, components of explanation of etiology:

1. Biology and genetics
2. Personality and behavior
3. Social group membership and culture

With that assumption, we will demonstrate that there are one-discipline theories, two-discipline theories, and multifactorial-biopsychosocial theories of etiology.

One-Discipline Theories

In traditional psychoanalytic theory, "drug addiction" is seen as "rooted in an oral dependence on outer supplies. . . . All other features are incidental" (Fenichel, 1945). Alcoholics are characterized by their "oral and narcissistic pre-morbid personalities" created by difficult family constellations.

Currently, one-discipline theories are likely to be more biological and/or genetic. Goodwin (1982) argues that multifactorial theories exist because "there is a bind of unspoken gentlemen's agreement that since experts from diverse backgrounds study alcoholism, alcoholism must have diverse origins" (p. 168), and that the evidence for multiple causes of alcoholism is no better or no worse than the evidence for a single cause, and concludes: "Who knows? Maybe alcoholism also has a single switch. Maybe it could be turned off if we knew how" (p. 169).

Korenman (1989) does indeed believe that we know how. Arguing that "the concept persists that addiction is a behavioral disorder," Korenman states that the "cure for addiction" lies in molecular and cell biology, and major research investment in these areas would permit us "to return brain cells to their pristine state and eliminate the craving that permanently victimizes the user."

Perhaps there should be some other term for those explanations that are integrative in one sense although they lie entirely *within* biology, behavior, or culture. Thus, there are biomedical researchers who speak of "multidisciplinary" study as involving genetics, neurology, biochemistry, and molecular biology. There are psychologists who believe they are integrative theorists because they have combined principles of ego psychology and behaviorism.

Two-Discipline Theories

There are a number of combination etiological theories: combinations of biology/genetics + psychology, biology/genetics + sociocultural factors, psychology + sociocultural factors, and so on. Bry, McKeon, and Pandina (1982) suggested a multiple-risk-factors hypothesis that seeks to explain different variables significantly related to substance abuse found by different investigators as a function of "the *number* of etiological factors instead of a particular set of them." According to Bry, the "established psychosocial precursors" include a person's past history (experience and behavior), current need state of deprivation, available reinforcers, other current contingencies, and genetic predisposition. Such a compendium offers a two-factor explanation of etiology, that is, a psychological + genetic explanation.

Studies of Swedish identical twins by Cloninger and his colleagues have distinguished two types of alcoholism, which differ according to kind of parental alcohol abuse, dependence on alcohol, age of onset, and related behaviors such as fights and guilt (Cloninger, 1987). The two types of alcoholism are distinguishable, among other ways, in terms of "personality traits."

Cloninger, Sigvardsson, and Bohman (1988) report from a Swedish longitudinal study that "childhood personality predicts alcohol abuse in young adults." The three personality features included in this theory are harm avoidance, novelty-seeking, and reward dependence.

> Specific predictions from a neurobiological learning theory about the role of heritable personality traits in susceptibility to alcohol abuse were tested in this prospective longitudinal study. . . . The three dimensions (of childhood personality variation), i.e., novelty-seeking, harm avoidance, and reward dependence, were largely uncorrelated with one another, and each was predictive of later alcohol abuse. (p. 494)

Whether Cloninger's typology or the personality dimensions stand the test of further research investigation remains to be seen. For our purposes, the main point is the attempt made to incorporate the biological/genetic factor + the psychological factor in a single etiological theory about alcohol abuse.

There are also some two-discipline theories that come from a single discipline and which are considered theories within that discipline. Among sociologists, for example, symbolic interactionism is an attempt to integrate both psychological and sociocultural factors. "There is an interaction between the object—the conditions of alcohol use—and the subject—those who are mobilized to define and react to alcohol as something related to unwelcome conditions" (Gusfield, 1985, p. 72).

Symbolic interactionists speak of "predisposing factors" and "orienting factors," that is, of psychological and sociocultural conditions that permit prediction of alcohol problems.

Dismissing etiological hypotheses that present alcoholism as "primarily" a symptom of psychological instability, Vaillant and Milofsky (1982) offer a two-factor viewpoint: The development of alcoholism is based on ethnicity + "the number of alcoholic relatives." Ethnicity may produce particular attitudes toward alcohol use and abuse, and the number of alcoholic relatives is a measure of hereditary factors. Vaillant (1982) is unique in offering a two-factor theory of genetics + culture. He sees all the behaviors manifested by the alcoholic patient when he or she presents at a rehabilitation facility as the *effect* of the drinking rather than the cause. The fallacy of *post hoc, ergo propter hoc* has been suggested for a long time:

> X behavior is observed in patients who have been drinking and getting into difficulties for the last 10 or 20 years and it is therefore assumed that X is a causative factor in their alcoholism. To know that X behavior exists may be of enormous value in treating the patient but it does not necessarily follow that it antedated and led to the alcoholism. (Lisansky, 1960, p. 316)

But the long-debated search for "the alcoholic personality" appears to terminate in Vaillant's work by throwing the baby out with the bath. In dismissing the findings of prealcoholic behaviors and traits, such as passivity and low self-esteem (McCord & McCord, 1960), elevations in the depression and psychopathic deviate scales of the Minnesota Multiphasic Personality Inventory (MMPI; Kammeier, Hoffman, & Loper, 1973), and more self-confidence and aggression than nonalcoholic peers (Loper, Kammeier, & Hoffman, 1973), the search for the characteristic behaviors and personality traits of the prealcoholic person is terminated, and all behaviors reported retrospectively are dismissed as consequence, not etiology. Although the burden of proof rests on those who would defend the existence of prealcoholic personality patterns as relevant and necessary to predict alcoholism, it does seem premature to dismiss out of hand the search for these patterns. The significance of impulse control, measured in a variety of behaviors, is reported in a comparison of alcoholic women and matched, nonalcoholic women (Gomberg, 1986). Block, Block, and Keyes (1988) report "under control and lower ego-resiliency" as antecedent to later drug usage, observed in children as young as three and four years old. The former is a cross-sectional study, the latter a longitudinal study.

Some researchers in alcohol/drug studies go further in suggesting that not only should the search for antecedent psychological variables be abandoned but the search for *any* antecedent, etiological variables is fruitless.

> No single biological, behavioral or psychosocial variables can account for the development of alcohol abuse and alcoholism, and it is probably unrealistic to search for any one determining factor. The great diversity of developmental and social experiences of people with alcohol related problems suggests that efforts to unravel the origins of alcoholism may prove less productive than attempting to understand how alcoholism is maintained. (Mello, 1982, p. 467)

We have different nihilistic viewpoints. Vaillant believes that the scientific search for antecedent psychological patterns of behavior is fruitless and Mello believes that all attempts to search for "the origins of alcoholism" are better if directed toward study of maintenance of alcoholism.

Currently, the most popular of two-discipline theories of etiology are those that include biology/genetics + sociocultural factors. This is clearly stated: Alcoholism is seen as "a polygenic and multifactorial disorder . . . a number of different types of genetic vulnerabilities interact with cultural and social factors, such as availability of alcohol (including the price of alcohol and distributing laws) and attitudes toward drinking and drunkenness" (Schuckit, 1986).

It is of interest that *psychological vulnerability* is the rejected portion of the two-discipline equation of prediction. One might speculate about the reasons for this, but the main point is that much of current etiological theory-making is two-discipline.

Three-Discipline Theories

One sociologist who sees "interdisciplinary biobehavioral research" as a concept whose time has come emphasizes the need for thinking that integrates the biological and behavior sciences (Straus, 1988). In the examples given, however, Straus seems to elucidate "biobehavioral" as biological + sociocultural. Applied to studies of women's drinking, for instance, he cites "interest in hormonal differences and endocrine function, a major body of research on alcohol-related fetal effects, studies of differences in the genetic impact on sons and daughters of alcoholic father and mothers, and studies of changing norms and practices."

The clearest call for a three-discipline etiological theory has been made by two psychologists (Zucker & Gomberg, 1986). Responding to Vaillant's view that explanation lies in biology + ethnicity, Zucker and Gomberg argue that such theories, "understate the role of personality influences and dismiss childhood effects out of hand." Presenting evidence to support their view that antisocial behavior is part of personality and plays a significant etiological role, the authors argue that childhood antisocial behavior is consistently related to later alcoholic outcome. In making the case for a biopsychosocial process, Zucker and Gomberg argue that the understanding of etiology involves understanding the processes by which alcoholism does *not* develop; in studies of high-risk populations, for example, less than half the high-risk sample manifests symptoms of alcohol abuse. One possible way of understanding the development of problem behavior is through psychological characteristics (e.g., antisocial behavior, poor impulse control), which may facilitate or moderate genetic endowment, just as the sociocultural environment may make it more likely or less likely that the person in the particular environment will or will not develop alcohol-related problems.

It is interesting to note historical changes. After decades of etiological explanation in terms of family dynamics and/or cultural environment, the shift toward explanations of alcoholism in terms of biology/genetics is part of a milieu in which constitutional, biological factors predominate in explanations. It will be of interest to see whether psychological/behavioral/personality explanations become part of major etiological theories again.

References

Block, J., Block, J. H., & Keyes, S. (1988). Longitudinally foretelling drug usage in adolescence: Early childhood personality and environmental precursors. *Child Development, 59,* 336-355.

Bry, B. H., McKeon, P., & Pandina, R. J. (1982). Extent of drug use as a function of number of risk factors. *Journal of Abnormal Psychology, 91,* 273-279.

Cloninger, C. R. (1987). Neurogenetic adaptive mechanisms in alcoholism. *Science, 236,* 410-416.

Cloninger, C. R., Sigvardsson, S., & Bohman, M. (1988). Childhood personality predicts alcohol abuse in young adults. *Alcoholism: Clinical and Experimental Research, 12,* 494-505.

Fenichel, O. (1945). *The psychoanalytic theory of neurosis.* New York: Norton.

Gomberg, E. S. L. (1986). Women and alcoholism: Psychosocial issues. In *Women and alcohol: Health-related issues* (NIAAA Research Monograph No. 16, pp. 78-120). Washington, DC: Government Printing Office.

Goodwin, D. W. (1982). Alcoholism and heredity: Update on the implacable fate. In E. L. Gomberg, H. R. White, & J. A. Carpenter (Eds.), *Alcohol, science and society revisited* (pp. 162-170). Ann Arbor: University of Michigan Press.

Gusfield, J. R. (1985). Alcohol problems—an interactionist view. In J. von Wartburg, P. Manenat, R. Muller, & S. Wyss (Eds.), *Current in alcohol research and the prevention of alcohol problems* (pp. 71-81). Berne, Switzerland: Hans Huber.

Kammeier, M. L., Hoffman, H., & Loper, R. G. (1973). Personality characteristics of alcoholics as college freshman and at times of treatment. *Quarterly Journal of Studies on Alcohol, 34,* 590-599.

Korenman, S. G. (1989, March 28). We need research in the biology of addiction. *New York Times*, p. 18.

Lisansky, E. S. (1960). The etiology of alcoholism: The role of psychological predisposition. *Quarterly Journal of Studies on Alcohol, 21*, 314-343.

Loper, R. G., Kammeier, M. L., & Hoffman, H. (1973). MMPI characteristics of college freshmen males who later become alcoholics. *Journal of Abnormal Psychology, 82*, 159-162.

McCord, W., & McCord, J. (1960). *Origins of alcoholism*. Palo Alto, CA: Stanford University Press.

Mello, N. K. (1982). An examination of some etiological theories of alcoholism. *Academic Psychology Bulletin, 4*, 467-474.

Schuckit, M. A. (1986). Genetic and biological markers in alcoholism and drug abuse. In N. C. Braude & H. M. Chao (Eds.), *Genetic and biological markers in drug abuse and alcoholism* (NIDA Research Monograph No. 66, pp. 97-108). Rockville, MD: National Institute on Drug Abuse.

Straus, R. (1988). Interdisciplinary biobehavioral research on alcohol problems: A concept whose time has come. *Drug and Society, 2*, 33-48.

Vaillant, G. E. (1982). *The natural history of alcoholism*. Cambridge, MA: Harvard University Press.

Vaillant, G. E., & Milofsky, E. S. (1982). The etiology of alcoholism: A prospective viewpoint. *American Psychologist, 37*, 494-503.

Zucker, R. A., & Gomberg, E. S. L. (1986). Etiology of alcoholism reconsidered: The case for a biopsychosocial process. *American Psychologist, 41*, 783-793.

PART III

Treatment Modalities

13

SELF-HELP GROUPS

Within a broad framework, Katz and Bender (1976) define self-help groups as "voluntary small group structures formed by peers who have come together for mutual assistance in satisfying a common need, overcoming a common handicap or life-style disrupting problem and bringing about desired social and/or personal change." Although this definition can be seen as encompassing a multitude of groups, self-help groups can essentially be described in terms of four major issues (Levy, 1976).

The first type is concerned with conduct reorganization or behavioral control. Organizations of this type are Alcoholics Anonymous (AA), Narcotics Anonymous (NA), and Synanon, among others.

Groups such as Parents Without Partners and Recovery aim at the amelioration of stress by teaching how to do something about a stressful situation that cannot be avoided.

The third type of organization is formed for what Levy calls survival purposes. Here the group labeled deviant by the mass of society because of different life-styles and values, or people who are discriminated against for racial or other reasons meet to help members maintain self-esteem and survive hostile social settings. Gay self-help groups are examples of this type.

The fourth type is interested in personal growth and self-actualization. T-groups (therapeutic groups) and sensitivity groups typify this category.

The focus of this chapter is to examine the self-help movement as it relates or might relate to treatment and aftercare needs of substance-abusing populations. It is therefore necessary to understand the rationale underlying the upsurge of the self-help model.

What makes the self-help movement a viable one in general, and for the substance-abusing population specifically? What does it offer that the professionally directed services cannot provide?

The first and most obvious advantage is that of economics. The self-help approach adds a significant manpower resource to the human services system, which has been, is, and possibly will be for a long time, experiencing a manpower shortage. A second reason for the upsurge in the self-help process can be traced to the consumer movement, which recognizes that the existing institutions have not provided nurturance and social support for the needy, the stigmatized, and the generally excluded groups (Katz & Bender, 1976). This exclusion has, to some extent, actually forced these groups to form minisocieties as a reaction to the exclusion and as a defense against the perceived onslaughts of the larger society.

Another related reason is that the professional community is seen as having failed with the populations with which self-help groups are concerned. AA avers that "almost no recovery from alcoholism has ever been brought about by the world's best professionals, whether medical or professional" (Alcoholics Anonymous, 1953).

Finally, the self-help movement is legitimized by theory/research/practice, which is more aware of the importance and benefits of involving the client or consumer in his or her own learning, relearning, or socialization. The significance of having the client share in the determination of his or her own fate is increasingly recognized and accepted in the human services field.

General Self-Help Characteristics

Although a literature review suggests a variety of perceptions as to the definition of self-help groups, depending upon the kind of self-help group being looked at, there are some characteristics common to most, if not all, self-help groups. Katz and Bender (1976) have identified a number of what they call underlying motifs. Self-help groups are voluntarily joined and formed by a group of peers who manifest or experience common needs that are not met by the existing social institutions. These groups are generally concerned with providing material as well as emotional assistance to the members of the group, and each member is sensitized to his or her responsibility and concern for his or her fellow members as the result of consistent interactions. The interactions and the fact of group membership are designed to enhance each member's state of personal identity.

An exploratory conference on nonresidential self-help organizations and the drug abuse problems sponsored by the National Institute on Drug Abuse (1978) identified the following self-help group characteristics:

1. Self-help organizations (SHOs) are voluntary groups whose origin usually is spontaneous.
2. SHO members are peers in that they share a common problem/need/handicap.

3. SHOs are formed by the members for the purpose of coming together to deal with/overcome their shared problem/need/handicap and to initiate a desired change (social and/or personal).

4. SHO members perceive that the needs inherent in their shared problem/need/handicap are not being met by or through established resources.

5. An SHO provides help and support through its members' efforts, skills, knowledge, and concern, and without the aid of professionals.

6. The help and support process involves face-to-face interactions.

7. The members are responsible for and have control of the group. Parenthetically, it might be added that although SHOs might have been stimulated or even started by professionals, self-determination and control must become a reality in a short time.

8. If professionals and government agencies are involved, they function only in a secondary role and at the pleasure of the members.

Dynamics of the Self-Help Process

In a brief review of the historical and theoretical background of self-help programs, Glaser (1971) pointed out that the theoretical roots could be traced to a number of sources. Some of these are Alfred Adler's departure from a narrowly focused intrapsychic approach and his recognition of the part social forces played in determining behavior; Lewin's field-theory approach, which emphasized the here and now and influenced the encounter group movement; existential philosophy, which negates the proposition of immutable essences and holds that man is responsible for his essence; and learning theories that postulate that behavior can be shaped via a system of appropriate reinforcement schedules—these are recognized as being some of the major theoretical and intellectual underpinnings of the self-help movement. In addition, the work of Maxwell Jones (1975) in the development of therapeutic milieu to treat personality disorders provides some of the procedural bases of residential self-help programs. The therapeutic milieu or community concept assumes that a setting in which all of the participants, staff, and patients could openly and honestly discuss and resolve community issues would provide the basis for an effective therapeutic process. This egalitarian, participative therapeutic community approach provided new and refreshing treatment concepts and made a significant dent in the established hierarchical treatment and social systems in psychiatric settings.

The foregoing theoretical underpinnings provide the backdrop for an analysis of the dynamics of self-help groups. What makes self-help groups effective and useful?

The first reason for the efficacy of the self-help modality relates to the sharing of common life experiences and problems. There is clearly an assumption that because all group members have "been there," they understand, at a basic gut level, each other's problems. There is therefore a high sense of trust and sensitivity among the group members. In addition, having "been there" reduces the possibility that a group member can "con" another, a possibility that is seen as great between a professional and his client. Self-help group members often see the professional as someone who can be conned, simply because the professional finds it difficult to be authoritative in dealing with the "victims of society." This difference from the usual professional-client quality has been labeled the aprofessional dimension (Riessman, 1976) and refers to an activist orientation and a greater understanding and identification with consumer/client problems.

A second reason is that the self-help situation permits the individual to participate in and to derive the benefits of the total helping situation, both as a receiver and as a giver. Maximum participation in making decisions about group issues, focusing upon the attempt to increase control over issues that affect one personally, and making decisions that count in an accepting situation should all increase one's sense of independence as well as one's decision-making ability. Helping others and being important to others defines one's sense of worth. The simple process of helping others provides a social legitimacy to a group of individuals for whom that legitimization has been lacking. Riessman (1976) refers to this process as the helper-therapy principle.

Another critical aspect of the efficacy of self-help groups is the development of a support network or system. The program may be a residential one, or it may be one in which members come together on a scheduled basis. Group membership may change, but membership status is determined by each member. A member may move in and out, but the group support is there when he or she needs it and chooses to use it.

The self-help group also provides a vehicle for defining a different set of values, a different life-style, and a milieu that reinforces those changes. In effect, the self-help group process not only provides support for and rewards associated with change but also serves to maintain those changes. The group that enabled the individual to make changes becomes the stabilizing reference group. The group provides a sense of community, belonging, and acceptance that is so vital to individuals who have experienced a continuous chain of isolating, rejecting events.

Finally, Antze (1976) points out that self-help groups are fixed communities of belief. Because self-help members are often those who are least likely to benefit from professional therapy and are in the throes of despair, they are in a state of ready acceptance of a new belief system. As these individuals relate to group members who are sensitive to their needs, and who appear to have resolved their own problems, the persuasive quality of the group advice and admonitions is greatly increased.

Examples of Self-Help Organizations

It would be difficult to overemphasize the importance of Alcoholics Anonymous not only to the field of alcoholism but to the self-help movement generally. As will be discussed below, it provided the stimulus and the model for the development of Narcotics Anonymous, which remains the single most significant self-help organization for drug abusers. Moreover, it has helped spawn a number of self-help organizations in its image or closely resembling it. Inasmuch as AA forms the basis for a consideration of many self-help groups concerned with conduct reorganization, AA will be used to explore the structure and functioning of that group and those other self-help groups that have been developed through a use of its model.

Alcoholics Anonymous

As has been described, Alcoholics Anonymous is the model upon which many nonresidential self-help groups are organized. There are over 30,000 local AA groups in 92 countries, consisting of over 1 million members. Each group is autonomous except in matters affecting other AA groups or the AA fellowship as a whole. Groups are run by short-term steering committees to avoid permanent leadership and dominance. The basic tenets of AA can be found in its 12 steps:

1. We admitted that we were powerless over alcohol, that our lives had become unmanageable.
2. We came to believe that a power greater than ourselves could restore us to sanity.
3. We made a decision to turn our will and our lives over to the care of God as we understood him.
4. We made a searching and fearless moral inventory of ourselves.
5. We admitted to God, to ourselves, and to another human being the exact nature of our wrongs.
6. We were entirely ready to have God remove all these defects of character.
7. We humbly asked Him to remove our shortcomings.
8. We made a list of all persons we had harmed, and became willing to make amends to them all.
9. We made direct amends to such people wherever possible, except when to do so would injure them or others.
10. We continued to take personal inventory, and when we were wrong, promptly admitted it.
11. We sought through prayer and meditation to improve our conscious contact with God, as we understood Him, praying only for knowledge of His will for us, and the power to carry that out.

12. Having had a spiritual awakening as a result of those steps, we tried to carry this message to others and to practice these principles in all our affairs (Alcoholics Anonymous, 1953).

In addition to the 12 steps, there are 12 traditions:

1. Our common welfare should come first; personal recovery depends on AA unity.
2. For our Group purpose there is but one ultimate authority—a loving God as He may express himself in our Group conscience; our leaders are but trusted servants, they do not govern.
3. The only requirement for membership is a desire to stop drinking.
4. Each Group should be autonomous, except in matters that affect other groups, or AA as a whole.
5. Each Group has but one primary purpose—to carry the message to the alcoholic who still suffers.
6. An AA Group ought never to endorse, finance, or lend the AA name to any related facility or outside enterprise, lest problems of money, property, or prestige divert us from our primary purpose.
7. Every AA Group ought to be fully self-supporting, declining outside contributions.
8. Alcoholics Anonymous should remain forever nonprofessional, but our Service Centers may employ special workers.
9. AA as such ought never be organized; but we may create service boards or committees directly responsible to those they serve.
10. AA has no opinion on outside issues; hence the AA name ought never be drawn into public controversy.
11. Our public relations policy is based on attraction rather than promotion; we need always maintain personal anonymity at the level of press, radio, and films.
12. Anonymity is the spiritual foundation of all our Traditions, ever reminding us to place principles before personalities (Alcoholics Anonymous, 1953).

Research designed to evaluate and/or understand the effectiveness of AA has been limited and at times simply self-serving. Two reports worthy of note are those of Leach (1973) and Madsen (1974). Leach reports on four studies of AA conducted in New York, London, Finland, and the United States/Canada. These four studies consisted of self-report questionnaires from 12,946 AA members. They were not scientifically controlled studies, nor did they involve pre- or postmeasures. Self-reported abstinence was the only measurement of effectiveness. Large numbers of AA members, moreover, also reported concurrent treatment in addition to AA. Therefore, it cannot be concluded that AA was solely responsible for the recoveries found in the studies.

The studies report that alcoholics began to maintain unbroken sobriety in AA after an initial period of AA membership marked by relapses. In the largest of the four studies, which was conducted in the United States and Canada and involved 11,355 subjects, 38% were reported as abstinent from 1 to 5 years.

Madsen (1974) did an ethnographic investigation of AA in California using participant observation procedures and making extensive use of questionnaires, biographies, and taped interviews. He concluded that "in comparison with other therapies, the AA success rate is really miraculous."

The literature, scientific and otherwise, on AA has been reviewed by Bebbington (1976), who pointed out the difficulties in assessment of the efficacy of the organization. The problems include the anonymous membership with resultant difficulty in counting members and determining their progress, self-selection related to motivational factors affecting outcome, the fluctuating number of members with varying degrees of affiliation and commitment, and the influence of additional treatment from other sources. Bebbington concluded that the characteristics of AA make it unlikely that it can be assessed by proper scientific methods.

Narcotics Anonymous

This first, and still major, self-help group for the support of drug abusers had its origins in alcoholics anonymous. NA is a nonprofit organization, which was formed in 1953 by a group of drug abusers who felt that the AA fellowship did not offer a program of recovery from drug addiction. AA's concern with drugs has traditionally been limited. It has viewed alcohol as the major issue for individuals abusing both drugs and alcohol.

NA's goal has been that of drug abstinence. Like AA, NA does not speak of cures, but of recovery. The organization is wedded to the AA model and has incorporated the 12 steps of AA as its philosophical base.

As with AA, because of anonymity there are no statistics on NA members. It is suggested that there is no single predominating drug among persons coming to NA. NA claims that the type of drug used is irrelevant—whether pills or heroin, one's life is being controlled by drugs and the fight for abstinence is therefore the same. Moreover, NA warns against the substitution of alcohol for other substances.

The NA program is viewed as following a 24-hour plan such that all effort is expended on remaining drug-free for 24 hours and thereby getting through life one day at a time. Experienced members are portrayed as models for new members and act as "buddies" to new members to help prevent relapse into drug use. It is the NA meetings, however, that are viewed as integral to the individual group member's recovery (Narcotics Anonymous, 1976b).

Like AA, NA states "once an addict, always an addict" (Narcotics Anonymous, 1976a). The individual is unable to use drugs normally and must resist temptation ever to use drugs again.

NA has also reported that even those who relapse show marked gains from their efforts to achieve abstinence. These individuals are viewed as having dropped many of the behaviors supportive of drug abuse that have characterized them in the past. In this sense, the NA experience is described as analogous to climbing up a tower, one step at a time until reaching the top. One may slip down a few stairs without necessarily reaching the bottom and having to start all over again. The NA influence can remain, and a relapse need not mean all has been lost. Indeed, the relapse and resulting dissatisfaction with oneself may provide an impetus to seek larger personal gains. In this sense, even relapse can be seen as instrumental to recovery (Narcotics Anonymous, 1976a).

Women for Sobriety

Women for Sobriety was formed largely because some women felt that their needs were not being adequately met by AA. The organization was started in 1975 by Jean Kirkpatrick, a recovered alcoholic. This self-help group helps alcoholic women rebuild their self-concept and self-esteem focusing on "self-power" rather than on any higher spiritual power. The member must rid herself of "negative emotion," create new ideas about herself and her world, and act rather than react. The group has 13 steps to aid in the development of self-esteem and the building of positive social networks:

1. I have a drinking problem that once had me.
2. Negative emotions destroy only myself.
3. Happiness is a habit I will develop.
4. Problems bother me only to the degree I permit them to.
5. I am what I think.
6. Life can be ordinary or it can be great.
7. Love can change the course of my world.
8. The fundamental object of life is emotional and spiritual growth.
9. The past is gone forever.
10. All love given returns twofold.
11. Enthusiasm is my daily exercise.
12. I am a competent women and have much to give others.
13. I am responsible for myself and my sisters.

Women for Sobriety is not based upon anonymity among its members, but provides anonymity for those who wish it. It is a voluntary, self-supporting organization.

Residential Therapeutic Communities

The AA movement spawned the self-help therapeutic communities for drug addicts. The therapeutic community model was essentially the child of Charles Dederich, who broke away from AA because he found it to be too restricting. With some friends from AA, he set up a "free-association" discussion group in 1958. This group attracted and retained an increasing number of drug addicts. The influx of drug addicts culminated in a break with the alcoholic members and led to Dederich's total involvement with and championship for addicts. Thus, Synanon was launched. Synanon has, in turn, become the prototype for the development of a host of other therapeutic communities for addicts. Daytop in New York is perhaps the most widely known community organization. The usual arrangement is to employ a proportion of staff who have never been on drugs, but formerly drug-dependent persons also play an important role. Both Synanon and Daytop require new residents abruptly to cease taking all drugs on admission. The opioid abstinence syndrome is made more tolerable by reassurance and psychological comfort from other members who have gone "cold turkey," but its prospect must deter some drug takers from admission. Others, even after the withdrawal stage, prematurely terminate their rehabilitation. Synanon has been reluctant subsequently to discharge those who remain back into the community at large, making the forecast, which has proven self-fulfilling, that full return to society would lead to relapse. Daytop has developed a scheme of phased re-entry into the community for former drug users (O'Brien, 1973).

A follow-up study of former Daytop residents contacted 64% of the subjects who had completed rehabilitation and 39% of those who had dropped out at some stage after the initial 6 months of treatment (Collier & Hijazi, 1974). Of the contacted Daytop graduates, 84% were no longer taking drugs or abusing alcohol, were not again arrested, and were either employed or engaged in furthering their education. Using the same criteria, 46% of the drop-outs who were contacted had a satisfactory outcome. In a study of a comparable community, Romond, Forest, and Kleber (1975) found statistically significant differences in follow-up between the graduates and those who had left prematurely; the former were more likely to remain nondependent on drugs, to be free from new convictions, to continue employment or education, and to attend drug therapy programs as clients or as staff. The researchers did not claim a causal relationship between the length of time in treatment and the outcome.

A review of the other follow-up reports of therapeutic communities in the United States and Britain has been undertaken by Smart (1976), who noted deficiencies in many of the studies. Among the defects was a paucity of control groups consisting of comparable subjects who did not receive a rehabilitative regime. It was also unfortunate that, although communities differed in the proportion of residents who were polydrug users or who were not dependent on opioids, the possible resultant variations in prognosis were not considered. In the reports, subjects who had completed rehabilitation tended to be relatively few, often representing less than 15% of the admissions; the recovery rates of these subjects varied from 33% to 92%, compared with 22% to 50% among dropouts, but it was not possible to determine which program characteristics were related to favorable outcomes. Smart suggested that therapeutic communities return too few residents to employment in working roles other than in drug treatment or social service activities. Another criticism that has sometimes been leveled against certain rehabilitative communities for heroin takers is that their residents consist of a disproportionately high number of middle class or White clientele who are unrepresentative of the majority of heroin-dependent persons.

The therapeutic communities (TCs) have a number of factors in common. TCs developed in response to the needs of drug addicts; they are based on the belief that addicts need to stop blaming social situations over which they have little control and need to take responsibility for their own actions. Therefore, it is proposed that members must learn to accept and carry out personal responsibilities and to see themselves as persons who are accountable for their own behavior.

Being honest is considered an essential requisite to personal growth and to the assumption of a productive life-style not dependent on substance abuse. Techniques were developed to strip the person of the old identity and to build a new one based on an honest assessment of oneself.

Admission into TCs is voluntary, but once admitted, the individual enters into a very authoritative and almost prescriptive community structure and participates in highly structured programs that usually employ ex-addict staff and provide a total living-in situation within a highly structured framework of "family" and community. TCs usually have established focal points:

- A "self-help" therapeutic milieu in which every activity is oriented toward staying "clean" and learning to be a productive member of society. This may include a progression in terms of complexity of work and extent of responsibility assigned first within the therapeutic milieu and later in the outside community. The drug abuser is aided by peers and alumni in reaching the goals of therapy.
- Group sessions that are usually led by an ex-addict and include techniques such as verbal confrontations or encounters. The ex-addict is often seen both as serving as a model for drug-abuse residents and as someone who cannot easily be "conned" by the drug abusers' "games."

Although all TCs are ostensibly treatment organizations, many TCs have become permanent subcultures from which transition to the larger culture is infrequent.

Self-Help and the Treatment Cycle

The question arises as to the point in the treatment cycle at which a self-help group may be most effective and the role to be assumed by the self-help group. The self-help initiative may occur at any of several points, with each of several objectives:

1. Prevention (prior to taking drugs, or while drug taking is still in the experimental stages)
2. Primary treatment (change would be mediated through the self-help group only)
3. Support for ongoing treatment (self-help would supplement treatment in a formal drug abuse program)
4. Aftercare services (self-help would be initiated only after the formal treatment program has been completed)
5. Some combination of all or any of the above

Most of the groups that were discussed in this chapter see themselves as providing the primary treatment. In fact, many make claims of attaining success through the self-help group after previous treatment failure. Yet many residential as well as outpatient treatment programs incorporate the self-help model into their treatment program, often requiring attendance at a 12-step program as part of the client's treatment plan.

For the youthful experimenter, or for the trouble-prone adolescent, self-help as prevention/early intervention may be highly appropriate. Self-help groups may be of particular importance for prevention or primary treatment in rural communities that have little or no prevention/treatment dollars.

In the case of multiple drug use, self-help groups may be an appropriate form of primary treatment for those who may not wish an association with a treatment program. However, a heroin addict may have needs—for instance, detoxification, vocational rehabilitation, medical care, education, and so on—that preclude the use of self-help in isolation. In this case, self-help may be more appropriate as part of a complex of ongoing treatment (National Institute on Drug Abuse, 1978). In this regard, methadone clients may pose a special concern. The clients cannot immediately achieve, and may not wish to achieve, a goal of abstinence. Consequently, they cannot ally themselves with abstinent group members, and they may therefore require a separate self-help group structure.

The need for self-help groups to undertake the task of aftercare appears to many a crucial element in the treatment process for drug addiction. The use of self-help groups as alumni associations to permit the development of prosocial friendships and negotiation of the nonaddict community may help prevent client recidivism. Self-help groups as a form of aftercare support may prove to be the most important "last step" in the treatment cycle. For those clients leaving the protective environment of the therapeutic community, re-entry is clearly an essential part of the treatment cycle. Because residential treatment clients live in a relatively artificial environment, it may be helpful for clients who are approaching graduation to attend self-help meetings off site. This may allow an easier adaptation to a new community structure upon exiting from the therapeutic community. For those leaving methadone maintenance or outpatient drug-free programs, community re-entry is not as pronounced an event. It is at program completion, however, that community resources must be identified and coordinated on behalf of the ex-drug abuser to give support to a drug-free adjustment. The self-help group can provide a new base of friendship and support for the former addict who remains in virtually the same environment that helped to stimulate and/or support his or her drug-abusing behavior.

In summary, self-help groups are viable at any point in the treatment cycle. Their appropriateness at a particular phase in the cycle depends on the individual's need and the community's resources.

Additional Resources

Alcoholics Anonymous
Box 459
Grand Central Station
New York, NY 10017

Narcotics Anonymous
World Service Office
P.O. Box 662
Sun Valley, CA 91352

Women for Sobriety, Inc.
Box 618
Quakertown, PA 18951

References

Alcoholics Anonymous. (1953). *Twelve steps and twelve traditions.* New York: Alcoholics Anonymous World Services.

Antze, P. (1976). The role of ideologies in peer psychotherapy organizations: Some theoretical considerations and three case histories. *Journal of Applied Behavioral Sciences, 12*(3), 323-344.

Bebbington, P. E. (1976). The efficacy of Alcoholics Anonymous: The elusiveness of hard data. *British Journal of Psychiatry, 128,* 572-580.

Collier, W. V., & Hijazi, Y. A. (1974). A follow-up study of former residents of a therapeutic community. *International Journal of the Addictions, 9*, 805-826.

Glaser, F. B. (1971). Gaudenzia, Inc.: Historical and theoretical background of a self-help addiction treatment program. *International Journal of Addiction, 6*(4), 615-626.

Jones, M. (1975). The treatment of personality disorders in a therapeutic community. *Psychiatry, 20*, 211-220.

Katz, A. H., & Bender, E. I. (1976). Self-help groups in western society: History and prospects. *Journal of Applied Behavioral Sciences, 12*(3), 265-282.

Leach, B. (1973). Does AA really work? In P. G. Bourne & R. Fox (Eds.), *Alcoholism: Progress in research and treatment* (pp. 245-284). New York: Academic Press.

Levy, L. H. (1976). Self-help groups: Types and psychological processes. *Journal of Applied Behavioral Sciences, 12*(3), 310-322.

Madsen, W. (1974). *The American alcoholic.* Springfield, IL: Charles C Thomas.

Narcotics Anonymous. (1976a). *Recovery and relapse.* Sun Valley, CA: Narcotics Anonymous World Service Office.

Narcotics Anonymous. (1976b). *We made a decision.* Sun Valley, CA: Narcotics Anonymous World Service Office.

National Institute on Drug Abuse. (1978, July). *Nonresidential self-help organizations and the drug abuse problem: An exploratory conference* (Services Research Report, No. ADM 78-452). Rockville, MD: Author.

O'Brien, J. (1973). Quantum leap toward 1984. *Journal of Drug Issues, 4* (4), 354-358.

Riessman, F. (1976). How does self-help work? *Social Policy, 7* (2), 41-45.

Romond, A. N., Forrest, C. K., & Kleber, H. D. (1975). Follow-up of participants in a drug dependence therapeutic community. *Archives of General Psychiatry, 32*, 369-374.

Smart, R. G. (1976). Outcome studies of therapeutic community and halfway house treatment for addicts. *International Journal of the Addictions, 11*, 143-159.

14

MEDICAL ASPECTS OF
TREATMENT

The Alcohol Withdrawal Syndrome and
Medical Detoxification

Alcohol "detoxification" refers to "treatment intended to rid the organism of alcohol and to promote recovery from its effects," whereas alcohol "detoxication" refers to "the condition of recovery from the effects or alcohol in the organism" (Keller & McCormick, 1968). Despite these differences, the terms are used interchangeably by clinicians.

Alcoholics are often able to check a phase of drinking, and endure the attendant withdrawal symptoms, without entering a hospital or detoxification center. Some achieve this without help from doctors or social workers, through their own determination or with encouragement from relatives or members of Alcoholics Anonymous. Other alcoholics appreciate the prescription of a drug or drugs to counteract the distress of the withdrawal period. Others again need withdraw to from alcohol in a hospital or detoxification center because their physical or mental health has required admission, or because they wish to stop drinking at least temporarily but are unable or unwilling to tolerate the withdrawal symptoms while in the community.

Syndromes of mild withdrawal include irritability, sleeplessness, and tremor. Symptoms of severe withdrawal (delirium tremens) include marked tremulousness, sweating, hallucinations (predominantly visual), seizures, and delirium (labile affect, and impaired orientation, memory, intellectual functions, and judgment). Increased catecholamine production as a result of the stress of withdrawal may result in tachycardia and low-grade fever. Although mild withdrawal symptoms typically appear 48 to 60 hours after withdrawal, there is great overlap and variation in their manifestation (Sellers & Kalaut, 1976). Frequently withdrawal symptoms may appear following trauma, infections (such as pneumonia), or gastritis. Patients with concurrent medical problems are at high risk for the development of delirium tremens.

Drug treatment of physical dependence relieves symptoms and reduces the likelihood of severe withdrawal features in the form of convulsions or delirium tremens. Drug administration also has a placebo effect in reassuring the alcoholic patient that undue suffering will not develop. The placebo effect has benefit even in the case of hospitalization, where the usual procedure is to withdraw the patient at once from alcohol.

Patients with mild withdrawal symptoms can be treated effectively with oral minor tranquilizers, multivitamins, a good diet, and observation in a relatively quiet environment. The presence of severe withdrawal symptoms is indicative of a potentially fatal physiological process. Management of such patients typically involves hospitalization and medication.

Benzodiazepines. By a wide margin, the most favored medications used by clinicians are the benzodiazepines (Favazza & Martin, 1974). The benzodiazepines relieve anxiety and promote sleep; in the doses usually given, their effect on clarity of consciousness is slight, so benzodiazepines are sometimes described as minor tranquilizers. They show an anticonvulsive effect; this property could be beneficial in the prevention of alcohol withdrawal seizures. Paradoxically, benzodiazepines can on infrequent occasions produce aggression, but their main disadvantage is their potential for abuse and dependence. Benzodiazepines are much less likely to induce dependence than barbiturates, but when administered to cover alcohol withdrawal, they should only be given for a maximum period of 2 weeks, and in decreasing dosage during their time of administration. The benzodiazepines are effective, relatively free of side effects, easy to administer, and well accepted by patients (Greenblatt & Shader, 1974).

Major tranquilizers. Many other medications are relatively effective in treating severe alcohol withdrawal syndrome, but each is problematic in some way, and none is superior overall to the benzodiazepines. Members of the phenothiazine group of major tranquilizers counteract alcohol withdrawal, and, unlike the benzodiazepines, they do not produce dependence. However, phenothiazines are associated with such side effects as lowering the seizure threshold, hypotension, and frightening extrapyramidal reactions.

Beta-adrenergic blockers. It has been suggested that drugs that compete with catecholamines for occupation of beta-adrenergic receptor sites and so block noradrenaline transmission at these sites are beneficial in alcohol withdrawal.

Beta-adrenergic blockers ("beta-blockers") act to prevent noradrenaline stimulation of receptors in the heart. They thus reduce the increased cardiac rate, force, and output that are found during alcohol withdrawal (Carlsson, 1969) and that are perceived by the patient as palpitations. Beta-blockers also control the tremor characteristic of alcohol withdrawal. The employment of a beta-blocker does not obviate the need for sedative, tranquilizer, or anticonvulsant medication. A beta-blocker therefore complicates treatment, possibly to an undesirable degree.

Propranolol (Inderal) is the most widely employed beta-blocker. Propranolol is contraindicated for patients who have asthma, cardiomyopathy, chronic obstructive respiratory disease, and diabetes requiring insulin (conditions frequently found in alcoholics).

Conclusion

When alcohol is withdrawn under medical supervision, it is desirable to prescribe drugs briefly in order to relieve withdrawal symptoms and to prevent the development of delirium tremens or convulsions. Either of these complications may prove fatal; convulsions can be followed by the organic brain syndrome (Walsh, 1961). But it is likely that the pharmacological actions of drugs provide a comparatively minor contribution to the relative ease with which most alcoholics withdraw from alcohol in the hospital. More influential factors are the benign course of the abstinence syndrome, and psychological features such as motivation, the placebo effect of drugs, and reassurance by staff and peers.

The Role of Drug Therapies in the Context of Alcoholism

The use of psychoactive medication for the treatment of the chronic phase of alcoholism has been the subject of research, speculation, and controversy for many years. Although there have been many studies purporting to demonstrate the effectiveness of psychoactive medication in this patient population, methodological problems in most of these studies prevent any general conclusions from being drawn. Viamontes (1972) reviewed 89 British and American studies that attempted to evaluate the effectiveness of psychotropic medication in the rehabilitation of chronic alcoholics and found the majority of these studies to be uncontrolled and representing the clinical impressions of the investigators rather than objectively valid, research-based evaluations. He concluded that no drug has proven better than placebos in the treatment of chronic alcoholics.

This conclusion should not imply that there are no alcoholics who can be helped by the use of psychoactive medication. Quite the contrary: there are alcoholics who suffer a variety of specific psychiatric disorders for which psychoactive medication is clearly indicated. In these, as in any other psychiatric patients, medication is often indicated and should be prescribed judiciously and monitored closely, particularly if the patient continues to drink. The use of medication in these patients has been demonstrated to be effective if (a) the patient's psychiatric condition is carefully diagnosed, and (b) treatment with psychoactive medication is based upon this diagnosis. On the other hand, the evidence implies that as a routine aspect of treatment for alcoholic patients, psychoactive medication appears to be generally ineffective and, in most cases, probably harmful.

Disulfiram Treatment

Disulfiram, best known in the United States under the trade name Antabuse, was reported by Hald and Jacobsen in 1948 to be a drug sensitizing the organism to ethyl alcohol. While taking the drug themselves for experimental purposes, they accidentally discovered unpleasant physiological responses to drinking alcohol. When first introduced, the medication tended to be given in what today would be considered excessively high doses. Also, early on many therapists felt that the patient should first be sensitized with the drug and then given alcohol as a means of convincing him or her as to the unpleasantness of the response should drinking occur. This technique is rarely, if ever, employed today. Instead, the patient's cooperation is enlisted and a convincing description of the disulfiram-ethanol reaction (DER) is given.

Mechanism. Disulfiram is an inhibitor of adelhyde dehydrogenase. Because acetaldehyde is the first metabolic breakdown product in the metabolism of alcohol, patients who have been treated with the drug experience acetaldehyde toxicity. The DER is not unlike the acetaldehyde toxicity seen in many Asian subjects when they consume beverage alcohol (Ewing, Rouse, & Pellizzari, 1974).

Disulfiram-Ethanol Reactions. Ideally, the DER is to be avoided. Nevertheless, it can occur accidentally, due to lack of judgment, because of giving in to impulse, and as a suicide attempt. Although hundreds of thousands of patients have taken millions of doses of disulfiram over more than 30 years, the literature contains only about 20 deaths. However, the DER does call for medical intervention in most cases.

The patient may experience flushing of the skin, particularly on the face. A throbbing headache is common. Respiratory distress and hyperventilation can be followed by respiratory depression. Complaints of pain in the chest can simulate a myocardial infarction, and the patient may be aware of palpitations and be suffering from arrhythmias. Typically, the blood pressure falls, there is sweating and sometimes nausea and vomiting. The patient may complain of apprehensive feelings, weakness, and dizziness and can display confusion. Severe reactions can go on to heart failure, unconsciousness, convulsions, and death.

Treatment is basically that of the treatment of shock, including the administration of oxygen. Ephedrine can be administered to maintain blood pressure. If the patient is vomiting and can get rid of any alcohol remaining in the stomach, this is bound to be beneficial because it will mean less acetaldehyde buildup.

Drug Withdrawal

Whether initially or at a later phase in therapy, the stage is often reached when the drug user is prepared as a practical step to undergo drug cessation. At this point, if physical dependence is present, it is necessary to overcome withdrawal symptoms and signs before dealing with adverse emotional and social factors.

Hallucinogens and volatile inhalants do not produce physical dependence and withdrawal symptoms; neither do simple analgesics unless the preparations also contain the opioids codeine or dextropropoxyphene. Stimulant drugs produce a degree of physical dependence that is mild, so despite some genuine withdrawal distress on their cessation, there is no need for their prescription. In case of opioids and general sedatives it is desirable, if the patient is in the hospital, for the doctor to prescribe an appropriate member of whichever of these sedative classes the subject was consuming; the selected drug is given in decreasing doses so that the withdrawal symptoms at no time become excessive.

The withdrawal of general sedatives and opioids is more likely to succeed if the patient is first admitted to a hospital. In a hospital setting it is possible to control drug intake, while the patient receives support from staff in an environment unassociated with previous drug usage.

Treatment of the Opioid Abstinence Syndrome

The intensity of distress of the opioid abstinence syndrome has been likened to that encountered in a bout of the flu; the patients and their medical advisers often take an exaggerated view of the severity of the symptoms and signs. But in order to spare patients from discomfort it is not the custom to withdraw opioids abruptly from patients admitted to the hospital. It should also be noted that sudden withdrawal of opioids from the elderly or physically ill can prove hazardous.

Opioid users who have taken a preparation that produces relatively mild physical dependence, such as codeine or a cough medicine containing a morphine-like drug, can be given the same preparation after admission in decreasing quantity and frequency of dosage; over a period of 7 to 10 days the product is gradually and fully withdrawn.

Methadone is the drug of choice for inpatient withdrawal of persons who are likely to possess marked physical dependence; they may, for instance, have been regular consumers of heroin, morphine, or methadone itself. On admission the patient is given oral methadone in a dose sufficient to suppress all or the greater part of the abstinence syndrome; no other medication is required. The effects of oral methadone endure longer than 24 hours, but it is customary during detoxification to give the drug initially on two or three occasions a day. During the ensuing days the level and frequency of administration are both progressively lowered until the drug is completely stopped. It is feasible to complete methadone withdrawal over a 10-day period; the symptoms developed on such a regime are not severe, but in a voluntary setting patients tend to take their discharge after methadone is withdrawn in this short a time. They give various excuses for leaving, but in fact they depart to obtain opioids. More gradual reduction, over a 3-week period, ensures that the patient is likely to remain in the hospital. The slower pace of withdrawal allows drug craving to subside and permits time for development of a positive relationship between patient and hospital staff; that relationship is the necessary basis for a constructive mutual examination of the drug intake and emotional problems of the patient.

Patients who have been taking opioids (or other drugs) by oral or nasal routes should never receive prescribed drugs by injection. Administration by injection strengthens physical and psychological dependence because of more rapid and complete drug absorption and because of the mental associations that are attached to use of the "needle".

Withdrawal of General Sedatives

Individuals who are physically dependent on barbiturates or other nonopioid depressants should be withdrawn from drugs in a hospital by means of a phased reduction of drug intake. Abrupt withdrawal produces distressing and dangerous consequences. Convulsions, for example, are a hazardous feature of the abstinence syndrome of the barbiturate and general sedative type; it is doubtful if anticonvulsants prevent fits in this syndrome.

In regard to choice of prescribed medication, the safest method is to employ in oral form the drug that the patient has been using, or a very similar drug; the amount given is decreased each day or on alternate days until after 10 to 14 days the medication has been fully withdrawn. The administration of an oral anticonvulsant may be beneficial and can do no harm, even though the efficiency of this procedure in the prevention of withdrawal fits is uncertain. If convulsions occur, they are treated with diazepam or phenobarbital. Withdrawal fits or delirium necessitate a brief increase in the quantity of prescribed sedative and postponement for a day or two of further decrements to its dosage.

Adjuncts in Treatment

Opioid Antagonists. The euphoric effects of heroin or morphine are almost completely inapparent if the user is taking an opioid antagonist. The antagonists naloxone, cyclazocine, and naltrexone have been used as prolonged therapy to prevent relapses among opioid-dependent persons who have undergone detoxication.

Naloxone might be considered the most dangerous antagonist, because it lacks concomitant antagonist effects and its withdrawal is unaccompanied by abstinence features. But the required dose is large, the expense of naloxone is considerable, and supplies are difficult to obtain.

Cyclazocine has received more extensive employment. Withdrawal of cyclazocine produces minor abstinence symptoms, but physical dependence on the drug has not led to its abuse (World Health Organization, 1975). During the early stages of administration of cyclazocine unpleasant effects can develop, consisting of slowing of thought, motor incoordination, irritability, or hallucinations; the undesirable clinical features can be minimized by slow administration of the drug.

Naltrexone is longer acting; although its daily use is feasible, Goldstein (1976) recommends its administration three times a week. Naltrexone possess slight opioid antagonist features; yawning, stretching, and a stimulant effect on thought and speech have also been noted. But naltrexone produces troublesome side effects less frequently than cyclazocine.

Long-term therapy by opioid antagonists is less popular with opioid users than methadone maintenance, though volunteers for therapy with an opioid antagonist do not commonly challenge its blocking effect by taking heroin.

Methadone Maintenance

Long-term chemotherapy with the synthetic opioid methadone was introduced for the treatment of heroin dependence in the mid-1960s (Dole & Nyswander, 1965; Dole, Nyswander, & Kreek, 1966). The immediate goal of methadone maintenance therapy is to provide a dose of methadone that will suppress opioid abstinence symptoms for the entire 24-hour period between doses without producing euphoria, sedation, or dulling of consciousness (Senay, 1983). Another goal of methadone therapy is to engage the addict in a therapeutic relationship both with a counselor and with a program. "Therapeutic" is defined here broadly to include the provision of social, vocational, legal, or other services in addition to psychological help. Maintenance therapy also aims to improve the health status of addicts.

The long-range goal of opioid substitution therapy varies. Some programs are based on a philosophy that affirms indefinite maintenance, and other programs aim specifically for short periods of maintenance (i.e., a few months to 2 years) and then require an attempt to become drug-free. Because we have less than 2 decades of experience with opioid substitution therapy, we have no data that would indicate which of these clinical postures is superior. Certainly the latter is more popular with addicts seeking treatment, whereas the former becomes more acceptable once addicts are in treatment.

Methadone maintenance is claimed to possess several advantages over a policy of avoiding prescriptions of opioids to outpatients:

1. Methadone in adequate dosage suppresses withdrawal symptoms from deprivation of other opioids. A legal supply of methadone reduces the reliance on illicit drugs of the opioid-dependent person; the supply checks criminal behavior required to obtain drugs or to obtain the money or valuables to purchase drugs.

2. Methadone withdrawal symptoms do not appear until 24 hours after consumption of the drug; by contrast, with heroin withdrawal features begin within 3 to 4 hours of taking heroin. In distinction from heroin, the drug user who receives methadone does not need to take the drug several times a day, and his state of well-being is more in equilibrium.

3. Again unlike heroin, methadone is effective when consumed orally. The patient does not need injections, which possess an intense euphoric effect, other psychological attractions, and physical risk.

4. In high dosage methadone blocks the euphoric effect of heroin so that there is no advantage to the subject if the latter substance is also taken.

5. Patients who are on methadone evolve a more stable life-style and develop no fresh physical complications (Kreek, 1973; Kreek, Dodes, Kane, et al., 1972). It is claimed that they incur fewer convictions, improve their morale, and form better marital and occupational adjustments (U.S. Department of Justice, 1973).

6. It is hoped that by means of methadone programs the heroin black market is curbed, that there are fewer new recruits to illegal drug usage, that crime is checked, and that welfare costs are reduced (U.S. Department of Justice, 1973).

Evaluation

The National Institute on Drug Abuse has sponsored large nationwide evaluation studies. The largest of these, the Drug Abuse Reporting Project (DARP), has been carried out by Sells and co-workers (Sells, 1979). The data base consists of approximately 44,000 drug-abuse treatment clients admitted to treatment between 1969 and 1973. Studies on this cohort have now been extended to a 6-year period, and longer periods of follow-up were projected.

Stratified random samples taken from the cohort have been studied, and, given the large size of the cohort, at least a moderate degree of generalizability can be inferred. Basic DARP findings have been that over 50% of the methadone maintenance clients were retained in treatment for 1 year or more and that rates of illicit opioid use and criminality decreased sharply in comparison to pretreatment rates. Employment rates improved in methadone maintenance clients; 39% were employed before treatment, and 62% were employed in the year after leaving treatment.

A second, independent evaluation of a large nationwide cohort was carried out by the National Institute on Drug Abuse on 12,000 patients entering treatment in 1979, 1980, and 1981 (Craddock et al., 1982). Again, substantial changes were noted in illicit drug use and criminality when pre- and posttreatment periods were compared. Employment rates improved a little, but because employment was affected negatively by the recession of the period, even modest positive changes are significant. This study added a feature not present in DARP, namely, evaluation of the psychological status of patients. Depression indicators, found to be high in addicts coming for treatment, were shown in this study to improve during treatment. Other findings, of both clinical and administrative importance, were that clients received many social, vocational, legal, and educational services, and that clients, in general, were quite satisfied with the treatment they received.

Why, in the face of truly massive data acquired on thousands of patients studied over many years is there such a disparity between what the data say and the attitudes of the public about this method of treatment? A General Accounting Office (GAO) report of the U.S. Congress cites lack of dissemination of the outcome data as the chief culprit, and it is an important factor (Comptroller General, 1980). But there are other factors equally potent and as yet apparently insuperable. One is the factionalism in the field of drug-abuse treatment. The judgment that providing legal opioids is unethical or sinful and in any event, ineffective—"it's like giving an alcoholic bourbon"—is widespread, particularly in the alcoholism treatment community and among therapeutic community workers. The funding structure frequently reinforces the divisions caused by this philosophic split by pitting methadone programs against therapeutic communities in the struggle for economic survival.

Because methadone, historically speaking, is relatively new and because regulatory efforts are sometimes too weak and sometimes too strong, a few clinics have been poorly operated, which has created justifiable concern. This has sometimes created a local image that all methadone programs are ineffective and poorly organized. Usually the parties involved are not aware that nationwide studies on evaluation have been carried out and that the results are favorable. The disparity between data and opinion is so wide that some communities have banned methadone programs.

Still another hurdle for legal opioid substitution is the notion of "cure." Although it is true that there are heroin experimenters and, in some instances, occasional users, it is also true that heroin use is associated with large numbers of dysfunctional abusers whose use becomes chronic, who are criminally active, and whose activities and health needs have a large impact on the quality of life for the communities in which they are imbedded. There are, to put it another way, large numbers of heroin users who develop careers with heroin or frequently with heroin and multiple other intoxicants. The fact is that there is no way to do anything other than to try to engage them in careers of treatment that will reduce crime, improve health, shorten runs of heroin use, reduce time in jail, and lessen contact with the criminal justice system. To demean what can be done because it is not a cure is destructive and has serious negative consequences for public health, as careers untreated are much more pathologic than careers treated, both for the addict and for the communities concerned.

There are then many reasons for the disparity between the data concerning methadone and public perception. The foregoing analysis implies that this disparity will not be reduced soon, and perhaps never, if institutions, national and international, do not improve communication about the data and take action to reduce the impact of the other factors that contribute to the disparity.

Conclusion

Traditionally, health care has been equated with medical care—implying a physician diagnosing and treating a patient's illness or physical complications. In more recent years, an interdisciplinary team of health-care professionals has been utilized with increasing acceptance. The emotional and social components of even the most medicalized illnesses, such as cancer, diabetes, heart disease, and stroke, have been recognized as legitimate areas for psychosocial family intervention and treatment (Huberty, 1974). Likewise, the emotional, social, and physical interrelated components of alcoholism and drug dependency are increasingly recognized as requiring a multidisciplinary team approach to achieve any maximum benefit for the chemically dependent patient.

References

Carlsson, C. (1969). Haemodynamic studies in alcoholics in the withdrawal phase. *International Journal of Clinical Pharmacology,* (Suppl. 3), 61-63.

Comptroller General. (1980). *Report to the Congress by the Comptroller General of the United States, April 14, 1980. Action needed to improve management and effectiveness of drug abuse treatment* (HRD-80-32). Washington, DC: General Accounting Office.

Craddock, S. G., et al. (1982). *Summary and implications: Client characteristics, behaviors and intreatment outcome 1980 TOPS admission cohort.* Research Triangle Institute Project 23U-1901.

Dole, V. P., & Nyswander, M. E. (1965). A medical treatment for diacetylmorphine (heroin) addiction. *Journal of the American Medical Association, 193,* 646-650.

Dole, V. P., Nyswander, M. E., & Kreek, M. J. (1966). Narcotic blockage: A medical technique for stopping heroin use by addicts. *Archives of Internal Medicine, 118,* 304-309.

Ewing, J. A., Rouse, B. A., & Pellizzari, E. D. (1974). Alcohol sensitivity and ethnic background. *American Journal of Psychiatry, 131,* 206-210.

Favazza, A., & Martin, P. (1974). Chemotherapy of delirium tremens. *American Journal of Psychiatry, 131,* 1031-1033.

Goldstein, A. (1976). Heroin addiction: Sequential treatment employing pharmacological supports. *Archives of General Psychiatry, 33,* 353-358.

Greenblatt, D. J., & Shader, R. I. (1974). *Benzodiazepines in clinical practice.* New York: Raven Press.

Hald, J., & Jacobsen, E. A. (1948). A drug sensitising the organism to ethyl alcohol. *Lancet, 255,* 1001-1004.

Huberty, D. (1974). Adapting to illness through family groups. *International Journal of Psychiatry in Medicine, 5,* 231-242.

Keller, M., & McCormick, M. A. (1968). *A dictionary of words about alcohol.* New Brunswick, NJ: Rutgers Center of Alcohol Studies.

Kreek, M. J. (1973). Medical safety and side effects of methadone in tolerant individuals. *Journal of the American Medical Association, 228,* 665-668.

Kreek, M. J., Dodes, L., Kane, S., et al. (1972). Long-term methadone maintenance therapy: Effects on liver function. *Annals of Internal Medicine, 77,* 598-602.

Sellers, E. M., & Kalaut, H. (1976). Alcohol detoxification and withdrawal. *New England Journal of Medicine, 294,* 757-762.

Sells, S. B. (1979). Treatment effectiveness. In R. L. Dupont, A. Goldstein, & J. O'Donnell (Eds.), *Handbook on drug abuse.* Washington, DC: Government Printing Office.

Senay, E. C. (1983). *Substance abuse disorders in clinical practice.* Littleton, MA: John Wright.

U.S. Department of Justice. (1973). *Methadone treatment manual* (pp. 1-6). Washington, DC: Government Printing Office.

Viamontes, J. A. (1972). Review of drug effectiveness in the treatment of alcoholism. *American Journal of Psychiatry, 128,* 1570-1571.

Walsh, P. J. F. (1961). Korsakov's psychosis precipitated by convulsive seizures in chronic alcoholics. *Journal of Mental Science, 108,* 560-563.

World Health Organization. (1975). *Evaluation of dependence liability and dependence potential of drugs. Report of a WHO scientific group* (Report Series No. 577, p. 25). Geneva, Switzerland: Author.

Chapter 15

INDIVIDUAL TREATMENT
APPROACHES

A wide range of therapeutic techniques has been used in the treatment of drug abuse. In general, the conditions under which one approach might prove to be more effective than another are still unclear. Several authors have discussed various approaches to treatments, such as behavior therapy (Lesser, 1976; Ulmer, 1977), reality therapy (Schuster, 1978-1979), autogenic training (Roszell & Chaney, 1982), and the role of counseling in general (Weiner, 1975; Weiner & Schut, 1975). Although a thorough review of all the individual approaches to substance-abuse treatment is beyond the scope of this book, an attempt will be made to review some of the better-documented interventions.

Psychotherapy

This treatment is an analytically oriented, focal psychotherapy modeled after that described by Malan (1963) and Sifneos (1972) and after a form of therapy used for many years at the Menninger Foundation (Wallerstein, Robbins, Sargent, et al., 1956). The two main techniques are supportive and expressive. The expressive ones aim to help the client identify and work through problematic relationship themes. The therapist identifies these (transference) themes via the relationship with the client and via parallels with what the client says about other important relationships, such as those with his/her parents, spouse, or other family members. Special attention is paid to the meanings the client attaches to the drug dependence.

The usefulness and advantages of individual psychotherapy with substance abusers have been documented in two studies (Woody, Luborsky, McLellan et al., 1983; Woody et al, 1984). These studies and a number of clinical reports (Khantzian, 1978, 1982; Wurmser, 1984) suggest that the type and degree of psychopathology associated with substance abuse can be identified, that suitable subjects may be effectively dealt with in a psychotherapeutic relationship, and that the addition of this modality is more efficacious than drug counseling alone. However, individual psychotherapy for substance abusers should be broadly defined to include all those interventions and roles a therapist must play in assuring that a substance abuser's physical and psychological needs are understood and managed.

The initial multiple roles that the therapist must play with substance abusers may be likened to the functions a primary-care physician assumes. Accordingly, in this aspect of our work the intervening clinician may be conceived of as a primary-care therapist whose aggregate roles and responsibilities for care accrue to what is psychotherapeutic (Khantzian, 1985). In this respect it is essential in early phases of treatment that a therapist be concerned and involved with the vitally important matters of safety, stabilization, and control. Carefully obtaining a drug history, including the amounts and patterns of drug(s) used and the empathic exploration of the drug effects sought and experienced, can contribute significantly to a strong treatment alliance with the client. Identifying and modifying external/environmental precipitants and aggravants, especially within the family, that predispose and worsen the substance abuse can also help to instill added stability and further strengthen the treatment relationship. Also, it is important for the therapist to involve himself or herself early and to follow through with decisions about and support for confinement, detoxification, involvement with Alcoholics Anonymous (AA) and/or Narcotics Anonymous (NA), and pharmacological treatment modalities.

In addition to mediating and facilitating other interventions, a major area of attention in early phases of treatment should be to monitor the client's capacity to benefit from individual psychotherapy and to tolerate and endure exposure to groups. In the case of some clients, the therapist can play an important role in helping to overcome their fears and resistance to AA and NA, thereby providing crucial added safety and support that are essential. In other instances the therapist may determine that coexistent psychopathology and other symptomatic or characterologic difficulties make referral to self-help and/or traditional group treatment undesirable, but that other treatment alternatives are acceptable and indicated.

As stabilization is achieved, one can begin to ascertain the capacity to develop a more traditional psychotherapeutic relationship. However, this may involve a protracted period of months to years as a person makes the internal psychological and external adjustments involved in establishing a drug-free life. Furthermore, substance abusers' difficulties with affect recognition and modulation often require increased therapist activity, initially and subsequently in helping them to label and tolerate their feelings.

It is frequently maintained that addicts and alcoholics are poorly motivated, lack insight, and develop destructive and unworkable psychotherapeutic relationships (i.e., negative transference/countertransference reactions). However, these characterizations may be more the result of excessive passivity and neutrality on the part of therapists, and an outmoded model of therapy that rests on uncovering techniques alone. More contemporary psychotherapeutic approaches appreciate the importance of structure, activity, warmth, flexibility, and empathy in helping these clients to identify and better manage their difficulties in the context of a caring relationship. Once stability has been well established and allowances made for the vulnerabilities unique to substance abusers, then the vicissitudes and complications of psychotherapy are not too different from those encountered when treating patients with character pathology and other severe neurotic and affective disturbances (Khantzian 1980, 1982).

Silber (1970), in a series of papers on the modified psychoanalytical approach to the treatment of alcoholism, indicated some success with uncovering techniques along with the therapist's "lending the alcoholic some of his or her own ego." In Silber's view, alcoholism is a symptom of underlying psychological conflict and can be modified by analyzing the transference and developmental conflicts of the alcoholic clients.

Other authors support a more direct intervention with substance abusers (Fox, 1958; Tiebout, 1962). In this approach, it is necessary to stop the drinking before psychotherapy can proceed. The client is confronted with the fact that he or she is an alcoholic (substance abuser) and is provided with the evidence supporting the diagnosis. Clients are told that the drinking/drugging must be removed before any effective therapy can be utilized to help them maintain sobriety in the face of their psychological and other problems. A contract based on this goal is initially established.

The major requirement in this interventionist approach to individual psychotherapy is to eliminate the use of substances initially, as indicated. However, directive psychotherapy by its very nature requires intervention in other aspects of the substance abuser's life during the early stages of recovery. The art of psychotherapy with substance abusers is learning what aspects of the client's life and defense mechanisms need intervention, at what point in time, and how the intervention should be accomplished. In addition, it is important that one recognizes that there are many aspects of the substance abuser's life and defense mechanisms that should not be interpreted or intervened against; rather, they should be redirected or left alone. Such processes of intervention or nonintervention should be based on a complete understanding of the client's current life situation, family, developmental, and drinking/drugging history and personality makeup. The closeness achieved in individual psychotherapy and the therapeutic alliance can facilitate this intricate knowledge of the client's needs, conflicts, and defenses and can make interventions much more successful.

Wallace (1978) described the preferred defense structure and personality characteristics of the alcoholic as follows: denial, projection, all-or-nothing thinking, conflict minimization and avoidance, rationalization, self-centered selective attention, preference for nonanalytic modes of thinking and perceiving, passivity versus assertion, and obsessional focusing. Wallace described these defense mechanisms and characteristics in detail and indicated that the therapist should selectively reinforce and encourage these defenses in the service of the goal of abstinence. The therapist should not explore, confront, or interpret these defenses early in the therapeutic process, but rather should redirect them, much as the reactive grandiosity is sublimated by AA members. Therefore, considerable skill and experience is needed in the psychotherapy of substance abusers, based on knowledge of the underlying psychological conflicts and needs of the substance abuser, the particular client's situation at a particular point in time, and the client's stage of recovery.

Cognitive Behavioral Interventions

Relaxation/Biofeedback Training

Over the past 2 decades, a variety of techniques subsumable under the broad label of "relaxation training" have been used to treat an exceedingly diverse array of clinical problems, including substance abuse (Hillenberg & Collins, 1982; King, 1980). Despite their popularity, however, the empirical efficacy of these techniques, and in particular their long-term efficacy, remains equivocal. Nevertheless, clinical applications of relaxation training have proliferated. The theoretical rationale underlying these applications has usually consisted of two assumptions: (a) that the problem behavior is caused or exacerbated by tension or anxiety, and (b) that relaxation training can effectively deal with the problem either by reducing anxiety or by increasing the individual's sense of perceived control in stressful situations.

A number of studies have reported that meditation is an effective means of reducing alcohol use in general. However, the subjects of these studies were not alcohol abusers, thus limiting the generalizability of any conclusions regarding the utility of meditation as a treatment (Benson & Wallace, 1972; Monahan, 1977; Shafii, Lavely, & Jaffee, 1975; Winquist, 1977). Longitudinal studies by Lazar, Farwell, and Farrow (1977) and by Katz (1977) again reported meditation to be effective in reducing alcohol use.

The data from somewhat more systematic studies, largely focusing on the effect of muscular relaxation on alcohol abuse (rather than mere use) have been inconclusive. Steffen (1975), in an inpatient study, found that electromyographical (EMG), biofeedback-assisted muscular relaxation was effective relative to a placebo condition in reducing both anxiety and blood alcohol level (although not the number of drinks ordered) in four alcoholics given access to alcohol in their rooms and in a simulated bar. Strickler, Tomaszewski, Maxwell, and Suib (1979) reported that following relaxation instruction for heavy social drinkers, there was a reduction in anxiety and a concomitant reduction in both drinking rate and amount in an experimental stress situation relative to a no-treatment control. Olson, Ganley, Devine, and Dorsey (1981) compared a "behavioral package" of covert sensitization plus progressive relaxation to transactional analysis and to a "milieu therapy" control treatment with chronic alcoholics. The behavioral package produced lower drinking and higher abstinence rates than did transactional analysis up to 18 months after treatment but not afterwards (up to 4 years), and it never differed from the control "milieu" therapy at any point. Moreover, because all subjects received milieu therapy in addition to any other treatment, the milieu treatment could well account for the initial positive changes shown by the behavioral-treatment group.

Other studies have found relaxation training to have little effect on alcohol use (Jacobson & Silverskiold, 1973; Marlatt & Marques, 1977; Wong, Brochin, & Gendron, 1981; Zuroff & Schwarz, 1978).

In summary, the evidence regarding the utility of relaxation as a treatment for alcohol abuse is equivocal.

The available evidence on the treatment of drug abuse with relaxation techniques is sparse and follows a pattern similar to the alcohol abuse literature. The series of studies discussed above, on the effects of meditation on alcohol use, also reported decreased use of other drugs (e.g., marijuana, tobacco, narcotics, tranquilizers, etc.). However, the subjects were not classified as drug abusers. A study by Brautigam (1977) evaluated the efficacy of meditation as a treatment for drug addiction using random assignment to meditation and control (group counseling) conditions, and found that the meditators decreased their use of both "soft" and "hard" drugs in the 3 months following the initiation of meditation while the controls' drug use remained at a high level. However, the short length of the follow-up period and discontinuation of meditation by 4 of the 10 experimental subjects again weakens the positive results, especially because the author reported that in the 2-year period after the study periodic relapse to drug use occurred for 80% of the meditators. It is therefore impossible, on the basis of the existing literature, to formulate any conclusions regarding the efficacy of relaxation training as a treatment for drug abuse.

Assertiveness/Social Skills Training

Researchers have given drug or alcohol abusers assertiveness/social skills training with the notion that deficits in these skills may predispose drug use or make readjustment to a drug-free environment difficult.

The studies reviewed, whether single-case, multicase, or groups, are uniform in their finding that alcohol- and drug-abuse clients can learn increased assertiveness. The link between increased assertiveness and decreased alcohol/drug use is less well established. Two controlled studies have positively correlated assertiveness/problem solving-training with decreased substance use. Chaney, O'Leary, and Marlatt (1978) found that randomly assigned alcoholics given assertiveness/problem-solving training had better outcomes at 1-year follow-up (fewer days drunk, less total alcohol consumption, shorter length of drinking episodes) than subjects in discussion or no-additional treatment groups. Ferrell and Galassi (1981) reported that assertiveness training produced better sobriety outcomes at 2-year follow-up than "human relations" training. Though these data are encouraging, the value of assertiveness training in decreasing drug/alcohol use requires testing in more controlled studies before firm conclusions about its effectiveness can be drawn.

Behavioral Interventions

Techniques Employing Aversive Stimuli

Of all the behavioral interventions for substance abuse, aversive techniques have the longest and most extensive history. In these techniques, aversive stimuli (such as shock or nausea) are contingently paired either with drug-related conditional stimuli (classical aversive conditioning) or with drug-related behaviors (operant punishment). Though theoretically these two paradigms are distinguished by the presence of a stimulus contingency (classical aversive conditioning) or a response contingency (operant punishment), in classical practice these distinctions have blurred considerably. The aversive agent is often necessarily paired with both stimulus and behavior aspects of the drug preparation/ingestion or injection ritual, whether the researcher/clinician realizes it or not. For this reason we review the aversive techniques together, noting procedural distinctions when they occur.

Use of Chemical and Electrical Stimuli in Alcohol and Drug Abuse

More than 40 years ago researchers (Lemere & Voegtlin, 1950; Thimann, 1949; Voegtlin & Lemere, 1942) reported on the clinical outcome of alcoholic patients treated by pairing emetine-induced nausea with several ingestions of the patient's preferred alcoholic beverages. The goal of treatment was to produce a classically conditioned aversion to alcohol that would help the patient curb his or her drinking. The reported outcomes of these studies were impressive: abstinence rates in the 50% to 60% range at 1-year follow-up.

Unfortunately, the lack of control groups in all of these studies makes interpretation of the positive results ambiguous. They might have occurred as a result of (a) the other supportive treatments given at each facility, or (b) the self-selected type of alcoholic patient who was functioning well enough to undergo the very aversive procedures (Neuberger, Matarazzo, Schmitz, & Pratt, 1980), or both. In addition, the studies relied almost totally on self-report as a measure of abstinence, and none of the studies had independent measures of whether the presumed conditioned aversion to alcohol in fact developed as a result of the procedures.

Until 1979 there was no clear demonstration that (a) a conditioned aversion to alcohol could be established, or (b) that, if established it could contribute to a positive clinical outcome. More recent studies provide physiological and subjective evidence of a conditioned aversion to alcohol using emetine plus syrup of ipecac as the nauseating agent (Baker & Cannon, 1979) and using lithium carbonate as the emetic agent (Boland, Mellor, & Revusky, 1978). Though both the Baker and Boland data report smaller effects on abstinence than the earlier uncontrolled clinical studies, their findings probably more accurately represent the actual impact of the aversive conditioning: modest results, but statistically significant, reproducible, and possibly useful as part of a treatment package for highly motivated clients.

Criticism over the uncontrolled parameters in emetine conditioning (Rachman, 1965) led to the use of electrical shock in aversive conditioning paradigms. However, the results of aversive conditioning with electric shock are even less encouraging than the results with chemical stimuli. Although early studies announced positive results, the interpretation of these results is unclear due to lack of appropriate controls (Blake, 1965) or equal outcomes between conditioning groups and pseudoconditioning controls (Vogler, Lunde, & Martin, 1977). Later studies have reported no evidence of a conditioned aversion to alcohol using shock as the aversive stimulus. Other research groups have shown that patients receiving electrical aversive conditioning did not reduce alcohol consumption compared to those receiving group therapy (McCance & McCance, 1969), to other control groups (Miller, Hersen, Eisler, & Hemphill, 1973), or to their own preconditioning baseline (Wilson, Leaf, & Natan, 1976).

There have been no studies using chemical or electrical stimuli with drug abusers that have demonstrated physiological evidence of a conditioned aversion. Though some of the reported treatment results are positive, they are largely uninterpretable due to the reliance upon single case reports (Boudin, 1972; Lesser, 1976; Lubetkin & Fishman, 1974; O'Brien, Raynes, & Patch, 1972; Spevack, Pihl, & Rowan, 1973; Wolpe, 1965) and the complete absence of appropriately controlled group studies (Lieberman, 1969; Raymond, 1964; Thompson & Rathod, 1968).

Use of Covert Aversive Stimuli in Alcohol and Drug Abuse

In covert sensitization (Cautela, 1967; Cautela & Rosenstiel, 1975) or verbal therapy (Anant, 1968), the client is asked to imagine strongly aversive stimuli (usually vomiting) in association with imaginal drug-related cues, scenes, and/or behavior. In practice, the distinction between "operant" and "classical" covert procedures is quite blurred, because the "stimuli" and "response" in the treatment situation occur at the level of imagination.

Though several case reports suggest that covert aversive techniques could be effective in the treatment of alcohol/drug abuse, others have found them ineffective, and their utility has not yet been established in controlled group studies.

Additional evidence (Elkins, 1975, 1980) suggests both (a) that conditioned nausea can occur to imagined drinking scenes, and (b) that subjects who develop conditioned nausea (about 69% of those treated) maintain significant periods of abstinence posttreatment.

There have been no controlled studies on the use of covert aversive techniques in the treatment of drug abusers. In single-subject studies using covert aversion, several investigators report positive outcomes, with drug-free periods (by self-report) extending up to 18 months (Anant, 1968; Kolvin, 1967; Palakow, 1975; Wisocki, 1973). Other investigators have had disappointing results (Droppa, 1978), finding that covert aversive stimuli required chemical (Maletzky, 1974) or hypnotic (Copeman, 1977) enhancement to be effective.

Contingency Management

In situations where the client's therapist, family, spouse, or employer has control of significant reinforcers/punishers, response contingencies may be set up that encourage control of drug or alcohol use. In some instances, contingencies may also be used to shape adaptive, prosocial behaviors that facilitate client management and/or re-entry into society.

In single- or multicase studies with alcoholics, therapists have used spouse contracts (Miller, 1972), direct payments (Miller, Hersen, Eisler, & Watts, 1974), refundable security deposits (Bigelow, Strickler, Liebson, & Griffiths, 1976), "community reinforcers" (Azrin, 1976; Hunt & Azrin, 1973), or contingent access to other potent reinforcers, such as methadone (Liebson, Bigelow, & Flame, 1973), to reinforce abstinence and/or compliance with disulfiram (Antabuse) treatment. All of these studies reported reduced drinking while the contingencies were in effect, with some studies finding additional positive impact on employment and arrests (Liebson, Tommasello, & Bigelow, 1978).

With opiate abuse clients, therapists have attempted to reduce illicit drug use with reinforcers such as direct monetary payments, methadone dose self-regulation, or take-home methadone, contingent upon drug-free (Hall et al., 1979; Milby et al., 1978) or opiate-free urines (Stitzer et al., 1980), or reduced benzodiazepine use (Stitzer, Bigelow, & Liebson, 1979). In general, these studies demonstrate that contingent reinforcers, especially take-home methadone, can produce change in the target behavior, though the change is sometimes small (Hall, 1979; Milby, Garret, English, Fritschi, & Clarke, 1978) and usually confined to the period during which the contingency is in effect (Stitzer et al., 1980).

In summary, both alcohol- and drug-abuse clients will respond to behavioral contingencies involving important reinforcers. That clients are, in fact, responding to the reinforcement contingencies is indicated by the relative ineffectiveness of contracts or contingencies without potent reinforcers (Beatty, 1978; Vannicelli, 1979) and by the frequent reversal of behavior to baseline levels when the contingencies are removed (Robichaud, Strickler, Bigelow, & Liebson, 1979; Stitzer, Bigelow, & Liebson, 1980). This reversibility poses no particular problem in structured settings where management is the goal and where powerful reinforcement contingencies may be easily maintained by the treating agent, but it does raise questions about the usefulness of these techniques for producing long-term change that will generalize to the "real world," where the contingencies may be different or absent. If significant "real world" reinforcers can be controlled (through contract or agreement), the results can be positive. Miller (1975) found that even skid row alcoholics could increase control over their drinking when community services were made contingent upon relative sobriety.

Extinction and Desensitization

Extinction (classical). Stimulus cues paired either with actual pharmacological withdrawal or with drug-compensatory states produced by drug administration may become classically conditioned stimuli capable of eliciting withdrawal-like symptoms and drug craving. Opiate abuse patients viewing drug-related slides or videotapes (Sideroff & Jarvik, 1980; Teasdale, 1973) or handling drug-related objects (Ternes, O'Brien, Grabowski, Wellerstein, & Jordan-Hayes, 1979) experience subjective craving and withdrawal-like changes in physiological measures. Alcoholics also report increased craving when exposed to environmental stimuli associated with alcohol ingestion (Ludwig, Wilker, & Stark, 1974; Mathew, Claghorn, & Largen, 1979).

Because craving and withdrawal may predispose drug/alcohol use, some researchers have attempted to extinguish these conditioned responses by presenting drug-related stimuli in the absence of drug effects. Though the procedure is conceptually simple, in practice it is quite a bit more difficult, given the numerous cues (environmental, sensory, and proprioceptive) that may have become conditioned stimuli for craving. With alcoholics, Blakey and Baker (1980) first compiled an individualized history of stimuli that triggered craving/alcohol ingestion. Extinction was carried out by systematically exposing patients to the "trigger" stimuli without allowing drinking. Five or six patients reported decreased desire over the course of the extinction and maintained the craving/withdrawal elicited from a single drink of alcohol by being given repeated exposures to alcohol cues (taste, smell, etc.) without following the cues with sufficient amounts of alcohol to produce a "high."

Extinction of psysiological and subjective craving in opiate abuse patients has also been attempted (O'Brien, Greenstein, Ternes, McLellan, & Grabowski, 1979). These clients were asked to perform double-blind cook-up and self-injection rituals in which the opiate administration was either omitted (saline trials) or pharmacologically blocked due to the antagonist treatment. Although this procedure was designed primarily to allow for classical extinction of environmental and proprioceptive stimuli that elicit craving, it also provided an opportunity for operant extinction of the nonreinforced self-injection behavior. Clients often found the initial self-injection trials mildly pleasurable, but this experience was soon replaced by strong dysphoria, withdrawal, and craving. The unreinforced self-injection procedure resulted in a high dropout rate, with no subject completing extinction of physiological and subjective responses. Nonetheless, there was some suggestion that subjects who completed more trials had somewhat better outcomes at 6-month follow-up than other non-extinction naltrexone subjects (O'Brien et al., 1979; see also Childress, McLellan, & O'Brien, 1983, 1984).

Desensitization. A few researchers have used systematic desensitization to reduce conditioned anxiety that might trigger drug/alcohol use. In this procedure, clients are usually first relaxed, then given repeated exposure to a graded hierarchy of anxiety-producing stimuli (real or imaginal). Though early theorists (Wolpe, 1958) believed prior relaxation was an essential part of the procedure, later reviewers (Emmelkamp, 1982) have found this not to be the case. Thus, desensitization is perhaps most simply viewed as a classical extinction paradigm.

In a series of case studies, Kraft used desensitization to treat various social anxieties presumed to underlie alcohol and drug abuse (Kraft, 1968, 1969). The outcome of these case studies was uniformly positive, with clients experiencing decreased anxiety and decreased alcohol/drug use. Follow-up, however, was relatively minimal and dependent upon self-report. The impact of desensitization in other case studies is difficult to assess given similar lack of controls and the use of multiple treatment interventions (O'Brien et al., 1972; Spevack et al., 1973) or the lack of drug use outcome data (Paynard & Wolf, 1974). The only group using systematic desensitization found that it marginally, but not significantly, enhanced self-reported alcohol abstinence (Lanyon, Primo, Terrell, & Werner, 1972).

In summary, there is recent suggestive evidence (a) that conditioned craving/withdrawal can be extinguished by repeated nonreinforced exposure to alcohol- or drug-related cues, and (b) that the extinction may have a positive impact on subsequent use/relapse, though promising extinction techniques have not been widely used, and their utility needs to be more fully explored in well-controlled treatment outcome studies (e.g. Childress, McLellan, & O'Brien, 1983, 1984). Case studies report that reduction in anxiety through systematic desensitization (extinction) may have a positive effect on drug/alcohol use, but these techniques have not been adequately studied with controlled group designs.

Anxiety and other dysphoric states can become powerful conditioned stimuli that elicit drug/alcohol craving (Ludwig & Stark, 1974; Mathew et al., 1979; Paulos, Hinson, & Siegal, 1981). One ready implication of this finding is that desensitization or other techniques that reduce anxiety could help control the drug use. A second, more subtle, implication is that anxiety (or other emotional states) may have become such an integral part of the stimulus complex that elicits craving that extinction techniques that focus exclusively upon drug-related stimuli may be effective only under the emotional state in which the extinction takes place. It remains to be seen whether extinction effects can generalize across the various mood states thought to play an important part in drug use (i.e., anger, depression, anxiety, etc.). Optimal effects might be achieved by conducting extinction with drug-related stimuli while the client is in the mood states that may form part of a "compound" conditioned stimulus for craving/withdrawal.

Herbal Therapy and Nutrition

In the past 10 years, many holistic alternatives have begun to be applied in the treatment of substance abusers (Nebelkopf, 1981a). These alternatives include herbs (Nebelkopf, 1981b), acupuncture (Wen & Cheung, 1973), nutrition (Williams, 1981), bodywork (Acampora & Nebelkopf, 1983), and a variety of other innovative methods. In these programs nutrition, relaxation, stress reduction, and physical exercise are important in the overall treatment plan (Nebelkopf, 1981c).

The relation of nutrition and substance abuse has been explored in several places (Free & Sanders, 1979; Land, 1985; Nebelkopf, 1981b; Pawlak, 1974; Saifer & Zellerback, 1984; Smith, 1979; Weiner, 1983; Williams, 1981; Worden & Rosellini, 1979).

Drug addicts and alcoholics are notorious for their poor diets, and drugs such as heroin, methadone, tobacco, coffee, and alcohol deplete the body's store of essential vitamins and minerals. Drugs may produce dietary deficiencies by destroying nutrients, preventing their absorption, or increasing their excretion (Worden & Rosellini, 1979).

Unfortunately, sugar products are the staple ingredients in the diet of many addicts. M. O. Smith (1979) suggested that the abnormally high rate of sugar consumption by narcotic addicts is due to several factors, including (a) intestinal spasms caused by narcotics, which make digestion and absorption of more complex foods difficult; (b) a strain on the liver caused by injected toxins, leading to reduced food assimilation and glycogen storage function; and (c) the addictive component of hypoglycemia, which stems from the "sugar-overreactive insulin-more sugar" cycle.

The condition of hypoglycemia is very common among drug abusers and alcoholics. In order to combat this condition, Airola (1974) recommends six to eight small meals a day with whole grains, seeds, nuts, and fresh vegetables forming the basis of a diet. All refined and processed foods, including white sugar, white flour, pastries, cookies, ice cream, candy, coffee, doughnuts, soft drinks, and salt, should be given up.

The prevention and treatment of alcoholism through nutrition has been a focus of Williams (1981), who recommends several vitamin and mineral formulas and the amino acid glutamine for alcoholics. Alcoholism is seen as a metabolic disease in that it changes the body's biochemistry. Eating high-quality foods, avoiding low-quality foods, doing exercises to promote internal nutrition, using nutritional supplements, cultivating moderation and inner peace, and using glutamine as a supplement are suggested as means of preventing trouble with alcohol.

Hoffer (1982), a pioneer in the field of orthomolecular psychiatry, believes that alcoholism and drug addiction respond to orthomolecular medicine. High doses of niacin have been used successfully with schizophrenics and are recommended for addicts (Pawlak, 1974). Libby and Stone (1977) and Free and Sanders (1979) report that high doses of vitamin C are effective in opiate detoxification.

Land (1985) discusses the principle of high-level or optimal recovery through holistic nutrition. The relationship of nutrition to chemical dependence needs to incorporate concepts of food allergies (food addictions), the link between eating disorders and drinking disorders, drinking to relieve symptoms of poor nutrition, unusually high nutritional needs that if unmet contribute to psychological and behavioral disorders, and psychosocial causes of substance abuse linked to nutrition and biochemical individuality. Many alcoholics in early recovery experience functional hypoglycemia, and this can be treated through diet. The identification of food allergies, food addictions, and hypersensitivities is important, for these can trigger symptoms that lead to a desire to drink. Land recommends that whole foods would be added to the diet and processed foods eliminated, that alternative sweeteners such as honey should be substituted for sugar, that whole grains should be used instead of white flour, and that herb teas be used instead of coffee.

Weiner (1983) describes a step-by-step program of nutrition and exercise for getting off cocaine, utilizing a variety of multivitamin and mineral formulas as well as several amino acid supplements, including glutamine, phenylalanine, and tyrosine to provide energy during the "down" phase of cocaine detoxification. Passion flower herb is used as a tranquilizer and gotu kola is used as a sedative, diuretic, and tonic.

According to Dr. Halfdan Mahler (1977), director-general of the World Health Organization:

> Modern medicine has a great deal to learn from the collector of herbs. Many of the plants familiar to the wise woman really do have the healing powers that tradition attaches to them. And already, a number of Ministries of Health, in the developing countries especially, are carefully analyzing the potions and decoction used by traditional healers to determine whether their active ingredients have healing powers that science has overlooked. Whatever the outcome of such scientific testing, there is no doubt that the judicious use of such herbs, flowers and other plants for palliative purposes in primary health care can make a major contribution towards reducing a developing country's drug bill. (p. 1)

Farnsworth (1985) studied 119 drugs obtained from plant sources and found a .74 correlation between the traditional uses of the plant and the therapeutic use of the plant-derived drug. He concluded that a fairly high percentage of useful plant-derived drugs were discovered as a result of scientific follow-up of well-known plants used in traditional medicine.

Research efforts like those proposed by Mahler (1977) and carried out by Farnsworth (1985) are needed scientifically to demonstrate the efficacy of a wide variety of herbs. Once this is established, specific research on which herbs are most effective in the detoxification from different drugs should prove most useful. It also appears that detoxification from drugs is not the most difficult variable in dealing with the drug problem. It is "staying clean" that is hardest. Relapse prevention is an area that needs further research. The establishment of an alternative life-style in which herbs and whole foods play a significant part may help to prevent disease and increase longevity. This is another potential area for further research. The acceptance of herbs as effective natural healers by drug program professionals and paraprofessionals, the medical establishment, and the general public is leading to a greater understanding of the nature of health and is having an impact on the drug problems the world faces today.

References

Acampora, A., & Nebelkopf, E. (1983). The methadone-to-abstinence program at Walden House. In *Proceedings of the 6th World Conference of Therapeutic Communities*. Manila, Philipines: Drug Abuse Research.

Airola, P. (1974). *How to get well*. Phoenix: Health Plus Books.

Anant, S. S. (1968). Treatment of alcoholics and drug addicts by verbal conditioning techniques. *International Journal of the Addictions, 3*, 381-388.

Azrin, N. H. (1976). Improvements in the community-reinforcement approach to alcoholism. *Behavior Research and Therapy, 14*, 339-348.

Baker, T. C., & Cannon, D. S. (1979). Taste aversion therapy with alcoholics: Techniques and evidence of a conditioned response. *Behavior Research and Therapy, 17*, 229-242.

Beatty, D. B. (1978). Contingency contracting with heroin addicts. *International Journal of the Addictions, 13*, 509-527.

Benson, H., & Wallace, R. K. (1972). Decreased drug use with transcendental meditation: A study of 1,862 subjects. In S. J. D. Zarafonetis (Ed.), *Drug abuse: Proceedings of the international conference* (pp. 369-376). Philadelphia, PA: Lea & Febiger.

Bigelow, G., Strickler, D., Liebson, I., & Griffiths, R. (1976). Maintaining disulfiram ingestion among outpatient alcoholics: A security-deposit contingency contracting procedure. *Behavior Research and Therapy, 14*, 378-381.

Blake, G. B. (1965). The application of behavior therapy to the treatment of alcoholism. *Behavior Research and Therapy, 3*, 75-85.

Blakey, R., & Baker, R. (1980). An exposure approach to alcohol abuse. *Behavior Research and Therapy, 1*, 319-325.

Boland, F. J., Mellor, C. S., & Revusky, S. (1978). Chemical aversion treatment of alcholism: Lithium as the aversive agent. *Behavior Research and Therapy, 6*, 401-409.

Boudin, H. M. (1972). Contingency contracting as a therapeutic tool in the deceleration of amphetamine use. *Behavior Research and Therapy, 3*, 604-608.

Brautigam, E. (1977). Effects of the transcendental meditation program on drug abusers: A prospective study. In D. W. Orme-Johnson & J. T. Farrow (Eds.), *Scientific research on the transcendental meditation program: Collected papers* (Vol. 1, pp. 506-514). Livingston Manor, NY: MIU Press.

Cautela, J. R. (1967). Covert sensitization. *Psychological Reprints, 20*, 459-486.

Cautela, J. R., & Rosenstiel, A. K. (1975). The use of covert conditioning in the treatment of drug abuse. *International Journal of the Addictions, 10*, 227-303.

Chaney, E. F., O'Leary, M., & Marlatt, G. A. (1978). Skill training with alcoholics. *Journal of Consulting and Clinical Psychology, 46*, 1092-1104.

Childress, A. R., McLellan, A. T., & O'Brien, D. P. (1983). Measurement and extinction of conditioned withdrawal-like responses in opiate-dependent patients. In *Proceedings of the 45th annual meeting of the Committee on Problems of Drug Dependence* (pp. 212-219). Rockville, MD: National Institute on Drug Abuse.

Childress, A. R., McLellan, A. T., & O'Brien, D. P. (1984). Assessment and extinction of conditioned withdrawal-like responses in an integrated treatment for opiate dependence. In *Proceedings of the 46th annual Meeting of the Committee on Problems of Drug Dependence*, St. Louis, MO.

Copeman, C. D. (1977). Treatment of polydrug abuse by covert sensitization: Some contraindications. *International Journal of the Addictions, 12*, 17-23.

Droppa, D. C. (1978). The application of covert conditioning procedures to the outpatient treatment of drug addicts: Four case studies. *International Journal of the Addictions, 13*, 657-673.

Elkins, R. L. (1975). Aversion therapy for alcoholism: Chemical, electrical, or verbal imagery. *International Journal of the Addictions, 10,* 157-209.

Elkins, R. L. (1980). Covert sensitization treatment of alcoholism: Contribution of successful conditioning to subsequent abstinence maintenance. *Addictive Behavior, 5,* 67-89.

Emmelkamp, P. M. G. (1982). Anxiety and fear. In A. Bellack, M. Herson, & A. Kazdin (Eds.), *International handbook of behavior modification and therapy* (pp. 349-395). New York: Plenum.

Farnsworth, N. (1985). Medical plants in therapy. *Bulletin of the World Health Organization, 63*(6).

Ferrell, W. L., & Galassi, J. P. (1981). Assertion training and human relations training in the treatment of chronic alcoholics. *International Journal of the Addictions, 16*(3), 959-968.

Fox, R. (1958). Antabuse as an adjunct to psychotherapy in alcoholism. *New York State Journal of Medicine, 58,* 1540-1544.

Free, V., & Sanders, P. (1979). The use of ascorbic acid and mineral supplements in the detoxification of narcotic addicts. *Journal of Psychedelic Drugs, 11*(3), 217-222.

Hillenberg, J. B., & Collins, F. L. (1982). A procedural analysis and review of relaxation training research. *Behaviour Research and Therapy, 20,* 251-260.

Hoffer, A. (1982). Nutritional therapy. In L. Hippchen (Ed.), *Holistic approaches to offender rehabilitation* (pp. 207-236). Springfield, IL: Charles C Thomas.

Hunt, G. M., & Azrin, N. H. (1973). A community reinforcement approach to alcoholism. *Behavioral Research and Therapy, 11,* 91-104.

Jacobson, D. D., & Silverskiold, N. P. (1973). A controlled study of hypnotic method in the treatment of alcoholism, with evaluation by objective criteria. *British Journal of Addiction, 68,* 25-31.

Katz, D. (1977). Decreased drug use and prevention of drug use through the transcendental meditation program. In D. W. Orme-Johnson & J. T. Farrow (Eds.), *Scientific research on the transcendental meditation program: Collected papers* (pp. 536-543). Livingston Manor, NY: MIU Press.

Khantzian, E. J. (1978). The ego, the self and opiate addiction: Theoretical and treatment considerations. *International Review of Psychoanalysis, 5,* 189-198.

Khantzian, E. J. (1980). The alcoholic patient: An overview and perspective. *American Journal of Psychotherapy, 34,* 4-19.

Khantzian, E. J. (1982). Some treatment implications of the ego and self disturbances in alcoholism. In M. H. Bean and N. E. Zinberg (Eds.), *Dynamic approaches to the understanding and treatment of alcoholism* (pp. 163-188). New York: Free Press.

Khantzian, E. J. (1985). Psychotherapeutic interventions with substance abusers: The clinical context. *Journal of Substance Abuse Treatment, 2,* 83-88.

King, N. J. (1980). The therapeutic utility of abbreviated progressive relaxation: A critical review of implications for clinical practice. In M. Hersen, R. M. Eisler, & P. M. Miller (Eds.), *Progress in behavior modification* (Vol. 10). New York: Academic Press.

Kolvin, T. (1967). "Aversive imagery" treatment in adolescents. *Behavior Research and Therapy, 5,* 245-248.

Kraft, T. (1968). Successful treatment of a case of drinamyl addiction. *British Journal of Psychiatry, 114,* 1363-1364.

Kraft, T. (1969). Successful treatment of a case of barbiturate addiction. *British Journal of the Addictions, 64,* 115-120.

Land, D. R. (1985). *Eat right!* Minneapolis, MN: Hazledon.

Lanyon, R. I., Primo, R. V., Terrell, F., & Werner, A. (1972). An aversion-desensitization treatment for alcoholism. *Journal of Consulting and Clinical Psychology, 38,* 394-398./

Lazar, Z., Farwell, F., & Farrow, J. T. (1977). The effects of the transcendental meditation program on anxiety, drug abuse, cigarette smoking, and alcohol consumption. In D. W. Orme-Johnson

& J. T. Farrow (Eds.), *Scientific research on the transcendental meditation program: Collected papers* (pp. 524-535). Livingston Manor, NY: MIU Press.

Lemere, F., & Voegtlin, W. L. (1950). An evaluation of the aversion treatment of alcholism. *Quarterly Journal of Studies on Alcohol, 11,* 199-204.

Lesser, E. (1976). Behavior therapy with a narcotics user: A case report: Ten-year follow-up. *Behavior Research and Therapy, 14*(5), 381.

Libby, A., & Stone, I. (1977). The hypoascorbemia-kwashkiorkor approach to drug addiction therapy: A pilot study. *Journal of Orthomolecular Psychiatry, 6*(4), 300-308.

Lieberman, R. (1969). Aversive conditioning of drug addicts: A pilot study. *Behavior Research and Therapy, 6,* 229-231.

Liebson, I., Bigelow, G., & Flame, R. (1973). Alcoholism among methadone patients: A specific treatment method. *American Journal of Psychiatry, 130,* 483-485.

Liebson, I., Tommasello, A., & Bigelow, G. (1978). A behavioral treatment of alcoholic methadone patients. *Annals of International Medicine, 39,* 342-344.

Lubetkin, B. S., & Fishman, S. T. (1974). Electrical aversion therapy with a chronic heroin user. *Journal of Behavior Therapy and Experimental Psychiatry, 5,* 193-195.

Ludwig, A. M., & Stark, L. H. (1974). Alcohol craving: Subjective and situational aspects. *Quarterly Journal of the Study of Alcohol, 35,* 899-905.

Ludwig, A. M., Wilker, A., & Stark, L. H. (1974). The first drink: Psychobiological aspects of craving. *Archives of General Psychiatry, 30,* 539-547.

Mahler, H. (1977). The staff of Aesculapius. *World Health.*

Malan, D. (1963). *A study of brief psychotherapy.* Philadelphia: J. B. Lippincott.

Maletzky, B. M. (1974). Assisted covert sensitization for drug abuse. *International Journal of the Addictions, 9,* 411-429.

Marlatt, G. A., & Marques, J. K. (1977). Meditation, self-control and alcohol use. In R. B. Stuart (Ed.), *Behavioural self-management: Strategies, techniques and outcomes.* New York: Brunner/Mazel.

Mathew, R. J., Claghorn, J. L., & Largen, J. (1979). Craving for alcohol in sober alcholics. *American Journal of Psychiatry, 136,* 603-606.

McCance, C., & McCance, P. F. (1969). Alcoholism in northeast Scotland: Its treatment and outcome. *British Journal of Psychiatry, 115,* 189-198.

Milby, G. L., Garret, C., English, C., Fritschi, O., & Clarke, C. (1978). Take-home methadone: Contingency effects on drug-seeking and productivity of narcotic addicts. *Addictive Behavior, 3,* 315-320.

Miller, P. M. (1972). The use of behavioral contracting in the treatment of alcoholism: A case report. *Behavior Therapy, 3,* 593-596.

Miller, P. M. (1975). A behavioral intervention program for chronic public drunkenness offenders. *Archives of General Psychiatry, 32,* 915-918.

Miller, P. M., Hersen, M., Eisler, R. M., & Hemphill, D. P. (1973). Electrical aversion therapy with alcoholics: An analogue study. *Behavior Research and Therapy, 11,* 491-497.

Miller, P. M., Hersen, M., Eisler, R. M., & Watts, J. G. (1974). Contingent reinforcement of lowered blood/alcohol levels in an outpatient chronic alcoholic. *Behavior Research and Therapy, 12,* 261-263.

Monahan, R. J. (1977). Secondary prevention of drug dependence through the transcendental meditation program in metropolitan Philadelphia. *International Journal of the Addictions, 12,* 629-784.

Nebelkopf, E. (1981a). Drug abuse treatment: A holistic approach. *Journal of Holistic Health, 6.*

Nebelkopf, E. (1981b). *The herbal connection.* Orem, UT: BiWorld Press.

Nebelkopf, E. (1981c). Holistic programs for the drug addict and alcoholic. *Journal of Psychoactive Drugs, 13*(4), 345-351.

Neuberger, O. W., Matarazzo, J. D., Schmitz, R. E., & Pratt, H. H. (1980). One year follow-up of total abstinence in chronic alcohoic patients following emetic counterconditioning. *Alcoholism, 4*(3), 306-312.

O'Brien, C. P., Greenstein, R., Ternes, J., McLellan, T., & Grabowski, J. (1979). Unreinforced self-injections: Effects of rituals and outcome in heroin addicts. In *Proceedings of the 41st Annual Meeting, Committee on Problems of Drug Dependence* (NIDA Research Monograph No. 27, pp. 275-281). Rockville, MD: National Institute on Drug Abuse.

O'Brien, J. S., Raynes, A. E., & Patch, V. D. (1972). Treatment of heroin addiction with aversion therapy, relaxation training and systematic desensitization. *Behavior Research and Therapy, 10*, 77-80.

Olson, R. P., Ganley, R., Devine, V. T., & Dorsey, G. C., Jr. (1981). Long-term effects of behavioral versus insight-oriented therapy with inpatient alcoholics. *Journal of Consulting and Clinical Psychology, 46*, 866-877.

Palakow, R. L. (1975). Covert sensitization treatment of a probationed barbiturate addict. *Journal of Behavior Therapy and Experimental Psychiatry, 6*, 53-54.

Paulos, C. X., Hinson, R. E., & Siegal, S. (1981). The role of Pavlovian process in drug tolerance and dependence: Implications for treatment. *Addictive Behavior, 6*, 205-211.

Pawlak, B. (1974). *Megavitamin therapy and the drug wipe-out syndrome.* Phoenix, AZ: Do It Now Foundation.

Paynard, D., & Wolf, K. (1974). The use of systematic desensitization in an outpatient drug treatment center. *Psychotherapy Theory, Research and Practice, 11*, 329-330.

Rachman, S. (1965). Aversion therapy: Chemical or electrical. *Behavior Research and Therapy, 2*, 289-300.

Raymond, M. (1964). The treatment of addiction by aversion conditioning with apomorphine. *Behavior Research and Therapy, 1*, 287-291.

Robichaud, C., Strickler, D., Bigelow, G., & Liebson, I. (1979). Disulfiram maintenance employee alcoholism treatment: A three-phase evaluation. *Behavior Research and Therapy, 17*, 618-621.

Roszell, D. K., & Chaney, E. F. (1982). Autogenic training in a drug abuse program. *International Journal of the Addictions, 17*(8), 1337-1350.

Saifer, P., & Zellerbach, M. (1984). *Detox.* Los Angeles, CA: Tarcher.

Schuster, R. (1978-1979). Evaluation of a reality therapy stratification system in a residential drug rehabilitation center. *Drug Forum, 7*(1), 59-67.

Shafii, M., Lavely, R., & Jaffee, R. (1975). Meditation and the prevention of alcohol abuse. *American Journal of Psychiatry, 132*, 242-245.

Sideroff, S., & Jarvic, M. E. (1980). Conditioned responses to a videotape showing heroin related stimuli. *International Journal of the Addictions, 15*, 529-536.

Sifneos, P. (1972). *Short-term psychotherapy and emotional crisis.* Cambridge, MA: Harvard University Press.

Silber, A. (1970). An addendum to the technique of psychotherapy with alcoholics. *Journal of Nervous and Mental Disease, 150*, 423-437.

Smith, M. O. (1979). Acupuncture and natural healing in drug detoxification. *American Journal of Acupuncture, 7*(April-June), 97-107.

Spevack, M., Pihl, R., & Rowan, T. (1973). Behavior therapies in the treatment of drug abuse: Some case studies. *Psychology Record, 23*, 179-184.

Steffen, J. J. (1975). Electromyographically induced relaxation in the treatment of chronic alcohol abuse. *Journal of Consulting and Clinical Psychology, 43*, 275.

Stitzer, M. L., Bigelow, G., & Liebson, I. (1979). Reducing benzodiazepine self-administration with contingent reinforcement. *Addictive Behavior, 4*, 245-252.

Stitzer, M. L., Bigelow, G. E., & Liebson, I. (1980). Reducing drug use among methadone maintenance clients: Contingent reinforcement for morphine-free urines. *Behaviors, 5,* 333-340.

Strickler, D. P., Tomaszewski, R., Maxwell, W. A., & Suib, M. B. (1979). The effects of relaxation instructions on drinking behavior in the presence of stress. *Behaviour Research and Therapy, 17,* 45-51.

Teasdale, J. D. (1973). Conditioned abstinence in narcotic addicts. *International Journal of the Addictions, 8,* 273-292.

Ternes, J., O'Brien, C. P., Grabowski, J., Wellerstein, H., & Jordan-Hayes, F. (1979). Conditioned drug responses to naturalistic stimuli. In *Proceedings of the 41st Annual Meeting, Committee on Problems of Drug Dependence* (NIDA Research Monograph No. 27, pp. 282-288). Rockville, MD: National Institute on Drug Abuse.

Thimann, J. (1949). Conditioned reflex treatment of alcoholism. *New England Journal of Medicine, 241,* 368-370, 408-410.

Thompson, I. G., & Rathod, N. H. (1968). Aversion therapy for heroin dependence. *Lancet, 31,* 382-384.

Tiebout, H. M. (1962). Intervention in psychotherapy. *American Journal of Psychoanalysis, 33,* 1-6.

Ulmer, R. A. (1977). Behavior therapy: A promising drug abuse treatment and research approach of choice. *International Journal of the Addictions, 12*(6), 777-784.

Vannicelli, M. (1979). Treatment contracts in an inpatient alcoholism setting. *Journal of Studies on Alcohol, 40,* 457-471.

Voegtlin, W. L., & Lemere, F. (1942). The treatment of alcohol addiction: A review of the literature. *Quarterly Journal of Studies on Alcohol, 2,* 717-803.

Vogler, R. E., Lunde, S. E., & Martin, G. T. (1977). Electrical aversion conditioning with chronic alcoholics: Follow-up and suggestions for research. *Journal of Consulting and Clinical Psychology, 45,* 467-479.

Wallace, J. (1978). Working with the preferred defense structure of the recovering alcoholic. In S. Zimberg, J. Wallace, & S. B. Blume (Eds.), *Practical approaches to alcoholism psychotherapy* (pp. 19-29). New York: Plenum.

Wallerstein, R., Robbins, L., Sargent, H., et al. (1956). The psychotherapy research project of the Menninger Foundation. *Bulletin of the Menninger Clinic, 20,* 221-280.

Weiner, H. (1975). Methadone counseling: A social work challenge. *Journal of Psychedelic Drugs, 7*(4), 381-387.

Weiner, H., & Schut, J. (1975). The interaction between counseling and methadone in the treatment of narcotic addicts: The challenge of the counseling relationship. *International Journal of Clinical Pharmacology and Biopharmacology, 11*(4), 292-298.

Weiner, M. (1983). *Getting off cocaine.* New York: Avon.

Wen, H. L., & Cheung, S. Y. C. (1973). Treatment of drug addiction by acupuncture. *Asian Journal of Medicine, 9.*

Williams, R. J. (1981). *The prevention of alcoholism through nutrition.* New York: Bantam Books.

Wilson, G. T., Leaf, R. C., & Natan, P. E. (1976). Aversive control of excessive alcohol consumption by chronic alcoholics in laboratory setting. *Journal of Applied Behavioral Analysis, 8,* 13-26.

Winquist, T. W. (1977). The transcendental meditation program and drug abuse: A retrospectice study. In D. W. Orme-Johnson & J. T. Farrow (Eds.), *Scientific research on the transcendental meditation program: Collected papers* (pp. 494-497). Livingston Manor, NY: MIU Press.

Wisocki, P. A. (1973). The successful treatment of a heroin addict by covert conditioning techniques. *Journal of Behavior Therapy and Experimental Psychiatry, 4,* 55-61.

Wolpe, J. (1958). *Psychotherapy by reciprocal inhibition.* Palo Alto, CA: Stanford University Press.

Wolpe, J. (1965). Conditioned inhibition of craving in drug addiction: A pilot experiment. *Behavior Research and Therapy, 2,* 285-287.

Wong, M. R., Brochin, N. E., & Gendron, K. L. (1981). Effects of meditation on anxiety and chemical dependency. *Journal of Drug Education, 11*, 91-105.

Woody, G. E., Luborsky, L., McLellan, A. T., et al. (1983). Psychotherapy for opiate addicts. *Archives of General Psychiatry, 40*, 639-648.

Woody, G. E., et al. (1984). Severity of psychiatric symptoms as a predictor of benefits from psychotherapy: The Veterans Administration-Penn study. *American Journal of Psychiatry, 141*, 1172-1177.

Worden, M., & Rosellini, G. (1979). Applying nutritional concepts in alcohol and drug counseling. *Journal of Psychedelic Drugs, 11*(3), 173-184.

Wurmser, L. (1984). More respect for the neurotic process: Comments on the problem of narcissism in severe psychopathology, especially the addictions. *Journal of Substance Abuse Treatment, 1*, 37-45.

Zuroff, D. C., & Schwarz, J. C. (1978). Effects of transcendental meditation and muscle relaxation on trait anxiety, maladjustment, locus of control, and drug use. *Journal of Consulting and Clinical Psychology, 46*, 264-271.

16

GROUP THERAPY

In the past two decades, evidence has mounted to support the idea that substance abuse is a disease with biological, psychological, and social causes and effects (Kissin, 1977; Secretary of Health, Education, and Welfare, 1971, 1974). Consequently, treatment has focused on a multimodal, multidisciplinary approach in which causal factors are isolated and a treatment plan is made that is specific to a given client's needs. One type of treatment that has been found to be especially useful for the psychological problems of many substance abusers is group psychotherapy. This may be justified by the presumed difficulty these clients have in developing an analyzable transference neurosis in individual therapy, by impulsive and acting-out propensities that threaten to disrupt or destroy individual treatment, and/or by the opportunities groups present for utilizing peer pressure to encourage desired changes. Although this chapter will not address specifically the issue of group versus individual treatment for substance abusers, it is our impression that many group approaches have arisen from clinicians' frustration and pessimism regarding individual approaches, rather than from a clearly articulated and substantiated rationale for group psychotherapy. Such a rationale requires a theoretical understanding of the problem of substance abuse that is consistent with current knowledge of human development and psychopathology, as well as a definition of group psychotherapy as distinct from other group approaches in task and methodology. Only then can a clear argument be formulated for the inclusion of group psychotherapy in a substance-abuse treatment program.

Models of Substance Abuse

Two ruling paradigms in the field of substance abuse are the medical/disease model and the legal/moral model. The disease model of substance abuse originated with respect to alcoholism. The disease model can be summarized as maintaining that certain afflicted individuals have the predisposition to progressive, addictive use of certain mood-altering chemicals. Given the presumed impossibility of such individuals moderating or controlling their use of intoxicants, the only acceptable treatment from this viewpoint is abstinence. This model does not make the substance abuser responsible for his illness any more than the patient with diabetes or kidney disease is responsible for his illness. Thus from the viewpoint of this model, psychological or motivational factors do not play an important role in the genesis of the illness.

In contrast to the disease model, the moral model holds the addict to be totally responsible for his addiction, which is a result of his own choices and selfish motivations. The treatment for a substance abuser, thus conceptualized, would be punishment for past transgressions and re-education to improve future choices. Although adherents of the moral model do not tend to publish their views, as such, in the professional literature, the impact of this model continues to be felt in the legal system as well as in many treatment programs.

Neither the disease model nor the moral model suggests the utility of psychotherapy with substance abusers, except perhaps as an auxiliary treatment to deal with the sequelae of substance abuse. In contrast, a psychological model, the self-medication model (Kaplan & Weider, 1974; Weider & Kaplan, 1969), argues for the centrality of psychotherapy in the treatment of substance abuse. This model views the substance abuser as an individual who is prone to becoming disorganized by painful affects, including rage, humiliation, shame, depression, anxiety, fear, boredom, and/or guilt (Wurmser, 1978). The psychopharmacologic properties of different drugs dictate that different classes of drugs especially attenuate different affective experiences, and it is suggested that an individual's drug of choice will be influenced by what affect or combination of affects he has the greatest need to dampen in order to maintain some feeling of psychological well-being. The hypersensitization to certain affects in compulsive substance abusers suggests that significant psychopathology is universal in this population (Wurmser, 1978).

Although each substance abuser has a unique set of biological, psychological, and social causes leading to the substance abuse problem, there are certain psychological themes that are commonly found in many drug and alcohol addicts. In one review, Kissin (1977) found that 70% to 80% of alcoholics who were given additional psychiatric diagnoses had a personality disorder and were generally antisocial, passive-aggressive, impulsive, or schizoid; 10% to 15% were diagnosed as neurotic, usually anxiety or obsessive-compulsive; and 10% to 15% had a psychosis, including schizophrenia or manic-depressive disorder. Although many substance abusers are not given secondary psychiatric diagnoses, some of them still have neurotic or characterological traits that affect their progress in treatment.

Kaplan and Weider (1974) posit three types of drug abusers: Type I uses drugs, particularly alcohol and marijuana, on occasion to heighten pleasurable experiences; Type II uses drugs in an attempt to cope, as a crutch to deal with difficult realities; Type III "takes drugs to escape the severe suffering of a chronically painful ego state" (p. 45). These latter users constitute the addiction-prone users, whose craving is determined by their need to find relief from extreme, unpleasant affects. An understanding of the profound psychological difficulties that produce Type III substance abuse should lead to an approach to treatment that gives primacy to psychotherapy.

Psychological Considerations

Psychodynamically oriented therapists have described this population as being fixated at the oral level of development, which results in narcissistic, passive-dependent, and depressive personality traits, sometimes with compensatory independence. Many have self-destructive tendencies, poor impulse control, and low frustration tolerance.

The tendency to flee uncomfortable or threatening situations is a common characteristic of substance abusers. This flight can take behavioral or emotional forms. Behavioral flight often entails the avoidance or physical leaving of situations. Emotional flight often entails the denial or repression of emotions surrounding a situation. Flight tendencies can often defeat individual or group treatment. Just as they may flee other emotionally charged situations, addicts often flee from the discomfort of treatment.

Substance abusers relying on flight and denial frequently do not develop the ability to perceive either the stress in situations or their reactions to stressful situations. Anxiety, guilt, and other uncomfortable feelings are common, and many substance abusers use drugs to anesthetize uncomfortable feelings (Fewell & Bissell, 1979).

Because of these tendencies, insight-oriented individual psychotherapy is difficult with substance abusers. Group psychotherapy offers an advantage in dealing with some of these difficulties. First, many authors have described how the substance abuser's narcissism, primitive object relationships, and poor frustration tolerance may lead him or her to develop a primitive transference relationship with a therapist that complicates the course of individual psychotherapy or causes the patient to leave treatment impulsively (Feibel, 1960; Stein & Friedman, 1971). However, the presence of other group members and the relative transparency of the therapist in a group psychotherapy model help diminish the intensity of the transference. Second, the massive denial found with many substance abusers causes them to tune out therapeutic interpretations or to refuse to acknowledge their problem with alcohol and/or drugs. In group psychotherapy, the presence of other clients who have been there and who can challenge this denial helps the addict become aware of the use of this defense mechanism. In addition, by being supportive and helpful, other group members encourage some gratification of narcissistic and dependency needs, which allows the substance abuser to feel safe enough to admit to and explore his or her addiction problem. Third, some addicts use substances to help them cope with anxiety or poor impulse control. Because the individual therapeutic situation may transiently increase a client's anxiety, the resulting emotional pain may be intolerable for many addicts and lead to impulse reactions such as drinking/drugging, suicidal behavior, or a flight from therapy. In the group psychotherapy setting, support and anxiety-reducing techniques can be used to modulate the anxiety level and discourage behavioral acting out.

Although substance abusers, generally, are not good candidates for the development of insight, many professionals support the benefits of interpersonal insight for this population (Yalom, Block, Bond, Zimmerman, & Qualls, 1978). Interpersonal insight refers to understanding family, social, and work situations that contribute to or cause excessive drinking (Steinglass, 1977). These situations are often referred to as antecedent conditions.

Situational insight development is a process that helps clients become aware of the antecedent conditions that result in substance use, after which the focus of treatment becomes helping clients anticipate and cope with these situations rather than drink or use drugs.

There are two major ways in which groups for interpersonal insight development can help clients become aware of and cope with their antecedents. First, by discussing their lives, group members can discover which situations create the stresses that lead to substance abuse. Thus the group becomes a means for treatment of antecedent conditions that exist outside the group. In group terms, situations from the lives of the members are referred to as situations in the *there-and-then* time sphere.

Second, by experiencing situations in the group that are similar to those outside the group, group members can become indirectly aware of some of the antecedents of substance use. Treatment groups can serve as a microcosm of the world outside. As a treatment group develops, members often experience reactions to the facilitators and other group members that are similar to reactions they experience in their lives outside the group. Because substance abusers are often poor observers and reporters on the life situations that cause them to use substances, the development of the same reactions to group situations can make their reactions more readily observable and understandable to the facilitators and the group members. With the support of the facilitators and the group, it is often easier for group members to learn how to cope with these situations in the group before they can alter their coping efforts in similar situations outside the group. In group terms, situations that develop in the group are referred to as *here-and-now* experiences.

Groups for treatment of substance abusers through interpersonal insight can use both the here-and-now and the then-and-there time spheres for developing awareness, anticipation, and alternatives for coping with antecedent conditions. In groups for treatment of substance abusers, change in behavior most often precedes insight. Learning to cope with difficult situations in the group frequently makes it easier for clients to develop awareness of antecedent conditions. It is often easier to understand a situation when it no longer poses a threat.

Group Psychotherapy Versus Self-Help

It is necessary to distinguish group psychotherapy from the proliferation of other group treatments of substance abuse, the most common of which are the self-help groups (AA and NA) and encounter groups (Lowinson, 1983). Scheidlinger (1982) defines group psychotherapy as

> a psychological process wherein an experienced one-to-one psychotherapist (usually a psychiatrist, psychologist, social worker, or nurse-clinician), with special additional group process training utilizes the emotional interaction in small, carefully planned groups to "repair" mental ill health, i.e., to effect amelioration of personality dysfunctions in individuals specifically selected for this purpose. (p. 7)

Group psychotherapy is a modality that is defined both by the training of the therapist and the primary task of the endeavor (Singer, Astrachan, Gould, & Klein, 1975). The psychological model of substance abuse outlined above stresses the difficulties these patients have in integrating and modulating their affective lives. In contrast to the self-help groups and encounter groups, group psychotherapy is conducted by a therapist who has a psychological model of substance abuse upon which to base decisions about group composition, intervention strategies, and therapeutic goals. Other group experiences, especially AA and NA, may provide crucial support to the client during periods of painful uncovering in group psychotherapy. Thus it is possible to see other groups as complementing the work of psychotherapy (Mack, 1981; Rosen, 1981).

Factors Influencing the Group Therapy Experience

One way of exploring the effectiveness of group psychotherapy for substance abusers is to examine the basic curative factors that are found in many psychotherapy groups. Yalom (1975) developed a Q-sort technique for studying these curative factors. He constructed statements that described each of 12 factors that he believed a priori were important in group psychotherapy. From these 12 factors he produced 60 different statements. He used his technique to study 20 psychiatric outpatients who had completed an average of 16 months of outpatient group psychotherapy, and he had them Q-sort the statements according to how helpful each was regarding the patient's group psychotherapy experience. Based on the patients' rank order of the statements, Yalom was able to construct a ranking of the curative factors: Interpersonal input (or the feedback that patients received from the group members and the therapists as to how they interacted with other patients), catharsis, group cohesiveness (or the feeling of being accepted by other group members), and insight were felt to be the four most important factors, according to the patients' evaluation.

Feeney and Dranger (1976) gave Yalom's Q-sort to 20 inpatient alcoholics who participated in a 90-day rehabilitation program. These patients similarly rank ordered Yalom's statements after an average of 49 days in group psychotherapy, and based on their statements a rank order of curative factors was constructed for this population. The first four curative factors in this population were identical to Yalom's outpatient psychiatric population.

Effectiveness of Group Psychotherapy for Substance Abuse

The anecdotal literature has generally been enthusiastic regarding the effectiveness of group psychotherapy for substance abusers. Stein and Friedman (1971) have stated: "Group psychotherapy is, in most instances, the treatment of choice for the psychological problems of the alcoholic" (p. 652), and they estimate that 60% to 70% of patients in group psychotherapy improve, versus 20% to 40% of patients receiving individual psychotherapy. Other anecdotal accounts (Doroff, 1977; Fox, 1962) have stated much the same thing, and substance abusers have been treated in a variety of therapy groups emphasizing different theoretical and technical principles, including psychoanalytic, assertiveness training, Gestalt, psychodrama, transactional analysis, aversion therapy, and insight-oriented theoretical principles. Despite these anecdotal accounts, a review of the literature has revealed few well-controlled studies measuring the effects of group psychotherapy with substance abusers.

Other Therapeutic Groups

A number of group formats have been found therapeutic for substance abusers, even though their primary goal is not insight into important intrapsychic and interpersonal issues. Nevertheless, important dynamic issues come up in these groups from time to time, and for this reason a brief description of some of them is outlined below.

The *education groups* are designed for three types of individuals: the general public; those who are at high risk for substance abuse, such as drunk drivers or children of substance abusers; and those who are diagnosed as alcohol or drug dependent (Freeman, 1985). The groups are usually closed-ended and meet on a time-limited basis—ranging from 6 to 20 weeks—depending on the setting. Many participate voluntarily, others are mandated to attend because of drunk driving, family violence, or drug-related criminal offenses. Some members may be referred to treatment groups later for follow-up. The combination of the two groups is very helpful for early-stage substance abusers.

The orientation-style drug education group in lecture-discussion format allows members either to speak up or to remain silent without experiencing group pressure to reveal themselves. Many inpatient and outpatient programs offer such didactic groups as a free service to the community.

The goal of most didactic groups is to change knowledge, attitudes, and behaviors related to alcohol and drug use or to encourage abstinence. Input on the physical, psychological, and social effects of drugs, causes of addiction, and alternatives to substance use are presented, often using a multimedia approach.

The first and most obvious positive result of lectures is what most people expect from education, information giving. One of the most basic and therapeutic pieces of information delivered is that alcoholism and other addictions are diseases. Both families and patients need to learn this in order to get beyond the judgmental and moralistic attitudes of most people.

Another crucial message is the nature of the 12 Steps of Alcoholics Anonymous. Patients learn that these are easily understood simple tools that are the principles of recovery. Explaining that alcohol is a chemical and a "drug" is another essential and common piece of knowledge included in educational programs. These and many other bits of knowledge assist the therapeutic process of surrender through the dismantling of intellectual defenses.

Secondly, lecturers who themselves are recovering people may assist the therapeutic experience of the client by being role models. Not only are these people capable of being sober, but they also are able to comprehend and articulate how and why they learned to control their disease. Lecturers and speakers model intellectual discipline, abstract thinking, organizational ability, and verbal skills that add depth to the role. Role models are critical elements in the "installation of hope," which is a vital aspect of group therapy identified by Yalom.

A third contribution of the lectures is to provide a vicarious therapy experience. Ever since the Greeks, people have been aware of the emotional catharsis an observer may have to an external experience such as a play. The lectures, films, and reading materials used in addiction treatment programs provide opportunities for vicarious therapeutic interactions. Just as group therapy gives clients a chance to identify with the person "on the hot seat," lectures offer clients an indirect yet potentially powerful experience to discover themselves. "Aha!" type insights happen in psychotherapy, but they also happen when people have the chance to discover themselves from a distance. Awareness of defense mechanisms often takes the indirect route of vicarious therapy.

Clients learn from the symbolic messages in lectures, as well as from the specific didactic content. Some of the most exciting and stimulating lecturers are those who generously sprinkle fact with stories and examples.

Self-help and support groups are intended to assist the members to grapple honestly with the role of alcohol or drugs in their lives. The group function is to support sobriety, to identify ways in which people sabotage themselves, and to break through denial. Such groups serve as sober support systems for the substance abuser, thereby countering isolation and loneliness (see Chapter 13).

Activity/resocialization groups are usually organized around a specific type of activity, usually of recreational or occupational nature; examples include sporting events, crafts, dance, and music. By encouraging abstinent interactions, clients relearn social skills and develop new social networks (Mallums, Godley, Hall, & Meyers, 1982).

Family therapy represents a type of group therapeutic experience in which the participants are all members of the same family. Much has been written regarding the substance-abusing family structure and systems approach to dealing with this problem. In some cases, multiple family groups have been organized where different families can share common problems and concerns involving substance abusing members (see Chapter 17).

References

Doroff, D. R. (1977). Group psychotherapy in alcoholism. In B. Kissin & H. Begleiter (Eds.), *The biology of alcoholism: Treatment and rehabilitation of the chronic alcoholic* (Vol. 5). New York: Plenum.

Feeney, D. J., & Dranger, P. (1976). Alcoholics view group therapy: Process and goals. *Journal of Studies on Alcohol, 38*(5), 611-618.

Feibel, C. (1960). The archaic personality structure of alcoholics and its indications for group therapy. *International Journal of Group Psychotherapy, 10,* 39-45.

Fewell, C. H., & Bissel, L. (1979). The alcoholic denial syndrome: An alcohol focused approach. *Social Casework, 59*(1), 6-14.

Fox, R. (1962). Group psychotherapy with alcoholics. *International Journal of Group Psychotherapy, 12,* 56-63.

Freeman, E. M. (1985). Multiple group services for alcoholic clients. In E. M. Freeman (Ed.), *Social work practice with clients who have alcohol problems*. Springfield, IL: Charles C Thomas.

Kaplan, E. H., & Weider, H. (1974). *Drugs don't take people, people take drugs*. Secaucus, NJ: Lyle Stuart.

Kissin, B. (1977). Theory and practice in the treatment of alcoholism. In B. Kissin & H. Begleiter (Eds.), *Treatment and rehabilitation of the chronic alcoholic* (Vol. 5). New York: Plenum.

Lowinson, J. H. (1983). Group psychotherapy with substance abusers and alcoholics. In H. I. Kaplan & B. J. Sadock (Eds.), *Comprehensive group psychotherapy* (pp. 256-262). Baltimore, MD: Williams & Wilkins.

Mack, J. E. (1981). Alcoholism, A.A., and the governance of the self. In M. H. Bean & N. E. Zinberg (Eds.), *Dynamic approaches to the understanding and treatment of alcoholism* (pp. 128-162). New York: Free Press.

Mallums, J., Godley, M., Hall, G., & Meyers, R. (1982). A social systems approach to resocializing alcoholics in the community. *Journal of Studies on Alcohol, 43*, 1115-1123.

Rosen, A. (1981). Psychotherapy and Alcoholics Anonymous: Can they be coordinated? *Bulletin of the Menninger Clinic, 45*, 229-246.

Scheidlinger, S. (1982). *Focus on group psychotherapy: Clinical essays.* New York: International Universities Press.

Secretary of Health, Education, and Welfare. (1971). *First special report to the U.S. Congress on alcohol and health.* Washington, DC: National Institute on Alcohol Abuse and Alcoholism.

Secretary of Health, Education, and Welfare. (1974). *Alcohol and health: New knowledge.* Washington, DC: National Institute on Alcohol Abuse and Alcoholism.

Singer, D. L., Astrachan, B. M., Gould, L. J., & Klein, E. B. (1975). Boundary management in psychological work with groups. *Journal of Applied Behavioral Science, 11*, 137-176.

Stein, A., & Friedman, E. (1971). Group therapy with alcoholics. In H. I. Kaplan & B. J. Sadock (Eds.), *Comprehensive group psychotherapy.* Baltimore, MD: Williams & Wilkins.

Steinglass, P. (1977). Family therapy in alcoholism. In B. Kissin & H. Begleiter (Eds.), *Treatment and rehabilitation of the chronic alcoholic.* New York: Plenum.

Weider, H., & Kaplan, E. H. (1969). Drug use in adolescents: Psychodynamic meaning and pharmacogenic effect. *Psychoanalytic Study of the Child, 24*, 399-431.

Wurmser, L. (1978). *The hidden dimension: Psychodynamics in compulsive drug use.* New York: Jason Aronson.

Yalom, I. D. (1975). *The theory and practice of group psychotherapy* (2nd ed.). New York: Basic Books.

Yalom, I., Block, S., Bond, G., Zimmerman, E., & Qualls, B. (1978). Alcoholics in interactional group therapy. *Archives of General Psychiatry, 35*, 419-425.

17

FAMILY SYSTEMS AND FAMILY THERAPY

Two separate literatures on families and substance abuse have evolved, one on the family and alcohol, and one on the family and drug abuse. There have been few attempts to synthesize these into a single cohesive theory. Until recently, most studies on the alcoholic family have focused on a male alcoholic in his 40s and his overinvolved spouse (Kaufman & Pattison, 1981). Most studies of drug abusers have focused on addicts in their teens and twenties and their parents (Kaufman, 1974, 1980). All too often, and unknowingly, these studies have focused on the same family. This is because families in which a parent is an alcoholic frequently produce drug-abusing and alcoholic children (Ziegler-Driscoll, 1977b). In addition, the incidence of drug abuse by alcoholics and alcohol abuse by primary drug abusers is increasing (Kaufman, 1981). This leads to further overlap of the two types of families.

The Alcoholic Family

One approach to the study of alcoholic families has been the study of marital interactional dynamics, role perceptions, and marital patterns of expectations and sanctions about the use of alcohol. Alcoholic couples demonstrate neurotic interactional behavior similar to that of other neurotic couples; both alcoholic and neurotic marriages differ from healthy ones. Thus marriages of alcoholics may not be unique but similar to other neurotic marriages in which alcoholism is part of the neurotic interaction (Becker & Miller, 1976; Billings, Kessler, Gomberg, & Weiner, 1979; Drewery & Rae, 1969; Hanson, Sands, & Sheldon, 1968). However, several studies have at least differentiated alcoholic families from control groups.

Studies of communication patterns have demonstrated several abnormalities in the families of alcoholics. Gorad (1971) has shown that male alcoholics exceed their wives, normal husbands, and normal wives in the use of responsibility-avoiding messages. Also, both the alcoholic and his wife are highly competitive in style, using more "one-up" messages and cooperating less than other couples. These "couples blame each other, put each other down, turn each other off and compete for dominance. They side-track each other, do not come up with solutions and then terminate communication, leading to the alcoholic's fleeing the scene to drink" (Paolino & McCrady, 1979, p. 357).

Jacob, Richey, Cvitkovic, and Blane (1981) compared alcoholic families to normal ones, both sober and under the influence of alcohol. They found that alcoholic-spouse interactions had more negative affect, which increased in the presence of alcohol. Orford, Oppenheimer, Egert, Herrman, and Gutline (1976) found that in alcoholic families the wives gave and received less affection, wives used few socially desirable adjectives in describing their "sober" husbands, and wives expected their husbands to use "hostile-dominance" adjectives or phrases.

Few studies have differentiated alcoholic couples from other dysfunctional couples. One finding that does differentiate alcoholic families from other families (except for those with drug abusers) is the high incidence of alcoholism in the families of origin of the alcoholic and his or her spouse (Cotton, 1979; Ziegler-Driscoll, 1977b).

Alcoholism and Children in the Family System

Much of the literature on alcoholic families has focused primarily on the marital partners while neglecting the roles and functions of children in the family and the consequences of alcoholism for children: Cork (1969) called them the "forgotten children." Children are often the most severely victimized members of the alcoholic family. They have growth and developmental problems (Chafetz, Blane, & Hill, 1971; El Guebaly & Orford, 1977). Further, these children are often subject to gross neglect and abuse. Teenage children are not immune to these adverse consequences, even though they are often considered less vulnerable. Just as significant are the long-term adverse consequences for personality patterning and identity formation and the possible development of dysfunctional attitudes toward alcohol (Kaufman & Pattison, 1981).

Moos and Billings (1982) have studied the children of alcoholics while the alcoholic is in recovery, as well as in relapse. They found that the children of recovering alcoholics functioned as well as control children, in contrast to the poor functioning in families where the alcoholic had relapsed. The family environments of the recovered alcoholic were not different from controls, but those of relapsed alcoholics were less cohesive and less likely to promote independence.

Regardless of the family system, alcoholism is a major stress on individual family members and the total family. Alcoholism is an economic drain on family resources, which threatens job security. Drinking behavior may interrupt normal family tasks, cause conflict, and demand adjustive responses from family members who do not know how to respond appropriately. In brief, alcoholism creates a series of escalating crises in family structure and function, which may bring the family system to an extreme catastrophic state (Kaufman & Pattison, 1981).

Drug Abuse and the Family

Family of Origin

Communication within families of drug abusers is characterized by unclear messages, vague information giving, lack of direct talk, avoidance of eye contact, frequent interruptions, and speaking for others (Bartlett, 1975; Stanton, 1979a). There is little, or only indirect, expression of positive or negative emotions as family members are very concerned with impulse control. Hostile feelings are usually defined as unacceptable and cause fear and guilt (Freidman, 1974; Kaufman & Kaufman, 1979; Kirschenbaum, Leonoff, & Maliano, 1974; Reilly, 1975). Thus, only by getting high can the addict experience and express strong feelings (Huberty, D., 1975).

Family members describe life at home as dull, lifeless, shallow, affectless, and without enjoyment, fun, and humor. Quite often, they experience feelings of love and hostility simultaneously. They feel encapsulated, separated, unaccepted, misunderstood, and confused (Kaufman & Kaufman, 1979; Kirschenbaum et al., 1974; Reilly, 1975), often defending against these emotions by heavy alcohol consumption, self-medication, or overeating, all of which serve as anesthetics, tranquilizers, and antidepressants. Thus there is a higher than average frequency of multigenerational alcohol abuse, chemical dependency, and compulsive disorders in families of addicts (Friedman, 1974; Huberty, C., & Huberty, D., 1976; Huberty, D., & Huberty, C., 1983; Kaufman & Kaufman, 1979; Klagsbrun & Davis, 1977; Reilly, 1975; Schwartzman, 1975; Stanton, 1979b; Stanton et al., 1978; Wolper & Scheiner, 1981), especially in one-parent families (Ziegler-Driscoll, 1979).

Parents of addicts not only rationalize their own misuse of legal drugs and medication but quite often deny their children's substance abuse. In some cases children's drug taking goes unrecognized by parents who get vicarious satisfaction from it; often, their attitudes condone or encourage the substance abuse (Huberty, C., & Huberty, D., 1976; Huberty, D., 1975; Kaufman & Kaufman, 1979; Klagsbrun & Davis, 1977; Stanton, 1979a, 1979c).

Sometimes parents are simply ignorant of chemical dependency, the effects of drugs, or the drug scene (Huberty, C., & Huberty, D., 1976; Ziegler-Driscoll, 1979). If parents have noticed substance abuse, neither they nor the addicts accept any responsibility for it. The parents blame each other, protect themselves by counterattacking, or name external explanations for the drug abuse. If they blame the addicts, it is usually with the implication that the fact of dependency absolves the addicts from accountability for their behavior (Huberty, D., 1975; Reilly, 1975; Stanton et al., 1978).

Parents often differ in child-rearing concepts. As a result, they fail to set clear and firm limits for their children—they fail to punish problem behavior, are inconsistent, or disagree over whether and how to discipline. There is little shared authority or emphasis on the children's responsibility for their own behavior (Gottschalk et al., 1970; Huberty, C., & Huberty, D., 1976; Huberty, D., 1975; Kaufman & Kaufman, 1979; Klimenko, 1968; Reilly, 1975; Stanton, 1979b). Sometimes parents are so moralistic and critical that their children reject their standards and values and select radically different activities and friends, for instance, on the drug scene (Kirschenbaum et al., 1974). In families of future addicts children are rarely praised, positively reinforced, nurtured, or validated. There is little expression of love and affection. Instead, there are high rates of negative and judgmental messages in the form of criticism, complaints, and nagging. Because the only available reinforcers are negative affective displays, children learn that the way to get attention is to cause trouble; this they can do by becoming addicted (Kaufman & Kaufman, 1979; Kirschenbaum et al., 1974; Klimenko, 1968; Reilly, 1975; Stanton, 1979a). Future drug addicts are either faced by their parents' low expectations (self-fulfilling prophecy) or by their high performance standards and achievement orientations. The latter often lead to fear of failure, task-avoidance, insecurity, and feelings of inferiority. By abusing drugs the addicts avoid facing these high expectations, being absolved of responsibility for their behavior (Hirsch & Imhof, 1975; Reilly, 1975; Schwartzman, 1975; Stanton, 1979c).

The independence, self-differentiation, identity-formation, and self-assertion of their children are rarely furthered by parents of future addicts. They have little tolerance for their children's individuality, do not provide them with personal space, react negatively to their attempts at establishing their own identity, and fail to validate them as unique persons (Bartlett, 1975; Kirschenbaum et al., 1974; Stanton, 1979c). Thus, these children are unprepared for the tasks of adolescence, and some try to avoid maturation, individuation, and separation by misusing drugs. In other cases, they try to reconcile the urge to leave home with pressure from enmeshed family members to stay. Their parents experience stress and intolerable anxiety when these children attempt to separate (especially in one-parent families). They fear the children's emancipation for its possible effects on their family; they see it as a threat to the family's homeostasis, are afraid of losing psychological resources, and are unwilling to enter a new stage of the family cycle. Sometimes a strong move toward individuation also stimulates conflict between the parents, reactivating old dependence-independence issues from early marriage or from the families of origin. Therefore, these parents covertly encourage their children to stay at home, invoke feelings of guilt or appeal to loyalty in order to curb striving for autonomy. Addicts then offer their problem as a way of avoiding separation (Stanton et al., 1978).

Quite often, individuation and separation have become problems because the drug abusers suffered a great emotional loss such as a parent dying, separating, or getting divorced. It is well documented that there is an above-average absence of one parent in the future addict's childhood or early adolescence (Gottschalk et al., 1970; Harbin & Maziar, 1975; Huberty D., & Huberty, C., 1983; Kaufman & Kaufman, 1979; Klagsbrun & Davis, 1977; Seldin, 1972; Stanton, 1979a, 1979c; Ziegler-Driscoll, 1977c). Abusing drugs would then be a way of combating the pain caused by this traumatic and sometimes unexpected loss, of showing one's loyalty to the remaining parent, or of guarding against the pain of a new loss.

In other cases, one or both parents have never worked through the powerful feelings caused by the death of their own parents. Thus they suffer from a deep sense of emotional deprivation, separation anxiety, suppressed grief, and delayed mourning. These feelings cause them to discourage the individuation and independence of the future addicts (Reilly, 1975).

Less frequently, addiction serves to keep the families of origin together. Many of these families are characterized by disengagement, isolation of subsystems, and lack of intimacy and affection. Communication is minimal except around the substance abuse. Especially when the addicts take drugs, their parents and other family members interact and argue with each other.

Scapegoating their drug-abusing children, blaming each other for their behavior, and discussing their treatment are the only causes that make these parents relate to each other. Thus family life becomes organized entirely around the substance abuse. Because it intensifies family bonds and unites the family, there is a strong investment in keeping the children addicted. This would explain the double messages, inconsistent limit-setting, and covert encouragement of substance misuse by these parents (Friedman, 1974; Gottschalk et al., 1970; Huberty, D., 1975; Huberty, D., & Huberty, C., 1983; Kaufman & Kaufman, 1979; Kirschenbaum et al., 1974; Klimenko, 1968; Reilly, 1975; Schwartzman, 1975; Stanton, 1977, 1979a, 1979c; Wolper & Scheiner, 1981).

Similar functions are served by drug abuse in families characterized by frequent marital conflict. If these arguments threaten the continuance of the family, children might become addicted in order to distract their parents from fighting. Later on, taking drugs may keep marital conflicts from crystallizing or becoming disruptive. The parents avoid the roots of their own dissension by shifting the focus to the substance misuse; they can also act out their problems through disagreements about the addicts without the danger of divorce. Once the danger of separation has passed, the children often stop using drugs. Then the refocusing of parental conflict on marital issues may cause a repetition of their children's attention-getting and self-destructive behavior.

In all these cases, the addict's behavior stabilizes the family. He is a "savior" who shifts the conflicts and pain between his parents onto himself (Stanton, 1978). Moreover, in their role of scapegoats, addicts often have to represent bad parental introjects. In compensation, they assume a central position within their families, are sometimes envied by their siblings for all the attention they get, and may enjoy the secondary gains and rewards of the "sick" role (Bartlett, 1975; Huberty, C., & Huberty, D., 1976; Kirschenbaum et al., 1974; Kupetz et al., 1977; Reilly, 1975; Schwartzman, 1975; Seldin, 1972; Stanton, 1978, 1979a, 1979c; Weidman, 1983).

If addiction is a family disease and a family problem, the drug abuser can be regarded as the identified client or patient, the symptom of a disturbed family. Substance abuse has an adaptive function for the family because it satisfies its desire for stability. The family adjusts to the addiction; it becomes the family's equilibrium and the center of family life. The family "then has a major psychological investment in maintaining that member as a drug abuser so as not to upset the family pattern" (Huberty, D., 1975, p. 183). Therefore, it tries to maintain the addict's role and is resistent to change (Hirsch & Imhof, 1975; Huberty, C., & Huberty, D., 1976; Kaufman & Kaufman, 1979; Kirschenbaum et al., 1974; Klagsbrun & Davis, 1977; Kupetz, Larosa, Klagsbru, & Davis, 1983; Stanton et al., 1978; Wolper & Scheiner, 1981).

Stanton and Todd (1982) have summarized the qualities of the dysfunctional family system in drug abusers that distinguish them from other dysfunctional families:

1. High frequency of multigenerational chemical dependency.
2. Primitive and direct expression of conflict with explicit alliances (unschizophrenogenic).
3. An illusion of independence in the addict because of active involvement with a drug-oriented peer group.
4. Mothers with symbiotic child-rearing practices extending into the child's later life.
5. An extreme incidence of premature, unexpected, or untimely deaths.
6. Addiction is a pseudoindividuation that maintains family ties through a facade of defiance and independence.

The Addict's Nuclear Family

When substance abusers marry, their newly formed families are often secondary to their families of origin. Roles and patterns of interaction established in the latter are carried over into the marriage, where relationships are quite often defined in the same way. The work of Kosten, Jahali, and Kleber (1982) demonstrated the lack of symmetrical role relationships in male heroin addicts and their spouses. They noted an alternative sequence of two complementary role relationships. The addict alternates from compliant child with a nurturing mother to rebellious son with a policing mother. These couples were intensely enmeshed so that threats of separation were very powerful. When a separation occurred, the husband returned to his own enmeshed family of origin. When this became too uncomfortable, he would return to treatment in order to re-unite with his wife.

In other cases, the parents may invoke a family crisis if they fear that they are losing their children. The addicts respond by starting a fight with their spouses, indicating to their parents that they have not lost them. Quite often the quarrels are used as an excuse to return home and help the parents (Bartlett, 1975; Huberty, D., 1975; Kaufman & Kaufman, 1979; Stanton, 1979a, 1979b; Wolper & Scheiner, 1981; Ziegler-Driscoll, 1979). According to Stanton (1978) "Marital battles thus become a functional part of the intergenerational homeostatic system, possessing both adaptive and sacrificial qualities" (p. 141).

A key issue in the families of women drug abusers is drug abuse by the spouse. Women heroin addicts tend to be living with an addicted partner. Among those entering drug treatment in Michigan, 93% of White women and 86% of Black women were living with men who used drugs, as compared to 75% of White men and 66% of Black men who entered drug treatment (Ryan & Mose, 1979). If both spouses misuse drugs, then they tend to form a supportive network to assist each other in continuing on the path of abuse and dependence. Despite this overt support, these relationships are rarely intrinsically loving and eventually deteriorate.

Mutual drug abuse provides a critical focus for the entire relationship. Drug abusing couples revolve their entire home experience and social lives around drugs. Heroin-addicted couples have a 24-hour relationship in which they do everything together including "hustling, scoring, fixing, sleeping and eating" (Rosenbaum, 1981). Although sexuality may be enhanced in the early phases of such relationships, it generally progressively dissipates into nonexistence.

Family Intervention

The first step of any intervention is to persuade addicts to initiate detoxification. Addicts must be led to take responsibility for their substance abuse and for remaining abstinent. To do so, they need help in resisting pressure from drug-abusing peers, dealers, and others on the drug scene (Bartlett, 1975; Kaufman, 1979; Kosten et al., 1983; Stanton, 1979a; Stanton et al., 1978; Ziegler-Driscoll, 1979).

Therapy must seek to make all members of the family of origin responsible for the drug problem and its solution, putting a stop to mutual shifting and blame and ensuring that everyone accepts a part in the detoxification process (Klimenko, 1968; Kosten et al., 1983; Stanton, 1979a, 1979d; Stanton & Todd, 1979b). Therapy also brings parents face to face with their own abuse of alcohol and medication; according to D. Huberty and C. Huberty (1983),

> because of the high incidence of parental and sibling substance abuse, we ask all family members in therapy to abstain from all mood-altering substances. In addition to detecting otherwise hidden parental and sibling drug or alcohol abuse, such an agreement also removes the double standard attached to the drug abuser in therapy. Parents are thereby allowed to experience the adult peer pressure, which often produces greater empathy. (p. 98)

In general, therapists see the whole family as the client and avoid the notion that the addict is the only sick or incompetent member. By exploring and discussing problems of other family members, therapists take the focus off the addict and show that drug abuse is actually a symptom of disturbed family functioning, that therapy is for the sake of all family members, and that everyone will have to change (Hirsch & Imhof, 1975; Howe, 1974; Klimenko, 1968; Reilly, 1975; Stanton, 1979a; Stanton & Todd, 1979a, 1979b).

Therapists must demand clear and explicit communication; therefore, they clarify mixed and ambiguous messages, remark upon private and nonverbal ones, and point out discrepancies between verbal and nonverbal behavior. In this way they serve as models for all family members. By encouraging family members to share their inner experiences and positive, negative, and ambivalent feelings, therapists fight alienation and show that openness is not dangerous, that family members still feel positively toward each other, and that negative emotions are normal. Therapists also help members to express anger constructively and deal with the resulting guilt. Moreover, they give permission to be serious, humorous, funny, sad, and so forth, increasing the range of permitted behavior, making companionship more enjoyable, and increasing satisfaction with family life (Campbell, 1983; Huberty, C., & Huberty, D., 1976; Huberty, D., & Huberty, C., 1983; Kaufman, 1979; Klimenko, 1968; Reilly, 1975; Wolper & Scheiner, 1981).

In most cases, the marriages of the addicts' parents need to be strengthened. Therapy plays a role in resolving marital conflicts, improving communication between spouses, building mutual support, and dealing with sexual problems. In order to make the parents relate again as partners, therapists often give homework assignments; for instance, they have the parents set specific times for a mutual activity or discussion. Therapy must also deal with the marital crises that can be expected when the addicts improve. It is of great importance that the drug abusers be freed from the responsibility for their parents' marriage and from roles as spouse surrogates. By detriangulation, by breaking alliances, and by establishing clear boundaries, therapy serves to keep them out of their parents' marital relationship and conflicts. It helps break the symbiosis between the addicts and their opposite sex parents and establishes generational lines; this changes incestuous relationships and their effects on the children. At the same time, the same-sex parents must be brought into a more central position in their families: Through therapy, they are encouraged to become involved with their addict children. Thus attitudes are improved, feelings clarified, and common interests discussed (Friedman, 1974; Huberty, C., & Huberty, D., 1976; Huberty, D., & Huberty, C., 1983; Kaufman, 1979; Reilly, 1975; Stanton, 1979c; Stanton & Todd, 1979b; Wolper & Scheiner, 1981; Ziegler-Driscoll, 1977).

Therapy must counter the opposite-sex parents' overprotection, indulgence, and infantilization of their drug-abusing children while trying to stop the scapegoating and blaming by the same-sex parents. Therapy must enable parents to accept their parental responsibility, take control, and improve their parental competence. They must be helped to set consistent limits and enforce them jointly, and thus to work as a team. The parents must be made to realize that they often have unrealistic expectations and give attention only to the problematic behavior of their drug-abusing children. Encouraged to notice admirable traits and to reward desired behavior, they can learn techniques of positive reinforcement. In many cases, parents must be taught to relate to their drug-abusing children as real persons. To do this, therapists interpret rejections, identifications, and attempts at object-conservation; deal with death themes, grief, and family secrets; discuss emotional losses, and let family members complete their mourning. They must also affirm family loyalties, showing that these will survive when children individuate, and resolve separation anxiety. Such interventions should lead to these parents accepting the individuality and difference of their children, seeing them as unique and separate persons, and allowing them to establish their own identity. In this way the parents get ready to let their drug-abusing children leave home (Campbell, 1983; Friedman, 1974; Huberty, C., & Huberty, D., 1976; Huberty, D., & Huberty, C., 1983; Kaufman, 1979; Noone & Reddig, 1976; Reilly, 1975; Stanton, 1979d; Ziegler-Driscoll, 1979).

Although the therapeutic focus remains on the family of origin, problems affecting the newly created families of procreation of married addicts must also be addressed. Parents must be persuaded to develop more positive and accepting attitudes toward spouses of their addicted children. It is more important, however, to establish clear boundaries between the two families. Only then is it possible to focus on the marital relationship of the addict, solve conflicts, improve the sex life, and help an addicted spouse. The marital roles, patterns, and relationship definitions, unconsciously carried over from the families of origin, must also be identified.

On the social level, therapists must deal with the peer relationships of addicts. The latter must be separated from drug-abusing friends and removed from the drug scene. On the other hand, peers might be included in some sessions in order to integrate the addicts in a supportive group, facilitate the separation from their parents, and discuss value conflicts (Callan et al., 1975; Campbell, 1983; Ziegler-Driscoll, 1979). In a few cases, relatives, friends, teachers, caseworkers, and other individuals may be invited to some sessions. In this way therapists can gather new information and clarify previous observations. In addition, addicts' families can be integrated into a social network whose members might serve as resource people and service providers, help with problem solving and decision making, reduce alienation, and maintain positive changes (Bartlett, 1975; Callan, Garrison, & Zerger, 1975; Howe, 1974; Klagsbrun & Davis, 1977; Klimenko, 1968). Similar goals can be reached by integrating the clients into longer-lasting support groups such as Families Anonymous. However, multiple family and parents' groups are more therapeutic because their members have similar problems and therefore feel understood. Moreover, they share feelings, support each other, offer help in crisis situations, learn by identification or analogy, and use the strengths of other families as models (Bartlett, 1975; Huberty, C., & Huberty, D., 1976; Huberty, D., & Huberty, C., 1983; Klimenko, 1968; Kosten et al., 1983; Ziegler-Driscoll, 1977a, 1979).

Efficacy of Family Therapy with Substance Abuse

This section does not attempt thoroughly to review the evaluation literature on family therapy of substance abusers. Stanton (1980) and Janzen (1977) provide the interested reader with excellent reviews of drug abuse and alcoholism, respectively. However, several examples of family therapy evaluation in this field will be presented here.

In drug abuse, Silver and his colleagues (Silver, Panepinto, Arnon, & Swaine, 1975) describe a methadone program for pregnant addicts and their addicted spouses in which 40% of the women became drug-free in treatment and the male employment rate increased from 10% to 55%. Both rates are much higher than those achieved by traditional methadone programs without family treatment. The problem with this study, as with most evaluations of family approaches to drug abuse, is the lack of follow-up data and control groups.

Ziegler-Driscoll (1977a) has reported a study that found, on a 4- to 6-month follow-up, no difference between treatment groups with family therapy and those without. However, the therapists were new to family therapy and the supervisors new to substance abuse. As the therapists became more experienced, their results improved. Stanton and Todd's (1982) evaluation of family therapy with heroin addicts on methadone is perhaps the most outstanding with hard-core addicts. They compared paid family therapy, unpaid family therapy, paid family movie "treatment," and nonfamily treatment. The results of a 1-year posttreatment follow-up were that the two family therapy treatments produced much better outcomes than nonfamily treatments in abstinence from drugs. The nonfamily treatment and movie groups did not differ from each other.

Hendricks (1971) found at 1-year follow-up that narcotic addicts who had received 5½ months of multiple family therapy (MFT) were twice as likely to remain in continuous therapy than addicts not responding to MFT. Kaufman's work has shown that adolescent addicts with MFT have half the recidivism rate of clients without it (Kaufman & Kaufman, 1977). Stanton (1980) noted that of 68 studies of the efficacy of family therapy of drug abuse, only 14 quantify their outcome. Only six of these provided comparative data with other forms of treatment or control groups.

Four of the six studies (Hendricks, 1971; Scopetta, King, Szapocznik, & Tillman, 1979; Stanton, 1980; Wunderlich, Lozes, & Lewis, 1974) showed family treatment to be superior to other modes. Winer, Lorio, and Scrofford (1975) and Ziegler-Driscoll (1977b) found no superiority of family treatment. Stanton (1980) concluded that "family treatment shows considerable promise for effectively dealing with problems of drug abuse" (p. 16).

Stanton and Todd (1982) have provided the field with one of the best-documented controlled studies to date of family therapy of drug abuse. They emphasize concrete behavioral changes that include a focus on family rules about drug-related behavior and the utilization of weekly urine tests to give tangible indications of progress. They are concerned with interrupting and altering the repetitive family interactional patterns that maintain drug-taking.

In their family treatment groups, they found on 1-year follow-up that days free of methadone, illegal opiates, and marijuana all shifted favorably compared with a nonfamily treatment group. However, there was no significant decrease in alcohol abuse nor increase in work or school productivity. They noted a high mortality rate of 10% in nonfamily therapy cases but only 2% with those who received family therapy.

Although there has been more detailed evaluation of the family therapy of alcoholism than of drug abuse, Janzen, in a 1977 review, stated that "it is not possible to show that family treatment is as good or better than other forms of treatment for alcoholism" (p. 124). However, he also stated that such treatment has advantages to the family and the alcoholic that other treatments do not offer. Despite their methodological shortcomings, all the studies he cited reported positive results. Meeks and Kelly (1970) reported the success of family therapy with five couples, but no comparison group couples were included. They described abstinence in two alcoholics and "improved drinking pattern" in the other three, but with no objective measures of family functioning. Cadogan (1973) compared marital group therapy in 20 couples with 20 other couples on a waiting list. After 6 months of therapy, nine couples in the treatment group but only two couples in the control group were abstinent. However, again, there was no follow-up or use of objective, externally validated measures.

Steinglass (1979), utilizing a comprehensive battery of evaluative instruments with alcoholic families before treatment and at a 6-month follow-up, found that five of nine alcoholics were drinking less at follow-up. Overall positive changes in psychiatric symptomology were minimal. However, when the results of the two therapies were analyzed, the directive, forceful therapist was found to be more successful than the passive one. Steinglass also proposed that brief, intense family therapy programs may shift rigid systems but may not provide sufficient time for beneficial shifts to be permanently incorporated.

Conclusion

Many new family therapy techniques have evolved over the past decade. The field of substance-abuse treatment has been fortunate to be in the forefront of the implementation of these techniques. It is erroneous to claim that family therapy alone is superior to other treatment methods. The relative value of family therapy compared to other modalities in the treatment of substance abuse awaits the results of further studies. However, family therapy is a valuable, if not essential, component of treatment. In order to be effective, family therapy must be tailored to each individual family and its specific needs. However, family therapy should not stand alone in the treatment of serious substance abusers, but should serve as a valuable and often essential adjunct to such treatment—particularly when integrated into a comprehensive program. Thus, in addition to family therapy, a successful treatment program should offer a full range of services.

References

Bartlett, D. (1975). The use of multiple family therapy groups with adolescent drug addicts. In M. Sugar (Ed.), *The adolescent in group and family therapy.* New York: Brunner/Mazel.

Becker, J. V., & Miller, P. M. (1976). Verbal and nonverbal marital interaction pattern of alcoholic and nonalcoholic couples during drinking and nondrinking sessions. *Journal of Studies on Alcohol, 37,* 1616-1624.

Billings, A. G., Kessler, M., Gomberg, C. A., & Weiner, S. (1979). Marital conflict resolution of alcoholic and nonalcoholic couples during drinking and nondrinking sessions. *Journal of Studies on Alcohol, 40*(3), 183-195.

Cadogan, D. A. (1973). Marital group therapy in the treatment of alcoholism. *Quarterly Journal of Studies on Alcohol, 34,* 1184-1194.

Callan, D., Garrison, J., & Zerger, F. (1975). Working with the families and social networks of drug abusers. *Journal of Psychedelic Drugs, 7,* 19-25.

Campbell, P. G. (1983). Streit family workshops creating change in a family environment. *Journal of Drug Education, 13,* 223-227.

Chafetz, M. E., Blane, H. T., & Hill, M. J. (1971). Children of alcoholics: Observations in a child guidance clinic. *Quarterly Journal of Studies on Alcohol, 32,* 687-698.

Cork, M. R. (1969). *The forgotten children.* Toronto: Addiction Research Foundation.

Cotton, N. S. (1979). The familial incidence of alcoholism: A review. *Journal of Studies on Alcohol, 40,* 89-116.

Drewery, J., & Rae, J. B. (1969). A group comparison of alcoholic marriages using the interpersonal perception techniques. *British Journal of Psychiatry, 115,* 287-330.

El-Geubaly, N., & Orford, D. R. (1977). The offspring of alcoholics: A critical review. *American Journal of Psychiatry, 134,* 357-365.

Friedman, P. H. (1974). Family system and ecological approach to youthful drug-abuse. *Family Therapy, 1,* 63-78.

Gorad, S. L. (1971). Communications styles and interaction of alcoholics and their wives. *Family Process, 10,* 475-489.

Gottschalk, L. A., et al. (1970). The Laguna Beach experiment as a community approach to family counseling for drug abuse problems in youth. *Comprehensive Psychiatry, 11,* 226-234.

Hanson, P. G., Sands, P. M., & Sheldon, R. B. (1968). Patterns of communication in alcoholic marital couples. *Psychiatry Quarterly, 42,* 538-547.

Harbin, H. T., & Maziar, H. M. (1975). The families of drug abusers: A literature review. *Family Process, 14,* 411-431.

Hendricks, W. J. (1971). Use of multifamily counseling groups in treatment of male narcotic addicts. *International Journal of Group Psychotherapy, 21,* 34-90.

Hirsch, R., & Imhof, J. E. (1975). A family therapy approach to the treatment of drug abuse and addiction. *Journal of Psychedelic Drugs, 7,* 181-185.

Howe, B. J. (1974). Family therapy and the treatment of drug abuse problems. *Family Therapy, 1,* 89-98.

Huberty, C. E., & Huberty, D. J. (1976). Treating the parents of adolescent drug abusers. *Contemporary Drug Problems, 5,* 573-592.

Huberty, D. J. (1975). Treating the adolescent drug abuser: A family affair. *Contemporary Drug Problems, 4,* 179-194.

Huberty, D. J., & Huberty, C. E. (1983). Drug abuse. In M. R. Textor (Ed.), *Helping families with special problems.* New York: Jason Aronson.

Jacob, T., Richey, D., Cvitkovic, J. F., & Blane, H. T. (1981). Communication styles of alcoholic and nonalcoholic families when drinking and not drinking. *Journal of Studies on Alcohol, 42*(5), 466-482.

Janzen, C. (1977). Families in the treatment of alcohol. *Journal of Studies in Alcohol, 38,* 114-130.

Kaufman, E. (1974). The psychodynamics of opiate dependence: A new look. *American Journal of Drug and Alcohol Abuse, 1,* 349-370.

Kaufman, E. (1979). The application of the basic principles of family therapy to the treatment of drug and alcohol abusers. In E. Kaufman & P. Kaufman (Eds.), *Family therapy of drug and alcohol abuse.* New York: Gardner.

Kaufman, E. (1980). Myth and reality in the family patterns and treatment of substance abusers. *American Journal of Drug and Alcohol Abuse, 7*(3, 4), 257-279.

Kaufman, E. (1981). Family structures of narcotic addicts. *International Journal of the Addictions, 16,* 106-108.

Kaufman, E., & Kaufman, P. (1977). Multiple family therapy: A new direction in the treatment of drug abusers. *American Journal of Drug and Alcohol Abuse, 4*(4), 467-478.

Kaufman, E., & Kaufman, P. (1979). From a psychodynamic orientation to a structural family therapy approach to the treatment of drug dependency. In E. Kaufman & P. Kaufman (Eds.), *Family therapy of drug and alcohol abuse.* New York: Gardner.

Kaufman, E., & Pattison, E. M. (1981). Differential methods of family therapy in the treatment of alcoholism. *Journal of Studies on Alcohol, 42,* 951-971.

Kirschenbaum, M., Leonoff, G., & Maliano, A. (1974). Characteristic patterns in drug abuse families. *Family Therapy, 1,* 43-62.

Klagsbrun, M., & Davis, D. J. (1977). Substance abuse and family interaction. *Family Process, 16,* 149-164.

Klimenko, A. (1968). Multifamily therapy in the rehabilitation of drug addicts. *Perspectives on Psychiatric Care, 6,* 220-223.

Kosten, T. R., Jalali, B., & Kleber, H. D. (1982). Complimentary marital roles of male heroin addicts: Evolution and intervention tactics. *American Journal of Drug and Alcohol Abuse, 9*(2), 155-169.

Kosten, T. R., et al. (1983). Family denial as a prognostic factor in opiate addict treatment outcome. *Journal of Nervous and Mental Diseases, 171,* 611-616.

Kupetz, K., et al. (1977). The family and drug abuse symposium. *Family Process, 15,* 325-332.

Kupetz, K., Larosa, J., Klagsbru, M., & Davis, D. (1983). Family drug abuse symposium and editorials. *Family Process, 16*(2), 141-147.

Meeks, D. E., & Kelly, C. (1970). Family therapy with families of recovering alcoholics. *Quarterly Journal of Studies on Alcohol, 31,* 399-413.

Moos, R. H., & Billings, A. G. (1982). Children of alcoholics during the recovery process: Alcoholic and matched control families. *Addictive Behavior, 7,* 1551-1563.

Noone, R. J., & Reddig, R. L. (1976). Case studies in the family treatment of drug abuse. *Family Process, 15,* 325-332.

Orford, J., Oppenheimer, E., Egert, S., Herrman, C., & Gutline, S. (1976). The cohesiveness of alcoholism: Complicated marriages and its influence on treatment outcome. *British Journal of Psychiatry, 128,* 318-319.

Paolino, T. J., & McCrady, B. (1979). *The alcoholic marriage: Alternative perspectives.* New York: Grune & Stratton.

Reilly, D. M. (1975). Family factors in the etiology and treatment of youthful drug abuse. *Family Therapy, 2,* 149-171.

Rosenbaum, M. (1981). *Women on heroin.* New Brunswick, NJ: Rutgers University Press.

Schwartzman, J. (1975). The addict, abstinence, and the family. *American Journal of Psychiatry, 132,* 154-157.

Scopetta, M. A., King, O. E., Szapocznik, J., & Tillman, W. (1979). *Ecological structural family therapy with Cuban immigrant families.* Unpublished manuscript.

Seldin, N. E. (1972). The family of the addict: A review of the literature. *International Journal of the Addictions, 7,* 97-107.

Silver, F. C., Panepinto, W. C., Arnon, D., & Swaine, W. T. (1975). A family approach in treating the pregnant addict. In E. Senay (Ed.), *Developments in the field of drug abuse* (pp. 401-404). Cambridge, MA: Shenkman.

Stanton, M. D. (1977). The addict as savior: Heroin, death, and the family. *Family Process, 16,* 191-197.

Stanton, M. D. (1978). Family therapy. *Drug Forum, 6,* 203-205.

Stanton, M. D. (1979a). The client as family member: Aspects of continuing treatment. In B. S. Brown (Ed.), *Addicts and aftercare: Community integration of the former drug abuser* (pp. 81-102). Beverly Hills, CA: Sage.

Stanton, M. D. (1979b). Drugs and the family. *Marriage and Family Review, 2,* 1-10.

Stanton, M. D. (1979c). Family treatment approaches to drug abuse problems: A review. *Family Process, 18,* 251-280.

Stanton, M. D. (1979d). Family treatment of drug problems: A review. In R. L. Dupont et al. (Eds.), *Handbook of drug abuse* (pp. 133-150). Washington, DC: National Institute on Drug Abuse.

Stanton, M. D. (1980). Some overlooked aspects of the family and drug abuse. In B. G. Ellis (Ed.), *Drug abuse from the family perspective.* Rockville, MD: National Institute on Drug Abuse.

Stanton, M. D., et al. (1978). Heroin addiction as a family phenomenon: A new conceptual model. *American Journal of Drug and Alcohol Abuse, 5,* 125-150.

Stanton, M. D., & Todd, T. C. (1979a). *Family characteristics and family therapy of heroin addicts: Final report, 1974-1978: (NIDA Grant No. RD1 DA 01119). Rockville, MD: National Institute on Drug Abuse.*

Stanton, M. D., & Todd, T. C. (1979b). Structural family therapy with drug addicts. In E. Kaufman & P. Kaufman (Eds.), *Family therapy of drug and alcohol abuse.* New York: Gardner.

Stanton, M. D., & Todd, T. C. (1982). *The family therapy of drug abuse and addiction.* New York: Guilford.

Steinglass, P. (1979). An experimental treatment program for alcoholic couples. *Journal of Studies on Alcohol, 40,* 159-182.

Weidman, A. (1983). The compulsive adolescent substance abuser: Psychological differentiation and family process. *Journal of Drug Education, 13,* 161-172.

Winer, L. R., Lorio, J. P., & Scrofford, I. (1975). *Effects of treatment on drug abusers and family.* Report to SOADAP.

Wolper, B., & Scheiner, Z. (1981). Family therapy approaches and drug dependent women. In A. M. Beschner, B. G. Reed, & J. Mondanaro (Eds.), *Treatment services for drug dependent women* (Vol. 1, pp. 343-407). Washington, DC: U.S. Department of Health and Human Services.

Wunderlich, R. A., Lozes, J., & Lewis, J. (1974). Recidivism rates of group therapy participants and other adolescents processed by a juvenile court. *Psychotherapy: Research and Practice, 11,* 243-245.

Ziegler-Driscoll, G. (1977a). Family research study at Eagleville Hospital and Rehabilitation Center. *Family Process, 61,* 175-189.

Ziegler-Driscoll, G. (1977b). The similarities in families of drug dependents and alcoholics. In E. Kaufman & P. Kaufman (Eds.), *Family therapy of drug and alcohol abuse.* New York: Gardner.

Ziegler-Driscoll, G. (1979). The similarities in families of drug dependents and alcoholics. In E. Kaufman & P. Kaufman (Eds.), *Family therapy of drug and alcohol abuse.* New York: Gardner.

PART IV

Special Populations

18

CHILDREN AND ADOLESCENTS

Incidence and Trends in Drug Use

For a variety of reasons, including lack of agreement on definitions of drug-taking behavior, the extent of problematic drug use in children and adolescents is difficult to determine with accuracy (Lavenhar, 1979; National Institute on Drug Abuse, [NIDA], 1980b). However, several national surveys have indicated that psychoactive drug use by school-age children and young adults is extensive (NIDA, 1985, 1986 see Table 18.1).

Among 18- to 25-year-olds, use of all psychoactive drugs increased in the past decade, sometimes dramatically. However, recent data indicate that use of most drugs may be leveling off. Although these signs are encouraging, use nevertheless remains high and is a cause of acute concern (NIDA, 1987).

According to survey data from the National Institute on Drug Abuse (1985), the drugs used most widely by adolescents are also the most socially acceptable, namely, alcohol, marijuana, and nicotine. The use of alcohol, marijuana, and tobacco is associated with more morbidity and mortality than use of all other drugs combined.

Studies of adolescent drinking differ in their definitions of drinking behavior, but there is general agreement that alcohol use is widespread among adolescents. In 1984 Lloyd Johnson reported that 67% of high school seniors surveyed had used alcohol in the past month, and 39% reported having had five or more drinks on at least one occasion in the 2 weeks prior to the survey (NIDA, 1985).

Of the high school seniors surveyed, 5% reported using marijuana daily (NIDA, 1985). It is estimated that daily marijuana users smoke an average of 3.5 joints per day. Of a cohort of daily users, 50% reported continuing use of marijuana at follow-up 3 years later (NIDA, 1980a).

SPECIAL POPULATIONS

TABLE 18.1 Extent of Drug Use Among 12- to 17-Year-Olds and 18- to 25-Year-Olds and Among 1984 High School Graduates

Drug	% Ever Using Drug		% Using in Past Month		% 1984 High School Graduates Using Drug 20 or More Days in Past Month
	12-17	18-25	12-17	18-25	
Alcohol	65	95	27	68[a]	4.8
Marijuana	27	64	12	27[a]	5
Tobacco	50	77	12	38[a]	18.7
Amphetamines	7	18	3	5	0.6
Hallucinogens	5	21	1	2	<.5
Cocaine	7	28	2	7	<.5
Inhalants	NA[b]	NA	NA	NA	<.5
Tranquilizers	5	15	1	2	<.5
Sedative-Hypnotics	6	19	1	3	<.5
Analgesics	4	12	1	1	<.5
Phencyclidine	2	11	NA	NA	<.5
Heroin	<.5	1	<.5	<.5	<.5

SOURCE: NIDA, 1985.
a. By comparison in the past month, 56.1% of older adults had used alcohol, 6.6% had used marijuana, and 34.1% had used tobacco (NIDA, 1985).
b. Not available.

Nicotine is beginning to be acknowledged to be a highly addictive drug with severe long-term health consequences. The 1984 survey of high school seniors found that nicotine in the form of cigarettes was used daily by 19% of respondents, making it the most used drug class (NIDA, 1985). Since 1984 there has been a slight downward trend in the use of cigarettes by adolescents.

The popularity of other psychoactive drugs among adolescents varies by region. For example, there is little phencyclidine (PCP) used in most of the Midwest. Use of PCP in rural areas has remained below the use in some large cities, particularly those on the west coast. LSD declined in popularity for a few years but has recently become popular again. Another disturbing trend in the street drug market is the use of illicitly manufactured stimulant drugs aggressively marketed as "legal stimulants." In size, shape, and color, these drugs are designed to mimic legitimately manufactured stimulants. They usually contain ephedrine, phenylpropanolamine, and caffeine. It is now uncommon to find young people using true amphetamines.

Use at Earlier Ages

Naturally, drug use was not introduced exclusively during the senior year of high school, and the respondents of the study by Johnson, Bachman, and

TABLE 18.2 Grade of First Use for Sixteen Types of Drugs, Class of 1980

Grade:	6th	7th–8th	9th	10th	11th	12th	Never Used
Marijuana	1.9	13.0	16.5	14.7	9.7	4.4	39.7
Inhalants	1.4	2.4	1.9	2.5	2.0	1.7	88.1
Amyl or Butyl Nitrates	0.1	1.2	2.2	2.6	3.2	1.8	88.9
Hallucinogens	0.1	0.8	2.2	3.5	4.3	2.4	86.7
LSD	0.1	0.5	1.4	2.2	3.3	1.7	90.7
PCP	0.2	1.0	1.9	2.7	2.6	1.0	90.4
Cocaine	0.1	0.5	1.7	3.3	5.6	4.3	84.3
Heroin	0.2	0.0	0.2	0.2	0.2	0.4	98.9
Other Opiates	0.4	0.5	1.8	2.1	3.4	1.6	90.2
Stimulants	0.3	1.5	4.3	6.6	7.3	6.3	73.6
Sedatives	0.3	0.9	2.5	3.3	4.8	3.2	85.1
Barbiturates	0.2	0.7	2.3	3.0	3.2	1.6	89.0
Methaqualone	0.1	0.3	1.3	1.8	3.3	2.8	90.5
Tranquilizers	0.3	1.6	3.0	3.3	4.4	2.6	86.8
Alcohol	8.0	22.2	24.8	19.3	11.9	7.0	6.8
Cigarettes	3.0	7.2	5.8	4.7	3.4	1.7	74.2

SOURCE: NIDA, 1980.
Note: This question was asked in two of the five forms (N \sic 6,000), except for inhalants, PCP, and the nitrates, which were asked about in only one form (N \sic 3,000).

O'Malley (1982) were asked to indicate the grade levels at which they first tried various illicit drugs. Findings include

1. Initial experimentation with most illicit drugs occurs during the final 3 years of high school.
2. For marijuana, alcohol, and cigarettes, most of the initial experiences took place before high school.
3. Nearly half of the inhalant users had their first experience prior to 10th grade.
4. For each illicit drug except inhalants and marijuana, less than half of the users had begun use prior to the 10th grade.
5. Marijuana use has been rising steadily at all grade levels down through eighth grade, but the trend lines show a decelerating curve.

Overall, the trend curves show a slackening of use over the years 1975 to 1984. The only questionable areas (use may in fact be increasing) are the stimulants and cocaine, but again, not enough data has yet emerged to draw definitive conclusions. (Table 18.2 summarizes the findings.)

Gender Differences

A number of studies concerning the use of alcohol, marijuana, cigarettes, and other substances by teenagers have demonstrated that there is a gender difference in regard to the frequency of use. Kandel (1980) concluded that males report more use than females of all substances except cigarettes. Five national surveys of high school seniors from 1975 to 1979 show that males use more alcohol and marijuana, but not more cigarettes (Bachman, Johnson, & O'Malley, 1981). Johnson and colleagues (1982) present further information with respect to substance abuse by gender. They find that for stimulant use, the annual prevalence and frequency rate is higher among females (22% versus 20%). Use of alcohol seems disproportionately concentrated among males. Despite this evidence of differences by sex, little attention has been paid to the origin of these differences.

Ensminger, Brown, and Kellam (1982) examined gender differences in substance use from a social adaptation/social bond perspective. They found early aggressiveness and early shyness to be related to later substance use for males, but not for females. For males, peer attachment and school bonds were of primary importance; for females, family bonds and school bonds ranked highest. These authors agree with Kandel (1980) and other researchers that cigarette use is practically the same across sexes. They propose that this may be caused by the greater acceptability, legally and socially, of smoking cigarettes as contrasted with the use of other substances.

Teenagers with strong social bonds to home and school are not as likely to be substance abusers as those with weaker bonds (Ensminger et al., 1982). Strong peer bonds seem to heighten use. Gender differences in the strength of social bonds did account for some of the differences in substance use, but major differences still remain unexplained by social control measures. The authors conclude that the developmental paths leading to substance use by females are the same as those for males.

Other Significant Factors

On a regional basis, there are no particularly significant differences. In general, substance use is more prevalent in the Northeast section of the nation than anywhere else, with lower rates usually occurring in the South.

As for population density, the figures (Johnson et al., 1982) are fairly predictable: Illicit drug use is highest in the large metropolitan areas and lowest in the rural or nonmetropolitan areas. Marijuana shows the largest difference, with a 56% rate in large metropolitan areas as opposed to 42% in nonmetropolitan areas. There seems to be little association with urbanicity with respect to use of tranquilizers, sedatives, stimulants, or cigarettes.

Other factors that appear to have little or no influence on teenage drug use include the family's socioeconomic status, the mother's current employment status, or the mother's current marital status (Miller & Rittenhouse, 1980).

Antecedents to Drug Use

There are several theoretical perspectives that dominate the literature on antecedents to drug use. Kandel's (1982) model describes different stages for drug use (beer and wine, hard liquor and cigarettes, marijuana, opiates, cocaine, and LSD), each stage being a likely antecedent for progression to the next stage.

Jessor and Jessor (1977) describe a very complex model. Adolescents are classified along dimensions of deviance that will, in turn, predict their drug use. The environment system (peer approval and models for drug use), behavior system (problem versus conventional behavior), and personality systems (attitudes, values, and expectations) interact to determine the risk of engaging in a wide range of adolescent problem behaviors including delinquency, early sexual experience, and drug use. In addition, there are factors that are closely related to drug use (parental use of approval or drugs) as well as distant causal factors such as parent-child relations. Longitudinal studies suggest that there is merit to these models. Analytic models have been used to describe the contribution of premorbid personality variables in an individual's choice of drug (Khantzian, 1980; Weider & Kaplan, 1984).

Sociodemographic variables do not clarify or explain initiation of drug use. Among intrapersonal characteristics, a predisposition toward rebellion, independence, and nonconformity, combined with the desire to appear more adult, consistently stand out as drug use precursors. In contrast, there is only weak or conflicting evidence supporting the importance of such personality traits as low self-esteem, external locus of control, and alienation (Kandel, 1978b; Orive & Gerard, 1980). Other studies suggest that adolescents who subsequently start using drugs develop favorable attitudes toward them before the onset of drug use (Jessor & Jessor, 1977, 1978; Kandel, Kessler, & Margulies, 1978; Mittlemark et al., 1983; Sadava, 1973; Sherman et al., 1983; Smith & Fogg, 1978). Most authorities agree that social factors play a major role in the spread of drug use among adolescents. Adolescents typically first try licit or illicit drugs with a friend, although relatives play a central role for alcohol (Orive & Gerard, 1980). The importance of peer and adult influence varies across substances. Peer influences encourage initial use of all drugs, especially marijuana. For both marijuana and cigarettes, the most important precursors are associating with peers who use the specific substance, as well as having favorable beliefs about it (Huba, Wingard, & Bentler, 1979, 1980; Jessor, Jessor, & Finney, 1973; Kandel et al., 1978; Rooney & Wright, 1982). Previous problem behaviors comprise the most important predictors of drinking hard liquor, whereas depression, lack of closeness to parents, and exposure to drug-using peers and adults maintain the strongest relationship with initiation into illicit drugs other than marijuana. Parental influences appear stronger for liquor. Parental attitudes affect drug use as well. Specific parental rules against drugs fail to prevent their adolescent's use, but parental tolerance of marijuana use or belief in the harmlessness of various drugs promotes experimentation (Jessor, 1976; Kandel, 1978a). Drug abuse is more likely among those teens whose mothers smoke cigarettes and/or drink moderately than among youths whose mothers abstain (Miller & Rittenhouse, 1980). Apparently, children learn general orientations toward or away from substance use in accordance with the mother's substance use, because this same research found a similar pattern for the stronger illicit drugs as well as for youthful use of alcohol and cigarettes.

Correlation data support the high school seniors' reports that widely used illicit drugs are more readily available than the less common drugs (Johnson et al., 1982).

Psychological Effects of Drug Use in Children and Adolescents

A consideration of normal child and adolescent development will provide the framework in which to study the special psychological effects of drugs. For purposes of this discussion, the developmental models of Freud (1964), post-Freudian ego psychology (Freedman & Kaplan, 1965), Erickson (1963), Kohlberg (1964), and Piaget (1952a, 1952b) will be used. In broad outline, these models offer complementary views of the developmental sequences. Freudian psychology and post-Freudian ego psychology address intrapsychic, interpersonal, and instinctual phenomena; Erickson, intrapsychic and interpersonal phenomena; Kohlberg, moral development; and Piaget, cognitive phenomena.

Later Childhood

In late childhood, the conflicts generated by earlier intense parental attachment have been mastered, suppressed, or sublimated. Superego functions are being consolidated, especially the inner controls derived from parental expectations and contraints. Ego functions with roots in middle childhood, specifically those of identification with and striving for the ideal, work to promote self-esteem.

Marked advances in children's cognitive abilities, combined with society's expectations that children will achieve academically, are central features of mental development during later childhood. Developmentalists of a variety of theoretical persuasions have emphasized the importance of intellectual accomplishments during these elementary-school years.

Erickson has proposed that the key developmental crisis of children ages 7 through 12 centers on children's learning to accomplish tasks well, including intellectual tasks. They want to earn recognition by producing something and gain the satisfaction of completing work by perseverance. If they are able to accomplish interesting and worthy tasks, they come through this period with a sound sense of industry. Children who have a preponderance of failure experiences during middle-school age run a risk of internalizing a sense of inferiority. When such children confront a difficult problem, they feel inadequate and unable to proceed with any solution.

In keeping with Erikson's view are Piaget's discoveries about the advance of mental processes during later childhood. Piaget posited two major periods of mental development prior to age six or seven—the sensorimotor (birth to age two) and the preoperational (ages two to seven). The third period—that of concrete operations—appears during the elementary-school years (around ages 7 through 11). The egocentrism that causes preschool children to see things only from their own viewpoint also changes as the elementary-school child gains language facility and becomes more allocentric, meaning that the child can now better understand perspectives of others. The child's thinking becomes objective rather than intuitive, with an ability to change perspective so as to fit the requirements of an external reality, to appreciate more than one dimension of a situation, and to detach one's self from the thing observed. This ability to detach in a cognitive sense, to view an action from a different perspective, becomes the basis not only for cognitive learning but also for moral judgment. Late childhood is a relatively unconflicted stage emotionally, with early childhood tensions submerged, with the rules of the game mastered and peer relationships facilitated, and with an active, increasing push toward learning and accomplishment.

Introduction of drugs at this stage can disrupt both emotional equilibrium and intellectual endeavors. The problems of concentration and attention dampen the normal efforts at mastery and achievement. The cognitive effects of impairment of memory and processing serve to increase the attentional deficits. Thus, the normal goal-oriented, achievement-oriented stage is prevented by both lack of will and lack of capacity. Lack of achievement, in turn, leads to failure to reach one's ego ideal, with consequent loss of self-esteem and loss of interest.

Early Adolescence

People who have studied adolescence closely have often observed that, for many young people, it is a particularly stressful period of life. Lewin (1935) described it as a stage of instability, a time of locomotion from one stable period (late childhood) to another stable but as yet poorly comprehended stage (adulthood). Lewin proposed that the adolescent's conception of life was forced into a fluid state by the puzzling bodily changes brought on by puberty, by the youth's growing intellect, and by new opportunities for social freedom offered by society. Emotional tensions arise from the conflict between the attitudes, values, and styles of life of the period being left behind (childhood) and the period vaguely seen ahead (adulthood).

At ages 12 through 14, developmental tasks are in a far more dynamic phase than in childhood, thus the effects of disruption are more dramatic. From a Freudian and post-Freudian perspective, the young adolescents are beginning anew to separate themselves from family and to assume a self-defined sense of identity. This process involves disengaging from childhood attachments, childhood ego ideals, and previously accepted parental values and developing new relationships, ideals, and values. Consequently, a greater or lesser degree of disorganization and disintegration occurs prior to restructuring and reintegrating at the new level. This process spans several years and absorbs large amounts of the adolescent's energies.

Marked physical changes occur at the onset of adolescence. The most dramatic of these changes is the development of sexual maturity during the period called *puberty.* Sexuality now emerges in specifically genital form, amplified by hormonal influences.

In Erickson's (1963) proposed stages of psychosocial development, a major threat to the older child's established sense of identity occurs with the advent of adolescence. At the onset of puberty, marked changes arise in the child's biological nature—the ripening of the sexual functions, rapid growth in height and weight, alterations in body contour, and growth of body hair. Acceptance of parental social and moral values, which usually continued strong during later childhood, often diminishes significantly during adolescence as peers and the images furnished by mass-communication media become increasingly important models for teenagers' social behavior. Strained relations can develop between parents and their adolescent offspring as the youths seek privilege and independence. At the same time, the youth's perception of the options offered by the world expands significantly, and the problem of selecting and preparing for a lifelong career looms large. The confluence of these forces can precipitate what Erickson has called an identity crisis, which is displayed in what he termed *identity confusion.* Therefore, a major task of adolescence becomes that of resolving the identity crisis, so that youths can enter adulthood with an increasingly secure set of values and a clearer conception of their appearance, physical and mental abilities, interests, social relationships, potentials, ambitions for the future, and individuality.

In Piaget's stages of mental development, the highest stage—that of *formal operations*—is entered during or sometime after the arrival of puberty. As teenagers achieve an increasing command of formal-operational thought, they are able to grasp concepts and employ cognitive strategies that eluded them during childhood. They can now imagine the conditions of a problem—past, present, or future—and develop hypotheses about what might logically occur under different combinations of factors.

In assessing the psychological effects of drugs on adolescent developmental progression, it is clear that cognition is extremely vulnerable. The attainment of skills and the mastery of new material, so important to the individual's self-esteem and academic progress, will be frustrated by the use of drugs. Moreover, a drug that impairs thought processes, integrating ability, and judgment and discrimination will compromise the critical transition from concrete to formal operations. A falling off in academic performance is an objective measure of the drug's effect. The acquisition of new information is impaired, as is the type of learning that requires abstract reasoning. Thus, academic achievement that requires anything beyond rote learning is hindered. Academic incapacity, in turn, leads to lowered self-esteem.

Abstract reasoning—enabling one to weigh alternatives, to think in reversible terms, and to make judgments—plays an essential role in the restructuring of the superego and the generating of an independently determined value system. Failure to develop a workable value system can lead to serious social conflicts and dislocations.

The process of separation from parents, with development of a new ego ideal and a new sense of identity, necessitates substitution of other attachments and affiliations. The youngster whose drug use leads to socially inappropriate behaviors has difficulty in developing and maintaining friendships. This inability to form meaningful new attachments may result in self-absorption and isolation, and may delay or altogether restrict the development of a stable sense of identity.

Another normal feature of the process of separation from parents and drive toward independence is oppositional and sometimes hostile behavior. When adolescents' substance use places them at odds with parental standards, their drug-related behavior can become the focus of severe conflict. The separation process then becomes overlaid with guilt and with irreconcilable differences. The younger person may interpret parental criticism as rejection and may respond with withdrawal, narcissistic preoccupation, and regression. Alienated from parents, burdened with guilt, and tenuously affiliated with the peer group, such an adolescent is highly vulnerable to the development of psychopathology.

Later Adolescence

The developmental tasks of later adolescence represent continued work on some of the early tasks of childhood, particularly sex-role identity and moral development. During later adolescence, these tasks are expanded and separated from their intimate bond with the parent-child relationship.

Strengthening gender-appropriate psychosexual identification and achieving satisfying heterosexual attachment and functioning are tasks of later adolescence, beginning in the middle teens and extending into early adulthood. Early adolescence is accompanied by heightened sexual drive and heterosexual awareness, but acting-out is usually limited to masturbation, sexual talk, transitory attachments, and crushes. These tentative activities come into sharper focus in midadolescence in the form of varying degrees of sexual exploration and experimentation, and in fleeting romantic attachments in which the beloved is idealized or is perceived as an extension of self. The goal is more one of self-gratification than of sharing. In late adolescence, sexuality and emotional attachment become unified in a relationship of mutual concern, sharing, and intimacy. This last phase is the prelude to a mature, lasting adult attachment.

During early- and middle-school age, morality consists primarily of recognizing the difference between right and wrong and learning to control one's behavior in anticipation of its moral consequences. During the stage of later adolescence, the young person is likely to have to exercise moral judgments in matters of much greater complexity than those confronting the early-school-age child. Further, the later adolescent is more aware of the multiple perspectives that are possible in a moral situation and of the principles of justice and fair play that need to be preserved in a moral decision.

Lawrence Kohlberg's (1964) theory of the development of moral thought includes three levels of moral reasoning, called preconventional (ages 4 to 10), conventional (ages 10 to 18), and postconventional (ages 18 and up). The post-conventional level of moral reasoning includes an awareness of the relativism of values and a commitment to either a personal or a universal set of moral principles. Turiel (1974) described a transitional stage between the conventional and postconventional levels during the late high school and early college years. At this time, old principles are challenged but new, independent values have not yet taken their place. This transition in moral thought closely parallels the general process of identity formation. The search for identity includes a search for a moral code that will preserve the adolescent's personal integrity.

Drug use can prove highly disruptive to these important developmental tasks. Not only does the weakened adolescent ego and tenuous sense of identity impair the establishment of a strong gender identity, but these failures, in turn, inhibit heterosexual attachments. For those adolescents who are insecure or frightened of their sexual strivings, drugs are used for their disinhibitory effect in overcoming self-consciousness and inhibition, or alternatively, for inhibiting sexual drive.

The impact of these drug effects on the developmental process is greater than can be appreciated by analyzing the various components. There are distortions and disruptions, but there is also omission of a vital, active engagement in the process of growing up—a failure to experience suffering, to come to grips with anxiety, to tolerate ambiguity and frustration. Thus, the individual emerges from adolescence without having experienced it, without being able to carry into adulthood a history of conflicts resolved, obstacles overcome, fears conquered, social skills mastered, values defined, and relationships established.

Treatment

Most viewpoints suggest that treatment of adolescents must address both substance abuse and other underlying problems in terms of concurrent psychiatric diagnosis, learning disorders, family interaction, internal conflicts, and normal developmental issues of adolescent development if treatment is to have long-term impact (Lettieri & Ludford, 1981). Prevailing opinion among drug treatment professionals requires readjustment of an entire life-style, not just treatment of physiologic drug dependence. Moreover, most adolescents never develop physical dependence or withdrawal symptoms.

Data describing the variety and degree of success of treatment facilities and the characteristics of those who attend remains incomplete as a result of the diversity and wide variety of modalities of care provided by governmental agencies, private charitable organizations, private-for-profit organizations, individual health care professionals, and concerned lay people. Furthermore, most youth treatment programs have not evaluated their services because of lack of resources and research capability.

Just as with drug treatment in general, few empirical studies have investigated the effectiveness of treatment for adolescent abusers. Findings of the few studies examining early intervention treatment did not provide evidence that this modality reduces drug abuse or prevents the effects of continued drug use (Blume & Richards, 1979; Chasanoff & Schrader, 1979; Gottheil et al., 1977; Iverson et al., 1978). Studies indicate that at least with alcohol and opiate abuse, family therapy has shown promising results (Cadogan, 1973; Stanton, Todd, et al., 1982). Polich and colleagues (Polich, Ellickson, Reuter, et al., 1984) conclude that adolescent drug abusers are typically not addicted to opiates and have less physical dependence on drugs than adult abusers. There are fewer high-rate users among adolescents. The extent of impairment is less. Adolescents are more likely to be detected as abusers by family or school and generally come to the attention of treatment only when they get into trouble. Moreover, the behavioral, family, and "life-style" problems of the adolescent drug abuser are as likely to be the cause as the effect of the drug abuse. It is critical, therefore, that a drug treatment for adolescents be oriented toward those problems. Although the consensus of researchers is that an interdisciplinary treatment approach is best suited for treatment of drug abuse, traditional treatments for drug abuse are limited to either biologic or psychological interventions. Furthermore, a full medical, neurologic, nutritional, and psychiatric evaluation is warranted given the high likelihood of concurrent or pre-existing psychiatric conditions as well as medical aftereffects of drug use.

Diagnoses on 153 patients discharged from a general adolescent inpatient psychiatric unit between 1982 and 1983 were reviewed to examine concurrent psychiatric diagnosis and a diagnosis of mixed substance disorder. Of the 153 patients, 46% had a diagnosis of mixed substance abuse disorder. In no case was this the only diagnosis. Not surprisingly, 72% had a diagnosis of conduct disorder. Other Axis I diagnoses included major depressive disorder (33%), attention deficit disorder (21%), intermittent explosive disorder (10%), schizoid disorder (7%), oppositional disorder (4%), and bipolar affective disorder (2%). Axis II diagnoses included specific developmental disorders 63% of the time; other personality disorders were borderline personality (30%), narcissistic personality disorder (8%), and schizotypal personality disorder (4%). As with the adult population, it is clear that to make a diagnosis of mixed substance abuse and to look no further is to miss other serious psychiatric pathology (Rounsaville, Weissman, Kleber, et al., 1982).

Many adolescents who reach the point of help generally have experienced a variety of serious problems in a short period of time. School performance is generally affected; the adolescent may have been suspended or expelled. Family relationships are noticeably impaired. The legal system may also be involved. Chronic substance abuse, similar to any severe disturbance of conduct, frequently requires at least a brief period of residential treatment to address the family dysfunction and the adolescent's impulsivity and tendency to act out. The presence of concurrent psychiatric conditions in addition to substance abuse (hyperactivity, learning disabilities, mental retardation, violence, suicidality, and psychosis) make outpatient treatment difficult at best. The focus of treatment during such residence is to address the misuse of substances, developmental dysfunction, and interpersonal relationships through educational sessions, group, individual, and family sessions. A 12-step Alcoholics Anonymous model is often quite helpful (Nelson & Noland, 1983).

The short-term goal in treatment of drug abuse is to help the adolescents become free of the serious negative consequences of drug use, understand the disorder, and achieve a physical and emotional state that provides them a reasonable chance of remaining abstinent. The ultimate goal of treatment is to enable them to achieve and maintain a drug-free life-style with which they can be reasonably comfortable. Clients who are dependent on drugs should be encouraged to practice lifelong abstinence.

Once any acute drug effects are resolved, the process of helping a client examine his or her drug use can begin. Clients should be encouraged to accept responsibility for their drug use and all other behaviors and to make a commitment to remaining abstinent.

When the client has accepted abstinence as a goal, treatment providers need to assess the problems the adolescent may encounter in attaining and maintaining abstinence as well as what skills the individual will require to deal with these difficulties. A plan to help the client cope with deficient skills should be developed. The intellectual, physical, and personality characteristics of the client and the dynamics of the family require thorough evaluation at this stage. Most adolescents who abuse or are dependent on drugs have poor self-esteem or other underlying problems that need to be identified during treatment. Many of these problems improve significantly with a few weeks of abstinence, but ongoing plans to work on them should be developed before the adolescent's release to an aftercare program (Niven, 1986).

Family members and significant others in the client's life should have at least an understanding of the nature of the drug problem and the treatment process. They should become familiar with the ways in which they may help or obstruct the client's progress. As a general rule they should be encouraged to participate in the adolescent's recovery program. The importance of total family involvement in treatment cannot be underestimated. The extent of appropriate family involvement quite often determines the success or failure of a particular treatment modality. Drug-abusing adolescents frequently come from families in which there are coexisting patterns of alcohol or drug abuse in either parents or siblings. Families frequently "enable" drug use by economically subsidizing their children or denying the extent of drug use or its damaging consequences. Families frequently allow themselves to be held "emotionally hostage" by believing that confronting their child will lead to an escalation of drug use and other self-destructive consequences. To return a child to such a home without addressing these issues is to allow a continuation of drug or alcohol abuse.

Prevention

Preventing a phenomenon can best be done with a clear understanding of the processes that cause it. When one examines the process by which adolescents initiate substance use, social and family influences predominate; that is, drug use typically starts among a group of friends or relatives. Drug use among family members presents a powerful message that substance use is acceptable. Frequently, parents will verbally discourage drug use among their children while drinking and taking benzodiazepines for anxiety and stress. Although educational appeals help, they are not sufficient to affect the behavior of potential drug-using adolescents. Adolescents are more interested in present-day issues, such as life at home, at school, or with friends, rather than possible future physical, social, or psychological consequences. New methods of drug prevention programs focus on social influence and peer group norms as primary motivating factors in initiating substance use among young people.

Primary prevention has the highest apparent likelihood of success. The longer a person delays initiating drug use, the less likely he or she is to become a chronic user (Brill & Christie, 1974; Davidson, Mellinger, & Manheimer, 1977; Kandel, 1978a). Prevention of experimental or regular drug use in adolescence may not ensure adult abstinence, but it may decrease the likelihood and the effects of future dependence. Polich and colleagues (1984) suggest targeting prevention programs at alcohol, marijuana, cigarettes, and stimulants based upon an index of harm theory, that is, choosing drugs that pose the greatest risk to the greatest number of adolescents based upon probability of use.

In addition, the ideal age for primary prevention by different drug classes is best determined by examining drug use rates by age. By age 16 or 17, between 20% and 30% of high school students have become users of cigarettes and marijuana. A prevention program for high school juniors or seniors thus has little relevance, but focusing on 12- to 13-year-olds addresses a group in which very few have started using. Targeting prevention activities on younger adolescents also takes advantage of a more positive group climate that exists when only a few of a child's peer group take drugs and most of them also do not approve of it. Alcohol has maintained a persistent and stable pattern of high use levels. Ten percent of all 12- to 13-year-olds and 25% of 14- to 15-year-olds have used alcohol in the past month. Alcohol prevention programs may require different timing and face less favorable odds of success given its common use among youths and adults as well as its firmly established social position in our culture.

As previously discussed, the most important antecedents of alcohol, marijuana, and other illicit drug use are the following:

- Peer drug use and approval
- Parental drug use and approval
- The adolescent's own beliefs and norms about drug use and its harmfulness
- A predisposition toward nonconformity, rebellion, and independence
- Low academic performance and motivation
- Engaging in "problem behaviors" that reflect deviance from traditional adult norms about appropriate adolescent activities

These findings have definite implications for designing prevention programs. The primary cause of initial drug use is social influence. Therefore, an important initial strategy is to help individuals resist social pressure. Programs should try to reinforce and secure social norms against drug use. Finally, the most effective appeals are likely to come from other adolescents, rather than from teachers, parents, or adult authorities. Adolescents are vulnerable to prodrug appeals because they wish to appear mature. Furthermore, adolescents are much more concerned about present-day issues, friendships, and activities than about future health problems. Therefore, prevention programs need to counteract the belief that drug use shows maturity and to concentrate on short-term consequences of drug use.

The optimal method to reach adolescents is through the school system. Schools contain natural social groups that can reinforce the program method and offer direct access to a major proportion of the adolescent population. There is empirical evidence that smoking cigarettes can be prevented by using school-based programs (Polich et al., 1984). At the age of 12, or seventh grade, fewer than 5% of children use cigarettes or illicit drugs at least once a month. The data on smoking prevention are so compelling that the marijuana prevention program by the American Lung Association is being built around the common dangers of marijuana and tobacco smoking. Thus, drug prevention programs should appropriately be targeted at junior high school students. Unfortunately, large numbers of seventh-grade students are already regular users of alcohol, a substance that, at least among adults, is broadly accepted. Programs designed to prevent initiation of drinking are unlikely to be successful. In order to work, the program must have the support of parents and administration.

The two approaches to prevention that must happen together are the creation of a drug-free support infrastructure and the identification of peer group forces that promote drug use and strategies to deal with them. Production and dissemination of informational materials, including brochures, pamphlets, print and broadcast announcements, as well as prepackaged information and teaching kits for teachers, physicians, and media personnel may assist in establishing a base of concern upon which direct initiatives can be built. Thus far, no scientific data base establishes the effects of information campaigns about illicit drugs (U.S. Senate, 1982).

Of course, testing and evaluation of school programs, parents action committees, and information programs is necessary. Resulting changes in target group knowledge and attitudes can be traced. Although it does not hurt to have a well-conceived "just say no" campaign on a national level, prevention programs that work well will be those that are local and have regular, almost daily influence on behavior.

References

Bachman, J. G., Johnson, L. D., & O'Malley, P. M. (1981). Smoking, drinking, and drug use among American high school students: Correlates and trends, 1975-1979. *American Journal of Public Health, 71,* 59-69.

Blume, R., & Richards, L. (1979). Youthful drug use. In R. I. Dupont et al. (Eds.), *Handbook on drug abuse*. Rockville, MD: National Institute on Drug Abuse.

Brill, N. W., & Christie, R. L. (1974). Marijuana use and psychosocial adaptation. *Archives of General Psychiatry, 31,* 713-719.

Cadogan, D. A. (1973). Marital group therapy in the treatment of alcoholism. *Quarterly Journal of Studies on Alcohol, 34,* 1187-1194.

Chasanoff, E., & Schrader, C. (1979). A behaviorally oriented activities therapy program for adolescence. *Adolescence, 14,* 569-577.

Davidson, S. T., Mellinger, G. D., & Manheimer, D. I. (1977). Changing patterns of drug use among university males. *Addictive Disease, 3,* 215-233.

Ensminger, M. E., Brown, H., & Kellam, S. G. (1982). Sex differences in antecedents of substance use among adolescents. *Journal of Social Issues, 38,* 25-42.

Erickson, E. H. (1963). *Childhood and society* (2nd ed.). New York: Norton.

Freedman, A. M., & Kaplan, H. I. (1965). *Comprehensive textbook of psychiatry* (Vol. 2, 2nd ed.). Baltimore: Williams & Wilkins.

Freud, S. (1964). New introductory lectures on psychoanalysis. In J. Strachey (Ed.), *The standard edition of the complete psychological workss of Sigmund Freud* (Vol. 22). London: Hogarth.

Gottheil, E., et al. (1977). An outpatient program for adolescent students: Preliminary evaluation. *American Journal of Drug and Alcohol Abuse, 4,* 31-41.

Huba, G. J., Wingard, J. A., & Bentler, P. M. (1979). Beginning adolescent drug use and peer and adult interaction patterns. *Journal of Consulting and Clinial Psychology, 47,* 265-276.

Huba, G. J., Wingard, J. A., & Bentler, P. M. (1980). Framework for an interactive theory of drug use. In D. J. Lettieri, M. Sayers, H. W. Pearson (Eds.), *Theories on drug use*. Rockville, MD: National Institute on Drug Abuse.

Iverson, D. C., et al. (1978). The effects of an education intervention program for juvenile drug abusers and their parents. *Journal of Drug Education, 8,* 101-111.

Jessor, R. (1976). Predicting time of onset of marijuana use: A developmental study of high school youth. *Journal of Consulting and Clinical Psychology, 44,* 125-134.

Jessor, R., & Jessor, S. L. (1977). *Problem behavior and psychosocial development: A longitudinal study of youth*. New York: Academic Press.

Jessor, R., & Jessor, S. L. (1978). *Theory testing in longitudinal research on drug use: Empirical findings and methodological issues*. Washington, DC: Hemisphere-Wiley.

Jessor, R., Jessor, S. L., & Finney, J. A. (1973). A social psychology of marijuana use: Longitudinal studies of high school and college youths. *Journal of Personality and Social Psychology, 26,* 1-15.

Johnson, L., Bachman, J., & O'Malley, P. (1982). *Highlights from student drug use in America 1975-1980*. Rockville, MD: National Institute on Drug Abuse.

Kandel, D. B. (1978a). Convergences in prospective longitudinal surveys of drug use in normal population. In D. B. Kandel (Ed.), *Longitudinal research on drug use: Empirical findings and methodological issues*. Washington, DC: Hemisphere-Wiley.

Kandel, D. B. (Ed.). (1978b). *Longitudinal research on drug use: Empirical findings and methodological issues*. Washington, DC: Hemisphere-Wiley.

Kandel, D. B. (1980). Drug and drinking behavior among youth. *Annual Review of Sociology, 6,* 235-285.

Kandel, D. B. (1982). Adolescent drug abuse. *Journal of the American Academy of Child Psychiatry, 20,* 573-577.

Kandel, D. B., Kessler, R. C., & Margulies, R. Z. (1978). Antecedents of adolescent initiation into stages of drug use: A developmental analysis. In D. B. Kandel (Ed.), *Longitudinal research on drug use: Empirical findings and methodological issues*. Washington, DC: Hemisphere-Wiley.

Khantzian, E. J. (1980). An ego-self theory of substance dependence. In D. J. Lettieri, M. Sayers, & H. W. Wallenstein (Eds.), *Theories of addiction* (NIDA Research Monograph No. 30, pp. 29-33). Rockville, MD: National Institute on Drug Abuse.

Kohlberg, L. (1964). Development of moral character and moral ideology. In M. L. Hoffman & L. W. Hoffman (Eds.), *Review of child development research* (Vol. 1). New York: Russell Sage.

Lavenhar, M. A. (1979). Methodology in youth drug research. In G. M. Beschner, & A. S. Friedman (Eds.), *Youth drug abuse problems: Issues and treatment*. Lexington, MA: Lexington Books.

Lettieri, D. J., & Ludford, M. S. (1981). *Drug abuse and the American adolescent* (NIDA Research Monograph No. 38). Rockville, MD: National Institute on Drug Abuse.

Lewin, K. (1935). *A dynamic theory of personality*. New York: McGraw-Hill.

Miller, J. D., & Rittenhouse, J. D. (1980). Social learning and drug use in family dyads. In J. D. Rittenhouse (Ed.), *National survey on drug abuse during the seventies: A social analysis*. Washington, DC: Government Printing Office.

Mittlemark, M. B., et al. (1983). *Adolescent smoking transition states over 2 years*. Paper presented at the annual convention of the American Psychological Association, Anaheim, CA.

National Institute on Drug Abuse. (1980a). *Marijuana and health*. Rockville, MD: Author.

National Institute on Drug Abuse. (1980b). *Theories on drug abuse: Selected contemporary perspectives*. Rockville, MD: Author.

National Institute on Drug Abuse. (1985). *Use of licit and illict drugs by American high school students 1975-1984*. Rockville, MD: Author.

National Institute on Drug Abuse. (1986). *National household drug use survey* (DHHS Publication No. ADM 87-1488). Washington, DC: Government Printing Office.

National Institute on Drug Abuse. (1987). *Cocaine use remains steady, other drug use declines among high school seniors* (DHHS Publication No. ADM 87-1488). Washington, DC: Government Printing Office.

Nelson, C. D., & Noland, J. T. (1983). *A twelve-step guide for teenagers*. Minneapolis, MN: Compare Publications.

Niven, R. G. (1986). Adolescent drug abuse. *Hospital and Community Psychiatry, 37*(6), 596-607.

Orive, R., & Gerard, H. B. (1980). Personality, attitudinal and social correlates of drug use. *International Journal of the Addictions, 15*, 869-881.

Piaget, J. (1952a). *Judgement and reasoning in the child*. New York: Humanities Press.

Piaget, J. (1952b). *The origins of intelligence in children*. New York: International Universities Press.

Polich, J. M., Ellickson, P. L., Reuter, R., et al. (1984). *Strategies for controlling adolescent drug use*. Santa Monica, CA: RAND.

Rooney, J. F., & Wright, T. L. (1982). An extension of Jessor and Jessor's problem behavior theory from marijuana to cigarette user. *International Journal of the Addictions, 17*, 1273-1287.

Rounsaville, B. J., Weissman, M. M., Kleber, H., et al. (1982). Heterogeneity of psychiatric diagnosis in treated opiate addicts. *Archives of General Psychiatry, 39*, 161-166.

Sadava, S. W. (1973). Initiation to cannabis use: A longitudinal social learning study. *Psychological Reports, 33*, 75-86.

Sherman, S. J., et al. (1983). *Becoming a cigarette smoker: A social-psychological perspective*. Paper presented at the annual convention of the American Psychological Association, Anaheim, CA.

Smith, G. M., & Fogg, C. P. (1978). Psychological predictors of early use, late use, and non-use of marijuana among teenage students. In D. B. Kandel (Ed.), *Longitudinal research in drug use: Empirical findings and methodological issues* (pp. 101-114). Washington, DC: Hemisphere-Wiley.

Stanton, M. D., Todd, T. C., et al. (1982). *The family therapy of drug abuse and addiction*. New York: Guilford.

Turiel, E. (1974). Conflict and change in adolescent moral development. *Child Development, 45,* 14-29.

U.S. Senate Subcommittee of Alcoholism and Drug Abuse. (1982, February 24). *Oversight and prevention activities of the National Institute on Alcohol Abuse and Alcoholism and the National Institute on Drug Abuse [Hearings]. Washington, DC: Government Printing Office.*

Weider, H., & Kaplan, E. (1984). Drug use in adolescents. *Psychoanalytic Study of Children, 24,* 399-431.

19

THE ELDERLY

The elderly are the segment of the population that is usually 65 years of age and older. They constitute approximately 11% of the American population and demographers predict that percentage will increase due to immigration patterns, birth rates, and longer life expectancy. The elderly are a heterogeneous group, even in age: Persons defined as elderly may be of any age between 65 and 95 and they are sometimes divided into "young old" and "old old." Unfortunately, the term *elderly* has come to be associated with decline, failing health, and loss, although a distinction can be made between this picture of aging and "successful aging" (Rowe & Kahn, 1987). When the marital and economic status of older persons is examined, there are interesting gender differences. The life expectancy of women is longer than that of men, so there is a larger pool of elderly women; of this pool, 40% of older women live alone whereas only 15% of older men live alone. Older women have higher rates of poverty: Poverty among elderly Americans living alone is primarily the poverty of widowed women ("Old, Alone and Poor," 1987).

Although older people constitute 11% of the population, they receive 25% to 30% of all prescriptions written. This is hardly surprising, considering that one feature of aging is the increasing presence of both chronic and acute disease: arthritis, hypertension, osteoporosis, rheumatism, diabetes, visual problems, hearing loss, and so on. Of the total personal health care expenditure in the United States, elderly persons represent 31% of expenditure. The patterns of use and nonuse of both prescription drugs and over-the-counter drugs raise the questions of noncompliance and compliance, and of drug interactions as well. Elderly persons are not likely to be purchasers or users of illegal substances although there are some heroin addicts who survive into old age (Pascarelli, 1985).

The drinking behavior of older people is of some interest. There is a sizable drop in the number of elderly women who are heavy drinkers; this drop occurs at about age 50. Males, too, show a decrease in the proportion of heavy drinkers at age 50 but it is a relatively minor decrease; men tend to show the most sizable decrease in heavy drinkers at age 65. There appears to be a small increase in alcohol problems among men at age 70, which may be related to the stresses of widowerhood and retirement. This may be a unique cohort effect (Gomberg, 1982), although the decreasing percentage of drinkers and heavy drinkers as people age is reported for a number of different countries and has seemed to hold up over time (Gomberg, 1990). The proportion of older people who are abstinent (who do not drink at all) rises. This may change in the future, and indeed it is reported that more older persons continue to drink than was true a generation ago (Glynn, Bouchard, LoCastro, & Hermos, 1984). As for alcohol abuse and alcoholism, reports from an epidemiological catchment areas study find a prevalence of 3.3% among males in New Haven, Baltimore, and St. Louis, and a prevalence of .4% among elderly women (Holzer et al., 1984).

Narcotics

It does not appear that illegal drugs are purchased or used by older people. It also appears that the life-style that accompanies the use of illegal or "street" drugs being what it is, not many people live to old age as drug abusers. There is, however, one exception: A number of heroin addicts survive to age 60 and older.

Pascarelli (1985), studying people participating in a methadone maintenance program in New York City, reported that 2% of those attending the program were 60 or older; this was in 1985 and it shows a clear increase from 1974 when the older addicts represented .005% of program participants. DesJarlais, Joseph, and Courtwright (1985) examined an older cohort attending New York City methadone clinics and found 286 patients in their late fifties, 262 in their sixties, 53 patients in their seventies, and 5 patients between 80 and 86 years of age. Patients whose history of addiction was 20 years or longer were interviewed, and several factors emerged as significant contributors to their longevity: having long-lived parents, living by their wits but avoiding violence, having access to heroin supplies, having a concern for cleanliness of needles, using a moderate amount of nonopiate drugs (alcohol in particular), and having the ability to hold drugs in reserve, that is, a kind of control in their use of the drug.

Interestingly enough, most of the elderly heroin addicts interviewed were in reasonably good health, and their health problems were similar to those found among their age peers. It is ironic that more than 90% of these older heroin addicts were heavy smokers at one point or another in their lives: smoking-related health problems were relatively frequent among those who were disabled. Most of the patients, living alone, used the methadone program as a neighborhood center, and many continued their concealment of their heroin habit into old age. Within the methadone clinic program these older addicts are model patients.

Smoking

Men are more likely to be smokers than women although the percentage gap between them has narrowed over time. In 1965, 28.5% of older men and 9.6% of older women were current smokers; by 1985, these percentages had become 19.6% for older men and 13.5% for older women (Public Health Services, 1987). The marked increase in female smoking after midcentury is reflected currently in cancer death statistics: in 1985, female deaths from lung cancer were greater than female deaths from breast cancer. Over the last quarter century, the percentage of women smokers in the age groups from 20 to 64 dropped, but both very young women and the female elderly actually show increases in the proportion who smoke.

In an interview study of people over 65 in Massachusetts (Branch, 1977), 23% reported themselves to be smokers. The people who were least likely to be current smokers included people living alone, people living with their children, those in the oldest age group, and those who reported their health as poor or fair.

We can only speculate about the role played by a history of smoking in the health status of older people. The effects of aging, smoking, and drinking alcoholic beverages are confounded, but clearly smoking contributes negatively to the health status of the elderly.

Medication

General

In the United States, the elderly, who constitute 11% of the total population, account for approximately 25% of the total national expenditure for medications. The most commonly prescribed/used medications include cardiovascular agents and psychoactive drugs such as sedatives and tranquilizers. Over-the-counter (OTC) drugs widely used include analgesics, laxatives, vitamins, and antacids.

There is some evidence that older persons are significantly more likely to show adverse drug reactions than younger patients (Vestal, 1982). There are more hospital admissions among older patients with adverse drug reactions.

Note that drug response will be related to the presence and severity of chronic disease (more common among the elderly), to the use of other medications (more common among the elderly), to the interaction drugs (more common among common the elderly), and to patterns of alcohol usage.

Any discussion of the use of prescribed medication by the elderly must note the phenomenon of noncompliance. The patient does not comply with instructions and there are a number of ways in which noncompliance is manifest: not obtaining the prescribed drug, discontinuing the regimen, altering the frequency or amount of medications, taking the medication along with other prescribed or OTC drugs, sharing the medication with family or friend, and so forth. Although noncompliance is usually attributed to the limitations of the elderly patient, there may be also other explanations (denial, autonomy, etc.; Gomberg, 1990). A survey by the American Association of Retired Persons (1984) found that most frequently reported noncompliance occurred, "when consumers stop taking a prescription drug mid-process" and that this behavior was attributed largely to the experience of unpleasant side effects.

Drug interaction is a complex subject and there may be drug-drug interactions, drug-nutrient interactions, drug-laboratory test interactions, and drug-alcohol interactions. There is a pharmacodynamic response that might be called drug-patient interaction in which an adverse drug reaction occurs because of individual sensitivity to a specific type of drug. As the term is commonly used, it most often means drug-drug interaction. It is important that anyone prescribing drugs for a patient asks about other medications the patient takes regularly; such a query should include questions about over-the-counter drugs as well as prescription medication.

There is some disagreement as to whether older people use over-the-counter drugs more than other age groups. One view is that the percentage of the elderly who use OTC medication may be as high as 75% or higher (Simonson, 1984). Another view is that, "compared with other age groups, the elderly do not use OTCs excessively" (Jones-Witters & Witters, 1983). It would be interesting and useful to know not only whether older people buy and use OTC drugs to a greater extent than other age groups, but whether they use "home remedies" to a greater extent—and what such "home remedies" include.

Psychoactive Drugs

Older persons have a higher rate of prescription and usage of psychoactive drugs than do people in other age groups. The mental disorders diagnosed most frequently among older persons are depression, dementia (including Alzheimer's disease), paranoia, hypochondriasis, and iatrogenic drug problems. The latter diagnosis frequently includes the elderly who are prescribed antidepressants or minor tranquilizers and who develop clear drug dependencies. Finlayson (1984) reports a study of 248 elderly inpatients in a private hospital: 86% were alcoholic, but 8% had drug dependency on a psychoactive prescription drug, and 6% were dependent on a combination of psychoactive drug and alcohol.

The duration of a drug dependency should be ascertained in an early interview. For some patients, dependence on a psychoactive drug for sedation, control of depression, and antianxiety effects has begun recently, but many older patients begin such drug dependency before their sixties; Finlayson (1984) believes that "stress intensified an established pattern of drug dependence" and that such drug dependence has been of fairly long duration.

More information is needed about depression and insomnia among older persons. Depression appears to be the most common mental disorder among older people with an estimated incidence of 10% among those 65 years and older. Depression in older individuals is not always easily diagnosed; apathy and disorientation, for instance, may be indicative of depression but they may also indicate brain syndrome. Malnutrition, memory impairments, and confusions also complicate the clinical picture. Depression may also go unrecognized when an older person presents with apathy, withdrawal, and self-devaluation, regarded by the diagnostician as an appropriate response to aging. Insomnia is another issue; it is a common concomitant of aging and one class of the most widely used psychoactive drugs are sedatives and hypnotics. Insomnia may be due to illness, psychiatric or emotional disorders, life-style patterns, and lessened need for sleep among older persons. Although insomnia per se is not life-threatening, sleeplessness may increase the person's feelings of isolation and depression. Psychoactive drugs used commonly with elderly patients include antidepressants and sedatives/hypnotics; antianxiety agents are also widely prescribed.

National surveys that include elderly people living in the community show a high usage of psychoactive drugs. An early survey found 32% of women and 21% of men to have used at least one psychoactive drug during the last 12 months (Parry, Balter, Mellinger, Cisin, & Manheimer, 1973). Prentice (1979) commented that older people receive "disproportionately higher percentages" of psychoactive drug prescriptions. Among older persons who use psychoactive drugs, 50% reported that they could not perform their regular daily activities without the medication. Morrant (1983) advised that the best policy with the elderly "may be to prescribe the fewest drugs in the lowest doses and for as short a time as possible."

In the United State, there are more people in nursing homes than in all acute care hospitals. Some surveys suggest that up to three fourths of the beds are occupied by elderly persons (most often women) with emotional, social, behavioral, and mental disorders. Many nursing homes have become institutions for the long-term care of the mentally ill, and multiple drug therapy is common practice (Vestal, 1982). Harper (1985) reports that approximately half of the residents who are given medication receive tranquilizers, although it is not clear whether a psychiatric diagnosis has been made or by whom. Psychoactive medication apparently figures importantly in nursing home treatment and a question may be raised whether a major reason for the use of such medication involves issues of care and maintenance and the minimizing of problems for the caretakers. Some might argue that this is humane treatment, but there must be some concern as to whether the interests of the patients or the interests of the caretakers are best served.

It is interesting to note that although women in all other age groups are more frequently prescribed psychoactive drugs, this seems to turn around among the elderly: more men 65 and older report use of sedatives, tranquilizers, and stimulants in the last 12 months than do women in the same age group (Robbins & Clayton, 1987). Might this datum be related to increased access to medical care and more use of medical facilities by older men?

Alcohol

Elderly problem drinkers must, first of all, be described in terms of the duration of the problem: There are early-onset alcoholics, persons who have been drinking for a good many years and who, in spite of the odds not being in their favor, have survived into old age; there are also recent-onset problem drinkers—sometimes described as those individuals who developed alcohol-related problems from age 55 or 60 on; there are also elderly problem drinkers who have had some history of heavy or problem drinking in the past but only intermittently.

Although recent-onset problem drinkers are generally agreed to constitute about one third of elderly problem drinkers in general, there is no agreement about the etiology. Much has been made of elderly stresses, for instance, loss of a spouse or role loss, as in retirement. Little is known, however, about changing biological sensitivity to alcohol, a delayed role of genetic endowment, the role of depression as antecedent, the role of health problems, or the social milieu in which the older person may find himself or herself. A question has been raised about some retirement colonies and the drinking patterns of persons who were abstainers or light drinkers when exposed to "life in the fast lane."

The frequency with which alcohol-related problems may be encountered among the elderly will vary widely with the setting in which one is looking. In hospital settings, for example, it is possible to find a sizable percentage of elderly patients with a history of heavy drinking and alcohol-related medical problems (Gomberg, 1980; Gomberg, 1982). Such studies do not often distinguish between a past history of heavy/problem drinking and a current, ongoing problem, so that numbers may range from 15% to over 40%. Of the 250 men in a mental health outreach program for older people, those with the average age of 68.7 who were referred to the program, approximately 17% had alcohol-related problems. When social agency personnel and health care providers are queried, estimates range from 7% to 14% of older persons seen as probably having alcohol-related problems. But surveys of older people living within the community, as in the epidemiological catchment area studies, estimate 3.3% of older men and .4% of older women to be diagnosable as manifesting alcohol abuse or alcoholism.

Nor do any of these reports deal with the population of the "chronic drunkenness offender," the elderly street alcoholic who would be arrested/released for public intoxication. In many cities, the issue of a Skid Row has disappeared, but the more general problem of "the homeless" includes this subgroup of alcoholic persons (Rubington, 1982).

A recent report (Holzer et al., 1984) examines the relationship between alcohol abuse in a community sample of 4,600 respondents 60 and older and marital status, education, and income. Marital status: For men, alcohol abuse is highest among the divorced and separated men, next highest among the widowed, and least among the married. For women in this age group, alcohol abuse is highest among the married. It appears that for men, abuse of alcohol is more likely to be associated with marital disruption (rather than loss per se), whereas for women, the question of alcoholism à deux may be raised, that is, older women drinking with the spouse or some other significant person. Education: In this general population sample, alcohol abuse among the elderly is more associated with low educational achievement than with high. Income: There are higher rates of alcohol abuse among the poorest, regardless of age or sex. Among older men, those who are employed report more alcohol abuse than those who are not working; for women, the rate is higher among the nonworking women.

Surveys of communities must deal with the question of underreporting. There is no empirical evidence that older people do more underreporting than younger people. Older people are sometimes more accurate than younger respondents, for instance, when responding to questions about their automobiles, and sometimes less accurate than younger respondents, for instance, in questions about their neighbors. Unfortunately, we do not have any information on the relative accuracy of older respondents when asked about drinking behaviors.

National differences may be of interest. Early studies of alcoholism rates suggested that the prevalence of alcohol abuse among English women is somewhat higher, in relation to male alcoholism, than is true for American women. In discussing elderly people with alcohol problems, it was suggested that women—with their greater longevity—might constitute a majority of the elderly alcoholic population (Rosin & Glatt, 1971). The reports from the United

Kingdom about older persons' alcohol problems continue to emphasize elderly women alcoholics (Merry, 1980; Wattis, 1981).

When one is considering the group of elderly alcohol abusers who are characterized by recent onset and relatively short duration, a question may be raised about the antecedents of the alcohol abuse. The question of stressful-events-as-precipitant is not resolved. For example, retirement seems to involve a complex adjustment, and blue-collar men tend to lower the amount of drinking, probably because so much of their drinking has been associated with the workplace and with other workers. On the other hand, among retired management and executive males, the fact of retirement does seem to play a significant role in the onset of late-life alcohol problems (Finlayson, Hurt, & Morse, 1985). It does seem simplistic to explain the onset of late-life drinking problems solely in terms of age-associated stresses; this omits family history, individual responses to alcohol, biological sensitivities, changes in use of time and in life-style and general adaptation to older-person status.

There is very little information involving comparison of personality variables or drinking patterns of older and younger problem drinkers. One study compared problem drinkers 40 to 59 years old with those 60 and older (Cahalan, Cisin, & Crossley, 1969): The older problem drinkers reported more interpersonal problems (spouse, relatives, friends, neighbors), more difficulty with the police, more accidents, more financial worries, and more binge drinking. The younger problem drinkers reported more problems associated with the workplace and more belligerence. It is generally agreed that elderly alcoholics may be more difficult to diagnose, when they appear in hospitals and clinics, than younger ones. Indicators may include self-neglect, falls and injuries, confusion, depression, and malnutrition. A few clinical reports have suggested that older problem drinkers probably drink to alleviate depression and feelings of isolation. Some of the dynamics of younger problem drinking (e.g., difficulties in impulse control, sensation-seeking, and unconventionality) do not appear to be relevant in describing the problem drinking of the elderly. When the elderly alcoholic is described as being more alienated from society than his or her age peers, it is unclear whether such alienation was antecedent to the heavy/problem drinking or whether it has followed as a consequence, or both.

When one adds the increasing number of medical problems that are likely to appear with aging to the medical problems produced by excessive use of alcoholic beverages, the medical consequences of elderly alcoholism probably appear more quickly after the onset than they do among younger problem drinkers. One issue that has received some research attention is the medical consequence of cognitive impairment. There is extensive literature on neuropsychological impairment (e.g., Grant, Adams, & Reed, 1984; Hartford & Samorajski, 1984). On tests of general intelligence, few differences appear between alcoholics and nonalcoholics; however, there are differences in specific cognitive functions: short-term memory, nonverbal abstracting, complex memory tasks, visual-spatial relationships, and the ability to process new information. There are probably differences between those older alcoholics who have been drinking heavily for decades and those whose heavy drinking began more recently. Tarter and Edwards (1986) have pointed out that alcoholic cognitive impairment often relates to "a lifestyle of abusive drinking . . . multisystem pathology induced by prolonged and excessive alcoholic beverage consumption."

Evaluation and Treatment

What are the signs that suggest that the older person may be drinking heavily? Such signs will, of course, depend on whether the person is living alone, living with a spouse or other relatives, living with nonrelatives, and the extent to which their living arrangements encourage or discourage isolation. Some of the suggestive indicators are:

1. Accidents, falls, injuries, bruises, coordination difficulties.
2. Change in nutritional habits; sudden weight loss or gain, spending less on food, offhand meals.
3. Withdrawal from accustomed social interactions and loss of interest in things that have normally been of interest to the person.
4. Memory: abnormally forgetful and forgetful about details in which the person has in the past been interested.
5. Behavioral changes, for instance, hassles with other people, usually argumentative and negative.
6. Health problems, such as gastritis or hypertension, where no previous history existed, or cardiac arrhythmias.
7. Symptomatic behaviors, such as depression, anorexia, psychomotor retardation, slurred or slowed speech, or paranoid ideation.
8. Self-neglect, manifest in appearance or in meal preparation.
9. Problems in communication with family members and friends where the individual changes his or her customary patterns.
10. Resentfulness, anger, irritation for no apparent reason.

It is a good idea, if possible, to obtain an alcohol-problem screening test, for instance, the Michigan Alcoholism Screening Test (MAST) or the CAGE. This is obviously not always possible, but in the case of older persons who are involved with some social agency or senior center, it may be possible to request—with tact—that the person take the test.

Treatment Issues

Are programs specifically designed for elder alcoholics a good idea? Some conclude that since there are "only a few age-related differences among alcoholics in treatment" there is little need for special programs (Janik & Dunham, 1983). Others believe that an elderly specific approach is "superior to 'mainstreaming' " (Kofoed, Tolson, Atkinson, Toth, & Turner, 1987). Whether or not the program is specifically designed for older problem drinkers, there are a number of issues in treatment of elderly problem drinkers that should be noted:

1. Avoid stereotyping or generalization ("that's the way the elderly are"): Each individual has a unique history, and the antecedents and patterns of problem drinking are his or her own.
2. Confrontation: Confrontation is not advisable in the face of massive denial, and it may be necessary to suggest "help" with problems and issues, not necessarily defined as substance abuse.
3. Health issues: Detoxification is a slower process with older adults, and it would be well to understand that and to allow more time, reassuring the patient during the process. In the same way, some of the cognitive effects of the heavy drinking may be reversible and here, once again, it is essential that both therapist and patient understand that patience is necessary.
4. Medication: Caution on the use and dosages of medications; a minor tranquilizer used with a younger person is liable to have more marked effects. There are mixed opinions about the use of antabuse with older alcoholics.
5. Education: Education about the effects of alcohol, about nutrition, about exercise, and about sleep may be useful and therapeutic.
6. Counseling: Counseling often involving reminiscence and life review, may involve facing losses and feelings about those losses.
7. Work: Is retirement an issue? Unfilled time? Lack of leisure interests?
8. Working with the family: What is the relationship of the patient to his or her family members, including the spouse? Can these be helpful? Can the family be involved in the treatment process?
9. Social supports: Does the patient have friends? Did he or she have friends before the heavy drinking began? Are his or her friends drinking companions or people who will be supportive of sobriety?
10. Coordination of agencies: Has the patient utilized the services of any other agency, hospital, clinic, or emergency room? Are there any other services in the community that may be useful in a treatment program (e.g., are there part-time or voluntary work groups in which the patient might be interested?)?
11. Alcoholics Anonymous or similar self-help groups: Whether it is a church group, a senior center, a club, or a service organization, are there groups within the community that reflect the person's interests?

12. It has been reported (although not verified empirically) that elderly patients are more likely to form attachments to their counselors. It would be well to explore this issue before assigning the patient to, for example, a counseling student, who will disappear after a few months.

13. As in all alcoholism treatment programs, the question of aftercare is critical; it is not good practice to detoxify a patient, give him or her some didactic and counseling sessions, and then call the therapy complete. Some form of aftercare needs to be a part of every treatment plan.

14. Barriers to treatment will appear from a variety of sources. The older patient himself or herself will not show any enthusiasm for treatment and the family may be disturbed by the idea of treatment for substance abuse problems in an elderly relative. These resistances must be recognized and discussed openly. There is, however, a kind of resistance, a barrier to treatment that the caretaker in a treatment facility is less likely to recognize: the principle of triage or, "I have so little time, better to work with younger patients who have dependent families." Clinicians who do not like working with the elderly should not do so.

15. And, finally, a caution that needs stating: The patients of the age group we have been discussing are very likely to be considerably older than the clinician. There is a very important issue about *dignidad,* recognition of the need for dignity of the elderly. This is all too often overlooked, and caretakers will address the patient by his or her first name, behaving like a somewhat impatient parent when the patient is slow or reluctant to respond. It must be remembered that the patient has lived a long life, has a variety of life experiences, and hopefully some wisdom, and although older people may try the clinician's patience, their dignity must be respected.

References

American Association of Retired Persons. (1984). *Prescription drugs: A survey of consumer use, attitudes and behavior.* Unpublished manuscript.

Cahalan, D., Cisin, I. G., & Crossley, H. M. (1969). *American drinking practices.* New Haven, CT: College and University Press.

DesJarlais, D. C., Joseph, H., & Courtwright, D. T. (1985). Old age and addictions: A study of elderly patients in methadone maintenance treatment. In E. Gottheil, K. A. Durley, T. E. Skoloda, & H. M. Wasman (Eds.), *The combined problems of alcoholism, drug addiction and aging* (pp. 201-209). Springfield, IL: Charles C. Thomas.

Finlayson, R. S. (1984). Prescription drug abuse in older persons. In R. M. Atkinson (Ed.), *Alcohol and drug abuse in old age* (pp. 61-70). Washington, DC: American Psychiatric Press.

Finlayson, R. S., Hurt, R. D., & Morse, R. M. (1985, April). *Clinical and outcome data in 224 elderly alcoholics.* Paper presented at the meeting of the Research Society on Alcoholism.

Glynn, R. J., Bouchard, G. R., LoCastro, J. S., & Hermos, J. A. (1984). Changes in alcohol consumption behaviors among men in the normative aging study. In G. Maddox, L. N. Robins, & N. Rosenberg (Eds.), *Nature and extent of alcohol problems among the elderly* (Research Monograph No. 14, pp. 101-116). Washington DC: The National Institute on Alcohol Abuse and Alcoholism.

Gomberg, E. S. L. (1980). *Drinking and problem drinking among the elderly.* Ann Arbor, MI: University of Michigan, Institute of Gerontology.

Gomberg, E. S. L. (1982). *Alcohol use and problems among the elderly (DHHS Publication No. ADM 82-1193, pp. 263-290). Washington, DC: Government Printing Office.*

Gomberg, E. S. L. (1990). Drugs, alcohol and aging. In L. T. Kozlowski, H. M. Annis, H. D. Cappell, F. B. Glaser, E. M. Sellers, M. S. Goodstodt, Y. Israel, H. Kalant, & E. R. Vingilis. (Eds.), *Research advances in alcohol and drug problems* (Vol. 10, pp. 171-213). New York: Plenum.

Grant, I., Adams, K. M., & Reed, R. (1984). Aging, abstinence and medical risk factors in the prediction of neuropsychologic deficit among long-term alcoholics. *Archives of General Psychiatry, 120,* 710.

Harper, M. S. (1985). Survey of drug use and mental disorders in nursing homes. In S. R. Moore & T. W. Teal (Eds.), *Geriatric drug use, clinical and social perspectives* (pp. 101-114). New York: Pergamon.

Hartford, J. T., & Samorajski, T. (Eds.). (1984). *Alcoholism in the elderly: Social and biomedical issues.* New York: Raven Press.

Holzer, C. E., III, Robins, L. N., Myers, J. K., Weissman, M. M., Tischler, G. L., Leaf, P. J., Anthony, J., & Bednarski, P. B. (1984). Antecedents and correlates of alcohol abuse and dependence in the elderly. In G. Maddox, L. N. Robins, & N. Rosenberg (Eds.), *Nature and extent of alcohol problems among the elderly,* (pp. 217-244). Washington, DC: National Institute on Alcohol Abuse and Alcoholism.

Jones-Witters, P., & Witters, W. L. (1983). *Drugs and society: A biological perspective.* Monterey, CA: Wadsworth Health Sciences.

Kofoed, L. L., Tolson, R. L., Atkinson, R. M., Toth, R. L., & Turner, J. A. (1987). Treatment compliance of older alcoholics: An elderly-specific approach is superior to "mainstreaming." *Journal of Studies on Alcohol, 48,* 47-51.

Merry, J. (1980). Alcoholism in the aged. *British Journal on Alcohol and Alcoholism, 15,* 56.

Old, alone and poor: A plan for reducing proverty among elderly people living alone. (1987). Baltimore, MD: Commonwealth Fund Commission on Elderly People Living Alone.

Parry, J. H., Balter, M. B., Mellinger, G. D., Cisin, I. H., & Manheimer, D. I. (1973). National patterns of psychotherapeutic drug use. *Archives of General Psychiatry, 28,* 769.

Pascarelli, E. F. (1985). The elderly in methadone maintenance. In E. Gottheil, K. A. Druley, T. E. Skoloda, & H. M. Waxman (Eds.), *The combined problems of alcoholism, drug addiction and aging* (pp. 210-214). Springfield, IL: Charles C Thomas.

Public Health Services. (1987). *Smoking, tobacco and health* (DHHS Publication No. CDC 87-8397). Washington, DC: Government Printing Office.

Robbins, C., & Clayton, R. R. (1987). Gender-related difference in psychoactive drug use among older adults. *Journal of Drug Issues.*

Rosin, A. J., & Glatt, M. M. (1971). Alcohol excess in the elderly. *Quarterly Journal of Studies on Alcohol, 32,* 53-59.

Rowe, J. W., & Kahn, R. L. (1987). Human aging: Usual and successful. *Science, 237,* 143.

Rubington, E. (1982). The chronic drunkenness offender on Skid Row. In E. L. Gomberg, H. R. White, & J. A. Carpenter (Eds.), *Alcohol, science and society revisited* (pp. 332-336). Ann Arbor: University of Michigan Press.

Simonson, W. (1984). *Medications and the elderly: A guide for promoting proper use.* Rockville, MD: Aspen Systems Corp.

Tarter, R. E., & Edwards, K. L. (1986). Multifactorial etiology of neuropsychological impairment in alcoholics. *Alcoholism: Clinical and Experimental Research, 10,* 128.

Vestal, R. F. (1982). Pharmacology and aging. *Journal of the American Geriatrics Society, 30,* 191.

Wattis, J. P. (1981). Alcohol problems in the elderly. *Journal of the American Geriatrics Society, 29,* 131.

20

WOMEN AND SUBSTANCE ABUSE

Freud called the psychology of women "a dark continent," and this continent is still relatively unexplored. Women are inadequately represented in the literature of substance abuse and alcoholism. In the last 20 years, for example, women have constituted only 7% of research subjects on treatment outcome (Vanicelli, 1984), and although there are more male substance abusers and alcoholics than female, the ratio is *not* 13:1!

Drugs may be used, misused, and abused. Drugs may also be classified as illegal or banned, prescription, or "social drugs" like nicotine or alcohol. We will discuss first those drugs that are acceptable *within limits*: nicotine, psychoactive prescription drugs, and alcohol; such drugs may be used, misused, or abused. When illegal drugs such as heroin or cocaine are involved, the drug-taking behavior per se is described as drug abuse. Alcohol is used within acceptable limits by two thirds of American adults, but it may also be abused so that the abuser is described as a problem drinker or alcoholic.

Drug/Alcohol Use and Misuse

Nicotine

Women did not begin smoking in large numbers until the 1940s. The men's peak exposure to nicotine occurred much earlier than that of women: Among men, lung cancer cases rose until 1986 when the rates leveled off, but lung cancer rates have risen steadily among women. Deaths from lung cancer surpassed mortality rates for breast cancer among women in 1985. The percent of white and black women 20 years of age and older who smoke has dropped, but at a considerably slower rate than men's. The occupations of women who smoke tend to be blue collar or pink collar; waitresses and cashiers have the highest percentage of smokers among women, whereas teachers and bank tellers have the lowest percentage.

Surveys of high school and college students show females a little more likely to smoke than their male counterparts in high school. Women in college are considerably more likely than college men to be smokers (Johnson, O'Malley, & Bachman, 1989). A great deal of concern has been expressed about the ineffectiveness of warnings and prevention efforts among young women, and Gritz (1986) has written about the relationship between smoking, weight control, and advertising among teenage girls. She has observed that "our smoking prevention programs today often do not address the lifestyle choices and values of those adolescent girls most likely to take up smoking—who are disinterested in school, not college bound, who are precocious in social and sexual behaviors, and who may especially value the images peddled by advertisements" (Gritz, 1986 p. 18).

Psychoactive Drugs

Lifetime prevalence of various drugs—sedatives, tranquilizers, stimulants, and analgesics, medically prescribed—shows a preponderance of female use except for the adolescent years. From ages 12 to 17, boys report more frequent use of sedatives, stimulants, and tranquilizers; for each drug, this turns around to more frequent report of female use from age 18 on (Clayton, Voss, Robbins, & Skinner, 1986). Males are more likely to report nonmedical use of these drugs, including obtaining a drug without prescription or misuse of a prescribed drug, males are more likely to report such behavior.

One of the issues that arose in the 1970s turned around the well-documented fact of more *prescriptions* written for women patients than for men patients. This was linked to higher rates for women of "neurotic illness," physical and mental symptoms, and help-seeking and medication-taking behavior (Cooperstock, 1976). It is relevant that women make more physician/clinic/hospital office visits than do men, and it is also true that women use more prescription drugs of all sorts than do men. We know little about health-care-seeking behaviors, and the epidemiology of psychoactive drug use may relate to frequency of office visits, physicians' stereotypes about men and women, women patients' wish for medication, and so on.

In an interesting study, Ambert (1982) examined psychotropic drug use in separated and divorced people as related to gender, parental status, and income. Contrary to other studies, she found higher drug use among men than among women. In early studies, distinctions had been made *within gender,* for instance, homemakers reported a higher level of psychoactive drug use than employed women, and men who were retired or unemployed used more such drugs than other men. Ambert's findings were that upper income men and women who had custody of their children had the lowest drug use, and lower-income men, few of whom had custody of their children, had the highest use (Ambert, 1982). These findings relate to another study of family roles and stressors related to gender differences in obtaining psychoactive drugs (Cafferata, Kasper, & Bernstein, 1983). Three explanations of the gender difference are examined: sex role theory, social support theory, and stress theory. The data support all three viewpoints to some extent. Although psychoactive drug use was affected for both men and women by "family role responsibilities," women were more likely to use. Women appear to be more sensitive than men to the effects of less supportive or more stressful family circumstances. Under these conditions, women are more likely to seek medical assistance, and physicians are more likely, under any circumstances, to prescribe psychoactive drugs for women patients than for men.

The suggestion has been made that men are more likely to respond to anxiety and depression with alcohol, whereas women are more likely to become psychoactive drug users (Parry, Cisin, Balter, Mellinger, & Manheimer, 1974).

Findings are consistent: Women are more likely to be users of prescribed psychoactive or psychotropic drugs. The relationship of female socialization, therapeutic drug use, and social sanction of the "sick role" for women in the past has been explored (Gomberg, 1982). It is of interest that when men assume nontraditional roles and approximate "the female role" with regard to work status or childcare, they also tend more frequently to be users of psychoactive drugs.

Alcohol

It is generally agreed that more men drink than do women, and that men drink larger quantities. It is not that simple, however, because there are differences in percentage of drinkers across the life span (Fillmore, 1987) and there are differences in the drinking behaviors of men and women, varying with education, marital status, income, employment, race, and religion. More drinking and higher frequency/quantity of consumption are associated with the young adult years, with nonmarried status, and with higher educational achievement. Among nonwhite minorities, the proportion of nondrinkers or abstainers among women is higher; this is true among Hispanics, Blacks, and Americans of Asian origin although there may be a question about gender differences among Native Americans.

A convergence hypothesis notes that the rates of drinking and problem drinking have increased faster for women over the last few decades and predicts that male and female rates will be the same. This hypothesis was rejected by Ferrence (1980), who found no clear evidence of convergence. Recent studies have reported differing results: Some reject the convergence hypothesis, but others note the increase in substance use (and in problems associated with that increase) among women. Some take the middle ground: Johnson et al., (1989) report that high school seniors in the United States show fewer occasions of heavy drinking for females than for males, "but this difference has been diminishing very gradually since the study began over a decade ago. . . . There also remains very substantial sex difference in alcohol use among college students and young adults generally, with males drinking more" (p. 13).

Among adolescents, there are several substances in which use is converging (e.g., nicotine) but generally, males are more frequent users and consume more alcoholic beverages than females in all age groups. The gender difference is, however, less wide than it was a generation ago.

Recent studies of adolescents and young women suggest that pleasure seeking is a primary motive for drinking, and the wish for excitement and sensation is often expressed in surveys of the young. Although some drink for escapist reasons and release of tension, hedonistic reasons for drinking are cited more frequently. One escapist reason for drinking is to modify feelings of depression, but clearly, alcoholic beverages are not, in the long run, good medicine for depression. They may minimize feelings of depression temporarily, but as time goes on, alcohol appears to increase feelings of depression.

In studies of expectancy, attitudes, and beliefs about alcohol, it appears that women show more anxiety when drinking with men than with other women, and they believe that alcohol makes them sexier and more vulnerable. Indeed, the association of drinking and sexual availability is still strong in people's belief systems, and George, Gournic, and McAfee (1988) have demonstrated with college student subjects that drinking women are viewed as different and more sexually available than nondrinking women.

Drug/Alcohol Abuse and Dependence

Narcotics and Heroin

A survey of 51,390 women who voluntarily admitted themselves to federally funded drug treatment programs during a 12-month period (Tyler & Frith, 1981) showed heroin to be the most abused drug.

Drugs of abuse studied include heroin, marijuana, barbiturates, amphetamines, sedatives, and tranquilizers; women who were never married and who were unemployed when admitted were the heaviest users of all drugs. More than half the sample had a first drug experience before age 18, but among heroin abusers, the largest proportion of clients admitted to drug treatment programs began using between 16 and 18 years of age. Age of onset differences for the different drugs are of interest: Significantly more marijuana abusers reported using it under 16 years of age than was true of any of the other drugs studied, whereas tranquilizer abusers reported first use after the age of 25.

The male-to-female ratio of opiate abusers is estimated to be 3:1 or 4:1; that is, women comprise approximately 20% to 25% of the addict population (Martin & Martin, 1980). Whatever information is available for both men and women narcotic addicts is drawn from treatment facilities, primarily federally funded community drug treatment programs. Historically, there has been an interesting turnabout. Prior to the passage of the Harrison Narcotic Act in 1914, the use of narcotics was higher among women, estimated to be twice as high as the use by men, but in the years following the criminalization of narcotics use, male use became more frequent than female use.

The question of ethnic differences among women narcotic abusers is qualified by the willingness of different groups to enter treatment and court-mandated treatment of different ethnic groups. A 1976 analysis of admissions to federally funded community drug treatment programs showed 25% of admissions to be women. There were variations in percentage in different ethnic groups: 31% of white admissions, 24% of black admissions, and 16% of Hispanic admissions were females.

Although research is sparse, it is generally believed that the actions of narcotics in men and in women are similar (Martin & Martin, 1980). There is a question about such similarity, but resolution awaits further research. Narcotic drugs have profound effects on endocrine function (most of the work has been animal studies) and heavy drug intake clearly affects the menstrual cycle and the fetus; obstetrical complications are common in female addicts. Because the estimate is that 80% to 85% of women addicts are of child-bearing age, the questions of fertility, pregnancy, fetal effects, and obstetrical complications are significant and, indeed, seem to be the major issues that are raised about women addicts.

A recent investigation (Marsh & Simpson, 1986) followed the addiction careers of 91 men and 84 women on methadone maintenance over a 12-year period. Reasons for beginning drug use were similar, with peer pressure cited frequently; reasons for quitting were similar, and there was no gender difference in the types of treatment sought. No significant differences emerged in drug use patterns, including use of alcohol, marijuana, and cocaine. Martin and Martin (1980) report that "the personality characteristics of many female addicts are in most respects similar to male addicts. They exhibit sociopathic behavior and may well have antisocial personalities" (p. 480). However, the relative psychiatric symptomatology of men and women narcotic addicts does appear to differ. Martin and Martin (1980) report women addicts to be "somewhat more neurotic and less psychopathic than male addicts." This is also reported by Marsh and Simpson (1986), who state that differences center on greater proportions of criminality among males and greater incidence of somatic complaints among females. Males are reported to act out more, and females tend to somaticize. Women addicts studied by Marsh and Simpson reported feeling more anxious and worried than the men.

A report of 546 heroin addicts in methadone maintenance programs in Southern California (Anglin, Hser, & McGlothlin, 1987) showed a number of gender differences:

1. Women took less time to become addicted; more women than men become addicted immediately after the initiation of drug use.

2. Female addicts tended to live with spouses or common-law partners who were likely to be narcotics addicts.

3. Women were less likely to be users of marijuana and/or alcohol (disagreement with the findings of Marsh and Simpson).

4. Women were less likely to be employed, more often on welfare, and less frequently dealing drugs than men.

5. Women were less likely to have been arrested/incarcerated.

These differences, as Anglin and colleagues point out, parallel traditional role expectations.

In one of the most extensive studies reported, 170 heroin-addicted women and 202 heroin-addicted men in treatment facilities in three large cities were interviewed (Binion, 1982; Colten, 1982; Tucker, 1982). In sum, this interview study reported the following:

1. Initial drug use was more closely related to interpersonal difficulties among women who sought out an addict peer group because of poor self-image and an unhappy family situation; men reported more difficulty in their early years with school, poverty, and peers. Men reported more peer group activity and more use of alcohol and other drugs. Both men and women described their mothers more positively than their fathers (Binion, 1982).

2. Differences between heroin-addicted mothers and a comparable group of nonaddicted mothers were minimal. Feelings about and perception of their children were very similar. Heroin-addicted mothers expressed more doubts about their adequacy as mothers and tended to rely on their own mothers more than did nonaddicted women. (Colten, 1982).

3. For heroin-addicted women, the absence of social support was associated with the use of nonsocial, potentially dysfunctional coping strategies, but a similar pattern does not exist for heroin-addicted men (Tucker, 1982).

A review of the literature and a report of the "changing profiles" of women's narcotic addiction (Nurco, Wegner, & Stephenson, 1982) shows that such addiction is viewed as more deviant in the white subculture than in the black subculture. Women addicts, too, are perceived as more deviant, perhaps in part because of the association of prostitution with female addiction. Nurco and colleagues emphasized the low self-esteem of the female addict, her guilt feelings, and feelings of despair, and her belief that she had little power over control and change.

In general, treatment modalities for men and women narcotics addicts are similar, and there is no evidence of poorer prognosis for one sex or the other. Treatment programs may include auxiliary services but, by and large, the major treatment is currently methadone maintenance programs. Marsh and Simpson (1986) have argued that treatment, particularly in therapeutic communities, has been male-oriented and that women tend to experience harsher confrontation and exploitation. The greater societal stigma associated with female addiction has been emphasized (Maglin, 1974; Marsh & Simpson, 1986), as well as the greater need among women addicts for financial assistance and job training. The studies reported above suggest that women have greater need for ancillary services, including counseling and support in their maternal roles.

Cocaine

The widespread abuse of cocaine is a phenomenon of the 1980s, and although some literature has appeared (e.g., Gawin & Ellingwood, 1988; Gawin & Kleber, 1986; Grabowski, 1984; Kozel & Adams, 1985), there has been very little on gender issues. Most attention to women cocaine abusers has been focused on the fetal effects of pregnant addicts' use of cocaine.

A recent study reports on comparison of 95 men and 34 women in a hospital treatment program for cocaine abusers (Griffin, Weiss, Mirin, & Lange, 1989). Comparison of some sociodemographics show the following: Women patients began cocaine abuse at a significantly younger age than the male patients, and entered treatment younger and with fewer years of abuse. With female onset at 15.6 years average, and male onset at 18.5 years average, they are clearly a young group; the great majority of patients are in their twenties. Drug-use patterns were similar for both sexes, for instance, different drugs used in the last 30 days or amount of cocaine used in the last 6 months. More men were married and men were more likely to be employed. The amount of money spent on cocaine differed, men having spent a much greater amount in the last 6-month period; this may be related to the fact that more women than men lived with a drug-dependent partner, frequently in a cohabitation arrangement.

Most of the cocaine abusers reported the use of cocaine to increase sociability, and the men and women did not differ in reports of cocaine effects on aggression, appetite, anxiety, or mood. The women gave as reasons for cocaine use depression, feelings of unsociability, family and job pressures, and health problems, and they were more likely than the men to cite *specific* reasons for use. The men, however, reported more intoxication effects, including decreased "ability to have sex." The impact of cocaine on guilt feelings differed by gender: Women reported decreased guilt, and men increased guilt.

Diagnostically, gender comparison shows a very similar pattern to alcohol abusers: Women were more likely to have other psychiatric symptomatology, particularly depression. Antisocial personality (Axis II, DSM-III-R) was reported only by men. Griffin and colleagues report that the gender difference in depression between men and women persists over time, and slower recovery from depression by women has remained constant: "Women cocaine abusers may experience more distress during early abstinence than men. This possibility is supported by our finding of poorer overall social adjustment among women" (Griffin et al., 1989, p. 125).

Generalizations from a single study of inpatients in a single institution, an inpatient psychiatric hospital, are of course limited. Nonetheless, these findings should be noted: Although both men and women patients are primarily in their twenties, women began use of cocaine earlier; the male patients were less depressed than the female patients, and the latter took longer for improvement of depressive symptomatology; the cocaine abstinence syndrome appears to be more severe with women abusers; and the guilt-relieving properties of cocaine seem to make this drug particularly reinforcing for some women.

Alcohol

The Diagnostic and Statistical Manual (DSM-III-R) of the American Psychiatric Association (1987) distinguishes between alcohol abuse and alcohol dependence. Alcohol abuse, as described in DSM-III-R, is analogous to *problem drinking,* and alcohol dependence to alcoholism. The average age of women in treatment for alcohol problems and alcoholism was reported in 1978 as the mid-forties (Armor, Polich, & Stambul, 1978), but more recent reports suggest that the average age in treatment facilities is younger, more likely to be in the thirties. Male:female ratios in alcoholism treatment facilities vary widely, depending on which subpopulation is being treated. Women are more likely to appear at middle-class and upper-class facilities (e.g., physicians' offices, private hospitals, and some outpatient facilities). They are less likely to appear in veterans medical centers, correctional facilities, and Skid Row shelters.

The antecedents of female alcoholism have been analyzed in terms of different life stages and by biological, personality, and sociocultural variables, as well as the drinking behaviors of family and peers (Gomberg & Lisansky, 1984). A question is sometimes raised about the history of child abuse as antecedent to female alcoholism. It is true that there are more positive family histories among alcoholic women than nonalcoholic women or alcoholic men (Gomberg, 1986), and in the limited literature on the question, a history of childhood abuse is reported more frequently by alcoholic women than by control women (Miller, Downs, Gondoli, & Keil, 1987). However, the alcoholic parent was rarely reported as perpetrator and the greater frequency of reported abuse seems to relate more to parental neglect.

Comparison of male and female alcoholics yields the following information:

1. In clinical populations and those who have attained sobriety, the proportion of women reporting positive family history is larger than is true of male alcoholics (Gomberg, 1986).

2. Males begin drinking earlier and develop alcohol-related problems earlier than do women. Women develop problem drinking later and come to treatment with a shorter duration of alcoholism than do men (Lisansky, 1957; Ross, 1989).

3. Women are more likely to cite a specific traumatic or stressful event as precipitant to their heavy drinking. Evidence on this question is ambiguous (Allan & Cooke, 1985; Lisansky, 1957).

4. Women are far more likely to report a spouse or lover who is a heavy/problem drinker than are men to report heavy/problem drinking by a spouse or lover. The importance of women's social environment is emphasized in the findings of Wilsnack, Wilsnack, and Klassen (1984) that women are likely to drink in ways similar to husbands, partners, close friends, and siblings.

5. At-home versus public drinking also differentiates men and women alcoholics. Although women vary by age (i.e., younger women are more likely to be drinking in public places than older women (Gomberg, 1986); taken in the aggregate, women are more likely to be drinking at home, either alone or with a significant other, than are men.

6. Cloninger's (1987) typology includes Type I, "milieulimited," and Type II, which is characterized by greater severity and antisocial behavior. Type II is seen only among males, whereas Type I, characterized by positive family history, relatively later onset, milder symptoms, and rare involvement in criminal activity, is seen among both men and women. Cloninger states that "women develop loss of control (Type I) alcoholism predominantly, with a later onset and more rapid profession of complications associated with guilt, depression, and medical complications.... Both types of alcoholism are common in men."

7. When men and women alcoholics are compared on marital status, more marital disruption is reported by women. Whether the heavy drinking comes *before* the marital disruption, or the other way around, is not known.

8. The use of other drugs is characteristic of both male and female alcoholics, but there is a good deal of variability by age and by drug. Generally, males are more frequent users of illegal or "street" drugs, and women are more frequent users and abusers of prescription psychoactive drugs such as sedatives or minor tranquilizers. Younger alcoholics of both sexes are more likely to report experience with banned substances and older alcoholics are more likely to combine abuse of prescribed drugs with alcohol.

9. Women have been described as having poorer prognosis in treatment and "the myth prevails that women have a poorer treatment prognosis than men" (Institute of Medicine, 1990). It has never been clear whether this view is based on (a) difficulties in managing the patient, (b) greater likelihood of dropping out of treatment, (c) outcome data, or (d) sex differences in dual diagnosis, or co-morbidity.

The question of co-morbidity is really several different questions:

1. Do men and women alcoholics differ in the *extent* to which they present dual diagnoses? Earlier work showed more psychiatric treatment history among women alcoholics than among males in the same facility, but recent work reports similar rates in the two sexes (Ross, Glaser, & Siasny, 1988).
2. Are the disorders that coexist with alcoholism the same for men and women? Women alcoholics do indeed manifest diagnoses of phobia, obsessive-compulsive, and panic disorders more frequently than do men, and there is general agreement that women's accompanying disorder more frequently is neurotic disorder. Males are more likely to be diagnosed as antisocial personalities. There is, however, disagreement as to whether depression is more characteristic of women alcoholics than of men. Bedi and Halikas (1985) report greater lifetime prevalence of depression among women alcoholics, and Hesselbrock, Meyer, and Keener (1985) report a larger percentage of depressed patients among hospitalized women alcoholics than men. Ross, Glaser, and Stiasny (1988) report no significant gender difference in the prevalence of affective disorder.
3. Do the other diagnostic disorders antedate the alcoholism, do they develop simultaneously, or does the psychiatric disorder follow from the heavy/problem drinking? Recent research with women alcoholics (Gomberg, 1986) shows age differences: Women alcoholics who are relatively young at onset of alcoholism show more impulsive, acting out behaviors, e.g. getting into difficulty with school/legal authorities.

Because they are a heterogeneous group with great differences not only in age at onset but in social class, ethnicity, marital status, employment status, etc., treatment plans for the woman patient should be individualized, keeping in mind the special needs of women substance abusers.

References

Allan, C. A., & Cooke, D. J. (1985). Stressful life events and alcohol misuse in women: A critical review. *Journal of Studies on Alcohol, 46,* 147-152.

Ambert, A. M. (1982). Drug use in separated/divorced persons: Gender, parental status, and socio-economic status. *Social Science Medicine, 16,* 971-976.

American Psychiatric Association. (1987). *Diagnostic and statistical manual of mental disorders* (3rd ed., rev.). Washington, DC: Author.

Anglin, M. D., Hser, Y. I., & McGlothlin, W. H. (1987). Sex difference in addict careers: 2. Becoming addicted. *American Journal of Drug and Alcohol Abuse, 13,* 59-71.

Armor, D. J., Polich, J. M. & Stambul, H. B. (1978). *Alcoholism and treatment.* New York: John Wiley.

Bedi, A. R,. & Halikas, J. A. (1985). Alcoholism and affective disorder. *Alcoholism: Clinical and Experimental Research, 9,* 133-134.

Binion, V. J. (1982). Sex differences in socialization and family dynamics of female and male heroin users. *Journal of Social Issues, 38*(2), 43-58.

Cafferata, G. L., Kasper, J., & Bernstein, A. (1983). Family roles, structure, and stressors in relation to sex differences in obtaining psychotropic drugs. *Journal of Health and Social Behavior, 24,* 132-143.

Clayton, R. R., Voss, H. L., Robbins, C., & Skinner, W. F. (1986). Gender differences in drug use: An epidemiological perspective. In B. A. Ray & M. C. Braude (Eds.), *Women and drugs: A new era for research* (NIDA Research Monograph No. 65.) Washington, DC: Government Printing Office.

Cloninger, C. R. (1987). Neurogenetic adaptive mechanisms in alcoholism. *Science, 236,* 410-416.

Colten, M. E. (1982). Attitudes, experiences and self-perception of heroin addicted mothers. *Journal of Social Issues, 38*(2), 77-92.

Cooperstock, R. (1976). Psychotropic drug use among women. *Canadian Medical Association Journal, 115,* 760-763.

Ferrence, R. G. (1980). Sex differences in the prevalence of problem drinking. In O. Kalant (Ed.), *Alcohol and drug problems in women.* New York: Plenum.

Fillmore, K. M. (1987). Women's drinking across the adult life course as compared to men's. *British Journal of Addiction, 82,* 801-811.

Gawin, F. H., & Ellinwood, E. H., Jr. (1988). Cocaine and other stimulants: Actions, abuse and treatment. *New England Journal of Medicine, 318*(18), 1173-1182.

Gawin, F. H., & Kleber, H. (1986). Pharmacological treatments of cocaine abuse. *Psychiatric Clinics of North America, 9,* 573-583.

George, W. H., Gournic, S. J., & McAfee, M. P. (1988). Perceptions of postdrinking female sexuality: Effects of gender, beverage choice, and drink payment. *Journal of Applied Social Psychology, 18,* 1295-1317.

Gomberg, E. S. L. (1982). Historical and political perspective: Women and drug use. *Journal of Social Issues, 38*(2), 9-24.

Gomberg, E. S. L. (1986). Women and alcoholism: Psychosocial issues. In *Women and alcohol: Health related issues* (DHHS Publication No. ADM 86-1139, pp. 78-120). Washington, DC: Government Printing Office.

Gomberg, E. S. L., & Lisansky, J. M. (1984). Antecedents of alcohol problems in women. In S. C. Wilsnack & L. J. Beckman (Eds.), *Alcohol problems in women* (pp. 233-259). New York: Guilford.

Grabowski, J. (Ed.). (1984). *Cocaine: Pharmacology, effects, and treatment of abuse* (DHHS Publication No. ADM 84-1326). Washington, DC: Government Printing Office.

Griffin, M. L., Weiss, R. D., Mirin, S. M., & Lange, U. (1989). A comparison of male and female cocaine abusers. *Archives of General Psychiatry, 46,* 122-126.

Gritz, E. R. (1986). Gender and the teenage smoker. In B. A. Ray & M. C. Braude (Eds.), *Women and drugs: A new era for research* (NIDA Research Monograph No. 65, pp. 70-79). Washington, DC: Government Printing Office.

Hesselbrock, M. N., Meyer, R. E., & Keener, J. K. (1985). Psychopathology in hospitalized alcoholics. *Archives of General Psychiatry, 42,* 1050-1055.

Institute of Medicine. (1990). *Broadening the base of treatment for alcohol problems.* Washington, DC: National Academy Press.

Johnson, L. D., O'Malley, P. M., & Bachman, J. G. (1989). *Drug use, drinking and smoking: National survey results from high school, college and young adults populations, 1975-1988* (DHHS Publication No. ADM 89-1638). Washington, DC: Government Printing Office.

Kozel, N. J., & Adams, E. H. (Eds.) (1985). *Cocaine use in America: Epidemiologic and clinical perspectives* (DHHS Publication No. ADM 85-1414). Washington DC: Government Printing Office.

Lisansky, E. S. (1957). Alcoholism in women: Social and psychological concomitants: I. Social history data. *Quarterly Journal of Studies on Alcohol, 18,* 588-623.

Maglin, A. (1974). Sex role differences in heroin addiction. *Social Casework, 55,* 160-167.

Marsh, K. L., & Simpson, D. D. (1986). Sex differences in opioid careers. *American Journal of Drug and Alcohol Abuse, 12,* 309-329.

Martin, C. A., & Martin, W. R. (1980). Opiate dependence in women. In O. J. Kalant (Ed.), *Alcohol and drug problems in women* (pp. 465-485). New York: Plenum.

Miller, B. A., Downs, W. R., Gondoli, D. M., & Keil, A. (1987). The role of childhood sexual abuse in the development of alcoholism in women. *Violence and Victims, 2,* 157-172.

Nurco, D., Wegner, N., & Stephenson, P. (1982). Female narcotic addicts. *Focus on Women, Journal of Addictions and Health, 3,* 62-105.

Parry, H. J., Cisin, I., Balter, M., Mellinger, G., & Manheimer, D. (1974). Increasing alcohol intake as a coping mechanism for psychic distress. In R. Cooperstock (Ed.), *Social aspects of the medical use of psychotropic drugs* (pp.119-144). Toronto: Alcoholism and Drug Addiction Research Foundation of Ontario.

Ross, H. E. (1989). Alcohol and drug abuse in treated alcoholics: A comparison of men and women. *Alcoholism: Clinical and Experimental Research, 13,* 810-816.

Tucker, M. B. (1982). Social support and coping: Applications for the study of female drug abuse. *Journal of Social Issues, 38*(2), 117-138.

Tyler, J., & Frith, G. H. (1981). Primary drug abuse among women: A national study. *Drug and Alcohol Dependence, 8,* 279-286.

Vanicelli, M. (1984). Treatment outcome of alcoholic women: The state of the art in relation to sex bias and expectancy effects. In S. C. Wilsnack & L. J. Beckman (Eds.), *Alcohol problems in women* (pp 369-412). New York: Guilford.

Wilsnack, R. W., Wilsnack, S. C., & Klassen, A. D. (1984). Women's drinking and drinking problems: Patterns from a 1981 survey. *American Journal of Public Health, 74,* 1231-1238.

Chapter 21

LESBIANS AND GAY MEN

The "Third Special Report to the U.S. Congress on Alcohol and Health" by the Department of Health, Education and Welfare (National Institute on Alcohol Abuse and Alcoholism, 1978) has a section on population groups that need special intervention. The report says: "It has been demonstrated that socio-cultural factors influence whether, how much, and why a person drinks" (p. 17). Mentioned are blacks, youth, women, Spanish, Indians, and the elderly. Gays are not mentioned, although they also fit the reason given for looking at special populations. In the "Fourth Report" (1981) gays are briefly mentioned, but they are again left out in the "Fifth Report" (1983). Besides women, gays are the category that are contained within all the other groups and thus have a great complexity of sociocultural interactions on their drinking. They are unique in that they are the only group who are able to hide in other minority groups or in the general society.

Researchers and therapists interested in all the causes of substance abuse problems (e.g., Brenner, 1980; Levinson, 1983; Rabow & Watts, 1983) mention every conceivable social variable that can be taken into account, but sexual preference is conspicuous by its absence.

This chapter often refers only to alcohol, and infrequently to all drugs, as alcohol is the more pervasive problem. In addition, the sources we found to review usually dealt only with alcohol. It is, of course, more difficult to study and deal with recreational use of other drugs because (a) they are illegal and, therefore, more covert, and (b) they are numerous and taken for various reasons with various consequences. Whenever interventions are described that are appropriate or necessary for alcohol problems, they are also often applicable to the area of other drugs. The two are interrelated problems with alcohol often masking the more complicated drug problems.

Incidence and Prevalence of Substance Abuse Problems

There is little research on lesbians and gays and alcohol (Nardi, 1982), and even less on gays and other drugs. However, it is impractical to treat alcohol problems and ignore the other drugs, for it becomes obvious to therapists working with gays and lesbians, and to any researcher familiar with the gay community, that there is high likelihood that alcohol will not be the only drug involved. This has been noted, for example, by Smith (1982) and Ziebold and Mongeon (1982). Reports on acquired immune deficiency syndrome (AIDS) patients and controls also show high and varied drug use among gays (e.g., Jaffe, Choi, Thomas, & Haverkos, 1983; Valdiserri, 1984). Sandoval (1977) in her observational and interview study of Spanish-speaking gays who attended bars in and around Dade County, Florida, estimated that 30% were active drug seekers. An observational study by Israelstam and Lambert (1984) found that drugs such as "poppers" (inhaled nitrites) and marijuana were very common, and all other recreational drugs besides heroin were prevalent on the gay bar scene in many cities of the world.

The incidence of alcoholism among lesbians and gay men is often a sharply debated question. Despite lack of accurate and detailed data, the few research efforts that have been done support one another's findings and suggest that alcoholism and/or alcohol abuse currently affect about one third of American gay men and lesbians. Saghir and Robins (1970) stated that 30% of gay men and 35% of the lesbians studied were dependent on alcohol or drank excessively. Weinberg and Williams (1974) found 19.4% of the male homosexual population they studied reported "drinking more than they should," that is, drinking nearly "all the time." Lohrenz and his associates (Lohrenz, Connely, Coyne, & Sparks, 1978) examined alcohol problems among gay males in four Midwestern cities. Their study revealed that 29% of the 145 respondents were categorized as alcoholic on the basis of their Michigan Alcoholism Screening Test (MAST) scores. Beatty (1983) reported on the findings of two gay counseling centers in Pennsylvania. Both centers discovered that 40% of their new admissions had MAST scores indicative of alcoholism.

The Fifield (1974) proposal submitted to the National Institute on Alcohol Abuse and Alcoholism estimated that over 97,000 of the estimated lesbian population of 320,000 residing in Los Angeles (30.3%) had an alcohol abuse problem. Saghir and Robins (1970) compared a nonclinical sample of 57 lesbians with a group of 43 unmarried heterosexual women. They found that 35% of the lesbians had reported a history of excessive drinking or alcohol dependence, as compared with only 5% of the heterosexual women. Other studies report comparable levels of alcohol abuse among lesbians. Sandmaier (1979), for example, presents a 1972 study of drinking habits among blacks in a St. Louis housing project that indicated that 36% of the lesbians living in the project were either heavy or problem drinkers.

These estimates of the incidence of alcohol abuse among lesbians and gay men, although by no means comprehensive, do indicate that approximately one third of lesbian women and gay men are alcoholics. As such, alcohol abuse among homosexuals constitutes a serious social problem whose parameters need to be investigated, outlined, and understood before effective treatment interventions can be developed and applied.

Theories of Lesbian and Gay Substance Abuse

The literature is certainly not lacking in speculation about factors that may account for the high incidence of alcoholism among gay men and lesbians, but empirical research remains almost nonexistent. Traditionally, studies have focused on intrapsychic factors and on establishing a causal link between homosexuality and alcoholism. Small and Leach (1977) comprehensively reviewed a number of such studies based on psychoanalytic theory and found "no clear evidence that alcoholism is caused by homosexuality." Nardi (1982) has further suggested that psychoanalytic theory has been the major source of false assumptions concerning the relationship between alcoholism and homosexuality: "Psychoanalytic research on alcoholism . . . has suffered from the use of oppressive and sexist concepts and methodologies" (p. 17).

At present, the sociocultural perspective appears to be by far the most widely favored explanation for the difference in rates of alcoholism between gay and straight populations. Ziebold and Mongeon (1982, p. 5) suggest that there is no evidence of a causal relationship between alcoholism and homosexuality. They posit that lesbian and gay alcoholics drink for basically two reasons: (a) they socialize primarily in gay bars; and (b) lesbians and gays drink to "hide from the world and to escape from their feelings of being different." Implicit in the author's argument is the notion that our culture lacks the support systems for those lesbian and gay alcoholics seeking recovery. They suggest that the high incidence of alcoholism among gay men and lesbian women would be significantly lower were there more appropriate places for homosexuals to meet and interact. They further state that until gays and lesbians feel comfortable in "coming out" to the heterosexual community, many will continue to use alcohol to manage discomfort.

Weathers (1980) has asserted that, basically, "lesbian women drink for the same reason anyone else drinks—alcohol's there and it works" (p. 144). Weathers suggests that the increased stress of belonging to an oppressed minority, as well as the limited opportunity for meeting and socializing with other lesbians, can lead to conditions that may encourage alcohol abuse. She then lists two factors that play a critical role in the lesbian alcoholic's experience: (a) societal condemnation of the lesbian life-style, which can lead to or exacerbate feelings of low self-esteem, depression, powerlessness, and isolation; and (b) the lesbian/gay bar is the major social institution in most lesbian communities: "While the relationship between drinking and socializing is a common thread running throughout American Culture, the emphasis on this relationship is exacerbated in the lesbian sub-culture due to a lack of alcohol-free alternatives and limited social options available to lesbians in the larger society" (p. 145).

Burke (1982) further supports the notion that sociocultural factors contribute to lesbian alcoholism. In a factor analysis comparing alcoholic and nonalcoholic lesbians and heterosexual women, Burke found support for the hypothesis that the lesbian bar in conjunction with the alienation and isolation experienced by lesbians in a heterosexually dominant culture is related to the high rate of alcoholism among lesbian women.

The alienation-oppression theme has also been explored by Nardi (1979). He saw the gay alcoholic as suffering from the double bind of homosexuality on the one hand and alcoholism on the other. He argues that many emerging homosexuals are afraid to confront their feelings and behaviors openly due to society's negative attitudes toward homosexuality. This homophobic society instills in those coming to terms with their sexuality a variety of feelings about the immorality and deviant nature of homosexuality.

> Self-hatred, fear of being different, and lowered self-esteem often lead to strong ego defenses and rigid denial techniques. Hiding one's feelings, sexual and otherwise, becomes normative. The homosexual coming out finds he or she must struggle not only against society's demands but also against his or her own defenses. The individual becomes alienated from his feelings. To cope with those blocked feelings the homosexual often, but not always, turns to alcohol. (p. 5)

Nardi mentions that heterosexuals also turn to alcohol to cope with similar feelings of low self-esteem and blocked feelings. The main difference, however, is that the gay person usually lacks other external sources of strength that are available to the heterosexual, such as family bonds and work-related relationships. The homosexual may become more vulnerable to addictive behavior as a source of comfort and coping. Alcohol usually then becomes that addiction. Therefore, Nardi views alcohol abuse as a symptom of the oppression that the gay person faces in society.

A consistent theme in the literature is the suggestion that the factors leading to alcohol abuse among gays and lesbians are mainly psychogenic in origin. Alcohol is seen as a way of coping with the psychic toll on the homosexual due to various forms of oppression that result in intrapersonal and societal alienation. Concomitants of this alienation and oppression are reduced self-esteem, frustration, anger, fear, loneliness, self-doubt, and inadequacy. Diamond and Wilsnack (1978), using intensive interviews with 10 lesbian alcohol abusers, discovered strong dependency needs, power needs, negative self-perceptions, low self-esteem, and feelings of depression.

Treatment Strategies and Issues

Weathers (1980) cites the unresponsiveness of alcoholism service agencies to the lesbian and gay alcoholic as a possible reason for the high rate of alcohol abuse in the homosexual community. She found that most of the alcoholism agencies staff questioned in a survey demonstrated judgmental and restrictive attitudes toward gays and lesbians and continued to regard homosexuality as a pathology. Such negative attitudes tend to deter the lesbian or gay alcohol abuser from seeking help for their drinking and may serve to reinforce contin- ued drinking. In particular, Weathers discovered three major types of negative interaction that characterized the lesbian alcoholics' experience with alcohol- ism agencies:

1. Refusal of services if the woman's lesbianism is known or suspected.
2. Provision of services on a limited basis, or with negative attitudes that are not conducive to support, growth, self-disclosure, or sobriety.
3. Provision of services directed toward isolating and "curing" lesbianism as the primary problem, with little or no attention directed to alcoholism.

Because of the prevalence of such negative attitudes, Weathers (1980) believes that the lesbian woman's chances for recovery in many alcoholism agencies may range from poor to nonexistent.

Beaton and Guild (1976) have drawn attention to the unique treatment needs of homosexual problem drinkers. They point out that the majority of such treatment approaches have been geared toward aversion therapy or psycho- analysis. The problem arose in that these methods of treatment stressed the psychopathology of homosexuality and acted in the belief that if you cured the homosexuality, you automatically cured the addiction to alcohol. This approach has been condemned by Beaton and Guild and others involved in treating homosexual alcoholics (i.e., Schultz, 1974; Weathers, 1980; Ziebold, 1979). They insist that the problem is addiction to alcohol and not the fact of being gay or lesbian. This is particularly important in beginning to work with lesbian and gay clients who may use their sexual and affectional orientation as an excuse to continue drinking. Denial and rationalizations need to be confronted. Recovery from alcoholism becomes attainable almost as soon as the client can view it as a condition causally independent of homosexuality (Small & Leach, 1977).

Most alcohol treatment facilities appear to have little awareness of the special needs of the homosexual alcoholic, although there is some evidence that this is changing. One response to the neglect of this population has been the development of separate treatment programs. In 1980, there were approximately 100 specialized programs for gay and lesbian alcoholics and over 300 gay Alcoholics Anonymous (AA) groups (Brandma & Pattison, 1982).

Weathers (1980) founded the "Alcoholism Center for Women" in Los Angeles with a view to isolating the unique treatment needs of the lesbian alcoholic and designing treatment services relevant to those needs. Based on the experiences, inputs, and observations of gay community service workers, recovered lesbian alcoholics, and concerned alcoholism professionals, she defined four major needs relevant to a social support perspective:

1. The need for a safe and nonjudgmental environment in which to share honestly and receive support.
2. The need for a peer support group, both during treatment and to facilitate community re-entry.
3. The need for full access to a wide range of services, including alcoholism-focused groups and counseling, vocational development, social welfare, and recovery home services.
4. The need for nontraditional support services to facilitate self-esteem, positive identity, and self-development. These include lesbian issues raps, C/R (consciousness raising) groups, assertion training, and alcohol-free social alternatives.

As previously noted, our society heavily stigmatizes both lesbianism and alcoholism in women, and this results in considerable damage to the self-esteem of lesbian alcoholics. Anger at societal rejection may be projected onto other lesbians or repressed, with resulting depression and feelings of powerlessness and isolation (Ziebold & Mongeon, 1980). Alcohol may be used to cope with negative feelings about being lesbian. Because alcohol is itself a depressant, however, its use only exacerbates problems with self-esteem. The client who has internalized society's negative attitudes toward homosexuality will need assistance in developing a positive lesbian identity (Hall, 1978). Woodman (1982) has suggested that the client should be helped to reassess internalized myths and stereotypes and explore involvement with other individuals or a group with similar interests.

Treatment modalities for alcohol abuse include individual, couples, family, and group therapy, and AA. There is little systematic research on the relative effectiveness of each modality with lesbian and gay alcoholics; most reports are anecdotal and involve small samples. However, with the increasing interest in viewing presenting problems within a systems perspective, individual treatment appears to be losing favor as a modality. There is a growing recognition of the role of the family in the maintenance of problem drinking and more interest in the use of conjoint and family therapy. It is important in all cases to identify significant others and family members who can lend support to the client (Anderson & Henderson, 1985).

Nardi (1982) has discussed three ways of conceptualizing the lesbian family: the family of origin, the extended close lesbian friends, and the intimate ongoing relationship with another woman. Relatively little has been published about the significant others of lesbian alcoholics, but it is known that interactions within the lesbian support system usually occur in the presence of alcohol. Nardi (1982) argues that the treatment of lesbian alcoholics must involve their lovers and that successful intervention "depends on restructuring the norms and roles of the extended family system" (p. 88).

The involvement of significant others in treatment is based on their role in maintaining the client's alcoholic drinking. Whitney (1982) has defined the co-alcoholic as the "person in the alcoholic's life who intervenes in such a way as to prevent the alcoholic from facing the consequences of his actions" (p. 37). The co-alcoholic is usually the alcoholic's lover but can also be a friend, employer, or relative. According to O'Donnell (1979), "the lesbian community is full of co-alcoholics. . . . Co-alcoholism is more elusive and may be more difficult to cure than alcoholism" (p. 78).

Ziebold (1978) sees peer group support for gay alcoholics as basic to recovery and feels that the gay community has to take over the role of the family. He says that concerned gays must go into the general community and seek out the socially isolated homosexual alcoholics.

The literature emphasizes the relationship between drinking and socializing in the gay and lesbian communities. It has also been suggested that the lesbian subculture may encourage or at least tolerate heavier levels of drinking (Diamond & Wilsnack, 1978). It would seem that the homosexual alcoholics' social networks are likely to revolve around the reinforced drinking behaviors. It is unlikely that any form of treatment will be successful with this population until alcohol-free social alternatives are made available to the client.

Some people believe that because of the negative experiences gay and lesbian alcoholics have had seeking help from nongay treatment agencies, only the gay community will be able to reach and treat the gay alcoholic effectively. Ziebold (1978) presents four points in support of this position:

1. The gay community could become the supportive surrogate family for the gay alcoholic without a supportive family structure.

2. If the intervention in the active drinking stage occurs in the gay community, there is a greater chance of reaching the socially isolated homosexual and less chance of exposing his or her orientation.

3. Alcohol-free re-entry into social relationships would be maximized by treatment in a gay setting.

4. A gay treatment agency would provide the role models essential for self-acceptance as a homosexual.

There are, however, problems inherent in separate facilities. This approach reinforces the isolation and alienation of the homosexual from the heterosexual community. If agencies develop a policy of referring to a lesbian/gay agency, nongay workers will have less and less contact with lesbian alcoholics and may become less inclined to examine their own attitudes about alternative life-styles.

Zigrang (1982) succinctly states the major disadvantage of gay alcohol treatment agencies: "Through their separation from the heterosexual majority they may ultimately contribute to the perpetuation of homophobic attitudes that appear to have significantly contributed to gay alcoholism in the first place" (p. 31).

The one element that characterizes the research on gay and lesbian substance abuse is a lack of empirical research. Clearly, if we are to develop successful treatment programs, we must first systematically study the etiologies of the problem and evaluate various treatment approaches.

Resources

National Association of Lesbian
and Gay Alcoholism Professionals
(NALGAP)

General Correspondence/Membership:
NALGAP
1208 East State Boulevard
Fort Wayne, IN 46805

Clearinghouse/Library/Bibliography/Directory:
NALGAP
204 West 20th Street
New York, NY 10011

International Advisory Council (IAC)
for Homosexual Men and Women in Alcoholics Anonymous
P.O. Box 492
Village Station
New York, NY 10014

National Lesbian and Gay Health Foundation (NLGHF)
P.O. Box 65472
Washington, DC 20035

References

Anderson, S. C., & Henderson, D. C. (1985). Working with lesbian alcoholics. *Social Work, 30*(6), 518-525.

Beaton, S., & Guild, N. (1976). Treatment for gay problem drinkers. *Social Casework, 9*(5), 302-308.

Beatty, R. (1983). *Alcoholism and the adult gay male population of Pennsylvania.* Unpublished master's thesis, Pennsylvania State University, University Park, PA.

Brandma, J. M., & Pattison, E. M. (1982). In J. M. Pattison & E. Kaufman (Eds.), *Encyclopedic handbook of alcoholism* (pp. 737-741). New York: Gardner.

Brenner, M. H. (1980). [Discussion of paper by R. Smart.] In T. C. Harford, D. A. Parker, & L. Light (Eds.), *Normative approaches to prevention of alcohol abuse and alcoholism: Proceedings of a symposium, 1977.* Washington, DC: Department of Health, Education and Welfare.

Burke, P. (1982, April). *Bar use and alienation in lesbians and heterosexual women alcoholics.* Paper presented at the 30th National Alcoholism Forum, Washington, DC.

Diamond, D. L., & Wilsnack, S. C. (1978). Alcohol abuse among lesbians: A descriptive study. *Journal of Homosexuality, 4,* 123-142.

Fifield, L. (1974). [Gay Community Services Center grant proposal] Submitted to the National Institute on Alcohol Abuse and Alcoholism, Los Angeles, CA.

Hall, M. (1978). Lesbian families: Cultural and clinical issues. *Social Work, 23*(5), 380.

Israelstam, S., & Lambert, S. (1984). Gay bars. *Journal of Drug Issues, 14,* 637-653.

Jaffe, H. W., Choi, P. A., Thomas, P. A., & Haverkos, H. W. (1983). National case-control study of Kaposi's sarcoma and pneumocystis-carinil pneumonia in homosexual men: 1. Epidemiologic results. *Annals of Internal Medicine, 99,* 145-151.

Levinson, D. (1983). An anthropological perspective on the behavior modification treatment of alcoholism. In M. Galanter (Ed.), *Recent developments in alcoholism* (Vol. 1). New York: Plenum.

Lohrenz, L., Connely, J. C., Coyne, L., & Sparks, K. E. (1978). Alcohol problems in several midwestern homosexual communities. *Journal of Studies on Alcohol, 39,* 1959-1963.

Nardi, P. M. (1979). *Double doors: Homosexuality and alcoholism.* Unpublished manuscript.

Nardi, P. M. (1982). Alcoholism and homosexuality: A theoretical perspective. In T. O. Ziebold & J. E. Mongeon (Eds.), *Alcoholism and homosexuality* (pp. 9-25). New York: Haworth.

National Institute on Alcohol Abuse and Alcoholism. (1978). *Third special report to the U.S. Congress on alcohol and health.* Washington, DC: Department of Health and Human Services.

National Institute on Alcohol Abuse and Alcoholism. (1981). *Fourth special report to the U.S. Congress on alcohol and health.* Washington, DC: Department of Health and Human Services.

National Institute on Alcohol Abuse and Alcoholism. (1983). *Fifth special report to the U.S. Congress on alcohol and health.* Washington, DC: U.S. Department of Health and Human Services, Public Health Service.

O'Donnell, M. (1979). Alcoholism and co-alcoholism. In M. O'Donnell et al. (Eds.), *Lesbian health matters* (p. 78). Santa Cruz, CA: Santa Cruz Women's Health Collective.

Rabow, J., & Watts, R. K. (1983). The role of alcohol availability in alcohol consumption and alcohol problems. In M. Galanter (Ed.), *Recent developments in alcoholism* (Vol. 1). New York: Plenum.

Saghir, M., & Robins, E. (1970). Homosexuality: IV. Psychiatric disorders and disability in the female homosexual. *American Journal of Psychiatry, 127,* 64-71.

Sandmaier, M. (1979). *The invisible alcoholics: Women and alcohol abuse in America.* New York: McGraw-Hill.

Sandoval, M. C. (1977). Patterns of drug abuse among the Spanish speaking gay bar crowd. In B. M. Du Toit (Ed.), *Drugs, rituals and altered states of consciousness* (pp. 169-187). Rotterdam: A. A. Balkema.

Schultz, A. (1974). Radical feminism: A treatment modality for addicted women. In *Developments in the field of drug abuse*. Cambridge, MA: Schenkman.

Small, J., & Leach, B. (1977). Counseling homosexual alcoholics. *Journal of Studies on Alcohol, 38,* 2077.

Smith, T. M. (1982). Specific approaches and techniques in the treatment of gay male abusers. *Journal of Homosexuality, 7,* 53-69.

Valdiserri, R. O. (1984). AIDS surveillance and health education: Use of previously described risk factors to identify high-risk homosexuals. *American Journal of Public Health, 74,* 259-260.

Weathers, B. (1980). Alcoholism and the lesbian community. In C. Eddy & J. Ford (Eds.), *Alcoholism and women.* Dubuque, IA: Kendall/Hunt.

Weinberg, M. S., & Williams, C. J. (1974). *Male homosexuals: Their problems and adaptations.* New York: Oxford University Press.

Whitney, S. (1982). The ties that bind: Strategies for counseling the male alcoholic. In T. Ziebold & J. Mongeon (Eds.), *Alcoholism and homosexuality* (pp. 37-41). New York: Haworth.

Woodman, N. J. (1982). Social work with lesbian couples. In A. Weick & S. T. Vandiver (Eds.), *Women, power, and change* (pp. 114-124). Silver Spring, MD: National Association of Social Workers.

Ziebold, T. O. (1978). *Alcoholism and the gay community.* Washington, DC: Blade Communications.

Ziebold, T. O. (1979, January). Alcoholism and recovery: Gays helping gays. *Christopher Street.*

Ziebold, T. O., & Mongeon, J. E. (1980, May). *Treatment strategies for homosexual alcoholics in recovery and reconstruction.* Paper presented at the meeting of the National Council on Alcoholism, Seattle, WA.

Ziebold, T. O., & Mongeon, J. E. (Eds.). (1982). *Alcoholism and homosexuality.* New York: Haworth.

Zigrang, T. A. (1982). Who should be doing what about the gay alcoholic. In T. O. Ziebold & J. E. Mongeon (Eds.), *Alcoholism and homosexuality.* New York: Haworth.

22

ETHNIC MINORITIES

The ethnic minorities with whom this chapter will be concerned are those federally mandated minorities within the United States: African Americans (blacks), Hispanic Americans, Asian/Pacific Americans, and American Indians and Alaska Natives. Minorities, in the 1980 census, constituted approximately 25% of the American population. Generally, health has improved among all Americans in the last serveral decades, but most of the minorities continue to have higher death rates from chronic diseases and to have lower life expectancies than the white segment of the population. Variations in drinking patterns, drinking problems, and drug abuse have been noted among different racial and ethnic groups for the last 20 years. What is presented here is a brief summary of what is known about each of the four minority groups about alcohol and drug abuse.

African Americans

African Americans, or blacks, constitute about 12% of the total American population, the largest racial minority group. Studies done in the 1960s and 1970s suggested that alcohol consumption patterns were reasonably similar for black and white males, but quite dissimilar for black and white women. Herd (1989) reported the results of a 1984 national survey that again indicate that black and white males show similar percentages of abstainers, moderate drinkers, and heavy drinkers. Black/white differences are more pronounced when results with women are compared. Nearly half (46%) of black women are abstainers, whereas only one third (34%) of white women report themselves as abstainers. Moderate drinking is reported similarly by black and white women,

273

but almost twice as many white women as black women were classified as "frequent high maximum drinkers."

When the data are analyzed by age group, there are some striking differences: Both men and women in the 18 to 29 year age group show the same results. White persons in that age group are more likely to be heavy and frequent drinkers. The age at which heavy/problem drinking is likely to appear among blacks is of interest: Blacks in middle-age cohorts show significantly more alcohol-related medical problems than do whites of comparable age. The heaviest alcohol consumption among whites is in the age group 18 to 29 years; heaviest alcohol consumption among blacks is in middle age.

The pattern of age-specific alcohol problems is quite different among blacks and whites. Heaviest alcohol consumption among whites occurs during the twenties; however, problems associated with drinking are more frequent among middle-aged blacks than among middle-aged whites. Herd (1990) has reported recently that "although black and white men appear to have very similar drinking patterns, the two groups of men may differ considerably when the relationship between alcohol use and some indicators of social and economic status are considered."

Those indicators include age (young white males have a much higher proportion of frequent heavy drinkers than young black males), income (high income status among blacks is associated with low rates of heavy drinking; among whites, income has little relationship to heavy drinking), and regional differences, which occur among whites but not among blacks.

Black/white differences in drinking behaviors are more pronounced when women are compared. The prevalence of heavy drinking occurs slightly more often among white women than black, but abstinence figures are reverse (i.e., there are more black abstainers than white abstainers) and this persist through all age groups, although the difference between black and white women becomes even greater when the women are 40 years of age or older. The difference in abstinence rates also persists in the four regions of the United States studied, although the rates of abstinence are almost identical for the north central region (Herd, 1989).

Although it used to be believed that black adolescents began drinking earlier and had many drinking problems, the epidemiological data suggest that fewer black than white adolescents drink at all, and that those who do drink less frequently, get drunk less often, and have lower rates of heavy and problem drinking than whites (Herd, 1989). Findings from that National Survey of Senior High School Students bear out these results (Harford & Lowman, 1989).

The incidence of medical problems, particularly cirrhosis, associated with drinking is high among blacks. Although there has been a decline in cirrhosis mortality, rates remain twice as high for nonwhite Americans as for whites. For both sexes, cirrhosis mortality among nonwhites peaks 10 years earlier than among whites. The only group for whom these figures are reversed are males over 65 years of age; white males in that age group are at greater risk of cirrhosis death than nonwhites.

Relatively little has been written on treatment of black alcohol abusers. Debate usually centers on the issue of need for culture-specific programs. Some argue that culture-specific treatment programs are justified when there is a large enough group of patients drawn from a particular ethnic group. Others believe that culture-specific treatment programs can be accomplished through individualized treatment programming (Maypole & Anderson, 1986-1987). A discussion of practical treatment issues, working with black alcoholics, has appeared recently (Brisbane & Womble, 1985-1986).

Some early studies suggested that black alcoholics were strongly motivated in seeking treatment and showed more cooperation in the treatment process (Strayer, 1961; Vitols, 1968). Selective factors operating in which black alcoholics sought treatment and the kinds of treatment sought make generalizations questionable. Several reports suggest that black women alcoholics (Strayer, 1961) have better prognosis than white women alcoholics in the same treatment program (Burtle, Whitlock, & Franks, 1974). A report of black and white women entering a treatment program (Corrigan & Anderson, 1982) reported that the black women were primarily drawn from lower-income groups, and the white group was drawn from a wide class range. The black women reported greater likelihood of drinking with others, were less likely to conceal their drinking, and less likely to use other drugs while drinking. Unlike other reports, Corrigan and Anderson found that black women do less well in treatment outcome than the white women. A pilot study of 40 black alcoholic women members of Alcoholics Anonymous (Brisbane, 1986-1987) showed 20 of them to have had alcoholic fathers and 14 of them to have had alcoholic mothers. An employed, middle-class group, the typical woman in this study considered that her intervention was produced by concern about and encounters with adolescent children, and she states that she used her faith in God and church attendance to help her stop drinking. Of some interest is the difference in the women's attitudes toward paternal and maternal alcoholism in their families of origin: The mother's alcoholism was viewed as "disgusting and unforgivable." They apparently experienced shame in talking about their mothers but displayed "a rather detached atttitude" about their fathers' drinking.

The role of the black church in recovery has been discussed (Prugh, 1986-1987); although the church may be a potent force in recovery, there are limitations. Younger persons may not be attending church in the same numbers as their elders. Those who get into the pattern of heavy drinking are not likely to be churchgoers.

Other Drugs. Historically, American blacks in the last century were associated with the use of cocaine ("happy dust"), although there is little evidence to support the supposition of association. A search for black/white differences in drug abuse has not been productive. The 38 studies tabulated in a National Institute on Drug Abuse review of drug abuse among minorities (Trimble, Padilla, & Bell, 1987) yield little more than a caveat that simplistic black/white comparisions are a questionable approach. Comparison simply on the basis of race is limited because there is, as one methodological issue, evidence of difference among subgroups in the same racial group, for instance, between American blacks and West Indian blacks (Kleinman & Lukoff, 1978).

The heroin situation has changed over the last several decades. Up to the 1980s, the profile of a heroin addict was a male adolescent, "disproportionately from minority groups, and living in the inner city area" (Kozel & Adams, 1986). How heroin entered the black urban world is well described in the autobiographical *Manchild in the Promised Land* (Brown, 1965). Currently, the composite picture of a heroin addict takes into account the increase in heroin dependence among young adults, women, and whites. Cocaine, as the drug of the 1980s, was originally considered the "champagne" of drugs, but the relatively low-priced accessibility of "crack" and the complex network of the drug business has created the current "war on drugs." Many—by no means all—of the casualties of the "crack" trade are in the inner city and belong to minority groups. The accessibility of treatment and prevention programs for poor and minority drug abusers is a problem—resources are inadequate for the size of the problem.

Hispanic Americans

The Hispanic Americans are the second-largest minority group in the United States. This diverse group consists of Mexican Americans, Puerto Ricans, Cubans, Dominicans, and other groups. The drinking patterns of Hispanics differ from other ethnic groups' patterns, and there appear to be more alcohol-related problems among Hispanics. The higher prevalence of heavy drinking and of alcohol-related problems among Hispanics is largely a male phenomenon. Hispanic women are less likely than non-Hispanic women to drink heavily or to report alcohol problems. Caetano (1989) has reported that only about a fifth of Hispanic men (vs. half of Hispanic women) are abstainers. Caetano has also pointed out that heavy drinking and drinking problems do not decline as Hispanic men move from their twenties to their thirties—in fact they increase. As is probably true with other ethnic groups, foreign-born Hispanics drink less than first-generation Hispanic men and women born in the United States.

There is general agreement among researchers that there is a higher lifetime prevalence of alcohol problems among Hispanics but there are several caveats: There is more study of Mexican Americans than of other Hispanic groups, and there are apparently regional differences even among Mexican Americans. The areas usually studied are Texas and California, and Gilbert (1989) points out that there are fewer abstainers among Mexican Americans in California than among their Texas counterparts. The higher prevalence is entirely a male issue, and there are fewer reports of alcohol-related problems among Mexican American women than among non-Hispanic white women.

Caribbean Hispanics (Cubans, Puerto Ricans, Dominicans) differ among themselves, and their drinking patterns and alcohol problems differ from those of Mexican-Americans. It is speculated that because they have migrated more recently, Caribbean Hispanics are more likely to maintain drinking practices from home, such as fiesta drinking or weekend binges.

Premature death from alcohol-related causes is high among Mexican-American men, and there are some very real needs for programs of prevention. Culture-specific programs are needed. The persistence of high rates of heavy drinking and problems among men age 30 and beyond suggests that drinking may be integrated into male socialization and development differently among Hispanics than in the general population.

Treatment issues raise the questions of cultural differences and the reluctance of many Hispanics to utilize the treatment facilities designated for substance abusers. For the children in families where the father may be a heavy or abusive drinker there is a double problem: acculturation and a heavily drinking parent (Figueroa & Oliver-Diaz, 1986-1987). Although Alcoholics Anonymous and its associated groups have made some effort to reach out to the Spanish-speaking heavy drinker/alcoholic, there is a major problem, namely that the idea of disclosing family problems in a public forum is unacceptable. For many Hispanic Americans deprived of a large extended family, some religious groups have served as substitute for family, and some fundamentalist groups have become primary systems of recovery. Other indigenous recovery systems involve traditional cultural systems (e.g., *curanderos*). Little information is available about the extent to which spiritual therapies are utilized. The limited data available suggest that Hispanic patients can do as well in treatment programs as Anglo patients. What is clearly needed in professional treatment facilities are Spanish-speaking counselors with cultural sensitivity.

A report on drug abuse among ethnic minorities (Trimble et al., 1987) presents the literature about the different Spanish-speaking groups.

Mexican Americans. An early study of Mexican-American heroin addicts (Chambers, Cuskey, & Moffett, 1970) who were admitted to the Public Health

Service Hospitals at Lexington, Kentucky, and Fort Worth, Texas, suggested that these heroin addicts, compared to white, black, and Puerto Rican addicts in the same hospitals, were more likely to be high school dropouts, to have begun opioid use earlier, and to be employed at the time of admission. More recent work is not more encouraging: Comparison of posttreatment outcomes among black, white, Mexican-American, and Puerto Rican patients in methadone maintenance programs found higher rates of Mexican-American dropout from the program, more arrests, and small reduction in opioid use—but a higher level of employment than members of other ethnic groups (Judson & Goldstein, 1982). Studies of adolescents have turned up widespread use of inhalants and high prevalence rates of marijuana use (Padilla, Padilla, Ramirez, Morales, & Olmedo, 1979); a later study showed a decline in inhalant use but increased use of alcohol and marijuana as well as prevalant use of PCP (Perez, Padilla, Ramirez, Ramirez, & Rodriquez, 1980). Limited information is available on cocaine use among Mexican Americans, but though Anglo deaths from cocaine doubled between 1982 and 1984, such deaths tripled among Hispanics. Alcohol is often used either as a substitute for or in addition to opioid drugs, which increases risks for Mexican-American drug abusers.

Puerto Ricans and Cubans. When the various Hispanic groups are compared for the number of drug abusers who enter federally funded programs, Mexican Americans show the largest percentage of opiate abusers (81.3%) but the Puerto Rican percentage is only modestly lower (77.1%). The proportion of Cuban Americans who abuse alcohol, marijuana, barbiturates, or amphetamines is the largest of the three Hispanic groups. Mexican Americans have the highest percentage of inhalant abusers of the three Hispanic groups.

Studies of Puerto Ricans need to differentiate among Puerto Ricans who remain on the island of Puerto Rico and those who migrate to the United States, particularly New York City. In New York City, the annual death rate due to drugs was 23.2 per 100,000 in the general population but 37.9 for Puerto Ricans living in the city (Alers, 1982). Recent figures indicate that Puerto Ricans constitute 28% of methadone maintenance program patients in New York City, but they constitute only 10.3% of the population. It is a realistic concern when Puerto Ricans in New York City report drug abuse to be the most important health problem in their community. Puerto Rican female drug abusers face a triple problem: pressures faced by all Puerto Ricans adjusting their value system to an American culture, pressure of cultural tradition and values for Puerto Rican women, as well as the pressures encountered by all drug abusers.

A problem drug for Cuban Americans living in South Florida is cocaine. This may be related to this area being a major place of entry for the cocaine trade and/or the relationship of this drug to Cuban-American value systems. Questions have been raised about engaging and treating Cuban-American drug users

(Trimble et al., 1987). Denial and fear of status loss make this a group difficult to reach or maintain in treatment, and in the Cuban-American community, parental influences combined with peer influences may create problems. Adolescents' peer groups are composed largely of children of the family's social network, which complicates the matter of peer influence in any given adolescent's drug abuse. One suggestion has been the utilization, in treatment, of family therapy techniques within a group treatment context. As with all Hispanic groups, the disruptive impact of acculturation must be considered in treatment planning. The Mariel refugees, recent Cuban immigrant arrivals, pose another set of questions for drug treatment service efforts.

A number of questions emerge: (a) Within a given ethnic group, which subgroups are most at risk for drug and alcohol abuse? (b) Although it has been common practice in drug and alcohol studies to compare "white" and "non-white" populations, such a division is grossly inadequate, and each ethnic group needs study; what is the efficacy of particular treatment and prevention strategies with different ethnic and different age groups? (c) What treatment modalities, indigenous and traditional, have been used in dealing with substance abuse, and how are such modalities perceived and responded to by different ethnic groups?

Asian/Pacific Americans

According to the 1980 census, Asian Americans and Pacific Islanders numbered more than 3.7 million and are one of the fastest-growing ethnic groups in the United States. This ethnic group, however, consists of 32 subgroups, of which only the Chinese, Japanese, Korean, and Filipino subgroups have received research attention; Americans from India, Pakistan, the Fiji Islands, Malaysia, Okinawa, Sri Lanka, Tibet, and so on have been relatively little studied. Some beliefs about this ethnic group in relation to drinking include viewing the group as predominantly nondrinkers and viewing all the subgroups as similar. Surveys suggest that there are clear differences between subgroups. Kitano and Chi (1989) report that in a Los Angeles study, Japanese and Chinese Americans had a higher porportion of drinkers than abstainers, but that the opposite is true for Korean and Filipino Americans; heavy drinking, mainly among males, was noted in each group, with the greatest amount of heavy drinking among the Japanese and the lowest among the Chinese.

The state of Hawaii has a very diverse population, the four largest ethnic groups being Caucasians, Japanese, Native Hawaiians, and Filipinos. A state-wide epidemiological study (Murakami, 1989) indicated that the largest consumers of alcohol were the Caucasians and the Native Hawaiians, who apparently experience similar symptoms and psychosocial problems linked to alcohol. Native Hawaiians appear to be at highest risk for alcohol abuse, but they are less inclined to seek professional help than the other subgroups. The Chinese and Filipino groups rank lowest on estimates of drinking prevalence and abuse, and the Japanese fall between the highest and lowest drinking subgroups. Alcohol use is far less frequent among females than among the males.

The significance of drinking among elderly Chinese has been little studied, but there is a report of a study done with clients 50 years or older who enter the Chinese-American Service League in Chicago (Yu & Liu, 1986-1987): Health was cited as the principal reason the elderly drink, but also as the principal reason they have stopped drinking. Those who drink for health reasons report folk beliefs about the benefits of alcohol; those who stopped drinking usually cited a chronic illness, such as diabetes or coronary disease. It is of interest that sex differences in abstinence in this age/ethnic group are small—it may be that at younger ages, Chinese women do not drink but that at older ages, the social acceptability of drinking permits them to drink, albeit moderately, ostensibly for health reasons. Two thirds of the elderly interviewed reported that they flush whenever they drink, but a quarter of them reported that they would continue drinking despite the flushing. The "Oriental flushing" reaction to alcohol presumably acts as a deterrent to excessive drinking. Because it is an uncommon reaction among Caucasians but prevalent among Chinese, Japanese, and other Asian populations, the latter groups' relatively low rates of alcoholism have been attributed to this reaction. Johnson (1989) has reviewed the literature on this question and notes that the association between the flushing reaction and lower alcohol consumption, though positive, is quite weak and occurs only under particular conditions. Among Koreans, for example, flushing is common, and there is a high rate of abstinence; however, Koreans who do drink frequently drink heavily. Flushing is also common among people with Asian backgrounds, such as American Indians and Eskimos, many of whom drink heavily. Johnson's research has demonstrated differences in the amount of alcohol necessary to produce the reaction. It is likely that the protective influence of the flushing reaction is seen primarily among those who flush after one drink or less.

A report from Los Angeles of Asian-American drinking practices (Kitano & Chi, 1986-1987) showed both differences and similarities among four subgroups: Chinese, Japanese, Korean, and Filipino. Drinking styles varied but similarities were found among those most likely to drink: men under 45 with relatively high social status and educational background, in professional or white-collar occupations, and with permissive attitudes and permissive friends. The authors make the point that in spite of evidence of "heavy drinking," there was little evidence of "problem behavior." Most drinking was done in social settings and on special occasions so that "drinking behavior was socially controlled."

Other Drugs. Because Asian Americans are perceived as "the model minority," substance-abuse issues tend to be overlooked or minimized. A California study in the 1970s indicated that of the approximately 1,000 Asian inmates in correctional institutions, about 90% were there for drug-related charges. A report from the state of Washington (Washington State Commission on Asian American Affairs, 1983) stated that evidence of drug use and drug problems in the Asian youth community "is much more serious than what is recorded by law enforcement agencies," and in New York City, the police and community organizations have expressed concern over the increase in youth gang activities. Because of the diversity of the Asian-American population (and one source of diversity among many is the recency of immigration), research generalizations are limited. The surveys that have been done are reported in a National Institute on Drug Abuse monograph (Trimble et al., 1987). In addition to all the other problems of such research, there are the added problems of history: the stereotype of the Chinese associating them with the use of opium, prostitution, gambling, and *tong* wars. One study (Ball & Lau, 1966) reports the typical Chinese opiate addict as an immigrant with limited English, a mean age of 53, and socially isolated; the Chinese were overrepresented in the patient population treated at the Public Health Service Hospital in Lexington, Kentucky, but Ball and Lau report that they constituted less than 3% of the addicts at Lexington. More recent statistics about Asian and Pacific Americans in San Francisco who utilized drug-abuse treatment showed them to comprise slightly over 3% in a city in which they constitute over 21% of the population. There is little certainty: It would be remarkable if there were no drug problems among Asian and Pacific American youth, but the question is whether there is disproportionately fewer, more, or the same numbers of problems as found among American youth in general.

American Indians and Alaska Natives

American Indians constitute less than 1% of the United States' population and are divided into approximately 280 separate tribal entities. Alaska Natives consist of 22 different ethnic groups. Among American Indians, alcohol abuse and alcoholism are several times higher than among the general population. Abstinence is practiced by a high percentage of Indian women in some tribes. Indian men between the ages of 25 and 44 have the highest rates of alcohol consumption. Among American-Indian women who drink, the rates of heavy drinking are high, and an extremely high incidence of fetal alcohol syndrome has been reported in some Indian groups (Dorris, 1989). Although Indian women generally consume less alcohol than the men (exception: Sioux women), they account for nearly half of all deaths from cirrhosis. Among Indian women, the death rate from cirrhosis is more than triple the rate for black women and about six times greater than the rate for white women (Spiegler, Tate, Aitken, & Christian, 1989).

Less is known about drinking behaviors among Alaska Natives, although some research on social indicators of alcohol problems in Alaska, such as hospital admissions, accident records, arrest records, and suicide rates, does indicate a disproportionately high rate of alcohol-related disorders in the native population. It is not altogether clear where the origin of the binge-drinking style or drinking party, in which alcoholic beverages are consumed until the supply is exhausted, lies. Some attribute the binge style to the high reward placed on alcoholic beverages in earlier times, others to the more recent prohibitions enforced for American Indians and Alaska Natives. Binge drinking is still prevalent among Indians who live on reservations or in rural areas in general, whereas "maintenance drinking," drinking heavily and regularly, characterizes much of urban Indian drinking (Weibel-Orlando, 1989).

Alcohol contributes directly to 4 of the 10 leading causes of death among American Indians: accidents, liver diease, homicide, and suicide (Heath, 1989). Accidents have been the leading cause of death among Indians of both sexes. Liver disease is the eighth leading cause of death among Indians. Homicide occurs at a rate more than double that in the overall population. Suicide rates are nearly twice the general age-adjusted rate, higher than that of the other nonwhite minorities (French & Hornbuckle, 1980). Morbidity and mortality linked to alcohol vary greatly from one tribe to the other.

Indian young people are at particularly high risk for heavy drinking and for alcohol problems, and the data show a steady increase in lifetime use of alcohol by young people over the last decade. Survey data show that significantly more Indian young people in junior and senior high school had used alcohol in the last 2 months than non-Indians of the same age, and nearly 40% of the 12-year-olds had used alcohol in the previous month, 8% on multiple occasions; a greater percentage of Indian high school youth reported getting drunk in the prior month, and they were more likely to have gotten drunk on multiple occasions. When Indians and non-Indian young people are compared, both groups report getting drunk for the first time at about the same age, but once they have started drinking, the Indian young people tend to get drunk more often (Spiegler et al., 1989).

Walker, Benjamin, Kivlahan, and Walker's (1989) study of alcohol treatment programs for Indians has yielded discouraging results. The Seattle study shows a low frequency of successful treatment outcome and a high recidivism rate, although most subjects were in treatment for "extensive time." Cross-cultural comparison and study has produced many hypotheses: Heavy drinking patterns may be associated with anxiety, dependency conflict, feelings of powerlessness, a hunting-gathering economy, and a relatively low degree of societal complexity. Leland (1976) has raised a question about the relevance of mainstream criteria for alcohol study of alcoholism treatment and client functioning in Alaska. Moore (1986-1987) suggests some avenues of treatment development: The most significant inpatient treatment variables were completion of treatment and amount of counselor time. Important pretreatment variables were the degree of impairment, prior experience with treatment, criminal record, and social support for heavy drinking from the social environment. The latter turns out to be one of the most important factors in maintaining sobriety.

Other Drugs. With survey data on a large sample of Indian young people, Oetting, Edwards, Goldstein, and Garcia-Mason (1980) reported alcohol as the most abused drug, but the next most used drugs were marijuana, cigarettes, inhalants, stimulants, and cocaine. Significantly more Indian young people have tried marijuana and inhalants than comparable age non-Indians, and the Indian young people are apparently exposed to drugs other than alcohol at younger ages. However, virtually all studies have been in the Southwest, and studies of urban Indian alcohol and drug abuse are minimal. Knowledge gaps are huge, but it is probably fair to conclude that alcohol and drug abuse is a major, if not *the* major, mental health problem for American Indians and Alaskan Natives. The challenge lies in how most effectively to treat and to prevent.

References

Alers, J. O. (1982). *Puerto Ricans and health.* New York: Fordham University, Hispanic Research Center.

Ball, J. C., & Lau, M. P. (1966). The Chinese narcotic addict in the United States. *Social Forces, 45,* 68-72.

Brisbane, F. L. (1986-1987). Divided feelings of black alcoholic daughters: An exploratory study. *Alcohol Health and Research World, 2*(2), 48-50.

Brisbane, F. L., & Womble, M. (Eds.). (1985-1986). Treatment of black alcoholics. *Alcoholism Treatment Quarterly, 2*(3/4), 1-270.

Brown, C. (1965). *Manchild in the promised land.* New York: Macmillan.

Burtle, V., Whitlock, D., & Franks, V. (1974). Modification of low self-esteem in women alcholics: A behavior treatment approach. *Psychotherapy: Theory, Research and Practice, 11,* 36-40.

Caetano, R. (1989). Drinking paterns and alcohol problems in a national sample of U.S. Hispanics. In D. L. Spiegler, D. A. Tate, S. S. Aitken, & C.M. Christian (Eds.), *Alcohol use among U.S. ethnic minorities* (NIAAA Research Monograph No. 18, pp. 147-162). Washington, DC: Government Printing Office.

Chambers, C. D., Cuskey, W. R., & Moffett, A. D. (1970). Demographic factors in opiate addiction among Mexican Americans. *Public Health Reports, 86*(6), 523-631.

Corrigan, E. M., & Anderson, S. C. (1982). Black alcoholic women in treatment. *Focus on Women: Journal of Addictions, and Health, 3*(1), 49-58.

Dorris, M. (1989). *The broken cord.* New York: Harper & Row.

Figueroa, R. L., & Oliver-Diaz, P. (1986-1987). Hispanic alcoholics' children need extra help. *Alcohol Health and Research World, 2*(2), 66-67.

French, L. A., & Hornbuckle, J. (1980). Alcoholism among Native Americans: An analysis. *Social Work, 25,* 275-280.

Gilbert, M. J. (1989). Alcohol-related practices, problems, and norms among Mexican Americans: An overview. In D. L. Spiegler, D. A. Tate, S. S. Aitken, & C. M. Christian (Eds.), *Alcohol use among U.S. ethnic minorities* (NIAAA Research Monograph No. 18, pp. 115-134). Washington, DC: Government Printing Office.

Harford, T., & Lowman, C. (1989). Alcohol use among black and white teenagers. In D. L. Spiegler, D. A. Tate, S. S. Aitken, & C. M. Christian (Eds.), *Alcohol use among U.S. ethnic minorities* (NIAAA Research Monograph No. 18, pp. 51-62) Washington, DC: Government Printing Office.

Heath, D. B. (1989). American Indians an alcohol: Epidemiological and sociocultural relevance. In D. L. Spiegler, D. A. Tate, S. S. Aitken, & C. M. Christian (Eds.), *Alcohol use among U.S. ethnic minorities* (NIAAA Research Monograph No. 18, pp. 207-222) Washington, DC: Government Printing Office.

Herd, D. (1989). The epidemiology of drinking patterns and alcohol related problems among U.S. blacks. In D. L. Spiegler, D. A. Tate, S. S. Aitken, & C. M. Christian (Eds.), *Alcohol use among U.S. ethnic minorities* (NIAAA Research Monograph No. 18, pp. 3-50) Washington, DC: Government Printing Office.

Herd, D. (1990). Subgroup differences in drinking patterns among black and white men: Results from a national survey. *Journal of Studies on Alcohol, 51*(3), 221-232.

Johnson, R. C. (1989). The flushing response and alcohol use. In D. L. Spiegler, D. A. Tate, S. S. Aitken, & C. M. Christian (Eds.), *Alcohol use among U.S. ethnic minorities* (NIAAA Research Monograph No. 18, pp. 383-396) Washington, DC: Government Printing Office.

Judson, B. A., & Goldstein, A. (1982). Prediction of long-term outcome for heroin addicts admitted to a methadone maintenance program. *Drug and Alcohol Dependence, 10,* 383-391.

Kitano, H. H. L., & Chi, I. (1986-1987). Asian-Americans and alcohol use: Exploring cultural differences in Los Angeles. *Alcohol Health and Research World, 2*(2), 42-47.

Kitano, H. H. L., & Chi, I. (1989). Asian-Americans and alcohol: The Chinese, Japanese, Koreans, and Filipinos in Los Angeles. In D. L. Spiegler, D. A. Tate, S. S. Aitken, & C. M. Christian (Eds.), *National Institute on Alcohol Abuse and Alcoholism: Research Monograph 18. Alcohol use among U.S. ethnic minorities* (pp. 373-382). Washington, DC: Government Printing Office.

Kleinman, P. H., & Lukoff, I. F. (1978). Ethnic differences in factors related to drug use. *Journal of Health and Social Behavior, 19,* 190-199.

Kozel, N. J., & Adams, E. H. (1986). Epidemiology of drug abuse: An overview. *Science, 234,* 970-1074.

Leland, J. (1976). *Firewater myths: Indian drinking and alcohol addiction.* New Brunswick, NJ: Rutgers Center of Alcohol Studies.

Maypole, D. E., & Anderson, R. E. (1986-1987). Alcoholism programs serving minorities: Administrative issues. *Alcohol Health and Research World, 2*(2) 62-65.

Moore, D. T. (1986-1987). Alcoholism treatment and client functioning in Alaska. *Alcohol Health and Research World, 2*(2), 68-69.

Murakami, S. R. (1989). An epidemiological survey of alcohol use, drug, and mental health problems in Hawaii: A comparison of four ethnic groups. In D. L. Spiegler, D. A. Tate, S. S.

Aitken, & C. M. Christian (Eds.), *Alcohol use among U.S. ethnic minorities* (NIAAA Research Monograph No. 18, pp. 343-354). Washington, DC: Government Printing Office.

Oetting, E. R., Edwards, R., Goldstein, G. S., & Garcia-Mason, V. (1980). Drug use among adolescents of five southwestern Native American tribes. *International Journal of the Addictions, 15,* 439-445.

Padilla, E. R., Padilla, A. M., Ramirez, R., Morales, A., & Olmedo, E. L. (1979). Inhalant, marijuana and alcohol abuse among barrio children and adolescents. *International Journal of the Addictions, 14,* 943-964.

Perez, R., Padilla, A. M., Ramirez, A., Ramirez, R., & Rodriquez, M. (1980). Correlates and chances over time in drug and alcohol use within a barrio population. *American Journal of Community Psychology, 6,* 621-636.

Prugh, R. (1986-1987). The black church: A foundation for recovery. *Alcohol Health and Research World, 2*(2), 53-54.

Spiegler, D. L., Tate, D. A., Aitken, S. S., & Christian, C. M. (Eds.). (1989). *Alcohol use among U.S. ethnic minorities* (DHHS, Publication No. ADM 89-1435) Washington, DC: Government Printing Office.

Strayer, R. A. (1961). Study of the Negro alcoholic. *Quarterly Journal of Studies on Alcohol, 22,* 111-123.

Trimble, J. E., Padilla, A. M., & Bell, C. S. (Eds.) (1987). *Drug abuse among ethnic minorities* (DHHS Publication No. ADM 87-1474) Washington, DC: Government Printing Office.

Vitols, M. M. (1968). Culture patterns of drinking in Negro and white alcoholics. *Diseases of the Nervous System, 29,* 391-394.

Walker, R. D., Benjamin, G. A., Kivlahan, D., & Walker, P. S. (1989). American Indian alcohol misuse and treatment outcome. In D. L. Spiegler, D. A. Tate, S. S. Aitken, & C. M. Christian (Eds.), *Alcohol use among U.S. ethnic minorities* (NIAAA Research Monograph No. 18, pp. 301-311). Washington, DC: Government Printing Office.

Washington State Commission on Asian American Affairs. (1983). [Report to the Governor]. Olympia, WA: Author.

Weibel-Orlando, J. C. (1989). Pass the bottle, bro!: A comparison of urban and rural Indian drinking patterns. In D. L. Spiegler, D. A. Tate, S. S. Aitken, & C. M. Christian (Eds.), *Alcohol use among U.S. ethnic minorities* (NIAAA Research Monograph No. 18, pp.269-290). Washington, DC: Government Printing Office

Yu, E. S. H., & Liu, W. T. (1986-1987). Alcohol use and abuse among Chinese-Americans: Epidemiologic data. *Alcohol Health and Research World, 2*(2), 14-18.

PART V

Special Issues

23

GENERAL ISSUES

Most of the controversies and issues to be discussed in these last chapters tend to be in the area of alcohol studies. The study of alcohol effects and alcohol-related problems is older than the study of other drugs of current concern, and there is far more research activity and clinical report surrounding the uses and abuses of alcohol rather than, say, heroin.

Alcohol studies have been characterized by controversy. It has in fact been described as "an ungrateful subject," in which partisans look to the literature for support of "their preconceived notions" (D'Abernon, 1920). American public attitudes have shifted from Pilgrim perception of alcoholic beverages as the good "creature of God" to later descriptions, particularly by temperance advocates, as "demon rum." In the twentieth century, we have had a Prohibition Amendment and, 35 years after repeal, a peak in per capita consumption. Currently, there has been a drop in per capita consumption of alcohol, possibly related to health concerns.

Issues related to treatment, policy, and prevention will be discussed in the following chapters. Here we will discuss the disease concept of alcoholism, the definition/diagnosis of alcoholism, problem drinking, alcohol abuse, alcohol dependence, views of etiology, and typologies and classifications of alcoholics.

The Disease Concept of Alcoholism

Alcohol has been available for many centuries, and its use and overuse have been noted in recorded history. Roman writings distinguish between drunken persons and those who apparently had no control over their drinking. One of the most poetic passages occurs in Proverbs in the Old Testament: "Who hath woe?

who hath sorrow? who hath contentions? who hath babbling? who hath wounds without cause? who hath redness of eye? They that tarry long at the wine . . . At the last, it biteth like a serpent and stingeth like an adder" (Prov. 23:29-32).

The early history of concern about alcohol in the United States dealt with "inebriety," and in the early settlements, a drunken man might be punished by being placed in stocks. It is interesting to note that the concern of the temperance movement was as much with the wife and children of the inebriates (there was no mention of female inebriates) as of the drinker himself. It was in the twentieth century that drinking, intoxication, and alcohol abuse became the province of scientists. Some early physiological work exists, but intensive biomedical and psychosocial study of alcohol and its effects on the individual and society is a product of the twentieth century.

At approximately the same point in recent time, in the 1930s, Dr. Jolliffe of Bellevue Hospital became the initiator of a Research Council on Problems of Alcohol, and two recovering alcoholics initiated Alcoholics Anonymous (Keller, 1962). Both of these developments assumed that alcoholism was indeed a disease. In 1956, the American Medical Association issued a statement directed toward hospitals urging them to admit alcoholic persons as patients; it was common hospital practice to refuse to admit alcoholic persons unless they had a demonstrable medical problem. This was hardly the first time physicians had defined alcoholism as disease—that goes back to a physician signer of the Declaration of Independence, Dr. Benjamin Rush. Medical interest persisted through the nineteenth century. The temperance movement and the Prohibition Amendment assumed that alcohol abuse and alcohol dependence would disappear but, as we know, it did not (Keller, 1962). The decades following repeal of Prohibition showed a slow but steady expansion of interest in research on alcohol and in treatment of alcohol-related problems. In 1945, when the movie *The Lost Weekend* appeared, there was no objection to the central character's girlfriend describing him as "a sick person."

At this moment, a majority of Americans—including the therapists—physicians, counselors, psychologists, and so on consider alcoholism to be a disease. The challenge to the idea of alcoholism-as-disease began with the social sciences, which described the "medicalization" of deviant behaviors and alcoholism as "the mythical disease" (Fingarette, 1988). In part, the challenge has arisen because of policy differences: There is a block, consisting primarily of social scientists, who believe that diminishing alcohol-related problems in a society can be accomplished with legal moves limiting the accessibility of alcohol beverages, such as taxes, price controls, controls over outlets, and the like. In part, the challenge has arisen as different schools of thought about therapeutic efficacy arose, and there is a high correlation between belief in "the mythical disease" and belief that abstinence is not the only goal of treatment. The challenge to the disease concept is based both on policy stances and theory about therapy.

This became more than an academic question when the U.S. Supreme Court was asked to render a judgment in a suit brought against the Veterans Administration (*Traynor v. Turnage,* 1988). The contention was that the plaintiffs' disease, that is, alcoholism, prevented them from using education benefits in the 10 years since military discharge. Extensions can be granted, but not based on "wilful misconduct." The Court ruled against the plaintiffs, arguing that even if alcoholism is genetically based and a disease, "the consumption of alcohol is not regarded as wholly involuntary." The problem is further complicated by the use of alcoholism-as-defense in cases of unacceptable behavior by business executives and politicians. Questions of free will may be raised: Is alcoholism "preordained by the genes?" (Wright, 1987).

The Supreme Court ruling, in spite of dire predictions ("Dark Clouds," 1987), changed little. Public belief in alcoholism-as-disease is little changed, and treatment policies and practices changed little. Other issues are brought into the debate about whether alcoholism is a disease: the usefulness of the idea as a therapeutic maneuver, responsibility for one's acts and choices (a variant of free will), legal suits over the disabling effects of alcoholism, the extension of the disease concept to people in the alcoholic's social environment (i.e., "codependents"), and so on. The debate continues among experts (Vaillant, 1990). One of the most cogent and sensible comments was made by a program director of a local council on alcoholism before the Supreme Court decision:

> From my viewpoint, the Justices will not simply decide that alcoholism is or is not a disease but will come down in the middle of the dilemma that is the physical, social, economic, spiritual, and mental ramifications of the alcohol syndrome. Solomon himself would have scratched his head on this one. (Tauriainen, 1988, p. 2).

Definition of Alcoholism/Alcohol Abuse

The problem of definition has been undertaken by at least three major groups: the Yale/Rutgers Center of Alcohol Studies, the World Health Organization, and the American Psychiatric Association.

The Yale/Rutgers Center of Alcohol Studies, where twentieth century research and treatment began, defined alcoholism in two sets of criteria (Keller, 1962). First there was "implicative" or suspicion-arousing drinking, which was repetitive or chronic. Second, there were alcohol-related effects on health, interpersonal relationships, and economic status. Interestingly, Keller specified that no single definition suited all purposes and that "a satisfactory medical definition is not adequate for epidemiological needs." The reasoning was that diagnosis could be made by taking an "adequate anamnesis," but that the public health worker or epidemiologist needed a behavioral-operational definition for survey purposes.

The World Health Organization's (WHO) Expert Committee on Alcohol has issued a series of reports (e.g., WHO, 1954). Adopting the definition of an addiction-producing drug from another WHO committee—the Expert Committee on Drugs Liable to Produce Addiction—it characterized drug addiction as having three components: (a) a compulsion, or overpowering desire or need to continue taking the drug and obtain it by any means; (b) a tendency to increase the dose; and (c) "a psychic [psychological] and sometimes a physical dependence on the effects of the drug." Distinguishing addiction-producing drugs from habit-forming drugs, the World Health Organization committee put alcohol "in a category of its own, intermediate between addiction-producing and habit-forming drugs." In 1965 a group associated with the World Health Organization committee (Eddy, Halbach, Isbell, & Seevers, 1965) challenged the idea of a single definition for all forms of drug addiction and habituation and suggested the concept of drug dependence, "psychic or physical or both." Drug dependence was defined as

> a state of psychic or physical dependence, or both, on a drug arising in a person following administration of that drug on a periodic or continuous basis. The characteristics of such a state will vary with the agent involved, and these characteristics must always be made clear by designating the particular type of drug dependence in each specific case; for example, drug dependence of morphine type, of barbiturate type, of amphetamine type, etc. (p. 722)

More recently, the World Health Organization Expert Committee on Problems Related to Alcohol and Consumption (WHO, 1980) has issued a report about problems related to alcohol consumption. The major thesis of this report was a rejection of the term *alcoholism* and the use of "alcohol dependence syndrome" in its place. The report states that

> until recently, there has been a widespread tendency to conceptualize the whole gamut of alcohol problems as manifestations of an underlying entity, alcoholism. . . . But there are many physical, mental and social problems that are not necessarily related to dependence. Alcohol dependence, while prevalent and itself a matter for serious concern, constitutes only a small part of the total of alcohol-related problems. (p. 17)

On the American scene, this 1980 report of the World Health Organization committee is encompassed in the recent report of the Institute of Medicine (1990); the Institute of Medicine committee noted that the focus of treatment needs to be expanded. "While maintaining and, indeed, increasing its present concern for individuals with severe problems, treatment must also address the vast and heterogeneous spectrum of problems that are of less than maximum severity" (WHO, 1980, p. 7). Alcohol problems, as defined by the Institute of Medicine committee, are "more inclusive" than terms such as "alcoholism" or "alcohol dependence syndrome."

The *Diagnostic and Statistical Manual of Mental Disorders III* (American Psychiatric Association, 1980) set out a list of diagnostic criteria for the terms "alcohol abuse" and "alcohol dependence;" this list was revised in 1987 (American Psychiatric Association, 1987). Abuse is defined as (a) maladaptive pattern of use, which may be either continued use in spite of problems related to the drug or recurrent use, and (b) the persistence of symptoms for a month or repeatedly over a longer period of time. Dependence is defined as (a) drug taken in larger amounts or over a longer period than intended; (b) persistent desire or one or more attempts at control; (c) actively getting, taking, and recovering from the drug; (d) frequent intoxication or withdrawal symptoms interfering with role obligations; (e) reduction of other life activities; (f) continued use in spite of persistent/recurrent drug-associated problems; (g) marked tolerance; (h) characteristic withdrawal symptoms; and (i) drug taken often to relieve/avoid withdrawal symptoms. Severity status includes mild, moderate, severe, in partial remission, and in full remission.

The DSM-III-R guidelines broadened the meaning of alcohol dependence so that it included not only tolerance and withdrawal (as specified in the 1980 guidelines) but a variety of behavioral indices of diminished control over alcohol use as well (Rounsaville & Kranzler, 1988). These guidelines—which are to be reviewed and revised in DSM-IV (in progress)—are of great importance to the clinician/practitioner, because they are an agreed-upon medical diagnosis, and because third-party payments are contingent on definitions of alcohol abuse and dependence as specified by the American Psychiatric Association.

The question of tests or checklists for the evaluation of patients' condition has been a less troublesome area. The number of available instruments is large: A compendium of 45 instruments was assembled by the National Institute on Alcohol Abuse and Alcoholism (Lettieri, Nelson, & Sayers, 1985). This collection of instruments was put together to suggest possible research instruments for use in treatment assessment research, but it includes the widely used Michigan Alcoholism Screening Test (MAST), the MacAndrew Alcoholism Scale, the Comprehensive Drinker Profile, the Addiction Severity Index, and others. Although many research foundations and researchers have developed questionnaires, scales, indexes, and inventories, this has not been a matter of dispute or conflict.

Views of Etiology

To a large extent, the differing views of etiology have been discussed in Part II. The wide range of etiological viewpoints is not unique to alcoholism and drug abuse. A recent description of a depressive breakdown (Styron, 1990) comments on the myriad theories that seek to account for depression, concluding that depression is probably based on abnormal biochemical response, genetics, and psychological disturbance based on loss.

A view of etiology that is complex and multifactored is rejected by some writers (Goodwin, 1982; Korenman, 1989). Goodwin comments about those who view alcoholism

> as a product of many forces: biological, sociological, psychological. To some extent, this may be a device to make all the students of alcoholism feel useful—the biologists, sociologists, psychologists. There is a kind of unspoken gentlemen's agreement that since experts from diverse backgrounds study alcoholism, alcoholism must have diverse origins. (p. 168).

Goodwin prefers "a single switch" theory. Korenman (1989) notes that "the concept persists that addiction is a behavioral disorder," but he hails the techniques of molecular biology as holding the answer to the riddle of etiology. For him, a "cure for addiction" lies in a major investment in the molecular and cell biology of addiction.

Other viewpoints involve two disciplines. There are many advocates of two-discipline theories and many writers who describe a "bio-behavioral approach." The biobehavioral viewpoint usually includes a biological, biochemical, and/or genetic component, and the behavior of the drug-using person. A less common approach is one that combines the biological, biochemical, and/or genetic component and sociocultural variables (Vaillant & Milofsky, 1982): "When ethnicity and heredity were controlled, childhood emotional problems and multiproblem family membership explained no additional variance" (p. 494).

A widely disseminated view of etiology involves at least three disciplines, a framework that includes physiological, behavioral, and sociocultural variables (Zucker & Gomberg, 1986). Of the various disciplines involved in this point of view, the evidence is recent and persuasive that there are biochemical and genetic factors that are predisposing, although these tend to be overstated (Lester, 1989). The evidence offered by the cultural anthropologists describes the role of ethnic background and the influence of cultural study (Bennett & Ames, 1985). The weakest link in the biopsychosocial approach is probably the psychological component of explanation. Although no one really speaks for "an addictive personality," it continues to be set up as a straw man. Explanations that lean on psychodynamic factors such as childhood deprivation have, in the past, been held up as the sole explanation of adult deviant behavior and have not done well in prediction studies. Antisocial behavior, however, is part of "personality" and as such it plays a significant etiological role (Zucker & Gomberg, 1986). There is some evidence that among women there may be an etiological role, not only for early antisocial behaviors, but, for early depression coupled with inadequate coping mechanisms (Gomberg, 1989a).

It does not appear likely that there will be unity and agreement among the different schools of explanation.

Typologies and Classifications

Although both clinicians and researchers often lapse into the usage in which "alcoholism" is described as though it were a unitary phenomenon, most would agree that there is no single syndrome, but rather a variety of disorders, so that one may speak of "the alcoholism." This has, in fact, been clearly spelled out in a recent report issued by the Institute of Medicine of the National Academy of Sciences (1990), a report titled *Broadening the Base of Treatment for Alcohol Problems.*

Approaching the question of typologies historically, Babor and Lauerman (1986) report on 39 typological formulations. Bowman and Jellinek (1941) summarized 24 typologies in an earlier paper, but the more recent historical summary presents the typologies by county of origin. We are probably most familiar with some of the American typological schemes. Knight (1938), for example, distinguished between "essential" and "reactive" alcoholics, with the former dating maladjustment and onset of alcoholic drinking as occurring early in life, and the latter as occurring relatively late in life as a response to stress. Knight also described "symptomatic alcoholics" who drank "only incidentally." To these categories, Menninger (1938) added "neurotic characters" who drank heavily as a manifestation of their disturbance, and "psychotic personalities" in whom the drinking is a symptom of a paranoid, schizoid, or psychotic disorder. (Clearly, the idea of dual diagnosis was not invented in the 1980s.) At the same time, Allen (1938) described "psychopathic" alcoholics and neurotic alcoholics, and it is of interest that so much research and clinical attention is now given to alcoholics and drug abusers who manifest antisocial personality (ASP).

An interesting distinction between different models for classification is made by Morey and Skinner (1986), who distinguish between dimensional models and categorical models. *Dimensional* models order individuals along an axis or axes, such as the World Health Organization's (1980) description of alcohol problems as existing along a dimension of *degree* in which alcoholism or the alcohol dependence syndrome is considered most serious. This model is also followed in the 1990 Institute of Medicine report. Another dimensional model is contained in Jellinek's (1952) description of stages or phases of alcoholism— here the dimension is time rather than severity. *Categorical* models attempt to identify internally consistent, nonoverlapping classes of problems drinkers (i.e., the American Psychiatric Association's [1987] Diagnostic and Statistical Manual III-R). Jellinek (1960) also contributed a categorical model for the typology of drinkers and his alpha, beta, gamma, delta, and epsilon is a typology based on "physical dependence," tolerance, withdrawal, "loss of control," and so on.

Alterman and Tarter (1986) have reviewed typologies as related to (a) hyperactivity, (b) childhood aggressive and antisocial behavior and adult sociopathy, (c) familial alcoholism, and (d) high risk/low risk individuals:

1. Hyperactivity appears to be a correlate of conduct disorder in children and sociopathy in adults, and it is apparently these disordered behavior patterns that are associated with the development of alcoholism.

2. Childhood aggressive and antisocial behavior and adult sociopathy form the basis for a distinction between ASP and non-ASP forms of alcoholism. The diagnosis of antisocial personality is reasonably reliable and objective, and there is some evidence that the course of alcoholism and the outcome of treatment may well differ between ASP and non-ASP groups.

3. Familial alcoholism has some merit as a basis for classification, according to Alterman and Tarter, but the evidence for a typology based on negative and positive family history is still inadequate. Considering that "positive history" covers a very wide variety of situations—variations of parental, sibling, and relatives' alcoholism, age at which persons are exposed to such alcoholism, extent of family disruption, and so on—it is clear that much work remains to be done.

4. There have been some positive findings in "high-risk" studies in which subjects with alcoholic first-degree relatives demonstrate lower blood acetaldehyde levels, lower levels of subjective intoxication, less behavioral and cognitive impairment, and less upper-body sway than subjects with no alcoholic first degree relative—following alcohol consumption. Such high-risk/low-risk investigations are at an early stage of development, and there are critical shortcomings (Sher, 1985). They may be important in studying etiology and eventually in the development of prevention programs.

A review of typologies by Hesselbrock (1986) distinguishes between those typological classifications derived empirically from personality measures and multivariate statistical techniques and those that are theoretically based. Jellinek's dimensional contribution to alcoholism typologies, the phasic development of alcoholism, and his categorical contribution of five distinct types (alpha, beta, gamma, delta, and epsilon) have been under attack for several decades, the major focus of the attacks being that his classifications do not deal adequately with the heterogeneity of alcoholics and the multidimensional nature of alcoholism.

Empirical approaches have frequently used factor analysis and clustering techniques. Classification of alcoholics may be based on personality inventories, alcohol use patterns, and/or treatment needs. Typically, analysis by personality inventory employs the Minnesota Multiphasic Personality Inventory (MMPI). Nerviano and Gross (1983) evaluated the "objective inventory" literature and suggested the following list of subtypes (Hesselbrock, 1986):

1. Conforming (compulsive-high impulse control and high social poise)
2. Impulsive (histrionic-low impulse control and moderate social poise)
3. Aggressive (impulsive and defensive)
4. Submissive (low dependency and dependent)
5. Avoidant (schizoid-low social poise and high autonomy)
6. Asocial (schizoid-independent but inhibited)
7. Narcissistic
8. Hostile (withdrawal-low social poise and high defensiveness)

Utilizing factor analyses, which derived four dimensions of drinking—general severity, tension relief, self-enchantment, and periodic drinking patterns—Horn, Wanberg, and Foster (1974) developed an Alcohol Use Inventory. This inventory includes questions about style of alcohol use, negative consequences, and perceived benefits of alcohol use. It is not clear, however, that the inventory responses produce a typology of the alcoholism; its major value seems to lie in a more finely tuned analysis of the subject's responses to alcoholic beverages per se.

Classifications based on treatment needs should be very useful in matching patients with optimal treatment plans. Attempts to study alcoholic patients with instruments designed to assess rehabilitation needs have been only modestly successful. One attempt (Kivlahan, Donovan, & Walker, 1983) to derive subtypes used age, social position, hours worked per week, duration of problem, drinking, alcohol dependence scale, neuropsychological functioning, vocabulary and arithmetic scales, and psychopathology. Complicated relationships exist among demography, patterns of drinking behaviors, neuropsychological functioning, and symptomatology.

Three areas have been selected by theorists to differentiate among subgroups of alcoholics: gender, psychopathology, and family history. The argument to be made for subgrouping alcoholics by gender seems self-evident: males and females are socialized differently, and the natural history of alcoholism seems to be different for men and for women. There is a body of work on gender differences in concomitant psychiatric symptomatology. Because there is relatively little work on treatment issues, it is not possible to say what gender variables are related to the initiation of treatment, the maintenance of treatment, and prognosis. That there are differences among alcoholic persons in terms of concomitant psychiatric symptomatology has been noted for a long time: note some of the earlier suggested typologies that described "neurotic" drinkers and the like.

The major forms of psychopathology associated with alcoholism include antisocial personality and depression. ASP alcoholics, in a study comparing alcoholics with the diagnosis of ASP and alcoholics without such a diagnosis (Hesselbrock, Hesselbrock, Babor, et al., 1983), showed the ASP alcoholics to be much younger at admission, to be less educated, to possess fewer occupational skills, to have a higher frequency of positive family history, and to manifest a different natural history of alcoholism. ASP alcoholics report significantly more childhood conduct problems and hyperactivity, began drinking earlier, progressed to alcoholism faster, and present with a longer duration of abusive drinking. A recent variation on the antisocial personality versus the non-ASP alcoholic is a differentiation between Type I and Type II alcoholics (Cloninger, 1987). Type II alcoholics have more positive family history, early onset, acting-out behaviors, and a triad of behaviors including low harm-avoidance, decreased reward-dependence, and high novelty seeking. Recent work has not been encouraging about validating Type II, and it is clear that what is needed is clear, unambiguous definitions of the type (Schuckit et al., 1990). Schuckit and his colleagues believe that the Type II alcoholic may be the antisocial-personality alcoholic with secondary alcohol and drug problem.

There are more problems with typologies that involve depression as a distinguishing pattern of behavior. One obvious problem is distinguishing depression antecedent to the onset of alcohol problems from depression that results from heavy alcohol consumption. It is not really clear whether alcohol does indeed relieve dysphoria: The situation may be complicated by different amounts of alcohol, different depressions, different stages of alcoholism, and so on. There is some evidence that depressed alcoholics are likely to do more binge drinking. The interaction of depression and suicide attempts is unclear. In a study of female alcoholics, there were few significant age differences among the women alcoholics in depression scores, but there were large, significant differences in suicide attempts. Suicide attempts that are made more frequently by younger alcoholic women (in their twenties) seem more related to issues of impulse control than to depression (Gomberg, 1986, 1989b).

Finally, grouping individuals by positive/negative family history has been suggested. Those with positive family history presumably show an earlier onset of alcoholism and more severe symptoms. Those alcoholic persons who have negative family histories have not been adequately studied. Although family history may be a promising way of typing alcoholics, the usefulness of such a typology has yet to be demonstrated in diagnosis, treatment, and prevention.

One is left with the impression although while the heterogeneity that exists among alcoholics has been recognized, typological classification has not progressed far beyond the work of Knight and Menninger 50 years ago.

References

Allen, E. B. (1938). Alcoholism as a psychiatric medical problem. *New York State Journal of Medicine, 38,* 1492-1503.

Alterman, A. I., & Tarter, R. E. (1986). An examination of selected typologies, hyperactivity, familial, and antisocial alcoholism. In M. Galanter (Ed.), *Recent developments in alcoholism* (Vol. 4, pp. 169-189). New York: Plenum.

American Psychiatric Association. (1980). *Diagnostic and statistical manual of mental disorders* (3rd ed.). Washington, DC: Author.

American Psychiatric Association. (1987). *Diagnostic and statistical manual of mental disorders* (3rd ed., rev.). Washington, DC: Author.

Babor, T. F., & Lauerman, R. J. (1986). Classification and forms of inebriety, historical antecedents of alcoholic typologies. In M. Galanter (Ed.), *Recent development in alcoholism* (Vol. 4, pp. 113-114). New York: Plenum.

Bennett, L. A., & Ames, G. M. (Eds.). (1985). *The American experience with alcohol: Contrasting cultural perspectives.* New York: Plenum.

Bowman, K. M., & Jellinek, E. M. (1941). Alcohol addiction and its treatment. *Quarterly Journal of Studies on Alcohol, 2,* 98-176.

Cloninger, C. R. (1987). Neurogenetic adaptive mechanisms in alcoholism. *Science, 236,* 410-416.

D'Abernon, The Right Honourable Lord. (1920). The scientific basis of drink control. *British Journal of Inebriety,* 73-85.

Dark clouds hang over disease concept validity [Editorial]. (1988). *U.S. Journal of Drug and Alcohol Dependence,* p. 3.

Eddy, N. B., Halbach, H., Isbell, H., & Seevers, M. H. (1965). Drug dependence: Its signficance and characteristics. *Bulletin of the World Health Organization, 32,* 721-733.

Fingarette, H. (1988). Alcoholism: The mythical disease. *The Public Interest, 91,* 3-22.

Gomberg, E. S. L. (1986). Women and alcoholism: Psychosocial issues. In *Women and alcohol: Health-related issues* (DHHS Publication No. ADM 86-1139, pp. 78-120). Washington, DC: Government Printing Office.

Gomberg, E. S. L. (1989a). Alcoholic women in treatment: Early histories and early problem behaviors. *Advances in Alcohol & Substance Abuse, 8,* 133-147.

Gomberg, E. S. L. (1989b). Suicide risk among women with alcohol problems. *American Journal of Public Health, 79,* 1363-1365.

Goodwin, D. W. (1982). Alcoholism and heredity: Update on the implacable fate. In E. L. Gomberg, H. R. White, & J. A. Carpenter (Eds.), *Alcohol, Science and Society Revisited* (pp. 162-170). Ann Arbor: University of Michigan Press.

Hesselbrock, M. N. (1986). Alcoholic typologies: A review of empirical evaluations of common classification schemes. In M. Galanter (Ed.), *Recent developments in alcoholism* (Vol. 4, pp. 191-206). New York: Plenum.

Hesselbrock, M. N., Hesselbrock, V. N., Babor, T. F., et al. (1983). Antisocial behavior, psychopathology and problem drinking in the natural history of alcoholism. In D. W. Goodwin, K. T. Van Dusen, & S. A. Mednick (Eds.), *Longitudinal research in alcoholism* (pp. 197-214). Boston: Kluwer-Nijhoff.

Horn, J. L., Wanberg, K. W., & Foster, F. M. (1974). *The Alcohol Use Inventory.* Denver, CO: Denver Center for Alcohol Abuse Research and Evaluation.

Institute of Medicine. (1990). *Broadening the base of treatment for alcohol problems.* Washington, DC: National Academy Press.

Jellinek, E. M. (1952). Phases of alcohol addiction. *Quarterly Journal of Studies on Alcohol, 13,* 673-684.

Jellinek, E. M. (1960). *The disease concept of alcoholism.* New Haven, CT: College and University Press.

Keller, M. (1962). The definition of alcoholism and the estimation of its prevalence. In D. J. Pittman & C. R. Snyder (Eds.), *Society, culture and drinking patterns* (pp. 310-329). New York: John Wiley.

Kivlahan, D. R., Donovan, D. M., & Walker, R. D. (1983). *Alcoholic subtypes: Validity of clusters based on multiple assessment domains.* Paper presented at the annual meeting of the American Psychological Association, Anaheim, CA.

Knight, R. P. (1938). Psychoanalytic treatment in a sanitorium of chronic addiction to alcohol. *Journal of the American Medical Association, 111,* 1443-1448.

Korenman, S. G. (1989, March 28). We need research in the biology of addiction. *New York Times,* p. 18.

Lester, D. (1989). The heritability of alcoholism: Science and social policy. *Drugs and Society: Current Issues in Alcohol/Drug Studies, 3,* 29-68.

Lettieri, D. J., Nelson, J. E., & Sayers, M. A. (1985). Alcoholism treatment assessment research instruments. In *NIAAA Treatment Handbook, Series 2* (DHHS Publication No. ADM 87-1380). Washington, DC: Government Printing Office.

Menninger, W. C. (1938). Treatment of chronic alcohol addiction. *Bulletin of the Menninger Clinic, 2,* 101-112.

Morey, L. C., & Skinner, H. A. (1986). Empirically derived classifications of alcohol-related problems. In M. Galanter (Ed.), *Recent developments in alcoholism* (Vol. 4, pp. 145-168). New York: Plenum.

Nerviano, V. I., & Gross, H. W. (1983). Personality types of alcoholics on objective inventories. *Journal of Studies on Alcohol, 44,* 837-851.

Rounsaville, B. J., & Kranzler, H. R. (1988). The DSM-IIIR diagnosis of alcoholism. *Review of Psychiatry, 8,* 323-340.

Sher, K. J. (1985). Excluding problem drinkers in high-risk studies of alcoholism: Effect of screening criteria on high-risk versus low-risk comparisions. *Journal of Abnormal Psychology, 94,* 106-109.

Styron, W. (1990). *Darkness visible.* New York: Random House.

Tauriainen, M. (1988, June). Alcoholism-disease-defense-dilemma. *Washtenaw Council on Alcoholism News and Views,* p. 2.

Traynor v. Turnage, 99 LED 2nd 618 (1988).

Vaillant, G. E. (1990). We should retain the disease concept of alcoholism. *Harvard Medical School Mental Health Letter.*

Vaillant, G. E., & Milofsky, E. S. (1982). The etiology of alcoholism: A prospective viewpoint. *American Psychologist, 37,* 494-503.

World Health Organization Expert Committee on Alcohol. (1954). *First report* (Tech. Rep. Series No. 84). Geneva, Switzerland: Author.

World Health Organization Expert Committee on Problems Related to Alcohol and Consumption. (1980). *Problems related to alcohol consumption* (Tech. Rep. Series No. 650). Geneva, Switzerland: Author.

Wright, R. (1987, December 14). Alcohol and free will: The Supreme Court reopens an old question. *The New Republic,* pp. 14-16.

Zucker, R. A., & Gomberg, E. S. L. (1986). Etiology of alcoholism reconsidered: The case for a biopsychosocial process. *American Psychologist, 41,* 783-793.

24

SOME TREATMENT ISSUES

There is no simple question: What is the best treatment for alcohol and/or drug abuse? As the review of typologies in the last chapter indicated, there are many different kinds of alcoholics. There are also many different types of treatment: counseling and therapy; Antabuse or other forms of chemotherapy; drug substitution, as with methadone maintenance or drug effect blocking; self-help groups; religious counseling; sexual therapy; didactic therapy; and so on. There are even different goals as the desired outcome of treatment. With cocaine dependency, the goal is termination of use and establishment of a life-style that works for the individual without cocaine. With heroin dependence, the goal may be abstinence or it may be methadone maintenance. With alcohol dependence, the goal may be abstinence or "controlled drinking."

Different Kinds of Drug/Alcohol Abuses

It is clear that there is a wide gulf between an alcoholic person who is homeless and lives in an urban Skid Row and an alcoholic person who chairs the board of a large corporation and lives in an expensive suburb. The same gulf exists between a young person, usually a member of a minority group living in an urban ghetto, who is heroin-dependent, and a thirtyish, European aristocrat living in the fast lane, also heroin dependent. Cocaine, which used to be called the "champagne" of drugs, can be used by urban sophisticates, but in another form, "crack," it is abused in urban ghettos. With such a wide range of social-class membership, it hardly makes sense to recommend the same treatment plan for all drug-dependent people.

There are other demographic variations among drug and alcohol abusers. There are *gender variations*: because socialization and social role assignment is different for men and for women, there will be variations in etiology, onset, manifestations, course, consequences, and entry into treatment. The last—entry into treatment—is influenced not only by gender variations but by availability of treatment programs and the facilitation or nonfacilitation of maintenance of treatment by social networks (Beckman & Amaro, 1984). Traditionally, women have been described as having poorer prognosis in therapy, and the modern form of that description is maintained in discussions of patient denial and in prognosis for cessation-of-smoking programs.

Clearly, there are *age variations* among drug abusers. Getting into difficulty with alcohol and/or drugs may occur during adolescence, early adulthood, middle age, or even among the elderly. Adolescents and young adults seem to create the greatest social concern, possibly because drug and alcohol abuse is so often concomitant with impulsive, acting-out behaviors of other kinds. Adults from 30 to 50 years of age make up the largest portion of hospital and clinical drug abusers in treatment and constitute over half of the members of Alcoholics Anonymous (Alcoholics Anonymous, 1987). Chapter 19 covers many of the issues concerning alcohol and drug problems among the elderly.

When drug abusers are in treatment, a family history is often part of the information gathering. Individual substance abusers vary not only in whether their family history is positive or negative, that is, whether there are genetically related relatives who drank alcoholically, but in whether their family history is positive or negative for depression, psychosis, and other forms of breakdown. It is significant that we think of variations in family history, for a generation ago, it was always assumed that all drug abusers had a disrupted family history. Although an early history of family disruption, conflict, and chaos is not uncommon, it is not always present, and some people become drug dependent with no apparent early family history of disruption. How the biochemical or genetic history relates to treatment is not really clear, and biologists are more prone to relate such histories to programs of prevention or early intervention. What is relevant in any treatment plan is the *current* status of family networks and whether such networks may be constructive or destructive (Gomberg, Nelson, & Hatchett, forthcoming). In the current scene, polydrug abuse is quite common, but the abuser usually has a primary *drug of preference*. It is relevant to treatment planning to know what that drug of preference is, its legal status, availability, and effects. Cocaine abusers may be using a variety of substances, but their first drug of choice is illegal, relatively short acting, but swift in its effects. The drug, the duration of abuse, the source from which it is obtained, the setting in which it is taken, and the multidrug-use patterns of a patient must be taken into account in treatment planning. There will be a good deal of variation between groups of drug abusers on this score.

There is some research dealing with the issue of severity and its relation to drug and alcohol abuse. The definition of "severity" is itself a problem, for severity can be defined in terms of duration; consequences in family, social, and work life; or medical complications. One may define severity in terms of craving or other vague concepts. There are measurements of severity (Lettieri, Nelson, & Sayers, 1987), and there may be a time when severity can be assessed and evaluated and utilized as one predictor of outcome.

Pattison's (1974) *multivariate-multimodel model of alcoholism* sought to determine the symptoms manifested by the patient, the stage of development, and the response under varying conditions of short-range and long-range effects. The model emphasizes treatment procedures that relate to the person's drinking environment, and it is designed with continuity of care as a major emphasis: identification, referral, short- and long-term treatment, and follow-up care.

Dual Diagnosis. A good deal of current attention is focused on dual diagnosis or comorbidity. The fact that alcoholic patients or persons addicted to various drugs manifest psychiatric symptomatology in addition to substance abuse has been noted for many years. In an early study, Brown (1950) had raters sort the psychological tests of state hospital admissions with diagnosis of chronic alcoholism without psychosis; these were divided into those who were "neurotic" and those who were "psychopathic." More recent work has linked substance abuse to affective disorder (Mayfield, 1985), to sociopathy (Kay, 1985), and to schizophrenia (Alterman, 1985). Alcoholic patients have been dual-diagnosed as manifesting alcoholism with antisocial personality and/or with depression (Hesselbrock, 1986). Schuckit has pointed out the confusion between alcoholism and sociopathy (Schuckit, 1973) between alcoholism and affective disorder (Schuckit, 1979), and between alcoholism and other psychiatric disorders (Schuckit, 1983). The problem of dual diagnosis has produced a large literature, sometimes emphasizing the drug-abusing behavior of persons in different psychiatric diagnostic groups (Alterman, 1985) and sometimes emphasizing the psychiatric symptomatology of alcoholics and drug abusers (Hesselbrock, Hesselbrock, Babor, et al., 1983). The relationship of dual diagnosis or comorbidity to treatment planning is evident: What does one treat first? Does one treat both behaviors concomitantly? What differences in treatment planning do the other psychiatric symptomatologies and syndromes necessitate?

Treatment Modalities

There are ways of categorizing treatment facilities, such as inpatient, outpatient, mixed, or medical. Most treatment programs begin with detoxification and, in most settings, go on to aftercare arrangement after the intensive part of the treatment has terminated. In better programs, there is recognition of the need for a continuum of care. Several books on alcoholism contain overview summaries of treatments (Estes & Heineman, 1986; Gomberg, White, & Carpenter, 1982; Royce, 1989).

Detoxification. Sugerman (1982) distinguished between inpatient and outpatient detoxification as well as a postwithdrawal phase. Issues surrounding the comparative effectiveness of inpatient versus outpatient detoxification have been raised by the work of Hayashida and associates (1989). Those who were detoxified on an outpatient basis remain in treatment for significantly fewer days than those detoxified as inpatients, and more of the inpatient group complete detoxification. Nonetheless, outcome evaluations at 1 month and 6 months after detoxification show "substantial improvement in both groups," and the authors conclude that outpatient medical detoxification is effective, safe, and costs less for individuals with "mild-to-moderate alcohol withdrawal syndrome." For the severely ill patient with threatening symptoms of alcohol withdrawal, clearly hospitalization is warranted; such patients, however, are a small minority of alcoholics who need detoxification.

Chemotherapy. Disulfiram (trade name, Antabuse) has been used in various treatment facilities since 1950. Although it is still in use, enthusiasm for it has waned, and it is less used at this time than it was several decades ago (McNichol & Logsdon, 1988). Disulfiram must be prescribed by a physician, based on medical examination and the patient's consent. It is taken to *prevent* alcohol intake, for it interferes with the metabolism of alcohol in the liver, so that drinking an alcoholic beverage while taking disulfiram usually permits a return to normal alcohol metabolism. It is, however, helpful for some alcoholics, particularly in the early stages of a treatment program. In Europe, a pellet of disulfiram may be implanted so that the person need not be on a medication regime, but this practice has not been approved in the United States. As pointed out by Royce (1989), "disulfiram is not a total therapy in itself but can be extremely useful in early stages of recovery" (p. 250).

For those who are heroin dependent, methadone maintenance might be considered a variation of chemotherapy. Methadone is substituted for the heroin, and the patient may appear at the methadone maintenance clinic daily for the drug. The concentration of methadone is kept above the threshold for withdrawal symptoms (Dole, 1980), and when taking the drug, the patient appears medically and functionally normal and does as well on tests of coordination and vigilance as he or she does when totally drug free. There are no euphoria effects. In the early history of methadone maintenance treatment, addict patients would occasionally try heroin, only to find it ineffective—apparently tolerance induced by daily methadone intake blocked the usual heroin effects. There are, additionally, some blockers of opiate effects and these include nalaxone and similar drugs.

Behavioral Modification Treatments. The oldest of these is aversive conditioning in which the sight, smell, and taste of alcoholic beverages is associated with an unpleasant stimulus such as elctric shock or a nausea-inducing chemical. Behavior treatments are more often operant, that is, the goal is reduced drinking or abstinence by manipulation of the consequences of the drinking. Behavioral modification techniques may include systematic desensitization, relaxation training, contingency management techniques, assertiveness training, biofeedback techniques, and other methods. One by-product of behavioral treatment has been contracting and subgoal definition, a clear communication of goals and subgoals often accompanied by a timetable between the therapist and the client. Emphasis is often placed on behavioral assessment, in which the circumstances that trigger a drinking episode may be studied and included as part of the relearning process. The 1970s produced a great many research and clinical reports that generated some fresh thinking and enthusiasm about behavioral treatment (e.g., Azrin, 1976; Briddell & Nathan, 1976; Miller, 1978). The focus in the 1980s seems to have been largely on "relapse prevention" (Marlatt & Gordon, 1985) and on further explication of behavioral methods (Marlatt, Baer, Donovan, & Kivlahan, 1988; Miller & Heather, 1986). There has been a very public controversy over some early work published by two behavior therapists (Sobell & Sobell, 1973), and the reported results of their early work have been sharply criticized (Pendery, Maltzman, & West, 1982). It is generally agreed that the earlier work in behavior modification was overly optimistic, and most behavioral therapists have moved toward a more integrated and inclusive approach to treatment than was true in earlier stages of behavioral modification treatment.

Psychotherapy. This includes individual counseling and group therapies, and it may take many forms. Individual counseling may range from the motivational counseling at intake through intensive sessions with a trained alcoholism therapist. There is general agreement that the first contact with the alcoholic is a critical point and there are a number of works that deal with the initiation and early stages of treatment (e.g., Liepman & Nirenberg, 1987).

Individual counseling has ranged from long-term psychoanalysis, which does not have a good success rate, to simplistic approaches that view the cessation of drinking as the end in itself. It is generally agreed that treatment cannot proceed until the patient does indeed stop drinking (even allowing for the good possiblity of relapse), but it is also agreed that by the time the alcoholic is involved in a therapeutic intervention, alcohol has created a large number of problems in his-her relationships and life that need to be dealt with. The efficacy of psychotherapy is still controversial, and a well- known study contrasted the effects of an intensive treatment program, which took several months, with the effects of a single counseling session attended by the alcoholic and spouse in which advice was given (Edwards et al., 1977). These investigators reported no difference in treatment outcomes, but the results have been described as "idiosyncratic to the English treatment scene. . . . Generalization of its results are problematic" (Nathan, 1982).

Group therapy has been popular in the treatment of alcoholism for many decades. The general acceptance by such a group, the understanding of those who have experienced similar problems, and the perception of defenses and denials seem to make group work reasonably effective.

A special form of psychotherapy that has become increasingly popular is marital and family therapy. Work with wives of alcoholics began relatively early, in the 1960s, and current work has emphasized marital interactions and communications. At this time, the trend is toward "family therapy" (Kaufman, 1984; Steinglass, 1982). A recent review of family therapy with chemically dependent women (Gomberg et al., forthcoming) has raised the question of evaluating the support offered by the family, pointing out that—particularly for women substance abusers—it cannot be assumed that the family always plays a constructive, supporting role.

There are a number of popularized views, often mass marketed, relating to the family of the substance abuser: children of alcoholics, enablers, codependents, and so on (Gomberg, 1989b). The dilemma posed to the professional help-giver is the fact that some of these movements, like revivalism, do indeed seem to offer solace to some, but most of them are fundamentally quasi-magical cures for unhappiness.

Self-Help Groups. The popularity of self-help groups such as Alcoholics Anonymous is beyond question and such groups are undoubtedly effective. The question is, what proportion of those who try Alcoholics Anonymous and similar self-help groups finds it unhelpful? Because no records are kept, there is no way of judging. For those who get the AA message, it can be an excellent source of support through the difficult months of achieving and maintaining sobriety. The most recent survey of the membership of Alcoholics Anonymous (a survey of membership is conducted every 3 years) shows that about a third of the members are women and that about 22% of the members are age 31 or younger. Professionals who are entering the substance abuse treatment field are probably wise to acquaint themselves with the operation of Alcoholics Anonymous by attending one of a local chapter's open meetings.

Galanter (1984) has proposed an innovative approach to ambulatory treatment for alcoholisms: self-help large-group therapy, which adapts the self-help principle to clinical settings. Based in part on Galanter's observations of psychological influences in contemporary charismatic religious sects, he has developed a self-help modality which—with adequate screening and selection of patients—can be quite cost effective. Comparison of patients assigned to large self-help groups with patients who underwent more conventional clinic treatment, that is, small-group therapy, showed little difference a year later in patient retention and visit rates.

Community Intervention. One promising avenue of treatment of alcoholism, the community reinforcement approach, was described by Azrin (1976). A variation has recently been reviewed by Shore and Kofoed (1984), who describe how community intervention "includes individual patient treatment and broader public health-community approaches that are addressed by specific policy measure" (p. 151). They review such community intervention approaches in several problem areas—the drunken driver, the public inebriate, and drinking by some Native-American groups—and conclude that such community intervention is a rapidly developing and promising approach.

Education. As utilized by treatment facilities, the assumption underlying didactic sessions is that it is necessary that patients understand how the body reacts to alcohol and just what alcoholism consists of. The nature of the "education" depends, of course, on the orientation of the educator, and a large number of treatment programs teach that alcoholism is a disease and that alcoholics are not weak-willed people who simply cannot drink like other people. The effectiveness of such educational material in the therapy and rehabilitation of patients is not often measured, but it is rarely the only component of a treatment program. The widespread educational efforts of treatment facilities and Alcoholics Anonymous are effective in the sense that people with alcohol problems usually know a great deal more about the beverage alcohol than people who do not have such problems.

Physical Rehabilitation. Most alcoholics enter treatment in a physically debilitated state, and they have rarely been living a healthy life-style. A rehabilitation program should include attention to diet and to exercise. Much of the treatment involves the restoration of the alcoholic person to good physical health. In addition to poor nutrition, most alcoholics have not been following any kind of exercise regime. Included under this category might be "recreational therapy," learning and relearning ways to spend leisure time. This might include sports, hobbies, arts and crafts, and the like.

Spiritual Therapies. A good deal of the program of Alcoholics Anonymous is concerned with a "higher power." With or without AA, spiritual counseling is often very useful in restoring order and sense to an alcoholic's life. The serenity prayer could be applicable to all of us: "God grant me the serenity to accept the things I cannot change, courage to change the things I can, and the wisdom to know the difference."

A variety of other techniques and modalities have been used by some therapists. These include acupuncture, hypnosis, relaxation, therapy, values clarification, and sexual therapies. LSD has been tried in treatment, as has mega-vitamin therapy. One technique that should probably be used more is parent effectiveness training.

The Goals of Treatment

The controversy over the question of moderate, acceptable drinking versus total sobriety and abstinence has lessened. There are some obvious advantages of the abstinence goal: less ambiguity, no choices or decisions, and fewer risks. The objection, however, felt by many behaviorally oriented clinicians was to the rigidity of the sobriety goal: Surely there must be alcoholics who can stop drinking in an uncontrolled way and learn to drink in a controlled, moderate fashion. The reasoning may be sound, but the problem is determining which alcoholics they are. There were indeed some behaviorists in the early stages who believed that *all* alcoholics could be taught to drink moderately, but they were a small minority.

The controversy over the goals of treatment has not included data from problem drinkers who recover without the aid of a therapeutic intervention. It is generally agreed that "spontaneous recovery" does occur, although some who believe in "once an alcoholic, always an alcoholic" would argue that those who recover were not really alcoholics in the first place. Several early outcome studies reported that some alcoholics who had been followed up after treatment reported controlled, moderate drinking (Davies, 1962); the first Rand Report also reported a small percentage of treated alcoholics who apparently were able to drink moderately 4 years after treatment (Polich, Armor, & Stambul, 1980). Some of these results have been challenged, and longer-term follow-up also shows a proportion reaching sobriety after a long period of time (Vaillant, 1988).

The assumption that all alcoholics remain alcoholism-prone for the rest of their days and that a single drink will trigger a drinking bout has been challenged, but it has not really been tested empirically. Study of the question is confused by the problem of self-fulfilling prophecy. The problem comes down to the question of whether some alcohol-dependent people can learn to drink moderately and who those people are. Even if the assumption is that such people indeed may relearn moderate drinking behaviors, we are no further along in distinguishing between alcohol-dependents who may and who may not be trainable. Considering the unknowns, the most sensible and least risky course of therapy is probably to encourage abstinence as the goal of treatment. The fact is that ethanol is not necessary for healthy body function, and people can live abstinently.

The most recent debate on the question of moderation as the goal of treatment for alcohol problems (Sobell & Sobell, 1986-1987) makes the point that "behavioral treatment does not advocate controlled drinking for all alcoholic persons." It views alcohol problems not as alcoholism versus nonalcoholism but rather as a continuum of drinking problems with different types of drinking problems responsive to different forms of treatment. The Sobells argue the need for dialogue about moderation and the excessive focus of the treatment field on the "severely alcohol dependent." There are indeed some behavioral therapists who conduct treatment with the goal of abstinence (Nathan & McCrady, 1986-1987). It is worth noting that in a critical review of related methodological issues (Taylor, 1986-1987), the first questions is "What consitututes alcoholism?"

Prognosis: Factors Determining Outcome

Factors that determine outcome may be divided into treatment factors and patient factors. Treatment factors relate to the choice of treatment, and sometimes patients may make their own choice without resort to any of our institutions of treatment, for instance, in religious conversion. There is a curious phenomenon in the treatment field: When different treatments or interventions are subject to empirical test, some do well, others not so well, but regardless of such empirical evidence, most treatment facilities continue to use the techniques familiar to their personnel. A resolution of this contradiction would probably follow if each treatment facility had available a variety of treatment approaches, and if each treatment facility would determine individual treatment plans for each incoming patient.

Patient Factors that have been assumed to predict treatment outcome include patient characteristics such as gender, age, motivation, degree of alcohol dependence, and personality; many of these have been challenged (Marlatt et al., 1988). The early literature often cited the "poorer prognosis" for women patients, but either as a result of shifts in patient populations or more rapport and concern with women, the prognosis, for outcome of treatment of women is no longer "poorer," and there may even be a slight trend toward better outcome with women patients. Younger patients were viewed as having poorer prognosis, but as the average age of those coming to treatment facilities has dropped (from approximately the mid-forties to the mid-thirties), this view of younger patients has been questioned. Several decades ago, patient "motivation" was considered essential, but this, too, is now questioned.

Good prognosis has been consistently associated with social stability and better cognitive and psychosocial functioning. These prognosis include not only obvious indicators such as marital status and employment but situational factors such as the work or family context of the patient: Supportive contexts make for better prognosis. The extent of comorbidity (dual diagnosis) is a predictive factor: Patients who are severely depressed after months of sobriety and patients who act out in antisocial ways are obviously poorer prognostically; absence of major psychiatric symptomatology is a positive prognostic indicator. Still to be studied more extensively is the amount of unavoidable stress in a patient's life situation and his or her mechanisms for dealing with stress. It is interesting that when alcoholic women in treatment are compared with matched, nonalcoholic women, early history shows little difference in stressors but significant differences in the *affect* generated in early years (Gomberg, 1989a). There are more negative events in the current lives of those two groups of women, but a good many of these negative events are generated by and are a consequence of the heavy drinking. The question is whether better coping mechanisms make for better prognosis, and study is needed.

A long-term follow-up study of 100 hospital-treated alcoholics and 100 heroin addicts (Vaillant, 1988) contributed to understanding of relevant prognostic indicators. The alcoholics (mean age 45; 17% female) showed severe alcohol dependence and social disability. The follow-up showed that good prognostic indicators at the time of hospital admission were living with spouse, employment, and no history of arrests. Factors related to relapse prevention included compulsory supervision, consistent aversive experience with alcohol (e.g., disulfiram or a painful medical problem), and entry into a new social support network, often an inspirational group.

Another study (Gallant, 1988) concludes that good prognostic signs include (a) stable employment history and higher than average income, (b) living with a spouse and/or involvement with social support network, (c) a compliant rather than assertive personality, (d) patient favoring abstinence rather than controlled drinking, and (e) no history of arrests.

It has been evident for many years that *social stability* is the key prognosticator in outcome of treatment. Those patients who have reasonably stable work records, adequate marriages, and some social networks other than drinking companions are more likely to do well in treatment. A record of arrests, particularly multiple arrests, which suggests either public intoxication or some criminal behavior, is an indicator of poor prognosis. The question of compulsory supervision as a positive indicator (Vaillant, 1988) is interesting because it touches upon an old debate: Is coercion into treatment and supervision helpful? When the patient's "motivation" was deemed essential for therapeutic success, the idea of coercion, any coercion, was rejected. But there is some evidence that coercion and supervision may indeed contribute to therapeutic success. This has some interesting possible interpretations: That the alcohol patient seeks some kind of control? That some alcoholic acting-out is a call for help? That aversive experience meets some wish for punishment?

Matching Patient and Treatment

There is a good deal of interest in matching patient and treatment. Recognition of the broad spectrum of alcohol-related problems and the heterogeneity of the alcoholic population, on the one hand, and the wide variety of treatment approaches available, on the other, raise a question: What is the best treatment plan for this particular patient? To ask, "Which treatment is best for alcoholics?" is simplistic. Instead, more attention needs to be given to patient evaluation, to clinical team staffing, to individualized treatment plans, and to expanding the range of modalities available in rehabilitation facilities.

Study of treatment effectiveness may indeed be hampered by the lack of patient/treatment matching. If a faculty has a treatment X available to which all patients are assigned, the patient pool will include those for whom X is indeed the best treatment and those for whom it is not. Follow-up results reflect this lack of discrimination. These issues have been discussed for about a decade (Gottheil, McLellan, & Druley, 1981; Institute of Medicine, 1990).

Treatment should be tailored to the needs of individual patients, and the current task is to study how this is best done. Some patients will need hospitalization—which ones? Some patients may benefit from disulfiram—which ones? Some patients will do well with brief contact—which ones?

Does Treatment Work?

It is clear that there is a wide range of problems relating to heavy alcohol intake, problems that can range from heavy drinking through problem drinking, alcohol abuse, alcohol dependence, and alcoholism. It is also clear that there are many treatment modalities in use. Therefore, the question, "Is treatment effective?" is simplistic to an extreme. The answer depends on the alcohol-related disorder, factors relating to the treatment facility and the treatment modality, and factors relating to the patient. But there are the realities of health-care costs, so questions must be raised: Should detoxification be done inpatient or can it be done less expensively on an outpatient basis? When is inpatient treatment significantly important in patient recovery? Is psychotherapy cost effective? Does one treatment modality produce the same results as another?

The role that alcohol abuse plays in the nation's health bill is a large one. Although the majority of alcoholics are still untreated, there is a huge cost in those who seek medical care for ailments associated with alcohol intake, such as liver disease, gastrointestinal disorders, coronary problems, certain cancers, psychiatric symptomatology, and so on. It is estimated that at least 25% of people in general hospital beds are there because of alcohol-related illness. The 1983 National Hospital Discharge Survey showed only 1.3% of discharges to have been diagnosed as a drug or alcohol problem, although epidemiological data suggest that a figure like 30% would be more accurate. This "hidden burden on the health care system" (Holden, 1987) is also manifested in data showing alcoholics utilizing health services at four times the rate of nonalcoholics, and their families incurring twice as many medical costs as other families. Treatment apparently does reduce health-care costs.

The question of *inpatient* alcoholism treatment and its costs was examined (Miller & Hester, 1986b), and the conclusion was that there is "no overall advantage for residential over nonresidential settings, for longer over shorter inpatient programs, and for more intensive (meaning cost-intensive) over less intensive interventions."

Miller and Hester (1986a) reviewed the research on effectiveness of different treatment modalities and summarized: mixed support for chemotherapy (antidepressants were noted as useful), ambiguous results about the effects of psychotherapy and membership in Alcoholics Anonymous, mixed results with aversion therapies, and some encouraging work in the area of marital and family therapy. In testimony before a Senate committee, Miller (1988) reported that "there is no one outstandingly effective treatment." The weight of research evidence favored brief advice/feedback intervention, the community reinforcement approach, social-skill training, and—in rank order—antidepressants, stress-management training, covert sensitization, and self-control training. To some extent, these results may be influenced by the fact that the behavioral therapies are usually researched by individuals more knowledgeable and sophisticated about research methods. This, membership in Alcoholics Anonymous, and general counseling rank as 0% of positive studies with three studies reported for each modality, all with negative results.

With the pressure on the health-care system and the shrinking availability of treatment dollars, it seems likely that there will be trends toward more *outpatient* treatment and "the social recovery model" (Holden, 1987) and toward shorter-term programs. There are, however, alcoholics and drug abusers who do need hospitalization, and research may clarify the criteria for hospitalization. This is, of course, a variation on matching, that is, identifying subgroups of alcoholics and drug abusers and matching them with needed and appropriate treatments. The undercurrent of stigma remains: Alcoholism goes unrecognized in many medical patients, caretakers are not always ready to refer recognized cases of alcohol/drug abuse, and there are many negative views about the efficacy of treatment. The fact remains that treatment, whatever its nature, is better than no treatment at all. If it does nothing else, it expresses societal concern about the alcohol- or drug-dependent person.

References

Alcoholics Anonymous. (1987). *AA membership survey.* New York: Alcoholics Anonymous World Service.

Alterman, A. I. (1985). Substance abuse in psychiatric patients: Etiological, development and treatment considerations. In A. I. Alterman (Ed.), *Substance abuse and psychopathology,* (pg. 121-136). New York: Plenum.

Azrin, N. (1976). Improvements in the community-reinforcement approach to alcoholism. *Behavior Research and Therapy, 14,* 339-348.

Beckman, L. J., & Amaro, H. (1984). Pattern of women's use of alcohol treatment agencies. In S. C. Wilsnack & L. J. Beckman (Eds.), *Alcohol problems in women* (pp. 319-349). New York: Guilford.

Briddell, D., & Nathan, P. (1976). Behavior assessment and modification with alcoholics: Current status and future trends. In M. Hersen, R. Eisler, & P. Miller (Eds.), *Progress in behavior modification* (Vol. 2, pp. 2-51). New York: Academic Press.

Brown, M. A. (1950). Alcoholic profiles on the Minnesota Multiphasic. *Journal of Clinical Psychology, 6,* 266-269.

Davies, D. L. (1962). Normal drinking in recovered alcohol addicts. *Quarterly Journal of Studies on Alcohol, 23,* 94-104.

Dole, V. P. (1980). Addictive behavior. *Scientific American* Offprint No. 735.

Edwards, G., Orford, J., Egert, S., Guthrie, S., Hawker, A., Hensman, C., Mitcheson, M., Oppenheimer, E., & Taylor, C. (1977). Alcoholism: A controlled trial of "treatment" and "advice." *Journal of Studies on Alcohol, 38,* 1004-1031.

Estes, N. J., & Heinemann, M. E. (1986). *Alcoholism: Development, consequences and interventions.* St. Louis: C. V. Mosby.

Galanter, M. (1984). Self-help large-group therapy for alcoholism: A controlled study. *Alcoholism: Clinical and Experimental Research, 8,* 16-22.

Gallant, D. M. (1988). A controlled study of advice versus extended treatment. *Alcoholism: Clinical and Experimental Research, 12,* 725-726.

Gomberg, E. S. L. (1989a). Alcoholic women in treatment: Early histories and early problem behaviors. *Advances in Alcohol and Substance Abuse, 8,* 133-147.

Gomberg, E. S. L. (1989b). On terms used and abused: The concept of "codependency." *Drugs and Society, 3,* 113-132.

Gomberg, E. S. L., Nelson, B. W., & Hatchett, B. F. (1991). Women, alcoholism and family therapy. *Journal of Family and Community Health, 13,.* 61-71.

Gomberg, E. S. L., White, H. R., & Carpenter, J. A. (Eds.). (1982). *Alcohol, science and society revisited.* Ann Arbor: University of Michigan Press.

Gottheil, E., McLellan, A. T., & Druley, K. A. (Eds.). (1981). *Matching patient needs and treatment methods in alcoholism and drug abuse.* Springfield, IL: Charles C Thomas.

Hayashida, M., Alterman, A. I., McLellan, A. T., O'Brien, C. P., Purtill, J. J., Volpicelli, J. R., Raphaelson, A. H., & Hall, C. P. (1989). Comparative effectiveness and costs of inpatient and outpatient detoxification of patients with mild-to-moderate alcohol withdrawal syndrome. *New England Journal of Medicine, 320,* 358-365.

Hesselbrock, M. N., Hesselbrock, V. N., Babor, T. F., et al. (1983). Antisocial behavior, psychopathology and problem drinking in the natural history of alcoholism. In D. W. Goodwin, K. T. Van Dusen, & S. A. Mednick (Eds.), *Longitudinal research in alcoholism* (pp. 197-214). Boston: Kluwer-Nijhoff.

Holden, C. (1987). Alcoholism and the medical cost crunch. *Science, 235*, 1132-1133.

Institute of Medicine. (1990). *Broadening the base for treatment of alcohol problems.* Washington, DC: National Academy Press.

Kaufman, E. (1984). Family systems variables in alcoholism. *Alcoholism: Clinical and Experimental Research, 8*, 4-8.

Kay, D. C. (1985). Substance abuse in psychopathic states and sociopathic individuals. In A. I. Alterman (Ed.), *Substance abuse and psychopathology* (pp. 91-120). New York: Plenum.

Lettieri, D. J., Nelson, J. E., & Sayers, M. A. (1987) Alcoholism treatment assessment research instruments. In *NIAAA treatment handbook Series 2* (DHHS Publication No. ADM 87-1380). Washington DC: Government Printing Office.

Liepman, M. R., & Nirenberg, T. D. (1987). Beginning treatment for alcohol problems. In W. M. Cox (Ed.), *Treatment and prevention of alcohol problems: A resource manual* (pp. 13-26). New York: Academic Press.

Marlatt, G. A., Baer, J. S. Donovan, D. M., & Kivlahan, D. R. (1988). Addictive behaviors: Etiology and treatment. *Annual Review of Psychology, 39*, 223-252.

Marlatt, G. A., & Gordon, J. R. (Eds.). (1985). *Relapse prevention: Maintenance strategies in the treatment of addictive behaviors.* New York: Guilford.

Mayfield, D. (1985). Substance abuse in the affective disorders. In A. I. Alterman (Ed.), *Substance abuse and psychopathology* (pp. 69-90). New York: Plenum.

McNichol, R. W., & Logsdon, S. A. (1988). Disulfiram: An evaluation research model. *Alcohol Health and Research World, 12*, 203-209.

Miller, P. (1976). *Behavioral treatment of alcohol.* New York: Pergamon.

Miller, W. R. (1988, June 16). *The effectiveness of alcoholism treatment modalities.* Testimony to the U.S. Senate Committee on Governmental Affairs, Washington, DC.

Miller, W. R., & Heather, N. (Eds.). (1986). *Treating addictive behaviors: Processes of change.* New York: Plenum.

Miller, W. P., & Hester, R. K. (1986a). The effectiveness of alcoholism treatment: What research reveals. In W. R. Miller & N. Heather (Eds.), *Treating addictive behaviors: Processes of change* (pp. 121-174). New York: Plenum.

Miller, W. R., & Hester, R. K. (1986b). Inpatient alcoholism treatment: Who benefits? *American Psychologist, 41*, 794-805.

Nathan, P. E. (1982). Human behavioral research on alcoholism, with special emphasis on the decade of the 1970s. In E. L. Gomberg, H. R. White, & J. A. Carpenter (Eds.), *Alcohol, science and society revisited* (pp. 279-294). Ann Arbor: University of Michigan Press.

Nathan, P. E., & McCrady, B. S. (1986-1987). Bases for the use of abstinence as a goal in the behavioral treatment of alcohol abusers. *Drugs and Society, 2/3*, 109-131.

Pattison, E. M. (1974). Rehabilitation of the chronic alcoholic. In B. Kissin & H. Begleiter (Eds.), *The biology of alcoholism* (Vol. 3, pp. 587-658). New York: Plenum.

Pendery, M. L., Maltzman, I. M., & West, L. J. (1982). Controlled drinking by alcoholics? New findings and a re-evaluation of a major affirmative study. *Science, 217*, 169-175.

Polich, J. M., Armor, D. J., & Stambul, H. B. (1980). *The course of alcoholism: Four years after treatment* (R-2433-NIAAA) Santa Monica, CA: RAND.

Royce, J. E. (1989). *Alcohol problems and alcoholism: A comprehensive survey.* New York: Free Press.

Schuckit, M. A. (1973). Alcoholism and sociopathy—Diagnostic confusion. *Quarterly Journal of Studies on Alcohol, 34*, 157-164.

Schuckit, M. A. (1979). Alcoholism and affective disorder: Diagnostic confusion. In D. W. Goodwin & C. K. Erickson (Eds.), *Alcoholism and affective disorders.* New York: SP Medical and Scientific Books.

Schuckit, M. A. (1983). Alcoholism and other psychiatric disorders. *Hospital and Community Psychiatry, 34,* 1022-1027.

Shore, J. H., & Kofoed, L. (1984). Community intervention in the treatment of alcoholism. *Alcoholism: Clinic and Experimental Research, 8,* 151-159.

Sobell, M. B., & Sobell, L. C. (Eds.). (1986-1987). Moderation as a goal or outcome of treatment for alcohol problems: A dialogue. *Drugs and Society, 1,* 1-171.

Steinglass, P. (1982). Alcoholism and the family. In E. L. Gomberg, H. R. White, & J. A. Carpenter (Eds.), *Alcohol, science and society revisted* (pp. 306-321). Ann Arbor: University of Michigan Press.

Sugerman, A. A. (1982). Alcoholism: An overview of treatment models and methods. In E. L. Gomberg, H. R. White, & J. A. Carpenter (Eds.), *Alcohol, science and society revisited* (pp. 262-278). Ann Arbor: University of Michigan Press.

Taylor, J. R. (1986-1987). Controlled drinking studies: Methodological issues. *Drugs and Society, 1,* 83-107.

Vaillant, G. E. (1988). What can long-term follow-up teach us about relapse and prevention of relapse in addiction? *British Journal of Addiction, 83,* 1147-1157.

25

POLICY AND PREVENTION

In examination of history and policy, a number of different viewpoints exist. One rather extreme position is that "a drug problem" did not exist until the passage of the Harrison Narcotic Act in 1914 (Szasz, 1974); it is the taboo that makes the problem. Others take the position that the use of psychoactive substances, such as alcohol, has created problems for humankind in all cultures and in all recorded history. Even if the term "alcoholic" did not exist, can one say that alcoholic beverages did not make for difficulties (problems) when consumed in large amounts? There is a history of Roman lack of moderation, comments about drunkenness in the Bible, passages in medieval literature and in the writings of Shakespeare. Another interesting viewpoint about drugs is that all people and animals use/need psychoactive substances.

There is government policy, there are policymakers, and there are efforts to influence policy. Generally, policymakers are the legislators, local, state, and federal, who will create legislation relating to the conditions under which substance X may be used (e.g., age, place, hours) or forbid the use of substance Y. Efforts to influence policy may be forthcoming from industry, the media, religious groups, research scientists, parents, community organizations, and individuals. The Volstead Act was a policy act, minimum-age-at-purchase of alcoholic beverages is a policy, drug testing is a policy. Public concern about "the drug problem" waxes and wanes: Often associated with youth problems, crime, and the breakdown of social controls, concern about drugs has, at several points in recent years, peaked and surpassed concern with other problems, such as AIDS, homelessness, or the national debt. Sometimes public concern focuses on legal drugs, as is the case with Mothers Against Drunk Driving (Sadoff, 1990); sometimes—as in the war on drugs—focus is primarily on a banned substance like cocaine.

Policy may also be made by an institution. Some churches allow drinking; others do not. A university is required, by federal mandate, to have a policy about the use of alcohol and other drugs, and such a policy must take into account existing laws dealing with age of purchase, sale of alcoholic beverages by licensed establishments, locations for the sale of alcoholic beverages and locations for the consumption of alcoholic beverages, laws relating to driving and drinking, social host laws, rules relating to advertising, on-campus and off-campus regulations, and so on.

Policy relating to alcoholic beverages has several unique features. Although opinions about heroin use are not often charged with affect, alcohol is not an obscure or neutral topic. Individual and institutional responses to drinking have varied (Moore & Gerstein, 1981), and a recent report on public opinion and alcohol policies suggests that there are "coherent underlying structures of opinion on alcohol policy issues among the public" (Wagenaar & Streff, 1990). The amount of scientific and quasi-scientific literature available about alcoholic beverages, their use, effects, and problems, is much larger than the literature about any other drug; it has been further complicated by increasing interest in the study of alcohol combined with other substances.

Four policy issues will be discussed briefly:

1. The war on drugs and the issue of drug testing
2. Proposed legalization of all banned substances
3. Drug abuse as a two-tiered problem
4. Policy and scientific findings

The War on Drugs and the Issue of Drug Testing:

For at least two decades, the federal government has fought a well-publicized war on drugs. Whether this war has had some success or whether it is a failure is difficult to judge. Clearly, the problem of illegal drug importation, sale, and use has not gone away, but what is unclear is the question of whether such illegal drug traffic has lessened. The war presumably has two major aspects: supply and demand. What has gained most of the media attention is the war on supply, that is, the attempts to wipe out the growing and processing of cocaine in several South American countries and the attempts to counter the importation of banned substances at the points at which they enter the United States. The war on demand is fundamentally those efforts made at treatment and at prevention of drug abuse. Whether or not one considers the war on drugs to have made significant gains depends, often, on the political viewpoint of the individual making the judgment. In the absence of useful solid data, more liberal judges of the war on drugs tend to pronounce it a failure and to call for a policy of more treatment and rehabilitation money. Less liberal judges may look at small gains, the drop in adolescent use of some substances and the drop in per-capita consumption of absolute alcohol. Judging whether changes in peoples' behavior as related to drugs (smoking, drinking, etc.) are directly linked with a government policy such as the war on drugs is difficult, and the best that can be said is that such policies and the expressed public concern do have a dampening effect on drug abuse.

The question of drug testing in the work place, that is, drug screening for job applicants and drug testing for employees, is a touchy one. The civil libertarian question, of course, is whether recreational use of a drug substance by an off-duty employee affects job performance. No one will argue that the use of alcoholic beverages, marijuana, or other drug substances is irrelevant when public safety is involved, and public anxiety is reinforced when there is a railroad, maritime, or airplane accident and the pilot or engineer is shown to have been using drugs while on the job. The issue is much more complicated when the question is raised whether U.S. government employees with access to confidential or secret information should be subject to drug testing. Drug testing is not well developed, and there are questions raised about its efficacy. There is also the question of whether such testing should be a one-time thing, a regular procedure, or a random testing. A recent decision by the United States Court of Appeals for the District of Columbia is relevant ("Court Rejects," 1990); the judges struck down regulations under which Agriculture Department employees could be tested if suspected of off-duty drug use, even if their job performance showed no impairment. The question of drug testing of government workers is by no means resolved.

A recent review of government intent and employer response to the Drug-Free Workplace Act of 1988 (Younger, 1990) comes to several conclusions. Among these conclusions are the following: (a) having a drug policy is the most common element of a drug program in any company; (b) most companies who drug test are more likely to do such testing on job applicants rather than employees; (c) the combination of familiarity with the Drug-Free Workplace Act and/or Department of Defense or Department of Transportation rules produces higher rates of drug program implementation; and (d) the respondents were familiar with the Act's existence but often less familiar with the requirements of the act. Younger also concludes that her survey "hint[s] at a possible, positive response from the private sector."

Proposed Legalization of Banned Substances

"Decriminalization" and "legalization" do not mean precisely the same things. To decriminalize a drug, criminal sanctions are removed against users but not necessarily against producers and sellers. Legalizing a drug is broader: Criminal sanctions are removed against users, producers, and sellers. The present legal status of various drugs might be described as specific-drug prohibition.

Legalization of banned substances may take many forms. All criminal penalties may be removed from the manufacture, sale, and use of all psychoactive drugs, or the relatively "safer" drugs such as marijuana might be legalized. Another alternative is to make all psychoactive drugs legally available but with intensive preventive programming that might limit their use and restrict consumption. Some advocate the inclusion of tobacco and alcoholic beverages in an overall plan, which would allow availability but educate for limited consumption.

Arguments in favor of legalization point to the costs and consequences of current drug prohibition laws: The relationship of drug prohibition laws and crime is quite clear. A real social problem exists in the *unregulated* nature of illegal drug use, including the lack of control over the purity of the drugs (no Food and Drug Administration supervision or honest-labeling laws!) and the large percentage of AIDS cases related to intravenous needle use. The arguments in favor of legalization assume that "most illegal drugs are not as dangerous as is commonly believed," and that those drugs that involve the most risk "are likely to prove appealing to many people precisely because they are so obviously dangerous" (Nadelman, 1989). Interestingly, those persons in public life who have spoken in favor of legalization represent a wide political spectrum: economist Milton Friedman, writer William Buckley, Mayor Schmoke of Baltimore, Police Chief McNamara of San Jose, psychiatrist Lester Grinspoon, and so on. There is no single position among those who would favor legalization. Some libertarians feel that governments should not be telling citizens what they may or may not put in their bodies. Other proponents argue that it is hypocritical to ban narcotics while allowing the sale of alcohol and tobacco. Some advocates argue that U.S. relations with the several Latin countries in which drugs are grown and processed for sale in the United States would improve with legalization. Some advocates argue that drug searches are a threat to individual freedom.

The major problem that advocates of legalization have to deal with is the vagueness of the details: Which drugs would be legalized? How would they be sold? What would be the age limits? Would there be limits set on the amount a customer could buy? There is general agreement among advocates and opponents of legalization that the increased availability and the legality of drugs would result in an increased number of users. The experience of Japan and Sweden with legalized amphetamines is sometimes cited; legalization involved an exchange of one set of problems for another and eventually, in both countries, the legalized drugs were banned.

Kaplan (1989) examined a number of policy options and concluded that "none of the policy options is attractive," and that we should choose the least bad policy. He argues that heroin and cocaine are indeed "dangerous drugs" and that the analogy to Prohibition of alcoholic beverages is a weak one: "Hard as it is to believe, the social cost of maintaining Prohibition was not only greater than that which heroin and cocaine currently impose upon us, it was even greater than that imposed by what is now our greatest drug problem—alcohol" (Kaplan, 1989, p. 33). Kaplan recommends a system with emphasis on treatment: Because compulsory treatment does work and because users who are both criminals and addicts are the heaviest consumers, he reasons that if treatments can bring usage/addiction under some degree of control, a major blow will have been dealt to the illegal distribution networks.

Others who argue against legalization state their argument simply: The costs are too high (Kondrake, 1989). At this time, it appears that most of the citizenry and most of the Congress are against legislation to decriminalize or legalize banned substances. The difficulty in the war on drugs focused on an attack on the supply is that it involves several sovereign nations, so perhaps the effort is doing as well as could be expected. And the war on demand is probably hampered as much by our inadequate knowledge of effective modalities of treatment of a drug habit and its concomitant life-style as by the inadequacy of funding and treatment facilities. Perhaps this will change in the next few years.

Drug Abuse as a Two-Tiered Problem

For the last years of the 1980s, the use of cocaine declined. This decline was largely a phenomenon of middle-class, White persons, and it was accompanied by a decline in the per capita consumption of alcohol. The media reported: "Rich vs. poor: Drug patterns are diverging" (Kerr, 1987). What the journalists were writing about was to two-tiered phenomenon: middle-class Americans who might be over the peak of experimentation with illegal drugs, and poor people who were not showing a decline in cocaine use (Isikoff, 1989).

In annual surveys of marijuana use among high school seniors, the use appeared to have peaked in 1978 and to have declined after that. It is not easy to make judgments about such trends, for the 1985 National Household survey of the National Institute on Drug Abuse (1988) showed that marijuana smoking among young people was more likely to be reported by high school dropouts. Among adults 35 and older, interestingly enough, it was the college-educated who were most likely to be marijuana users.

It is clear, however, that AIDS cases in intravenous drug abusers have occurred most frequently among innercity black people: The Center for Disease Control AIDS Weekly Surveillance Report of January 2, 1989, shows 59% of such cases to be black (American Public Health Association, 1989).

The issue is clearly a complex one, because factors of race and social class play an important role in the accessibility of treatment and in the motivation to seek treatment. Drug dependence or addiction is more likely to be viewed as criminal behavior among lower-class drug abusers. In Connecticut, for example, over 70% of prison inmates are reported to have serious alcohol/drug problems (Schottenfeld, 1990). Almost three-quarters of the prison inmates are black or Hispanic, whereas an estimated 30% of people admitted to public substance-treatment programs are black or Hispanic (Schottenfeld, 1990). The discrepancies in employment, income level, and other indices of social class between white and nonwhite clearly have an impact on public perception and availability of rehabilitation. It must also be recognized that for an undereducated, unemployed high school dropout living in a slum, the motivation to avoid drugs or seek treatment is less—for this drug abuser, there is less to lose.

Public policy has not explicity recognized the two-tiered nature of the drug problem and the need for effective prevention/treatment programs among lower-income people. Nor is this phenomenon exclusively American: In a report of changes in alcohol-related inpatient care in Stockholm county in relation to socioeconomic status, "the gap between blue collar workers and white collar workers widened" (Romelsjo & Diderichsen, 1989). This Swedish study linked data from national housing and population censuses and inpatient care registers in the late 1970s and early 1980s, a period during which alcohol consumption was declining in Sweden. The authors concluded that "the goal for national alcohol policy, suggested by the WHO—a reduction of per capita consumption—should be combined with additional measures that will reach all social groups" (Romelsjo & Diderichsen, 1989, p. 52).

Policy and Scientific Findings

Most researchers would like to have policymakers consider the findings of laboratories and epidemiological surveys. Those who plan prevention and those who plan and fund rehabilitation programs must have access to hard data and not rely on hearsay, stereotypes, and moral attitudes. Room (1988) has argued that "the relation between scientific research and policy claims is indeed problematic, with the science often distorted in the transmission" (p. 117). Heath has argued that scientists must be more careful and responsible in their use of data than they are currently (Heath, 1988). There have been a number of controversies among scientists in the alcohol/drug field that have received public attention. The National Institute on Alcohol Abuse and Alcoholism campaigned for *no* drinking at all during pregnancy, taking the position that even infrequent or moderate drinking could be harmful to the fetus; this was questioned by some researchers (Maugh, 1981). Another public controversy surfaced when the president of the National Academy of Sciences took issue with an academy panel's recommendations about marijuana, arguing that the data were insufficient to justify the panel's "value-laden" judgments (Walsh, 1982). The controversy over the goals of treatment (discussed in Chapter 24) is alive and well. A recent article by Maltzman (1989), one of the participants in an earlier controversy over controlled drinking as the goal of treatment, was published after a response was solicited from the Sobells (Sobell & Sobell, 1989). As Thomas Schelling (1990) has commented: Not many researchers are neutral on the policy issues.

Prevention

The first question must be, What are we trying to prevent: any drinking, heavy drinking, or problems associated with drinking? Prevention may be defined "as actions designed to keep from happening, to forestall, or to diminish the detrimental effects of alcohol . . . acute or chronic" (Gomberg, Breslow, Hamburg, & Noble, 1980). Prevention campaigns aim to reduce alcohol intake in order to minimize the negative consequences. Sometimes, as with adolescents and school children, the aim is not to reduce but totally to avoid drinking.

Prevention has been organized in a number of different ways. One way is to speak of primary, secondary, and tertiary prevention. Primary prevention has as its goal discouraging any drinking behavior, for instance, among underage persons or by the "appointed driver" at a party. Secondary prevention involves early recognition and intervention with persons who are at what may be described as middle-stage alcohol problems; employee assistance programs in the workplace are designed to assist people who have alcohol/drug or other problems while they are unimpaired enough to maintain themselves in a job. Tertiary prevention covers the treatment establishment and procedures with which we seek to help an alcohol-dependent or drug-dependent person.

Another way of organizing is in terms of agent, environment, and host:

Agent. The core of agent-directed techniques of prevention deal with the question of availability (Smart, 1980). Easier or more difficult ways of obtaining the agent (e.g., alcohol) are involved in methods such as raising the price, increasing the tax, controlling the number of outlets that sell the agent, and regulations about ingredients and minimum age for purchase. An extreme form of agent control is seen in the Prohibition Amendment, the "noble experiment." A less draconian form of agent control is changing the hours during which alcoholic beverages may be sold. A variety of such "normative approaches" were presented in a symposium (Harford, Parker, & Light, 1980).

Environment. This is a very broad concept encompassing family, school, the community, and the media. An environmental approach to prevention involves the institutions of the community and an attempt to minimize intake and consequences by working through these institutions. Traditionally, the most obvious place for such prevention programs has been the schools, and historically, the major approach was an educational one. The limitations of alcohol and drug education do change the amount of information the individual displays at the end of the educational effort; education may even change the individual's attitude. The problem lies in the minimal *behavioral* change that results from alcohol/drug education, (Bangert-Drowns, 1986). Prevention efforts that involve environmental manipulation more recently have focused on the media, particularly on television.

Host. Again, there are different approaches. The host may be the whole school or the whole community, or it may be a specific group within the larger body. Hosts may be high-risk subgroups within the population. There are special and unique aspects to addressing a prevention message to different subgroups, as for instance, children and adolescents, pregnant women, blue collar-workers, people in the armed forces, recently divorced/widowed persons, and the elderly. One group that has received a good deal of attention in the last decade has been "children of alcoholics"; clinical research has indicated that positive family history puts a person at somewhat higher risk than one with a negative family history. However, a very large number of people with positive family history do not develop alcohol-related problems. It is as though there were an equation with several variables that contribute to prediction of alcoholism, and positive family history is only one variable in that equation. There is another problem: Programs for children of alcoholics (COAs) may be laudable in intent but the emphasis seems to have resulted in negative stereotyping by mental-health professionals and peers (Burk & Sher, 1990). Considering the tentative state of our knowledge of high-risk and low-risk groups, it seems wise to proceed with caution in targeting specific groups.

It is also possible to analyze prevention strategies in terms of demand and supply. *Demand* techniques are directed toward the host, primarily, and the goal is to reduce the consumer market; approaches are usually directed toward the individual and his or her efforts as they contribute to minimizing demand. *Supply* techniques are usually community directed, involving the agent and the environment (Gerstein, 1984). Both techniques have the same end in view: change in *behavior.* The limitation of educational approaches is that they increase knowledge and may even modify attitudes, but they show minimal effectiveness as techniques of behavior change.

There are a number of methodological issues that make research in prevention a difficult task. If there are two groups, for example, and one group is exposed to technique X and the other is not, how do we evaluate the effectiveness of X? How long a period of time should elapse? Were there other factors that interacted with technique X so that the evaluation is not the effectiveness of X alone but the measure of X + other factors? Even when positive results are reported for a drug-prevention program (Ellickson & Bell, 1990), there are challenges that view the results as only "marginally effective" and not cost effective (Ferrence & Kozlowski, 1990).

In spite of the newness of the prevention approach and the methodological difficulties involved, there are a number of important things that have been learned:

1. A prevention campaign directed toward a *specific target* is more effective than a campaign where the target is diffuse. A prevention campaign that has as its goal no drinking during pregancy targets pregnant women or even women of childbearing age.

2. In a prevention campaign directed toward pregnant women, the goal is clear—no drinking during pregnancy (and probably not while breast-feeding). The clearer and more specific the goal, the greater the probability of success. One of the difficulties beseting prevention programs directed toward minimizing teenage pregnancies is do we ask young people to forego drinking/sexual behavior until they are young adults or do we ask them to be moderate and be careful?

3. A useful distinction has been made by Noel and McCrady (1984): "A primary level of intervention is aimed at prevention of drinking, or at least of excessive drinking. A secondary level of intervention is geared toward preventing some of the negative consequences of excessive drinking" (p. 58). These authors have identified *early-stage* intervention, or primary prevention, with etiology or antecedents or "presumed causes of excessive drinking," and *secondary-stage* intervention, or secondary prevention, with alcohol-related problems or consequences.

4. The use of self-help groups in prevention programs should be explored for its potential (Borman, Borck, Hess, & Pasquale, 1981). Although a beginning has been made, for instance, in utilization of rehabilitated alcohol/drug abusers in school peer counseling programs, there is a large source of personnel and motivation in self-help groups.

5. For more effective prevention efforts, specific groups should be targeted and campaigns of prevention devised that take into consideration the unique needs and cultural patterns of specific groups. Campaigns for women need to consider changes in normative sex-role behaviors, age group differences, and social class-religious-ethnic differences (Gomberg, 1989). All that has been learned about the characteristic drinking patterns and consequences for female heavy drinkers needs to be utilized (Noel & McCrady, 1984). A variety of programs has developed, some directed toward pregnant women, some directed toward alcohol-abusing women, and some toward women's tendency to combine minor tranquilzers and alcohol (Ferrence, 1984). From these, offshoot programs have developed that are directed toward women of child-bearing age in some Native-American groups where fetal alcohol syndrome has increased, and programs directed toward middle-aged and elderly women who counter solitude and/or rejection with inadequate coping mechanisms.

There is much to be learned in prevention techniques in studying the history of antismoking campaigns. Although scare tactics are of limited effectiveness, the mass of evidence linking smoking with a number of serious diseases and the constant reiteration of the message have had their effect. There are problems, of course: an antismoking campaign has as its end no smoking. Should an antialcohol campaign have as its end no drinking?

References

American Public Health Association. (1989). Illicit drug use and HIV infection. In *The nation's health* (p. 7). Washington, DC: Author.

Bangert-Drowns, R. L. (1986). *Meta-analysis of the effects of alcohol and drug education*. Unpublished doctoral dissertation, University of Michigan, Ann Arbor.

Borman, L. D., Borck, L. E., Hess, R., & Pasquale, F. L. (Eds.). (1981). Helping people to help themselves: Self help and prevention. *Prevention in Human Services, 1*, 1-129.

Burk, J. P., & Sher, K. J. (1990). Labeling the child of an alcoholic: Negative stereotyping by mental health professionals and peers. *Journal of Studies on Alcohol, 51*, 156-163.

Court rejects some drug testing of U.S. workers. (1990, November 18). *New York Times*, p. 20.

Ellickson, P. L., & Bell, R. M. (1990). Drug prevention in junior high: A multi-site longitudinal test, *Science, 247*, 1299.

Ferrence, R. G. (1984). Prevention of alcohol problems in women. In S. C. Wilsnack & L. J. Beckman (Eds.), *Alcohol problems in women* (pp. 413-442). New York: Guilford.

Ferrence, R. G., & Kozlowski, L. T. (1990). Drug abuse prevention programs. *Science, 250*, 740-741.

Gerstein, D. R. (Ed.). (1984). *Toward the prevention of alcohol problems: Government, business and community action*. Washington, DC: National Academy Press.

Gomberg, E. S. L. (1989). *Women and alcohol: Primary prevention*. Unpublished manuscript.

Gomberg, E. S. L., Breslow, L., Hamburg, B. A. M., & Noble, E. P. (1980). Report of panel five: Prevention issues. In Institute of Medicine, *Alcoholism, alcohol abuse, and related problems: Opportunities for research* (pp. 103-138). Washington, DC: National Academy of Sciences.

Harford, T. C., Parker, D. A., & Light, L. (Eds.). (1980). *Normative approaches to the prevention of alcohol abuse and alcoholism* (DHHS Publication No. ADM 79-847). Washington, DC: Government Printing Office.

Heath, D. B. (1988). Alcohol control policies and drinking patterns: An international game of politics against science. *Journal of Substance Abuse, 1*, 109-115.

Isikoff, M. (1989, January 6). Middle class shunning drug that devastates poor America. *Washington Post*.

Kaplan, J. (1989). Taking drugs seriously. *Drugs and Society, 3*, 187-208.

Kerr, P. (1987, August 30). Rich vs. poor: Drug patterns are diverging. *New York Times*, p. 1.

Kondrake, M. M. (1989). Don't legalize drugs. *Drugs and Society, 3*, 209-215.

Maltzman, I. (1989). [A reply to Cook, "Craftsman versus professional: Analysis on the controlled drinking controversy."] *Journal of Studies on Alcohol, 50*, 466-472.

Maugh, T. H., II (1981). Fetal alcohol advisory debated. *Science, 214*, 642-644.

Moore, M. H., & Gerstein, D. R. (Eds.). (1981). *Alcohol and public policy: Beyond the shadow of prohibition*. Washington, DC: National Academy Press.

Nadelman, E. A. (1989). Drug prohibition in the United States: Costs, consequences, and alternatives, *Science, 245*, 939-946.

National Institute on Drug Abuse. (1988). *National household survey on drug abuse: Main findings 1985* (DHHS Publication No. ADM 88-1586). Washington, DC: Government Printing Office.

Noel, N. E., & McCrady, B. S. (1984). Target populations for alcohol abuse prevention. In P. M. Miller & T. D. Nirenberg (Eds.), *Prevention of alcohol abuse* (pp. 55-94). New York: Plenum.

Romelsjo, A., & Diderichsen, F. (1989). Changes in alcohol-related inpatient care in Stockholm county in relation to socioeconomic status during a period of decline in alcohol consumption. *American Journal of Public Health, 79,* 52-56.

Room, R. (1988). Science is in the details: Toward a nuanced view of alcohol control studies. *Journal of Substance Abuse, 1,* 117-120.

Sadoff, M. (1990). *America gets MADD.* Irving, TX: Mothers Against Drunk Driving.

Schelling, T. (1990, October 16). *Licit/illicit substance abuse policy seminar.* Paper presented at the School of Public Health, University of Michigan, Ann Arbor.

Schottenfeld, R. S. (1990). Race, class and access to drug treatment. *Substance Abuse, 11,* 63-64.

Smart, R. G. (1980). Availability and the prevention of alcohol-related problems. In T. C. Harford, D. A. Parker, & L. Light (Eds.), *Normative approaches to the prevention of alcohol abuse and alcoholism* (DHEW Publication No. ADM 79-847, pp. 123-146). Washington, DC: Government Printing Office.

Sobell, M. B., & Sobell, L. C. (1989). Moratorium on Maltzman: An apppeal to reason. *Journal of Studies on Alcohol, 50,* 473-480.

Szasz, T. (1974). *Ceremonial chemistry: The ritual persecution of drugs, addicts, and pushers.* Garden City, New York: Anchor Press.

Wagenaar, A. C., & Streff, F. M. (1990). Public opinion on alcohol policies. *Journal of Public Health Policy, 11,* 189-205.

Walsh, J. (1982). Frank Press takes exception to NAS panel recommendations on marijuana. *Science, 217,* 288-229.

Younger, B. (1990). *The Drug-Free Workplace Act of 1988: Government intent and employer response.* Presentation at the Employee Assistance Professional Association annual conference, New Orleans, LA.

GLOSSARY

absorption, drug mechanisms by which a drug reaches the bloodstream from the skin, lungs, stomach, intestinal tract, or muscle.

abstinence syndrome a state of altered behavior observed following cessation of drug administration.

acetaldehyde the chemical product of the first step in the liver's metabolism of alcohol. It is normally present only in small amounts, for it is rapidly converted to acetic acid.

acetylcholine a neurotransmitter in the central and peripheral nervous systems.

acute effects the immediate, short-term response to a single dose of drug; compare to chronic effects.

additive effects an increased effect observed when two drugs having similar biological actions are administered. The net effect is the sum of the independent effects exerted by each drug.

adenosine a chemical believed to be a neurotransmitter in the CNS, primarily at inhibitory receptors. Caffeine may act by antagonizing the normal action of adenosine on its receptors.

administration, drug procedures through which a drug gains entrance into the body.

agonists drugs that activate the receptors in a manner that mimics the action of the natural neurotransmitter.

AIDS (Acquired Immune Deficiency Syndrome) a disease in which the body's immune system breaks down, leading eventually to death.

alcohol   generally refers to grain alcohol, or ethanol. A widely used sedative-hypnotic drug.

alcohol abuse   defined in the DSM-III as a pattern of pathological alcohol use that causes impairment of social or occupational functioning.

alcohol dehydrogenase   the enzyme that metabolizes almost all of the alcohol consumed by an individual. It is found primarily in the liver.

alcohol dependence   the DSM-III considers alcohol dependence to be a more serious disorder than alcohol abuse, in that dependence includes either tolerance or withdrawal symptoms.

aldehyde dehydrogenase   an enzyme that carries out a specific step in alcohol metabolism: the metabolism of acetaldehyde to acetate. This enzyme may be blocked by the drug disulfiram (Antabuse).

amotivational syndrome   a hypothesized loss of motivation that has been attributed to the effects of chronic marijuana use.

amphetamine   a behavioral stimulant.

analgesic   pain-relieving. An analgesic drug produces a selective reduction of pain, whereas an anesthetic reduces all sensation.

anesthetic   drug that causes loss of sensation or feeling, especially pain, by its depressant effect on the nervous system.

Antabuse   brand name for disulfiram, a drug that interferes with the normal metabolism of alcohol.

antagonist   drugs that occupy the receptors but do not activate them, thus producing a functional blockade of the postsynaptic neuron.

aphrodisiac   substance that will produce a sexually enhancing effect in a person who does not expect this result.

ataxia   loss of coordinated movement, for example, the staggering gait of someone who has consumed a large amount of alcohol.

autonomic nervous system   the branch of the peripheral nervous system that regulates the visceral, or automatic functions of the body, such as heart rate and intestinal motility.

aversion therapy   a form of treatment that attempts to suppress an undesirable behavior by punishing each instance of the behavior.

BAL   blood alcohol level, also called blood alcohol content (BAC). The proportion of blood that consists of alcohol.

barbiturate   a class of chemically related sedative-hypnotic compounds, all of which share a characteristic six-membered ring structure.

basal ganglia   also known as the corpus striatum. A part of the brain containing large numbers of dopamine synapses, it is responsible for maintaining proper muscle tone as a part of the extrapyramidal motor system.

behavioral tolerance   repeated use of a drug may lead to a diminished effect of the drug (tolerance). When the diminished effect occurs because the individual has learned to compensate for the effect of the drug, it is called behavioral tolerance.

benzodiazepine   the group of drugs that includes Valium and Librium. They are used as anxiolytics or sedatives, and some types are used as sleeping pills.

binding   the interaction between a molecule and a receptor for that molecule. Although the molecules float onto and off of the receptor, there are chemical and electrical attractions between a specific molecule and its receptor so that there is a much higher probability of the receptor being occupied by its proper molecule than by other molecules.

biological half-life   the amount of time required to remove half of the original amount of a drug from the body.

blackout   a period of time during which a person was physically conscious, but for which there is no memory.

blood-brain barrier   refers to the fact that many substances, including drugs, that may circulate freely in the blood do not readily enter the brain tissue. The major structural feature of this barrier is the tightly joined epithelial cells lining blood capillaries in the brain. Drug molecules cannot pass between the cells but must be able to go through their membranes. Small molecules and molecules that are lipid soluble cross the brain easily.

brainstem (hindbrain)   the enlarged extension of the spinal cord; it includes the *medulla oblongata,* the *pons,* and the *cerebellum.*

caffeine   a behavioral and general cellular stimulant found in coffee, tea, cola drinks, and chocolate.

caffeinism   habitual use of large amounts of caffeine.

cannabis   the marijuana, or hemp, plant.

carbon monoxide   a poisonous gas found in cigarette smoke.

cardiac arrhythmia   disturbance of the normal synchronized rhythm of the heartbeat so that the heart does not pump blood; fatal if not reversed.

catecholamine   class of biochemical compounds including the neurotransmitters dopamine, norepinephrine, and epinephrine.

central nervous system (CNS)   the neurons that are located in the brain and spinal cord.

cerebellum   part of the brainstem; concerned especially with the coordination of muscles and bodily equilibrium.

cerebrum (cerebral cortex)   the convoluted layer of gray matter that forms the largest part of the brain in humans; the highest neural center for coordination and interpretation of external and internal stimuli; contains sensory, motor, and association areas.

cholinergic   neuron that uses acetylcholine as a neurotransmitter.

cholinoceptive site   postjunctional receptor for acetylcholine, also affected by the agonists muscarine and nicotine.

chronic effect   the long-term response to repeated doses of a drug; compare to acute effects.

chronic obstructive lung disease   includes emphysema and chronic bronchitis. Cigarette smoking is a major cause of these disorders.

cirrhosis   a serious, largely irreversible, and frequently fatal disease of the liver. Usually caused by chronic heavy alcohol use.

codeine   a narcotic chemical that is present in opium.

concrete operations in Piaget's theory, a stage of cognitive development in which rules of logic can be applied to observable or manipulatable physical relations.

congener nonalcoholic constituents in alcoholic beverages, from the fermentation process, storage, the original plant material, or added substances.

convulsion an involuntary, violent, and irregular series of contractions of the skeletal muscles.

crack street term for a smokable form of cocaine.

cross-dependence a condition in which one drug can prevent the withdrawal symptoms associated with physical dependence on a different drug.

cross-tolerance a condition in which tolerance of one drug results in a lessened response to another drug.

DAWN The Drug Abuse Warning Network, a federal government system for reporting drug-related medical emergencies and deaths.

delirium tremens (DTs) a syndrome of tremulousness, with hallucinations, psychomotor agitation, confusion and disorientation, sleep disorders, and other associated discomforts, lasting several days after alcohol withdrawal.

dependence, drug state in which the use of a drug is necessary for either physical of psychological well-being.

depressant any of a large group of drugs that generally depress the CNS and at high doses induce sleep. Includes alcohol, the barbiturates, and other sedative-hypnotic drugs.

"designer drug" street term for illicit derivatives of fentanyl-type narcotics.

detoxification the process of allowing the body to rid itself of a large amount of alcohol or another drug.

direct action attachment of a drug to postsynaptic receptors to alter synaptic neurotransmission.

disinhibition a physiological state within the central nervous system characterized by decreased activity of inhibitory synapses, which results in a net excess of excitatory activity.

dose-response (dose-effect) relationship   the intensity and character of response to a drug depends on the amount administered and individual variability.

drug   any chemical substance used for its effects on bodily processes.

drug abuse   the intake of a chemical substance under circumstances or at dosage levels that significantly increase the hazard potential, whether or not the substance is used therapeutically, legally, or as prescribed by a physician.

drug disposition tolerance   the reduced effect of a drug that may result from more rapid metabolism or excretion of the drug.

drug interaction   the modification of the action of one drug by the current or prior administration of another drug.

endorphin   an opiate-like chemical that occurs naturally in the brains of humans and other animals. There are several proper endorphins, and the term is also used generically to refer to both the endorphins and enkephalins.

enkaphalin   an opiate-like chemical that occurs naturally in the brains of humans and other animals. The enkephalins are smaller molecules than endorphins.

euphoria   elevation of mood; a stimulant drug may cause a sensation of euphoria.

extrapyramidal   refers to a motor control system in the central nervous system that is responsible for maintaining muscle tone and posture.

fetal alcohol syndrome   a symptom complex of congenital anomalies seen in newborns of women who ingested high doses of alcohol during critical periods of pregnancy.

flashback   an experience reported by some users of LSD in which portions of the LSD experience reoccur at a later time without the use of a drug.

formal operations   in Piaget's theory, the final stage of cognitive development characterized by reasoning, hypothesis generating, and hypothesis testing.

freebase   when a chemical salt is separated into its basic and acidic components, the basic component is referred to as the freebase. Most psychoactive drugs are bases that normally exist in a salt form. Specifically, the salt, cocaine hydrochloride, can be chemically extracted to form the cocaine freebase, which is volatile and may therefore be smoked.

Gamma-aminobutyric acid (GABA)   an inhibitory amino acid neurotransmitter in the brain.

ganglia   groups of nerve cell bodies outside the central nervous system, such as along the spinal cord.

habituation   as defined in 1957 by the World Health Organization, a condition resulting from the repeated consumption of a drug, which includes these characteristics: (a) a desire (but not compulsion) to continue taking the drug for the sense of improved well-being that it engenders; (b) little or no tendency to increase the dose; (c) some degree of psychic dependence on the effect of the drug, but absence of physical dependence and hence no abstinence syndrome; (d) a detrimental effect, if any, primarily on the user.

hallucinogen   a drug that will consistently produce changes in thought, perception, and mood, alone or in concert, without causing major disturbances of the autonomic nervous system or other serious disability.

hashish   an extract of the hemp plant with a higher concentration of THC than marijuana.

heroin   a potent narcotic analgesic synthesized from morphine.

hypnotic   a central nervous system depressant that induces sleep; see also sedative.

identity confusion   the negative pole of psychosocial crisis of later adolescence in which a person is unable to integrate various roles or make commitments.

indirect action   an alteration in synaptic neurotransmission caused by a drug even though the drug does not attach to postsynaptic receptors.

indole   a type of chemical structure. The neurotransmitter serotonin and the hallucinogen LSD both contain an indole nucleus.

industry   a sense of pride and pleasure in acquiring culturally valued competencies. The sense of industry is usually acquired by the end of the middle childhood years.

inferiority   a sense of incompetence and failure that is built on negative evaluation and lack of skill.

intramuscular   a type of injection in which the drug is administered into a muscle.

intravenous   a type of injection in which the drug is administered into a vein.

lethal dose   the dosage that will kill; LD-50 means that this dose would be lethal to 50% of the test animals.

ligand   a molecule that binds to a receptor.

limbic system   a system of various brain structures that are involved in emotional responses.

liver microsomal enzyme   an enzyme associated with a particular subcellular component (the microsomal fraction) of liver cells. There are many such enzymes that are important for drug metabolism.

look-alikes   drugs sold legally, usually through the mail, that are made to look like controlled, prescription drugs. The most common types contain caffeine and resemble amphetamine capsules or tablets.

lysergic acid diethylamide (LSD)   a semisynthetic psychedelic drug.

mainline   injection of drug intravenously.

MAO inhibitor   a drug that inhibits the activity of the enzyme monoamine oxidase.

marijuana   a mixture of crushed leaves, flowers, and small branches of both male and female hemp plants.

MDMA   methylenedioxy methamphetamine, a catechol hallucinogen related to MDA. Called "ecstasy" on the street.

medial forebrain bundle   a group of neuron fibers that projects from the midbrain to the forebrain, passing near the hypothalamus. Now known to contain several chemically and anatomically distinct pathways, including dopamine and norepinephrine pathways.

medulla oblongata   part of the hindbrain (brainstem) between the spinal cord and pons; controls many vital functions, such as respiration, heart rate, and blood pressure; many depressant drugs have secondary toxic effects on the medulla.

mescaline   a psychedelic drug extracted from the peyote cactus.

mesolimbic system   a group of dopamine-containing neurons that have their cell bodies in the midbrain and their terminals in the forebrain, on various structures associated with the limbic system.

metabolism   the breakdown of drug molecules by enzymes, often in the liver.

methadone   a synthetically produced opiate narcotic.

monoamine oxidase (MAO)   an enzyme capable of metabolizing norepinephrine, dopamine, and serotonin to inactive products.

narcotic   one of a group of drugs similar to morphine, also referred to as opiates, and used medically primarily for their analgesic effects.

narcotic antagonist   a drug that is capable of blocking the effects of narcotic drugs. Used in emergency medicine to treat narcotic overdose, and in some addiction treatment programs to block the effect of any illicit narcotic that might be taken.

neurotransmitters   a chemical that is released by one neuron and that alters the electrical activity in another neuron.

nicotine   a behavioral stimulant found in tobacco that is responsible for its psychoactive effects and for tobacco dependence.

nitrosamine, tobacco specific   a group of organic chemicals, many of which are highly carcinogenic. There are at least four nitrosamines found only in tobacco, and these may account for much of the cancer-causing property of tobacco.

nucleus basalis   a group of large cell bodies found just below the basal ganglia and containing acetylcholine.

opium   a sticky substance obtained from the seed pods of the opium poppy and containing the narcotic chemicals morphine and codeine.

over-the-counter (OTC) drug pharmaceutical substance that can be purchased without a prescription.

parasympathetic the branch of the autonomic nervous system that has acetylcholine as its neurotransmitter and, for example, slows the heart rate and activates the intestine.

passive smoking inhalation of cigarette smoke from the air by nonsmokers near someone who is smoking.

PCP initials for the chemical name 1-(1-phencyclidine) piperidine. The generic name is phencyclidine. A hallucinogen often referred to as Angel Dust.

peptide a class of chemicals made up of sequences of amino acids. Enkephalins are small peptides containing only five amino acids, whereas large proteins may contain hundreds.

peyote a hallucinogenic cactus containing the chemical mescaline.

phantastica a term used to describe certain hallucinogens that produce altered perceptions but do not generally impair communication with the real world.

pharmacodynamics study of the interactions of drugs with the receptors responsible for the action of a drug in the body.

pharmacodynamic tolerance reduced effectiveness of a drug due to an altered tissue interaction to the drug.

pharmacokinetics study of the factors that influence the absorption, distribution, metabolism, and excretion of a drug.

physical dependence the habituation of body tissues to the continued presence of a chemical agent, revealed in the form of serious, even life-threatening, withdrawal symptoms following cessation of use.

postconventional morality in Kohlberg's stages of moral reasoning, the most mature form of moral judgments. Moral decisions are based on an appreciation of the social contract that binds members of a social system and on personal values.

potency the absolute amount of a drug required to produce a given pharmacological effect.

psychedelic drug any drug with the ability to alter sensory perception.

psychoactive drug any chemical substance that alters mood or behavior as a result of alterations in the functioning of the brain.

psychological dependence can be described as a tendency or craving for repeated or compulsive use of an agent because its effects are deemed pleasurable or satisfying, or because it reduces undesirable feelings, such as anxiety, insomnia, or depression.

psychotomimetic another name for hallucinogenic drugs.

puberty the period of physical development at the onset of adolescence when the reproductive system matures.

rebound effect or paradoxical effect a state of agitation or hyperactivity resulting from the withdrawal of a depressant drug.

receptors locations at which neurotransmitters or drugs bind, perhaps triggering a physiological response.

reuptake one process by which a neurotransmitter chemical may be removed from the synapse. The chemical may be taken back up into the cell from which it was released.

sedative-hypnotic drug any chemical substance that exerts a nonselective general depressant action upon the nervous system.

serotonin a synaptic transmitter both in the brain and in the peripheral nervous system.

side effect any drug-induced effect that accompanies the primary effect for which the drug was administered.

skin popping injection of a drug subcutaneously.

snorting application of a drug, such as cocaine, to the nasal mucosa or membranes by inhaling.

somatic system part of the nervous system that controls the voluntary, skeletal muscles, for example, the large muscles of the arms and legs.

spasticity　a state of abnormal increases in muscle tension, resulting in increased resistance of the muscle to stretching.

speed　methamphetamine or other amphetamine in an injectable form.

stimulant　any of a group of drugs that has the effect of reversing mental and physical fatigue.

sympathetic nervous system　part of the autonomic nervous system; stimulates structures generally concerned with the expenditure of body energy.

sympathomimetic　any drug that stimulates the sympathetic nervous system, for example, amphetamine.

synapse　gap between the end bulp (presynaptic terminal) of axon from first neuron to dendrite (postsynaptic membrane) of second, communicating, neuron, across which the neurotransmitter molecules diffuse.

synaptic vesicle　membrane-enclosed package of neurotransmitter found in the end bulb.

synergism (potentiation)　the combined action of two or more drugs, which is greater than the sum of the effects of each drug taken alone.

synesthesia　cross-sensing; the brain interprets a sensation incorrectly, such as "hearing" colors.

tachycardia　rapid heartbeat, such as from stress or stimulant drugs.

tardive dyskinesia　long-term effect of major tranquilizers in which, after years of use, the person has difficulty controlling voluntary movement, especially of the lips and tongue.

teratogen　an agent or factor that causes physical defects in a developing embryo.

tetrahydrocannabinol (THC)　a major psychoactive agent found in marijuana, hashish, and other preparations of hemp.

theobromine　a mild stimulant similar to caffeine, found in chocolate.

theophylline　a mild stimulant similar to caffeine, found in tea.

tolerance   refers to the development of body tissue resistance to the effects of a chemical agent so that larger doses are required to reproduce the original effect.

toxic effect   any drug-induced effect that is either temporarily of permanently deleterious to any organ or system of an animal or person to which the drug is administered. Drug toxicity includes both the relatively minor side effects that invariably accompany drug administration and the more serious and unexpected manifestations that occur in only a small percentage of individuals taking a drug.

tranquilizers, major   drugs used to relieve symptoms of severe psychosis.

tranquilizers, minor   psychoactive drugs with sedative and antianxiety effects; also used as anticonvulsants and muscle relaxants.

uptake   the process by which a cell expends energy to concentrate certain chemicals within itself. For example, precursor substances that will be synthesized into neurotransmitters must be taken up by the neuron.

vasocongestion   engorgement of blood vessels; more blood flows into than out of particular tissues, resulting in vasocongestion.

vasodilation   increase in diameter of blood vessels, causing increased volume of flow in that vessel.

withdrawal syndrome   the set of symptoms that occurs reliably when someone stops taking a drug; also called abstinence syndrome.

xanthine   the chemical class that includes caffeine, theobromine, and theophylline.

INDEX

ABOUT THE AUTHORS

Edith S. Lisansky Gomberg is Professor of Psychology at the University of Michigan Department of Psychiatry, School of Medicine, Medical Center Research Consultant at the Ann Arbor Veterans Administration Hospital neuropsychiatry unit, and Adjunct Professor of Psychology at the Rutgers University Center of Alcohol Studies. She has published extensively in the area of substance abuse: theories of etiology, female alcoholism, alcohol and medication problems among the elderly, and the effects of alcohol on behavior. She serves on the editorial boards of several journals and has served on federal committees, including those reviewing research proposals. Her teaching includes a course on drugs, society, and human behavior.

Rebecca Schilit is a graduate of the University of Michigan's Joint Doctoral Program in Social Work and Psychology. She is Assistant Professor at Arizona State University School of Social Work and a research consultant at the Tucson Veteran's Administration Hospital Social Work Department. Her teaching includes courses in human behavior and the social environment, research methods, and an elective course in substance abuse. She has published primarily in the areas of substance abuse problems among women and domestic violence. She also has an active consulting service, which provides assistance with the design and implementation of program evaluations, dissertations, and so forth.

Edith S. Lisansky Gomberg is Professor of Psychology at the University of Michigan Department of Psychiatry, School of Medicine, Research Consultant at the Ann Arbor Veterans Medical Center, and Adjunct Professor of Psychology at the Rutgers University Center of Alcohol Studies. She has published extensively in the area of substance abuse: theories of etiology, female alcoholism, Alcohol and medication problems among the elderly, and the effects of alcohol on behavior. She serves on the editorial boards of several journals and has served on federal committees, including those reviewing research proposals. Her teaching includes a course on drugs, society, and human behavior.

NOTES:

NOTES:

NOTES:

NOTES:

V